David Murray lives in Brisbane with his partner and their two sons. He has been a journalist since 1997, has won awards for news and investigative reporting and is a former Europe correspondent for News Corp. He is currently Crime and Courts Editor for *The Courier-Mail* and *Sunday Mail*.

T0363547

the murder of
ALLISON
BADEN-CLAY

DAVID MURRAY

EBURY
PRESS

An Ebury Press book
Published by Penguin Random House Australia Pty Ltd
Level 3, 100 Pacific Highway, North Sydney NSW 2060
www.penguin.com.au

Penguin
Random House
Australia

First published by Ebury Press in 2014
This edition first published by Ebury Press in 2017

Copyright © David Murray 2014
Part V and epilogue © David Murray 2017

The moral right of the author has been asserted.

All rights reserved. No part of this book may be reproduced or transmitted by any person
or entity, including internet search engines or retailers, in any form or by any means,
electronic or mechanical, including photocopying (except under the statutory exceptions
provisions of the Australian *Copyright Act 1968*), recording, scanning or by any
information storage and retrieval system without the prior written permission of
Penguin Random House Australia.

Addresses for the Penguin Random House group of companies can be found at
global.penguinrandomhouse.com/offices.

National Library of Australia
Cataloguing-in-Publication entry

Murray, David, 1976– author
The murder of Allison Baden-Clay/David Murray

ISBN 978 0 14378 160 8 (paperback)

Baden-Clay, Allison
True crime stories – Queensland – Brisbane
Murder victims – Queensland – Brisbane
Murder – Investigation – Queensland – Brisbane

Cover design by Luke Causby, Blue Cork
Front cover image © anonymous; believed to have been taken upon announcement of
Allison Dickie as Business Woman of the Year by Ipswich Chamber of Commerce
Map © Jonathan Bentley
Internal design by Midland Typesetters, Australia
Typeset in 11.5/15 pt by Midland Typesetters, Australia
Printed in Australia by Griffin Press, an accredited ISO AS/NZS 14001:2004
Environmental Management System printer

Penguin Random House Australia uses papers that are natural, renewable and
recyclable products and made from wood grown in sustainable forests. The logging and
manufacturing processes are expected to conform to the environmental regulations of the
country of origin.

For Catriona, Ned and Joe

CONTENTS

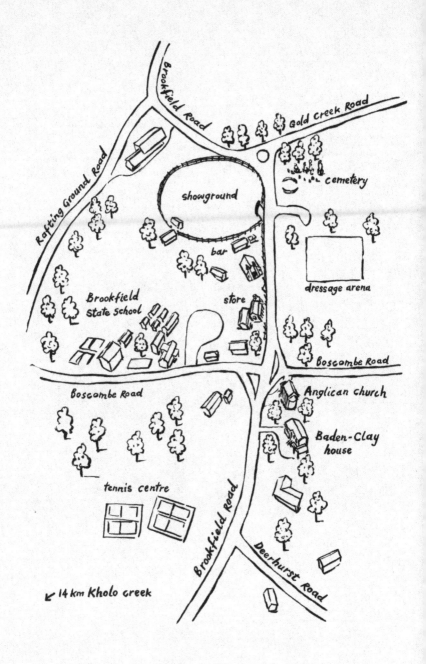

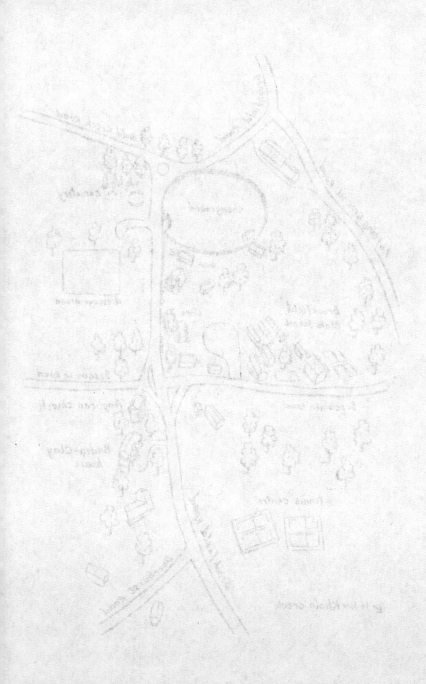

PART I – ALLISON AND GERARD

The bridge

The sun had yet to break the horizon, but a soft glow was lighting the morning. Along the banks of Kholo Creek, creatures were beginning to stir. Above, the rest of the world was waking too. Cars began rattling across the concrete-and-steel bridge spanning the creek. Wildlife heading to the water below had to negotiate a new presence that day. It was a woman – arms tangled in her jumper, running shoes laced. In the night her killer had come, leaving her on the muddy banks of this unremarkable little creek.

The Brisbane River snakes for more than 300 kilometres through south-east Queensland to empty into Moreton Bay. In 1823, New South Wales governor Sir Thomas Brisbane dispatched explorer John Oxley north to find a place to settle Sydney's worst convicts. Oxley, with the unexpected help of some shipwrecked convicts, found a broad waterway. He named it the Brisbane River, and a city rose on its banks.

Kholo Creek is a tiny tributary that feeds into the vast brown river before it wends its way through the CBD. Today, Kholo Creek Bridge spans the waterway, a 14-metre-high structure that supports an endless stream of cars, trucks and motorbikes travelling along Mt Crosby Road. Underneath, two large, ugly concrete pipes supply water to houses and businesses in the east. Steep creek banks and thick undergrowth keep bushwalkers away, while a fallen tree at the creek mouth renders it impassable at low tide. Few had the inclination or the means to venture up Kholo Creek. So the woman lay there, in plain view, yet unseen.

As the sun rose on that morning, 14 kilometres away, at her Brookfield home, the woman's absence triggered anxiety: when the three young Baden-Clay girls awoke, their mum, Allison, was nowhere to be seen. The worried girls had breakfast, got dressed and were shuttled off to school. By nightfall she still wasn't there.

Since childhood, Allison had been afraid of the dark, and as day turned to night Kholo Creek turned pitch black, with no street lights in sight. The headlights of cars whizzing back and forth on Mt Crosby Road cut through the darkness, but their beams did not reach down to Allison. Small fish breaking the surface of the creek, a lizard or snake rustling unseen through the undergrowth – these were her only witnesses.

With each passing hour, traces of her killer were lost to the earth. As the tide rose and fell, the water lapped her body. On the eighth night the rain came. It was a cloudburst that drenched the ground, parched from months of blue skies. Allison lay under the bridge but wind swept the deluge over her. Rivulets ran down the bank to the creek, washing more traces of him from her clothes, her body, her fingernails.

Somewhere, her killer was warm and dry. The sound of the heavy rain outside brought comfort. It would wash her clean. Perhaps even wash her away. Muddy brown floodwaters frothed, bubbled and gushed down the creek, gathering pace as they raced towards the Brisbane River. But stubbornly, steadfastly, Allison did not move. She stayed as if waiting for someone to find her.

Where are you?

Friday 20 April 2012

6.20 am

Gerard Baden-Clay tapped out a message on his iPhone, exclamation marks lending it a cheery tone: 'Good morning! Hope you slept well? Where are you? None of the girls are up yet! Love G.'

Gerard would say later he had woken just after 6 am. His wife, Allison, was not in bed. He padded through their house looking for her before deciding she must have headed out for an early-morning stroll. The couple's daughters, aged ten, eight and five, were waking.

In the ensuite of the master bedroom, Gerard lathered his face with shaving foam. When his middle daughter called out, he rushed into her room with a cloud of foam on his face. Surprised to be greeted this way, she wanted to know where her mother was.

'She's gone for a walk,' Gerard said, hurrying back to the bathroom to shave.

When she saw him next, the foam was gone, revealing a trail of angry scratches streaking down his right cheek. Daddy had cut himself shaving, he told her, asking her to play nursemaid and help put a bandaid on the wounds.

Together, they went through to wake the other two girls so they could begin getting ready for school.

Where was she? Again, Gerard tried calling Allison's phone but got no response. His wife was running out of time if she wanted to make a conference in the city that morning. He typed out another text, still with the jaunty exclamation marks: 'Al, getting concerned. [The elder girls] now up. I'm dressed and about to make lunches. Please just text me back or call! Love G.'

There was no reply. He phoned his parents at their nearby home. Within minutes his father and sister were on their way to help with a search of the local streets. When they came up with nothing, Gerard decided to hit the panic button, about an hour after he had woken to find his wife gone. He was around the corner from his home when he phoned 000.

7.15 am

Operator: Police Emergency. What's your location?

Gerard: Ah, good morning. Brookfield.

Operator: Whereabouts in Brookfield, sir?

Gerard: Ah, Brookfield Road, Brookfield.

Operator: And what's happening there?

Gerard: Um, I, I don't want to be alarmist. I tried the 131 number [the Policelink line] but, um, it went on forever.

Operator: Yeah.

Gerard: My, my wife isn't home. Um . . . I don't know where she is.

Operator: Okay. . . when did you last see her, sir?

Gerard: Um . . . last night . . . I went to bed. And I got up, ah, this morning and she, she wasn't there. And that's not unusual. She, she often goes for a walk in the morning.

Operator: Yeah.

Gerard: Um, I've texted her and called her a number of times. I think she has her phone with her.

Operator: Yeah. What time does she normally get back when she goes for a walk?

Gerard: Well, this morning she, she was planning to, she has a seminar in the city, so she was planning to leave by, you know, about seven.

Operator: Okay.

Gerard: And she's not back home yet. I'm now driving the streets. My, my father's come over and – to look after my children.

Operator:	Yeah, okay. So what was, what's your name first of all?
Gerard:	I'm sorry. Um, Gerard. G-E-R-A-R-D.
Operator:	And your last name Gerard?
Gerard:	Baden-Clay. B-A-D-E-N hyphen C-L-A-Y.
Operator:	And what's your wife's name?
Gerard:	Allison with two Ls.
Operator:	Okay. And how old is Allison?
Gerard:	Um, um, 44.
Operator:	Okay. So you didn't see her before she got up this morning?
Gerard:	No.
Operator:	All right. And how tall is your wife?
Gerard:	Um about five six, something like that, I think.
Operator:	Okay. And what colour hair's she got?
Gerard:	She just had it done last night. It's sort of blondie, brownie, reddish.
Operator:	Yep. And how long is it?
Gerard:	Ah, shoulder length.
Operator:	Okay. What I'm going to [do is] put a broadcast on for the police to keep a look-out for your wife. We'll get the police to come and see you.
Gerard:	I need to go home and get the kids ready for school.
Operator:	Yeah, all right, Gerard. I'll get the police to come and see you.

8 am

Constables Kieron Ash and Leah Hammond were on the road when their radio sprang to life with their call sign, M466. Their instructions were to check in with Gerard Baden-Clay about his absent wife. Every year, 6500 people are reported missing in Queensland. The vast majority are found safe and sound in the first 48 hours. There was no reason to suspect this would be any different.

5

Ash and Hammond saw the house was tucked between a small church and a childcare centre in Brookfield Road. A woman was walking three young girls down the front steps of the house, and for a moment it might have seemed the missing mum had turned up after all.

Gerard, close on the woman's heels, walked over to greet the officers. An older man came up behind him and casually put an arm over his shoulder. Gerard introduced his father, Nigel Baden-Clay. And the woman with the girls was his sister, Olivia Walton, not his wife, he explained. She was taking his daughters to school. Gerard was smartly dressed for a day at work – long pants, business shirt, tie and cufflinks. But what commanded the officers' attention were the painful-looking scratches trailing down his right cheek to his jawline. They were immediately on alert.

'Is it okay if we speak to you in private?' asked burly, bald-headed Ash.

Gerard asked his father to wait inside; Olivia left to take the girls to school.

Alone with the officers, Gerard expanded on what he'd told the emergency operator. There was nothing unusual to report from the previous night. His wife, Allison, was on the couch watching *The Footy Show* when he went to bed at 10 pm. By morning she had simply vanished.

Allison usually went for a 2-kilometre walk each morning, Gerard told the officers. He presumed that's where she was when he woke to find her gone. However, he told police he couldn't be certain she had gone to bed because she sometimes slept on the couch or in another room.

Ash's eyes were fixed on the red marks on Gerard's face. He asked if everything was all right between him and his wife.

'Look, there is something I should tell you,' Gerard said. Speaking softly, he told the officers he had been having an affair. Things weren't great at home. Allison had found out about his cheating and, although they were seeing a marriage counsellor, she no longer trusted him. He wanted the information kept strictly confidential – his father and sister did not know.

Absorbing the details, Ash queried Gerard about those vivid scratches.

Gerard said he'd cut himself shaving. He was distracted and in a rush to get the girls ready and off to school. As he described each step of his morning, he used an oddly coarse expression: he'd had a 'shit, shower and shave'. It seemed to clash with both his buttoned-down business attire and the gravity of the situation.

There was no set length of time for his wife's walks, but she should have been back long ago, Gerard told police. She had a conference to attend.

Ash registered that when Gerard spoke about himself, he confidently looked him in the eye. When talking about Allison, however, his eyes would drop to the ground and he would fidget.

Ash asked to go inside, so Gerard led the two officers up the front driveway.

In every direction there were sprawling acreage properties with grand entrances, sweeping drives and manicured lawns. Gerard and Allison's home was not one of these. Though Gerard was a prominent local real estate agent, the Baden-Clays had been renting their four-bedroom home for six years. It was an elevated, single-level house on a block that sloped down towards the road. The duck-egg blue paintwork was faded and peeling.

Thick vines had overtaken latticework at the front of the house, with spidery tendrils creeping over the steps and railings and spilling onto the unmowed lawn.

Constable Ash took note of the vehicles parked at the front of the house. Nigel's silver Holden Statesman with BWANA vanity plates and Gerard's white Toyota Prado with SETTLED plates were parked on the drive. Allison's silver Holden Captiva had been reversed into the carport to the right of the house.

It was autumn and the row of trees alongside the carport had shed their leaves. Their bare, straggly branches stretched over the corrugated roof. The unstoppable vines encircled the trees and the metal posts of the carport.

Constable Ash and Constable Hammond followed Gerard up the weathered front steps. The front door opened to a lounge room. A flat-screen television was perched on a wooden cabinet, next to a piano with a music book propped open above the keys. A black L-shaped couch and ottoman faced the TV. It was where Allison was supposedly curled up when Gerard last saw her. A blanket and basket of laundry sat on the end of the couch. Dated, dusty-pink carpet covered the floors. The white walls were dotted with scuffs and scrapes from the wear and tear of family life.

Photographs documenting Allison and Gerard's life as a couple and their growing family decorated the walls, cabinets and tables. The master bedroom lay to the left; the children's bedrooms were at the opposite side of the house, beside the carport. At the rear, the carpet gave way to terracotta tiles, running through a crowded home office, dining area and kitchen.

A glass sliding door opened to a back patio swathed in leaves, where a rusting gas barbecue was pushed up against the house. Thick clusters of fern thrust their way onto the patio from the overgrown yard, where an old Hills Hoist leaned at an angle. A line of mature trees along the back fence screened the house from neighbours. Gerard and Allison rented the house for $460 a week. It was dirt cheap for a family home in the prestigious suburb of Brookfield.

Hammond set about taking down some details about Allison. With Gerard's permission, Ash took the chance to have a look around. His instincts were telling him this was more than a frazzled mum gone AWOL. Alarm bells were ringing.

Ash went into the master bedroom. Strangely, in a house where the youngest child was five years old, there was a baby monitor on a bedside table. In the ensuite, he found no signs of a fight. Neither were there traces of bloodied tissues or toilet paper Gerard may have used to mop up after a shaving mishap. Something wasn't right. He didn't buy Gerard's story.

Gerard was cooperating so far, but the injuries on his face and his marital troubles couldn't be ignored. Ash went outside to the patrol car and phoned his supervisor, Senior Sergeant Narelle Curtis, the Brisbane West district duty officer, who was at Indooroopilly Police Station. He asked Curtis to come down and see for herself.

Gerard Baden-Clay, successful businessman, community leader, role model and happy family man had just become the focus of police suspicion. How had he ended up here? Over coming days countless strangers would wonder the same as they saw Allison's smiling face in newspapers and on news bulletins: the beautiful bride on her wedding day, posing for happy snaps on honeymoon, with her children.

As a child Allison had dreamt of being famous, but not like this.

Ballerina

The line stretched out the door of the Margaret Street dance studios in the Brisbane CBD when the Australian Youth Ballet Company (AYBC) held its inaugural auditions in July 1978. More than 220 girls and boys nervously waited to perform in small groups in front of a panel of eagle-eyed experts. The judge with the final word was a striking Eastern European dancer, Inara Svalbe. Dressed in a chic turtleneck, she wore her hair scraped back in an impossibly tight ponytail, not a strand out of place. Her knee-high boots clicked loudly on the thin wooden floorboards as she circled each new group, sizing them up.

Svalbe, the artistic director and co-founder of AYBC, had a grand vision. She planned to harvest the best of the best from established dance schools around the country, then run them through the same paces as professionals. Fewer than 30 dancers aged eight to 14 would be accepted. Children, and their parents, couldn't *grand jêté* fast enough to try out for the exclusive new company.

Along with the majority of hopefuls that year, ten-year-old Allison June Dickie didn't make the cut. She shouldn't have taken it personally – Svalbe didn't even select her own daughter, Krista Reeves, who was desperate for a place in the group too. Like Reeves, Allison did make a shortlist of reserves, who would be offered a place with the AYBC if another child quit or did not take up their position.

Before long, Allison, a pretty, reserved girl from Ipswich, a regional city 40 kilometres west of Brisbane, was called up. By May 1979, she was leaping across stage at the Twelfth Night Theatre in Bowen Hills in the AYBC's 'world premiere' of three original ballets. Supportive parents, word of mouth and adept marketing made for sell-out audiences. The show was scheduled to run at 8 pm on four consecutive nights but was so popular a 5 pm matinee was added.

Svalbe's origins were anything but glamorous. Born in a refugee camp in Bavaria, she moved with her family to Australia when she was two and grew up in Brisbane. She took up ballet at three and went on to dance with The Australian Ballet as a student, then performed soloist roles with the Royal New Zealand Ballet and principal roles with Ballet Theatre of Queensland. Svalbe started teaching at Oxley in 1968. Shortly after, she began running classes at a church hall in North Ipswich, where Allison Dickie was an early pupil.

Svalbe was the first to admit she herself never reached the lofty heights to which she aspired – nothing short of being the best was good enough for her. She brought this same determination and passion – almost obsession – to the AYBC. In the lead-up to performances she would regularly be up until 2 am or 3 am, finishing hundreds of elaborate costumes on her over-heated Elna sewing machine.

Svalbe likened herself to an artist with an unfinished masterpiece in her head. She couldn't rest until her ballet company was running exactly as she had envisioned. A *Sunday Mail* reporter who visited her home in Kenmore, in Brisbane's west, in the early 1980s found 'costumes everywhere. Not quite hanging from the ceiling, but over chairs, dangling from picture frames, in heaps on the floor, spilling over tables. Spangled tulle, sequined brocades, gleaming satins, rich brocades plus the occasional crown, some masks and ballet shoes'.

More than 30 years later, I knocked on the front door of the same house, unannounced. Daughter Krista, now in her 40s, opened the door, with her mum not far behind. Although the visit was unexpected, the two women welcomed me inside.

Her home was heavy with memories and mementoes. In a storage room, she pulled down five dusty, leather-bound photo albums and for the next hour we pored over photos and ballet reviews from the late 1970s and early '80s.

Each year Allison and the other dancers had to re-audition to keep their places at the company. Like everything else with the AYBC, the auditions were designed to replicate standards in the world of professional dance. So intense was the pressure that afterwards Allison and the other girls and boys would huddle together and cry their hearts out, convinced they wouldn't make the grade.

While there was pressure on everyone, Allison was a particularly sensitive young girl. Such was her distress at the prospect of failing that sometimes she would be physically ill before performances. But she always picked herself up, finding the strength to push through.

Allison and the other dancers travelled the country for performances that were often sold out. Co-founder Ken McCaffrey roped in a bevy of big names to lend their support. John Field, director of the Royal Academy of Dancing in London, and Australian ballet legend Sir Robert Helpmann became patrons. Invitations to perform started flooding in. One such invitation was to the 1980 International Festival of Youth Orchestras and Performing Arts in Aberdeen, Scotland.

Before the trip, Allison was profiled in her local paper, Ipswich's *Queensland Times*. The Redbank State School student was just 11 years old but was already ambitious, focused and prepared to work for what she wanted. Ballet lessons, she told the paper, grew progressively longer as the week went on: one hour on Monday, two hours on Wednesday and Thursday, two-and-a-half hours on Friday, three-and-a-half hours on Saturday, and a peak of nine hours on Sunday. All that training had made Allison supremely fit and rail thin.

Allison's parents, Priscilla and Geoff Dickie, were preparing to join her on the tour. Priscilla, speaking to the paper for the same article, told of the family's sacrifices for Allison to pursue her dreams.

'Geoff sometimes has to put up with meals on the run because we have to get Allison off to ballet classes . . . You have got to have determination for ballet and you have got to enjoy it and Allison does both.'

Allison grew up in a regular working-class family in an archetypal blue-collar neighbourhood. Geoff was a fireman and painted houses on his days off. Priscilla was a librarian at Allison's school. They lived in a modest house at 2A Spencer Street, Redbank, once a village named for the red soil of its riverbank, now a suburb of Ipswich. Redbank was home to Queensland's first coal mine, opened in 1843, and was the site of the state's first industrial strike. Over the years, Allison's large extended family had toiled in a local meatworks, brickworks, woollen mill and railway workshops.

Priscilla had grown up in a house in Church Street, a few doors down from where she set up home to raise her own children. She was the daughter of Bill and Lily Dann. Bill was a sociable railwayman and a dyed-in-the-wool Labor Party member. When a bright young policeman was eyeing a move into politics, Bill threw his weight behind him to get endorsed as a candidate. The policeman, Bill Hayden, went on to become Opposition leader from 1977 to 1983 and governor-general from 1989 to 1996.

When another Ipswich newcomer, Paul Tully, first ran for a seat on the local council in 1979, Bill handed out how-to-vote cards and drummed up support. Tully romped home in the vote and is today Queensland's longest serving local councillor.

'Billy Dann was the staunchest Labor supporter I ever had,' Tully tells me.

Bill and Lily had ten children: Priscilla, Noel, Julie, Kevin, Douglas, John, Stephen, Jeffrey, Louise and Bill. Money was tight and Lily was expert at stretching a dollar. She had just two cloth nappies for her babies. When one nappy was soiled she would wash it, hang it on the line and replace it with the other.

Bill built his house with the help of a neighbour. Initially the home had just two bedrooms, and four kids shared the one double bunk bed. The Danns were Methodists and their children went to Sunday school, all decked out in spotless white clothes.

Priscilla's father and brothers were soccer fanatics. They trained in the evenings on a strip of grass behind the railway workshops, with a single light strung up to break the darkness. It was the beginnings of the Redbank Seekers and Bill ran onto the pitch as the team's left back, with his eldest son Noel the centre forward. Noel was a Queensland under-18s representative player but gave up his place for religious reasons when they started playing on Sundays. Bill would have preferred his son to play, but respected Noel's decision.

Bill used to drive his big brood and their friends around in an old Whippet truck. Once, it broke down on the Indooroopilly bridge, when the Brisbane River crossing still had a toll. The toll master's eyes almost popped out when he found a group of 13 kids piled into the back, on their way to a soccer game. Bill tried to teach his wife to drive in the truck, but at a tiny 142-centimetres, or 4 feet 6 inches, Lily couldn't see over the steering wheel. Propped up on half a dozen pillows, she crashed during her lesson, and Bill threw in the towel.

Despite her small size, Lily was no pushover. With a glint in her eye she would always tell the story of seeing Bill walking down the street towards home with another woman by her side. When he made it to the front door, Lily belted him on the head with a frying pan as a warning shot.

When Bill died at 69 from leukaemia in 1989, 700 people turned up to his funeral. There were so many mourners, the highway through Redbank had to be closed off for the funeral procession. Bill Hayden, then Governor-General, sent a letter of condolence. Lily stayed on at Church Street into old age, when the government resumed her block to build a new highway. She eventually moved into a nursing home at nearby Riverview.

Allison's dad, Geoff Dickie, was also of Redbank stock; his parents James and Elizabeth Dickie lived there all their lives. Geoff's was a considerably smaller family; he had just one sibling – a sister, Julie. He and Priscilla have known each other for most of their lives, meeting at primary school in Redbank. Priscilla grew up to be a beauty. At 18, while on a seaside holiday with her family, she was crowned Miss Redcliffe 1959–60.

Geoff and Priscilla married in Redbank's Methodist church in September 1962. The couple went on to have three children: Vanessa, the eldest; Allison, their middle daughter; and a son, Ashley, the youngest. Priscilla and Geoff had notched up almost 50 years of marriage, were happily retired and were preparing to renew their vows when Allison vanished. Their planned celebration was cancelled in the end.

Geoff had always been a gentle, soft-hearted thinker. As adults, his children would say they'd hardly ever heard him raise his voice. Allison had inherited her father's thoughtful ways. Priscilla was a go-getter. She wanted her kids to have every opportunity in life, no matter the personal sacrifices she had to make. And there were plenty.

Along with many of the other ballet parents, Priscilla and Geoff pitched in as chaperones, drivers, carpenters, dressmakers and whatever else was needed to make the AYBC – and Allison's participation – work.

In July 1980, thanks to some committed fundraising from parents and children alike, enough money was raised for the AYBC to fly out of Australia for a month-long tour of the United Kingdom. It took in the youth festival in Aberdeen, Scotland, along with some other performances and sightseeing. Priscilla and Geoff joined their excited daughter on the flight.

The London performances went smoothly. 'Thunderous ovation for ballet,' read a headline back home after the first UK performance. When they reached Scotland, the AYBC dancers were the darlings of the festival. A full house watched their performance at Her Majesty's Theatre, Aberdeen. Ahead of the show, a photographer from the UK's *Evening Express* snapped Geoff Dickie carrying a 4-metre polystyrene prop through the streets of Aberdeen.

'We've brought this thing 12,000 miles [20,000 km] – and we've got to carry it for the last four,' he told the paper. Rolf Harris, at the time an untarnished star, met the dancers after one show and posed for photos.

It was lucky that the UK tour had gone so well. An incident at the dorm in London shortly after the contingent landed had threatened to derail everything. Inara Svalbe's daughter, Krista, had trained doubly hard to make the squad and was playing pool with one of the other dancers. The pair had an argument and Krista, enraged, hit the other girl before grabbing her bags and running into the streets. Allison set off in pursuit, determined to calm Krista.

Krista would never forget Allison running after her. Allison was like that: naturally thoughtful, decent and kind. Everyone was protective of Allison in return. Her occasional bouts of anxiety had not gone unnoticed. At rehearsals, Svalbe tells me, Allison would sometimes become worryingly withdrawn.

'We'd be doing "Sleeping Beauty",' says Svalbe, 'and she'd be a fairy and dancing beautifully and smiling – at rehearsal they didn't just do the steps; they did perform facially as well. They were smiling and acting. And then you'd find the next thing they'd have a break and she'd be sitting in the dressing room and she'd be rocking with her legs crossed. She'd be all withdrawn. That did worry me. In those days, you didn't know what to say or do.'

There never seemed to be a trigger, like a misstep or tiff with a friend – Allison was the least likely to argue with anyone. Afterwards, when the break was over, Allison would step back into rehearsals, bright and happy again, as if nothing had happened.

Allison's time with the ballet company came to an abrupt end in 1984. As she matured, she lost her lean figure, then lost her place in the AYBC.

'She got put on the short list. She'd put on weight,' admits Svalbe, who also cut Krista over her size. 'I was just so driven that everything had to be perfect.'

Allison, at 15, was out of the ballet company she had loved. She never returned, but her experiences would influence the rest of her life. So much about Allison as an adult could be traced back to her ballet years. In many ways she would always be that young ballerina – quietly determined, striving for perfection, dreaming of being on a stage. She had learnt how to push through the tough times and to smile for the world, even when she was in turmoil inside. And her training had instilled a belief that hard work and perseverance brought success – that if you failed, it was because you didn't try hard enough.

The ballet days shaped Allison's life in other ways too. The Europe trip, and other tours with the AYBC, gave Allison a taste of travel and the wide world beyond Ipswich. After finishing high school at Ipswich Girls' Grammar School, where she was deputy head girl, the 17-year-old headed back overseas for a year-long Rotary exchange in Denmark.

At a stopover in Japan, Allison shared a room with a fellow young Rotarian bound for Denmark, Linda Drinnan. Linda was from Camden, south-west of Sydney, and the girls became close friends. During their year abroad they travelled widely together. One whirlwind 18-day European tour took them to Paris, Venice, Vienna, Salzburg and Monte Carlo. Allison loved the romance of Paris more than anywhere.

Allison's best friend from school, Kerry-Anne Cummings, was also in Denmark on a student exchange. Both Drinnan and Cummings celebrated Allison's 18th birthday at her host family's home on the outskirts of Copenhagen. Drinnan, who later married and became Linda Ebeling, marvelled at Allison's outward composure on their hectic trips from one country to the next. Linda was always leading the charge, with Allison calmly and unhurriedly following. Linda would have a map in hand, always sure where she was and where she was going. Allison, on the other hand, had no idea and never seemed to care. If you were to spin Allison around three times, she'd be lost – but not stressed. She was easygoing and slow, in a good way, Linda remembered. On one such trip, Allison and Linda stopped at a small trinket shop and bought identical ring and bracelet sets. The floral pink jewellery was a cheap but priceless keepsake of friendship and adventure.

April 2012

Linda Ebeling was at home in Camden, New South Wales, as she read a late-night text message from her sister that made her chest tighten: 'Are you still awake? Allison from Brisbane is missing.'

Linda phoned back straight away. It was all over the news, her sister said. Linda and her husband, Stephen, went to their computer and clicked onto *The Courier-Mail*. There was a prominent story about Allison's disappearance.

Over the following weeks, Ebeling saw Allison's face on TV every day. At first she hoped Allison might appear at her doorstep. In the back of her mind she thought her friend might be running from something and need a safe haven.

While Ebeling waited for a knock on her door that would never come, she went to her jewellery box, where for 26 years she had kept the pink ring and matching bangle she and Allison bought together in Denmark. She knew Allison had kept hers too.

For the first time in all those years, Ebeling slipped on the cheap ring and bangle. It made her feel closer to Allison. She didn't take them off again for months.

May 2012

Krista Reeves reached for the light switch in the cold, dark storage room under her grandmother's house at Alderley, in Brisbane's north. Inara Svalbe had sent her daughter to see if one of Allison Baden-Clay's dresses from the AYBC was among a selection of outfits she'd stored away.

Allison had been found dead two days earlier and Svalbe hoped to find something to give her grieving parents from her ballet days. As Krista's hand reached for the light switch, there was a clatter in the room. Fearful she had disturbed a snake, she groped frantically for the light.

Flicking it on, Krista saw a yellow dress had fallen to the ground. Funny, yellow was Allison's favourite colour. She picked it up to hang it back on the rack and glanced at the name, faded but still visible, on the inside label: A. Dickie. There were 12 matching yellow dresses hanging in the storeroom – one for each dancer in the AYBC performance. Allison's had fallen to the floor.

First love

Maybe I am still harbouring regrets about getting married and
did I make the right decision? Was I ready to give of myself
and share or was I still self-centred. I didn't want to go overseas –
I wanted to change my career – to be FAMOUS!

Allison's private journal

Late 1990

When Allison June Dickie stepped off the high-speed catamaran
onto the jetty at Heron Island, the world was full of possibil-
ities. She was 22 years old, beautiful and had an Arts degree
majoring in psychology from the University of Queensland. The
girl from blue-collar Redbank had studied Japanese while at
university and was newly returned from a year teaching English
in Japan. At school and on her travels she had picked up varying
degrees of French, German, Danish and Swiss-German. With
these skills, she breezed into a job at Heron's tourist resort.

The 72-kilometre journey from the Queensland mining port
of Gladstone to Heron by boat takes two hours over choppy
waters. The island is but a speck in the ocean – 800 metres
long by 300 metres wide – formed by a build-up of sediment
on the southern Great Barrier Reef over thousands of years.
Captain Cook in 1770 and Matthew Flinders in 1802 both
missed the island, but Francis Blackwood anchored HMS *Fly*
off its shores in 1843 while surveying the reef. It remained uninhabited – the domain of the occasional birdwatcher and guano
miner – until the opening of a turtle soup factory in the 1920s.
Magnificent green turtles, 150 kilograms in weight and a metre
long, lumbered onto the island to lay their eggs, only to be
butchered, boiled and canned.

That was a bygone era. Since the 1930s, when Captain Christian Poulsen converted the cannery into a resort, the turtles have been a star attraction rather than a menu item. Arriving on the powdery white beaches from November, they nest at the same location where they hatched themselves. Resort guests can watch them burrowing above the high-tide line and see their shiny black hatchlings scamper from the sand to the sea. In the cooler months in the middle of the year, humpback whales on their annual northern migration pass the Heron jetty.

When Allison disembarked at the jetty, excitable Japanese tourists were alongside her, lugging bags that bulged with cameras and film. Her intention was to work at the Heron resort for a couple of months to save money and put her Japanese to good use.

Ian Drayton was a scuba-diving instructor who had kicked around in Heron's waters for two years. The freedom of his job was a world away from his regimented former career in the Australian Army. Before Heron, Drayton was a corporal in the 152 Signal Squadron at Perth's Campbell Barracks. The posting embedded him with the elite Special Air Service Regiment, whose motto is Who Dares Wins. Signallers serve side by side with Special Forces soldiers on their small patrols, providing specialist communications support.

Often, 'siggies' try out for full SAS selection. Drayton hurt his knee playing rugby for the army, which ruled out his chance at a beret. With peace breaking out during his six-and-a-half years in the military, he learnt to scuba dive and became a civilian instructor in his spare time. When he left the army, the reef drew him to Heron.

The warm waters around the coral cay teemed with hundreds of species of fish, manta rays, reef sharks and colourful coral. By day, Drayton's laid-back island life was filled with voyages into the ocean. By night, he had good company in the close-knit group of island staff.

Falling in love was not on Allison's itinerary when she left the mainland. She had high hopes of a successful career when she returned home, preferably on a stage somewhere. Drayton too was not looking to bring anyone into his life, but Allison immediately caught his attention. She had soft green eyes and long auburn hair. It might seem a peculiar thing for Drayton to have noticed, but Allison also had beautiful calves. The former ballerina always stood with one foot pointed behind the other, never flat-footed. It was like she was always ready to dance. Drayton soon fell head over heels and the pair began an island romance.

With no formal qualifications of his own and limited travel experience, he admired the achievements of the resort's newest recruit. He was also taken by her quirky nature. When it came to how the world worked, Allison could be as lumbering as the olive green turtles that waddled onto the island's beaches. Her naive comments about life were an endless source of amusement for her island friends. Eventually she would always end up laughing at herself too. She was easygoing, laid-back, happy.

As the relationship blossomed, Allison changed her plans and extended her stay on the island. She took up scuba diving, while Drayton started learning Japanese. Finally, she felt she could put off her life plans no longer and it was time to leave. Drayton wasn't going to let her walk out of his life. He gave up the island's best job and followed Allison south. They cemented their relationship by moving in together.

Their first home was a cheap, rented two-bedroom unit in Brisbane's western suburbs. Allison took a job in the city as a sales agent for Flight Centre, the travel firm founded by Queensland entrepreneur Graham 'Skroo' Turner.

The rise of the empire-building Turner is the stuff of legend. Raised on an apple orchard near Stanthorpe, on the border with New South Wales, Turner worked as a vet before leaving the country to go backpacking. Still in his 20s, he and two mates bought a double-decker bus, started a tour company, Top Deck Travel, and led expeditions to Europe, North Africa and Asia. The business grew to a fleet of dozens of buses, and Turner was on the road to riches. In Australia, he switched his focus to air travel and started Flight Centre with a single store in Sydney in 1982. The Flight Centre Travel Group eventually grew to more than 2500 stores in 11 countries, employing more than 15,000 staff. The company was a perfect fit for Allison, with her love of travel and languages.

Drayton, meanwhile, was unsure what to do with his life after his sudden decision to follow his new flame to Brisbane. He turned to a profession where his lack of formal qualifications, training and experience didn't matter: real estate. An army friend had a couple of real estate agencies and hired him as an agent in Redbank Plains, near Allison's childhood home.

Allison's parents, meanwhile, kept a watchful eye over their daughter. When Allison had gone to Heron, Priscilla and Geoff Dickie weren't expecting her to return with a boyfriend in tow. It was an even bigger deal for the family when Allison made one of the first major, independent decisions of her life and moved in with Drayton. They didn't rent for long, buying a house together at Malinda Street in the Ipswich suburb of Camira for $95,000 in March 1991. It was a large, brick, two-storey family home with a double garage and big yard, in anticipation of a life together.

Sometime around Allison's birthday, Drayton took the plunge. He'd booked a stretch limousine as a surprise. It arrived at their house and the chauffeur whisked the lovebirds off to a little restaurant in Chapel Hill, where Drayton had a table reserved for dinner. Weeks before, he had secretly picked out a diamond engagement ring, taking one of Allison's other rings to the jewellery store to get her size right. At the restaurant, over candlelight, he handed her the ring and proposed. Allison, who had no inkling of his plans until he popped the question, was overwhelmed. In tears, she accepted on the spot.

Family and friends celebrated the engagement at a party at the Ipswich home of her aunt and uncle, Julie and Don Moore, sharing beer and wine and plates of homemade food under a hired marquee.

Allison's best friend, Kerry-Anne Cummings, couldn't join them as she was living in London. Soon after, Allison and Drayton went and stayed with her at her Wimbledon flat, then the three of them spent a week on the road in Ireland. Allison took Drayton on to Denmark to visit the host family from her exchange trip at the end of school.

When travel agents were offered cheap fares to New Guinea, Allison and Drayton snapped them up. So did Allison's friend Linda from the Denmark exchange, who had followed her into a job at Flight Centre, and her boyfriend, Stephen Ebeling, who later became her husband. The four of them went on the holiday together, with Drayton leading the way on a scuba-diving trip over submerged plane wrecks and entertaining the group with tales about the SAS. Drayton, with his love of the outdoors, was a man's man. He and Stephen, a builder, got on like a house on fire.

Wise with their money, Allison and Drayton bought a second house together, at Serly Court in Bellbird Park, for $80,500 in October 1992, and rented it out. Financially, they were set up for a secure future. A wedding, family and long and happy life together seemed just over the horizon.

Second thoughts

The Miss Australia Awards was an event living on borrowed time when Allison Dickie entered in 1993. Organisers, desperate to keep up with the times, had changed its name from the Miss Australia Quest the previous year. Along with the name change, entrants could swap swimwear for business attire. The Miss Australia crown – made of silver, blue velvet and 800 pearls – had been ditched too, after 30 years of being balanced precariously on the heads of tearful winners. The satin sash and gleaming sceptre were also out.

In its heyday, the quest was broadcast live on TV with celebrity hosts such as Barry Crocker, Daryl Somers, Maggie Tabberer and Richard Wilkins. Winners made newspaper front pages and met royalty, presidents and popes. But despite raising tens of millions for the Australian Cerebral Palsy Association, a growing number felt the pageant was doing little for the cause of women's rights. Allison was following in the footsteps of her mum. When Priscilla had entered Miss Redcliffe back in the day as a petite teenager, her mother, Lily, got her to walk with books balanced on her head to improve her posture. Priscilla won, making the final of the then-exceedingly popular *Sunday Mail* Sun Girl Quest. A crowd of 10,000 cheered on the 16 finalists as they took to the podium in their swimsuits at Sutton's Beach, Redcliffe, for the Australia Day weekend of January 1960. The overall winner, Beryl, 17, from Gympie, took home a new car and was granted a television screen test.

Several decades later, Allison entered Miss Brisbane as a fun way to get back on stage for the first time since her ballet days, and to raise money for charity. The fundraising consumed most of Allison's spare time, but her efforts were rewarded. At a gala event at the Mayfair Crest Hotel on Roma Street on Friday 22 October 1993, Allison was named Miss Brisbane. Her mum was still working as a school librarian and had a young student with cerebral palsy. Accepting the award, Allison told the crowd she was absolutely thrilled. Her win made the news. 'Allison's fluent in compassion,' read one headline, picking up on her command of six languages. For a fleeting moment, she was the star she felt destined to be.

Six weeks later, Allison was back at the Mayfair Crest for the next stage, the Miss Queensland awards. The motto for the night was 'much more than a pretty face', in case anyone missed the message that this was more than a mere beauty pageant. In a field of 12, Allison lost out to a 23-year-old radiographer, but she'd had her moment in the sun. The awards limped on for a few more years before finally ending in 2000.

For Allison, the excitement of becoming Miss Brisbane was dampened by the deterioration of her relationship. Drayton was in the audience for her win but was no fan of the awards. He couldn't really fathom why Allison would want to enter.

Perhaps Allison reacted to his lack of support, or perhaps she was in two minds about whether the life mapped out in front of her was what she wanted, but she started having second thoughts. Although they were engaged, Allison and Drayton never got around to planning a wedding. In hindsight, Drayton knew it was a mistake to leave things open-ended. It made it too easy for Allison to leave. There were no blazing rows. They simply drifted apart.

Allison was the one who said it was over, and moved out. Drayton, devastated, quit real estate and went back to the Great Barrier Reef to nurse his wounds, this time to Lizard Island in Queensland's far north, where he returned to work as a dive instructor. Allison took one of their houses, and Drayton the other.

Allison set about moving on. She started a relationship with a dentist, who whisked her off on a European vacation. While they were away, her new lover abruptly abandoned her at a London train station. Standing alone on the platform, Allison didn't have a clue why he had run off. The answer came soon enough, but by bizarre coincidence. Instead of cutting short her holiday, Allison hooked up with her London-based best friend Kerry-Anne Cummings and continued her trip. The two friends were walking down a street in Prague when their jaws hit the floor – the runaway dentist was strolling towards them with another woman on his arm. Allison and Kerry-Anne could not stop laughing. He would forever be known as 'Dickhead Dan' the dentist.

Returning to Brisbane, Allison renewed contact with Drayton. Soon she was travelling 1600 kilometres from Brisbane to Lizard Island to visit him for a week, with Kerry-Anne in tow. Allison and Drayton fell back into each other's arms. Drayton thought it would be for good. But Allison was still unsure. She had kept it from Drayton, but someone new had come into her life.

The decision

Allison was rising up the ranks at Flight Centre. She'd been promoted to run an office at Ipswich before being elevated again to state human resources manager. Her new role was based on the second floor of a building in George Street in Brisbane's CBD. There, in 1995, she caught the eye of Gerard Baden-Clay, team manager of the company's new 24-hour call centre in the same building. Gerard was boyishly handsome with soft, almost feminine, features. He had been raised to have impeccable manners and to be polite and courteous.

Gerard oversaw a handful of staff who ensured clients could call at any hour to book flights, tours or accommodation. Allison was above him, literally. His desk, on the first floor, was directly below hers, and she outranked him in the company's pecking order.

They met when Allison was having trouble with her computer. Gerard, who majored in accounting at university but had an interest in computers, came to her rescue.

At first, Gerard tried to set Allison up with a friend of his, Ian Walton. Gerard had met Walton when both were working at accounting firm KPMG Peat Marwick, and now they were at Flight Centre together. Walton had expressed an interest in the company's sweet and beautiful HR boss. So one night, when they were all in Cairns for a managers' conference, Gerard organised a dinner and made sure Allison and Walton sat opposite one another.

Sparks flew that night, but not between Allison and Walton. Gerard, sitting nearby, had watched on enviously as the pair tested the water for a possible romance. He'd set up this meeting but now he wanted Allison for himself.

When the self-appointed matchmaker checked in later with his two colleagues, each was complimentary about the other but said they weren't really suited. Gerard seized the chance to walk Allison home on that balmy Far North Queensland evening. As Allison reached the top step before her hotel room door, he moved in closer. They kissed.

Allison invited Gerard to her family's annual Christmas gathering. Every year, her many uncles, aunts and cousins gathered at a family member's house. The happy, noisy get-togethers, void of airs and graces, could be intimidating for newcomers. The way to enjoy them was to give back as much as you got in the friendly banter and inevitable digs.

Gerard didn't get off to the best start with Allison's family. As about 50 of her relatives bustled around, Allison's new boyfriend retreated into a bedroom to work. She made excuses for him, saying he had a lot on at work and was always on call in the new 24-hour division. Gerard had set the tone for his interactions with Allison's family. He found the functions overwhelming, but left an impression he considered himself above them. Allison didn't feel that way. She found Gerard charming and she liked that he was hardworking and ambitious. Gerard treated her like a princess, and cast himself as her prince.

Allison's loyalties were divided. Ian Drayton had been down to Brisbane to see her and she could not make up her mind which man she wanted to be with. Drayton was safe, loving and smitten with Allison. But Gerard's relentless charm was almost impossible to resist. Somehow, Gerard always knew the right thing to say at the right time.

When Drayton visited Brisbane again, he and Allison met at a five-star hotel in the CBD. Privately, Allison was intent on making a decision – Drayton or Gerard. The stress took its toll. On the Sunday morning, before they were due to check out, Allison started struggling to breathe. Drayton thought she was having a life-threatening asthma attack and rushed her to hospital. In hindsight, it may have been a panic attack. The pair were in the emergency department for an hour or two before doctors cleared Allison to leave.

On their return to the hotel, Allison broke down in tears. She couldn't go through it again, she told Drayton. She was sorry. Drayton, knowing nothing about Gerard Baden-Clay, was blindsided. Allison left the hotel alone in her little red Nissan. As she drove off, she looked out the window and gave Drayton a wave. It was the last time they would see each other.

Allison later confided to her friends how, hopelessly divided, she eventually made up her mind between Ian Drayton and Gerard Baden-Clay that weekend. The decision was so split, she had resorted to a test.

In the hotel with Drayton in Brisbane, she had left some clothes on the bed and gone for a long shower. When she came out, the clothes were still there, crumpled and unmoved. On a recent night away with Gerard, when she'd put her clothes on the bed and gone for a shower, she returned to find Gerard had neatly ironed them and hung them in the cupboard.

What to some would seem slightly odd behaviour, perhaps evidence of a controlling nature, was the clincher for Allison. Gerard had picked up her clothes. Drayton hadn't. It might have been better to flip a coin, but that was how she came to make the most fateful decision of her life.

After making her choice, Allison phoned her friend Linda Ebeling to tell her all about Gerard. Ebeling would remember Allison excitedly relaying Gerard's family connection to Scouting founder Lord Baden-Powell. Clearly, Allison was swept up in Gerard's grand family history. Ebeling and her husband, Stephen, had a soft spot for Allison's previous fiancé, Drayton. But Ebeling thought her friend sounded happy with the new man in her life. Allison had always wanted to be doted on, and Gerard fitted the part perfectly.

Gerard was thoughtful and generous throughout their courtship. When Allison went away for work, she arrived at her hotel to find her favourite magazines waiting in her room. Gerard had phoned ahead to the hotel to arrange the small surprise.

April 2012

Ian Drayton froze in front of his TV. The bowl of cereal he'd been holding slipped through his fingers, shattering as it hit the tiles at his feet. He heard himself swear loudly at the screen. Tears flooded his eyes. At home in Canberra, Drayton had been getting ready for work. The former dive instructor and real estate agent now had two university degrees and was an executive at the Canberra Institute of Technology.

That morning he was half-watching the news when a familiar face flashed on the screen. The woman staring back at him was missing, presumed dead. Her name was Allison Baden-Clay but Drayton knew her as Allison Dickie, his former fiancée. They hadn't seen each other for 16 years. The truth was Drayton had never stopped caring for Allison.

A friend in need

20 April 2012

Her husband would be mad she hadn't had her phone with her all morning. *That's why they call it a mobile phone – because you can take it with you.* Kerry-Anne Walker returned to her desk in Flight Centre's Brisbane headquarters and retrieved it from next to her keyboard. Missed calls flashed on her screen. A couple from an unknown number. Another from her husband, Mark Walker. Allison's best friend from school, Kerry-Anne Cummings, had married but the pair had maintained their close friendship through the ups and downs of life and motherhood.

For most of that Friday morning, Walker had been on conference calls in a small office down the hallway from her second-floor desk in the CBD high-rise. She was finalising plans for the company's annual conference, which saw staff members converge from around the world. Before Kerry-Anne had a chance to call Mark back, he phoned again. She could hear concern in his voice.

'The police have been trying to call you. Allison's missing,' he said.

Kerry-Anne and Allison had been constants in each other's lives. They had gone to school together, had been to Denmark on their student exchange trips at the same time, and lived together at university. They had even both taken jobs at Flight Centre.

Dialling the number police had left for her, Kerry-Anne reached Detective Senior Constable Cameron McLeod from the Criminal Investigation Branch at Indooroopilly. Kerry-Anne told McLeod she didn't know where Allison was, but she could tell the detective it was very much out of character for her to be missing. It had never happened before.

Many times, Kerry-Anne had wished she was half the mother Allison was. Allison lived for her girls, channelling all her energy into them since putting aside her career for her marriage and family. The dedication Allison brought to her ballet as a child and that had made her such a success professionally in her 20s had been focused on her daughters – not on driving them to succeed, but on helping them to be happy. Allison's own battles with anxiety as a child had led her to become involved in a program to teach children resilience. Above all she wanted to equip her girls with the strength to make their own choices.

Kerry-Anne and Allison had been in touch only the evening before. Some months earlier, Allison had borrowed a couple of ball gowns from Kerry-Anne for a real estate awards night and still had them. Walker had sent her a text at 4.59 pm Thursday, reminding her about them: 'Al – hope you're well – can you bring the dresses into the office tomorrow? I need to collect. KAW.'

A reply from Allison's phone arrived at 7.50 pm Thursday. 'Of course! Sorry you had to chase them up. I am in the city all day at the convention centre so can drop them off on my way home about 6 pm?? Is that ok or do you need them for tomorrow night?? Al x'

At the time, Kerry-Anne's parents, sisters and brother had all been at her place for dinner, otherwise she would probably have phoned Allison back. Her mum and dad, Pam and Gary Cummings, had been visiting from Tasmania and it was a farewell dinner before their flight home in the morning.

Kerry-Anne replied at 9.25 pm, telling her friend it wasn't urgent: 'All good, just need for next week. Feel like I haven't seen you for ages. Hope everyone OK. We will have to have lunch soon.' There was no reply to the final message.

After the worrying conversation with police, Kerry-Anne kicked herself for sending text messages instead of phoning

Allison. Everything had seemed fine in the text from Allison, but how could she really know if they hadn't spoken?

Thinking Allison might answer a call from a friend, Kerry-Anne dialled her mobile phone. It rang out. She sent a text message. There was no reply.

Kerry-Anne usually didn't work on Fridays but had come to the office that day so she could park her car there, catch up on a few things at work, and then pop out for a special treat. A short stroll away was the five-star Marriott Hotel and, on the fourth floor, its luxurious day spa, the Dome Spa Retreat. Walker had a $500 gift voucher and had booked a massage and facial for that afternoon. A fluffy white dressing gown, glass of champagne and deck chair would be waiting for her at the outdoor pool adjoining the spa.

A day at the Dome was one of the most indulgent experiences the city had to offer and Kerry-Anne had a strictly limited chance to enjoy it. Her 12-month voucher was due to expire that afternoon. She had left her booking until the last day, savouring the occasion for a year. But now there was something far more important on her mind.

Kerry-Anne had phoned Allison's parents, Geoff and Priscilla Dickie, and they were already on their way to Brookfield from the Gold Coast, where they had settled in retirement. Kerry-Anne knew she had to join them. Grabbing her bag, she handed her spa voucher to a friend in the office and walked out. At least someone would enjoy it, she thought as she took the lift down to the basement car park.

There was no way Allison would ever walk out on her three daughters. That was an absolute. Something was terribly wrong. The drive from the CBD to Brookfield took just over 20 minutes. Kerry-Anne's anxiety grew with every minute of the journey, as word failed to arrive telling her it was all a mistake and Allison was safe and well.

Right to silence

20 April 2012

1 pm

Gerard was at the top of the long driveway as Kerry-Anne pulled up at the Brookfield Road house. The first thing she noticed was his meticulous business attire. His shirt was crisp and tucked into his neatly pressed trousers. It looked like he was ready for a regular day at the office. There were police cars out the front. Officers in uniform and in plain clothes milled around. Seeing her arrive, Gerard went over and gave Kerry-Anne a hug. She did a double take at the scratches down the right side of his face. The painful-looking wounds were weeping. After a quick hello, Gerard wandered off to talk to police.

Allison's parents had arrived before Kerry-Anne. Geoff and Priscilla had been at a church craft group on the Gold Coast when Gerard rang shortly before 10 am. Their son-in-law simply told them Allison had gone for a walk and hadn't come back. Immediately alarmed, the Dickies dropped everything and rushed back to their Paradise Point home, grabbing a change of clothes because they thought they might not be returning that night, and drove up to Brisbane.

The last time Priscilla had seen Allison was almost two weeks earlier, when her daughter was at Tallebudgera on the Gold Coast, spending the Easter weekend there with Gerard and the girls. The Dickies had set everything up for Allison so she and her family could walk straight into the camping and caravan park to enjoy their break. They had had lunch together on Easter Sunday before Allison, Gerard and the girls headed back to Brisbane.

When Geoff and Priscilla arrived at Brookfield about 11 am on the 20th, Gerard had greeted them casually.

'Hello, Dad. G'day, Mum,' he said. He shook Geoff's hand, and gave Priscilla a hug.

Allison's parents hated Gerard's habit of calling them Mum and Dad.

'What happened?' Priscilla asked. Gerard repeated the story he'd told all morning, then offered the stressed couple a cup of tea.

Inside the house, Priscilla was struck by how tidy the place was. She was used to seeing the home quite messy. Allison would always tell her not to worry about picking up after the girls, that tidying was for the end of the day. Today, her daughter's best teacups were laid out on the table. Priscilla had only ever had tea in a mug, not this fancy china. It looked too perfect. It didn't feel right.

Like most people who arrived at the house that morning, Priscilla and Geoff were also taken aback by the marks on Gerard's face.

'What's that?' Priscilla asked Gerard about the scratches.

He told his mother-in-law he cut himself shaving. Priscilla had been married to Geoff for 50 years and he had never hurt himself like that. Nor, for that matter, had her many brothers.

Police were coming and going, and Gerard was in and out of the house. At some point after Kerry-Anne arrived, Gerard had a request, asking her and the Dickies to join him in the house to talk in private. He led the way into the master bedroom. Turning to face Allison's parents and oldest friend, Gerard quietly dropped a bombshell. He'd spoken to a lawyer. He'd been told not to provide a formal statement. In situations like this, he said, the husband always came under suspicion. Police would most likely arrest him.

Kerry-Anne, Geoff and Priscilla were dumbfounded. Only a few hours had passed since Gerard reported Allison missing. All they could think of was finding her. Lawyers? Suspects? Arrests? It was way too soon for this kind of talk.

Kerry-Anne wanted to know what was going on. Why wasn't he cooperating with police? Gerard said he was cooperating, he just wouldn't be making a formal statement. Priscilla had more questions for Gerard. Did he hear Allison go to bed? Did he hear her get up? Gerard had nothing in the way of answers to offer her. Kerry-Anne asked if they'd had a fight.

'No,' he insisted. They'd had a discussion and then he went to bed, he said. 'She was watching TV.'

'Are you telling the police everything?' Kerry-Anne wanted to know.

Gerard started losing his cool. 'Keep your voice down,' he snapped. By now police were hovering outside.

Gerard told Geoff, Priscilla and Kerry-Anne he expected them to take Allison's side. He would do the same if something like this were happening to one of his daughters.

Gerard had been repeating the story, of waking to find his wife gone, over and over since early that morning: to his daughters, to his parents and sister, to an emergency operator, to the two police officers who first turned up on his doorstep, to two senior officers who followed, to detectives who came down his driveway next, and now to the Dickies and Kerry-Anne. It was proving difficult to follow his lawyer's advice to keep his mouth shut.

Suddenly, there was no time for any more questions. A police officer came into the room and ordered everyone outside. The house was being sealed off as a crime scene.

Outside, Kerry-Anne tried to find out more from the growing band of officers gathering at the home. 'What's happening? What about the scratches?' she asked a policewoman.

'We've seen the scratches, don't worry,' the officer replied, knowingly.

When she had a moment alone with Geoff and Priscilla, she asked them about the injuries too. Geoff repeated Gerard's shaving explanation.

Kerry-Anne phoned her parents, who had not long landed in Hobart, and told them what was happening. Her mum, who loved and adored Allison, got straight back on a plane to Brisbane.

Nothing that morning quite added up to the three of them. Other than his flash of anger when Kerry-Anne raised her voice in the bedroom, Gerard remained eerily calm. He did not look or act distraught. There was no sense of urgency. He wasn't rushing to look for Allison.

Scout's honour

When I was a boy at Charterhouse [one of Engand's top boarding schools] I got a lot of fun out of trapping rabbits in woods that were out of bounds. If and when I caught one, which was not often, I skinned him and cooked him and ate him – and lived. In doing this I learnt to creep silently, to know my way by landmarks, to note tracks and read their meaning, to use dry dead wood off trees and not off the ground for my fire, to make a tiny, non-smoky fire such as would not give me away to prying masters; and if these came along I had my sod ready to extinguish the fire and hide the spot while I shinned up some ivy-clad tree where I could nestle unobserved above the line of sight of the average searcher.

Robert Baden-Powell interview, *Listener Magazine*, 1937[1]

When Allison Dickie married Gerard Baden-Clay in 1997, she didn't marry a man, she married a dynasty. Gerard had always been immensely proud – some say too proud – to claim Scouting founder Lord Baden-Powell as his great-grandfather. It is a family fame forged on strength in adversity but also one that values living by your wits and, when necessary, using cunning and deception to outmanoeuvre an adversary.

It was 1899 and British Colonel Robert Stephenson Smyth Baden-Powell was surrounded and vastly outnumbered. The South African Republic had declared war on Britain, and Baden-Powell was charged with defending the British-held town of Mafeking. A force of up to 8000 Boer aggressors had cut off and laid siege to the town, but Baden-Powell held firm. With only a thousand men at his disposal, including untrained

The Baden Powell family tree

Reverend Professor Baden Powell (1796–1860),
Savilian Professor of Geometry at Oxford.
Married three times, had 14 children.

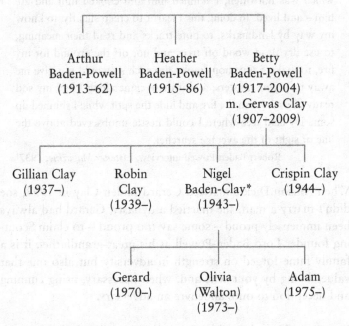

Lord Robert Stephenson Smyth Baden-Powell (1857–1941),
founder of the Boy Scouts movement.
Married Olave St Clair Soames.

Arthur
Baden-Powell
(1913–62)

Heather
Baden-Powell
(1915–86)

Betty
Baden-Powell
(1917–2004)
m. Gervas Clay
(1907–2009)

Gillian Clay
(1937–)

Robin
Clay
(1939–)

Nigel
Baden-Clay*
(1943–)

Crispin Clay
(1944–)

Gerard
(1970–)

Olivia
(Walton)
(1973–)

Adam
(1975–)

* Surname changed

townspeople, he turned to the art of deception, honed since his youth.

Aware the enemy was watching from a distance, he had his men bury empty boxes in a field to give the impression they were burying landmines. He wanted the enemy to have second thoughts about approaching. Men were also ordered to pretend to crawl under barbed wire on the perimeter, when none existed, to fool the forces in the distance into thinking they would have difficulty charging the town. Rifles were fired on one side of the outpost then rushed to the other and fired again to conceal a shortage of firearms. Similarly, searchlights were moved around to create the impression an assault from any direction would be exposed.

British journalists stranded in the town managed to smuggle out daily reports to readers back home telling of the heroic defence of Mafeking. For 217 days, Baden-Powell held the enemy at bay until a British relief force finally broke the siege in May 1900. At the age of 43, Baden-Powell became a national hero.

He returned to Britain to find a handbook he'd previously published for soldiers, *Aids to Scouting*, had become a hit with the general population. At the suggestion of Boys' Brigade founder William Smith, Baden-Powell wrote a new version for a younger audience. He tested his ideas at a camp on Brownsea Island in Poole Harbour, Dorset, in 1907 – the first Scout camp. *Scouting for Boys* was released in 1908. The power of his celebrity ensured the book was a runaway success. Spontaneously, boys throughout Britain and beyond began forming their own Scout patrols and troops.

At a meeting the next year at the Crystal Palace in South London, 11,000 Scouts turned up. 'Scouting started itself,' declared BP, as Baden-Powell became known. The presence of groups of girls in the crowd, declaring themselves the Girl Scouts, prompted him to write a new book for them, and Girl Guides was born.

Later, as well as BP's fame, his family would become accustomed to controversy too. Critics and biographers have condemned Baden-Powell for many things over the years. He's been labelled a mass murderer for starving Africans in Mafeking, and a brute for executing an African prisoner promised mercy.

He was a plagiarist and a charlatan in the eyes of others, for copying central ideas for the Scouting movement from British author Ernest Thompson Seton. Some suggest he had an ulterior motive for his movement, citing comments he made about photographs and artwork involving nude boys. Some suspect he was a repressed homosexual, pointing to an unusually close relationship with a male friend. His works are also often inherently contradictory. On the one hand he instructed Scouts not to follow the herd; on the other he told them to obey orders without question.

Perhaps the most dangerous challenge to his legacy, though, has been the revelation that some Scoutmasters have abused their trusted positions to prey on boys in their charge.

Still, Scouting has stood the test of time. According to the biography *Baden-Powell*, by author Tim Jeal, more than a decade ago 550 million people had been Scouts or Guides. Today there are 40 million Scouts in one million local Scout groups worldwide. There are 10 million Girl Guides and Girl Scouts. It is a huge legacy for his descendants to live up to.

Scouts – Gerard was among them – pledge to follow a Promise and Law based on Baden-Powell's original wording:

> On my honour I promise that I will do my best: To do my duty to God and the King; to help other people at all times; to obey the Scout Law.
>
> A Scout's honour is to be trusted; a Scout is loyal; a Scout's duty is to be useful and to help others; a Scout is a friend to animals; a Scout obeys orders of his parents, patrol leader or Scoutmaster without question; a Scout smiles and whistles under all difficulties; a Scout is thrifty; and a Scout is clean in thought, word and deed.

Scouts pledged to do a good deed every day, and adopted the motto 'be prepared'.

Meet the Clays

More than 100 years after Robert Baden-Powell defended the township of Mafeking from Boer invaders, his family was once again under siege. This time a nation's media surrounded them. The wife of Baden-Powell's great-grandson Gerard Baden-Clay was missing.

Under the glare of the media spotlight, Gerard retreated to the home of his parents, Nigel and Elaine Baden-Clay, in suburban Kenmore, a few kilometres from the home he shared with Allison. By then, more than a week had passed since his wife had vanished without trace. A command post had been set up to coordinate the search for Allison, but Gerard was keeping away from there. Allison's parents, Geoff and Priscilla Dickie, were permanent fixtures.

The public was becoming curious about the elusive Baden-Clays, who had circled their wagons around Gerard. Nigel and Elaine had chased journalists from their door and were aware news cameras were on their street around the clock to catch their son's comings and goings. Perhaps in an attempt to project an image of family unity, the couple engineered a display of affection for the cameras so baffling it was referred to by many simply as The Granny Pash. Uploaded to YouTube under the heading 'Baden-Clay parents pash for cameras', it would be watched thousands of times.

The footage was captured when Gerard arrived at his parents' home. After helping their son remove some things from the boot of the car, the couple leant in for a kiss in the carport. Nigel appeared to have expected a peck but his wife, Elaine, drew him in for a long and toe-curlingly awkward smooch. Channel Nine reporter Andrew Kos highlighted the scene in his report for that night's 6 pm news bulletin, telling viewers, 'As his parents, Nigel and Elaine, unpacked the car, a bizarre moment for a very public display of affection.'

The number plates on Nigel's car, BWANA, added to the family's air of oddity. From the African language Swahili, the word translated to master, boss or sir. Then there were the hunting trophies. Several sets of impressive antlers were mounted on the front wall of Nigel and Elaine's home; visitors had to pass them to get to the front door. The ostentatious display, visible from the street, included a majestic pair of spiral horns from a kudu antelope, commonly hunted in Zimbabwe.

An old profile of Nigel from when he was a Century 21 Westside salesman could still be found online. It described him, intriguingly, as an avid big game hunter, conservationist and marriage enhancement facilitator; he and Elaine helped organise retreats for couples wishing to reconnect. 'Nigel Baden-Clay's personal history reads like a list of people you'd like to invite to your next dinner party, but incredibly it is simply the compilation of one incredible life so far,' the website trumpeted.

And the surname? How could descendants of Baden-Powell have come to be called Baden-Clay? Truth is, they were plain old Clays until the 1980s, when the surname was changed by deed poll to the far more illustrious sounding Baden-Clay.

Even putting aside their famous ancestry, the Baden-Clays seemed determined not to behave like your average family. Now they were caught up in truly extraordinary circumstances.

Nigel Gerard Arden Clay married Elaine Isobel Nora Hughes in St Stephen's Anglican church in Bournemouth, south-west England, on 23 August 1969. On their marriage certificate, 26-year-old Nigel listed his occupation as 'tsetse fly control officer'. Elaine, then 25, was recorded as an advertising executive. Guest of honour was Nigel's grandmother, Olave Baden-Powell, the adored 80-year-old World Chief Guide and widow of Robert Baden-Powell.

Lady Baden-Powell had flown into the UK especially for the wedding. A day earlier, she had been addressing 1000 people in a hall in Finland, on one of her many tours, and had slipped and hit her face against a wall. A wide-brimmed hat concealed her two black eyes as Nigel and Elaine exchanged their vows.[1]

Lady Baden-Powell's famous husband had died in Nyeri, Kenya, in 1941, but she had continued his work. At London's 16th-century Hampton Court Palace, where she had a residence at the grace and favour of the Queen, Olave sent out an extraordinary 2000 Christmas cards a year; she was known for her prodigious memory for faces, names and places. Her palace apartment, which she called 'Hampers', had an annexe with 13 rooms, each named after a different country.[2]

Olave practised what she preached when it came to following the strong moral code instilled in Guides. On one occasion, Nigel's brother, Robin, spotted Lady Baden-Powell cleaning the back of her Guides badge ahead of a gathering at Wembley Stadium. He was puzzled. After all, no one would see the back once it was pinned to her jacket. She told him it was a reminder to always be clean, and not just in the visible ways.[3]

When Robin – Gerard's uncle – documented the Baden-Powell pedigree online, he finished up with a family tree which fills almost 50 printed pages and goes all the way back to a William Powle born around 1460 in Mildenhall, Suffolk.[4]

Robert Baden-Powell is not the only highly accomplished family member. His father, Baden Powell, was a Savilian professor of geometry at the University of Oxford. An overseas guest at one of Professor Powell's parties in 1857 recounted the privileged scene and extraordinary gathering of minds that greeted her. A servant welcomed her at the door, and another announced her arrival. Among other invitees were the likes of Peter Roget, of thesaurus fame, and mathematician Charles Babbage, known as the 'father of computing' for inventions that led to development of the modern computer.[5]

Robert Baden-Powell married late in life. He was 55 when he met Olave, then 23. It was 1912 and they were aboard the ocean liner SS *Arcadian*. The pair shared the same birthday, which they viewed as a sign they were meant to be together. They married later that year and had three children.

Their youngest child, Betty, met Oxford-educated Gervas Clay on a ship in 1936. When Betty discovered she and Gervas shared the same birthday,[6] the events were so strikingly similar to her parents' first meeting that it seemed fate had brought them together.

Gervas was a champion hurdler and member of the Achilles athletics club at Oxford. He was working in the British Colonial Service in Northern Rhodesia – now Zambia – and was expected back in Africa within months, so the couple hastily arranged to be married.[7]

Gervas Clay later told how his father asked him to check that Robert Baden-Powell owned long pants for the ceremony, because he was so frequently seen out in public wearing shorts. After the wedding, the couple headed immediately to Northern Rhodesia, where they lived for the next 30 years and raised their four children.[8] One of these children was Nigel, Gerard's father.

As Gervas rose up the career ranks, the family lived in 17 different houses.[9] He was posted as District Commissioner to Kitwe, Ndola and Broken Hill in Africa.[10]

A visit from royalty in 1960 added another chapter to the family's proud history. Gervas was then Her Majesty's Resident Commissioner for Barotseland, and the Queen Mother came to stay at his official residence in Mongu during a tour of Africa. Gervas later described to his son Robin how, during a garden party on the residency's lawns, he warned his royal guest about the presence of stinging ants.

The Queen Mother revealed that one was biting her at that very moment, so Gervas directed her to a private room, knelt down and removed her shoe. 'And there was a great soldier ant gnawing at her poor toe and drawn blood – and she had never shown a sign of it to the people,' Gervas told his son.[11] Robin documented the story, and many others, on websites devoted to his parents.

Betty, like her parents, documented her life in a daily diary and scrapbooks, and in one entry wrote of the Queen Mother attending a dance during the Mongu visit. The royal, wearing a tiara to please the crowd at Gervas's request, asked Betty if her husband danced.

'I said, "Yes",' wrote Betty, 'so she turned to him and asked him if he would dance with her – which he did very beautifully.'

A social disaster was narrowly averted when it was realised the record for the next dance was called 'The Lady is a Tramp', and it was replaced just in time, Betty wrote.[12] The Queen Mother must have been impressed with the hospitality during her three days as a guest of Gervas and Betty, because when she left she personally wrote a four-page thankyou note.

In Livingstone, Gerard's grandfather enjoyed a wonderfully civilised existence. Gervas would come home for lunch each day at 12.35 pm and enjoy a meal, game of cards and 30-minute nap before heading back to the office at 1.55 pm. He would be home again by 4.35 pm for a cup of tea, some cricket or a trip to the river with the dogs.[13]

Nigel, the third of Gervas and Betty Clay's four children, was born in Tanganyika – now Tanzania – East Africa, in 1943. In his eulogy to his father, which was read out at Gervas's funeral at the Parish Church of St John the Baptist in Somerset in 2009, Nigel described an idyllic childhood. His earliest memory, he recalled, involved hunting wildlife. He was three years old and Gervas had taken him shooting in Kitwe, Northern Rhodesia. His father shot a teal and couldn't find the bird. Nigel found it and was rewarded with a tickey, or thruppence. 'That was when the shooting bug infected him and Nigel has shared his father's love of shooting all his life.'[14]

For his secondary school education, Nigel was sent to a newly established boarding school at Peterhouse, Rhodesia, which developed a reputation as one of the finest in southern Africa. Like his father, he lived a highly regimented existence. At 6 am the bell rang and it was time to get up for showers. From 6.15 am to 7 am the students did their homework in their room, which had a small study nook with a table, chair, locker and books. From 7 am to 7.45 am it was breakfast, followed by morning prayers in the chapel until 8 am and then class.

The students were streamed according to ability in maths, physics, chemistry, French and Latin. Afternoons were spent playing sport – cricket in the summer and rugby and hockey in winter – or working around the school grounds. At 6.30 pm it was dinner, 7 pm to 8 pm was more study, and 10 pm was lights out. Boys who misbehaved were subjected to brutal canings.

When I track down Nigel's old Peterhouse classmates more than half a century later, they generally remember him fondly as one of the students in the top streams. A good friend from the school, Peter Pinder-Browne, tells me Nigel was 'always a very wide-awake kid'. Despite his Coke-bottle glasses, he was a keen sportsman who played hockey and cricket. As would be expected, Nigel was also strongly involved in Scouting.

Pinder-Browne and his twin brother, David, were once invited to Nigel's home in Livingstone for the Easter school holidays. It took two days by train to get there. The home was a regular government house, comfortable but not grand. The Clay family's cocker spaniel, memorably, could open and close doors. Like other expatriates in Rhodesia, the Clays had domestic help: a cook, cleaner and a couple of gardeners. It was standard for staff quarters to be separate, made up of sleeping rooms, a communal kitchen and toilet. Staff received wages and rations such as beans and maize meal, sugar and salt.

The Clays were excellent hosts and took their two young visitors to the breathtaking Victoria Falls. At a viewing platform, a locked iron gate blocked the way to a perilous walkway leading behind the wall of water plummeting from more than 100 metres above. It was an area normally off limits to the public, but Gervas Clay, as district commissioner, had a key and took Nigel and his friends through. It was the end of the rains and water levels were soaring. Nigel and his young friends were soon standing amid the spray, wind and thunder of water, conscious that they were enjoying privileged access.

Afterwards, the young boys tried to climb the famous thousand-year-old baobab tree nearby, but didn't make it far up the grand trunk. Another day, they went on a wildlife safari, spotting giraffe and zebra. It was a taste of paradise, an unforgettable holiday.

One day in 2013, Pinder-Browne was surfing the Internet and read that Nigel's son Gerard was facing trial for murder. 'It must be a catastrophe for the family. Even if he didn't do it – the name. The family were impeccable people,' he told me.[15]

Nigel would have other fond memories from childhood of his grandmother, Lady Baden-Powell. In particular, he held close a long walk with 'Granny' across a Swiss mountain, and a visit to a chalet where staff were shocked to see the World Chief Guide appear.[16]

While life was full of fun, there was always the family's strict moral code in the background. Nigel recalled in his eulogy to his father how Gervas once strongly rebuked him for trying to reuse a stamp that had not been postmarked: 'All of us, his children, are all in his debt for all that he taught us – about honesty, integrity, ethics, chivalry, respect for other people, love of animals (except for cats!), service to 'God and Queen', duty, and love of family.'

Some of the same words would be used to spruik a suburban real estate agency on the other side of the world.

Elaine Clay fell pregnant within months of marrying Nigel. The couple went to Johannesburg, South Africa, to share their big news with Olave Baden-Powell. Nigel's grandmother was on her last world tour. Coincidentally, Lady Baden-Powell had been in the same city 27 years earlier when daughter, Betty Clay, told her she was pregnant with Nigel.[17]

In England ahead of the birth, Elaine joined Lady Baden-Powell at her Hampton Court Palace apartment. Just as Allison would struggle many years later, Elaine found pregnancy harder than she had imagined. The publication *Guiding in Australia* mentions Elaine's time at 'Hampers': 'Elaine went to spend a short time with "Granny", the intention being to look after [Olave] as her servant was ill. However Elaine's role became reversed and she found she could not match Lady B.P.'s energy.'[18]

On 9 September 1970, Elaine delivered a healthy son. Gerard Robert Baden Clay was born at The Firs maternity home on Trinity Road at Bournemouth. The family was yet to change their name. Gerard's birth certificate, obtained through UK archives, shows the new parents were still named Nigel Gerard Arden Clay and Elaine Isobel Nora Clay. Nigel's employment was again listed as tsetse fly control, though on this document he added that he was a Zambian government supervisor.

Robin Clay, Nigel's brother, became Gerard's godfather.

Nigel, Elaine and their young son, Gerard, migrated south across the Zambezi River to Rhodesia – now Zimbabwe – in 1972. They were going into a country in the midst of a brutal, intensifying civil war. The Rhodesian government of Ian Smith had unilaterally declared independence from Britain in 1965. A white minority of 250,000 ruled a country of five million. Robert Mugabe's Zimbabwe African National Union, Joshua Nkomo's Zimbabwe African People's Union and the Rhodesia government were in a three-way battle for power.

Nigel was working for the Rhodesian government, and the family moved between various cities. Daughter Olivia Isobel Clay was born in Umtali, Rhodesia, on 26 September 1973, and another son, Adam Clay, was born on 23 December 1975, also in Umtali.

A striking family photograph from their time in Rhodesia, taken within a year of Adam's birth, can be found online. It shows Nigel dressed in camouflage fatigues, a rifle in one arm and his baby son, Adam, in the other. Gerard, who is about six years old, is standing slightly behind him, ramrod straight, with his shirt tucked neatly into his mustard-coloured shorts. Gerard, smiling broadly, is clinging to his dad's leg. Olivia is to the front, with a big grin, also holding her dad's leg. Nigel looks like a hero about to set off to battle. Presumably, Elaine Baden-Clay is behind the lens.

With Rhodesia at war, able-bodied young men were drafted into the army for mandatory service. There were some exceptions, such as civil servants who could not be spared from their day jobs. Nigel, 29 when he moved to Rhodesia, did his bit.

Many years later, when son Gerard came under suspicion for the murder of his wife, there was much talk about Nigel's military links. Some whispered he was a member of the infamous special forces regiment, the Selous Scouts.

Nigel may have been a Scout but he wasn't a Selous Scout. Published service rolls for the prominent regiment and the separate SAS do not include his name. When I consult Rhodesian military experts, at first they can find no record of Nigel. But eventually, one comes back with a match. On a 1978 roll, Nigel Clay – with a matching date of birth – is listed as a British South Africa Police reservist.

'In WWII parlance – Dad's Army,' the expert explained, in a reference to the British TV comedy of a bungling band of soldiers of advancing years. A separate record shows Nigel was one of almost 30,000 people awarded a Rhodesia General Service Medal.

I show the same expert the photo of Nigel in his camouflage fatigues, with his rifle in hand. The expert identified the weapon as an FN FAL rifle, commonly issued during the Rhodesian Bush War: 'Just the general appearance of his webbing . . . is how a relatively inexperienced soldier would have it. I do not think he would be anything other than "your average Joe",' he said.

As the battle for control of the country raged, blood was spilt on all sides. In one shocking incident in September 1978, a heat-seeking surface-to-air missile shot down an Air Rhodesia flight en route to the capital, Salisbury. Of the 52 passengers and crew on board, 38 died in the crash and a further ten were gunned down on the ground. A second Air Rhodesia flight was shot down in February 1979, killing all 59 aboard. The twin disasters hit home to Nigel and Elaine, who were fortunate not to have been aboard after flying the same route around that time.

An email from Nigel and Elaine to Robin Clay – sent decades after those incidents and published online – shows their memories of the time remain vivid: 'We flew to Kariba for a holiday without the children between the two [air] Disasters. In some ways it seems like yesterday, but in others it seems a lifetime ago.'[19]

In 1980, as the country gained independence and became Zimbabwe, the Clays joined the exodus of whites. Nigel, Elaine and their three children headed to Australia. Gerard was ten years old. Later, in a court affidavit, Gerard said the family made the move 'after forming the view that it would be safer to live in Australia'.

They spent ten days in Perth as guests of a woman who had been involved in Guiding for 60 years.[20] Links to Baden-Powell afforded them special treatment wherever they went. The family lived in Melbourne, with one of Nigel's cousins, for their first eight months, before moving to Toowoomba.

With the new start in a new country came another significant change – the Clays began calling themselves the Baden-Clays, in a nod to their famous ancestor.

Schoolboy

Toowoomba Grammar School headmaster William Dent had a reputation for memorable speeches and did not disappoint in his farewell to the class of '87. The year produced some of the best and brightest to graduate from the century-old private school. Among the students was 17-year-old Gerard Baden-Clay.

Despite the considerable academic and sporting achievements of pupils that year, Dent, as dry as they come, couldn't resist delivering a final rebuke. He bemoaned the 'remorseless tide of litter', the untucked shirts and 'raucous guffaws and uncouth bellows' in a speech which would have made him front-page news today.

'I have frequently imagined,' he deadpanned, 'what fun it might be one day to produce a gun and shoot stone dead the first boys I saw with their socks round their ankles, their shirt-tails hanging out, their hair uncombed or their elbows on the table. A few corpses scattered strategically about would not add much to our litter problem and would probably serve as a salutary warning to other potential offenders.'[1]

It was a speech the Baden-Clays, with their formal ways and appreciation for old-world etiquette, would have particularly appreciated. They had moved to Toowoomba – a conservative farming city west of Brisbane – in 1981. Here, Gerard attended Gabbinbar State School and then Toowoomba Grammar School. There were 696 students, 408 of whom were boarders, at Toowoomba Grammar when Baden-Clay was in his final year.

With parents who lived locally, Gerard had been in the dayboy minority. Charles Wiles was in the same year and social group at Grammar. He took away good memories of Gerard – though not of their old school or home town. As soon as he could,

Wiles left town and went on to run a contemporary arts centre in Cairns, about as far away as he could get from Toowoomba without leaving the state.

'I don't reckon he did it,' he volunteers when I phone around old classmates before Gerard's trial. 'I remember him being a really nice guy at school. There are a lot more people at school I would have thought would have turned out to be a murderer than him.'

Gerard's high school is one of nine Great Public Schools (GPS) of south-east Queensland, and was exactly how most would imagine a traditional, conservative school for boys. It could have been in England 100 years prior. The First XV rugby players were like gods, cheered on with a chant the rest of the school had to practise several times a week. Jason Little, a champion sportsman in Gerard's year, would become one of the greats of Australian rugby.

In the playground, it was boarders versus dayboys. Rugged farm boys, raised tough out west then shipped off to boarding school in the big smoke, patrolled like sharks looking for an easy kill. Dayboys, Gerard among them, hung in a group, counting on safety in numbers. They'd play handball in the lunch breaks. Every now and again a boarder would pick one of them off.

'It was classic bullying,' says Wiles. 'They'd grab you, hold you up against the wall and abuse you. Anyone who wasn't into sport was ridiculed.'

Gerard saw his share of school bullies after moving from Rhodesia to Australia. Soon after his arrival, he defended a newfound friend in the playground and was punched in the eye for his efforts. Trudging home that day, he had walked backwards into the house to try to hide his shiner from his mother, but she somehow knew straight away.

Friendships were forged among the dayboys that would stand the test of time. One of the high achievers from Gerard's grade immediately defends his former schoolmate when I contact him overseas. He tells me of having dinner in Brisbane with Gerard,

Allison and their daughters not long before Allison went missing. Accusations Gerard murdered his wife soon after the get-together are clearly a shock. 'I had an absolutely wonderful evening with Gerard and Allison and the kids,' he says. 'I think Gerard is an absolutely amazing father. I haven't seen any father be as good a dad to their kids as Gerard was.'

He adds: 'There's absolutely nothing in the childhood stuff.' I take that to mean there's no deep dark secret from his early days in Toowoomba. He was a nice enough kid from a decent family. In our brief conversation, the friend expresses anger at police for not returning his call after he phoned them about the dinner. 'You could probably ask the Queensland police why they don't follow up the basics.' He doesn't want to be named or to talk any more.

Julian Lancaster-Smith, co-founder of Toowoomba's Quality Desserts, is another student from Gerard's year.

'There were people in Toowoomba who were absolutely horrified,' he told me ahead of the murder trial. 'They thought there was no way in hell the guy we knew 25 years ago could do anything like that.'

Sometime after Gerard was charged, by chance, Lancaster-Smith and his wife were staying at the same caravan park as relatives of Allison. 'They asked me about him – was he as big an arsehole then, as he is now. The guy I knew back in Grammar was just a normal guy. He probably got bullied a bit like I did. [The murder charge] was something I wouldn't have predicted. Obviously he's innocent until proven otherwise.'

Not all of Gerard's schoolmates were so surprised. When I contact former classmate Fletcher Sigley, he reveals he phoned Crime Stoppers, while Allison was still missing, to nominate locations Gerard might have hidden her body. Particularly, he listed secluded areas Gerard knew from the Scouts and a stint of officer training in the army.

Sigley reasoned that pressure, stress, anxiety and depression could drive a person to do all sorts of things. Anyone could be capable of murder. The way he saw it, any man could be compared to a computer – it might run fine in standard conditions, but if you tried to open too many programs simultaneously, it slowed and could shut down completely. Gerard had always been very concerned about his image, and would have done everything to protect his good name. If Gerard had snapped and killed his wife he was unlikely to own up to it, Sigley thought.

I contact dozens of other boys from Gerard's senior year, tracking them down through school yearbooks, phone books and online. The majority don't remember Gerard, don't know him well enough to comment, or have only vague recollections about his double-barrelled surname and Scouting connection. Gerard simply doesn't stand out.

When I contact a former teacher, he's aware of the case but can barely recall Gerard. He says when news of Allison's disappearance started making national headlines, and word spread of a Toowoomba link, he had to drag out his old yearbooks to remind himself who Gerard was. 'He didn't stand out in any way, shape or form that could have given any indication of what would happen down the track,' he says.

Gerard's father made more of an impression. 'I wasn't totally rapt in his attitude, put it that way,' the teacher says of Nigel Baden-Clay. 'When people send their children to a private school, some do have a superior attitude to everybody, including the teachers. A number of parents were very snobby. It was just an impression I had. We had a couple of members of staff from Zimbabwe and South Africa. I'm not trying to be racist but the attitude that comes across sometimes is that "I'm better than you."'

He's not the only one left with this impression. The family moved into a home on the corner of Mackenzie Street and Range Street in Mount Lofty. It was a quiet, leafy street in an upmarket part of Toowoomba. Nigel was an insurance agent with AMP. Often he would pitch life insurance policies to neighbours and friends. The new arrivals and their prim and proper ways and proud family connections set off a wave of local gossip. One former neighbour was frank with his views about how the family fitted – or didn't – into Toowoomba's tight-knit community in the 1980s. 'I have met a great many people from all tiers of society and none have come close to matching the incredible superiority complex exhibited by Elaine and Nigel. They were so utterly full of themselves that others of us found discourse with them embarrassing. My father and I took delight in referring to Nigel as the "insufferable Boer". Elaine was far worse.'

The perception of the family wasn't helped when Mount Lofty residents became aware they had added the 'Baden' to their surname, which left the impression they were trying to gild the lily somewhat.

'As luck would have it,' says the former neighbour, 'the neighbourhood soon knew all about the "Baden" thing as a neighbour had been some sort of fashion editor on the *Women's Weekly* and had known Nigel's mother as "plain Betty Clay".'

Another neighbour, who, like Nigel, also worked in insurance, had a different view. 'I thought he was quite a decent fellow, Nigel. He was very hard working. He was fairly aggressive, I'd say, but you probably have to be, in insurance. He was typical of a South African or Zimbabwean.'

As far as Gerard and his siblings went, he said, 'there was no problem at all. They were quite well-behaved children, they were just normal kids.'

Regardless of what others thought of the family, Gerard, Adam and Olivia always had each other. They'd regularly play Marco Polo in their backyard swimming pool, noisily splashing about for hours. When Nigel's father, Gervas, visited, he could be heard for some distance as he playfully mimicked a hippo for his grandkids.

At the start of 1987, Gerard's final year of school, the family moved to nearby Withcott, where they bought a house on 2.8 hectares at Meadows Road for $150,000. While still at high school, Gerard worked part-time at a Toowoomba restaurant, Squatters, and also picked potatoes and strawberries in the Lockyer Valley. He graduated from school with a high tertiary entrance score of 900. With that mark, he enrolled in a Bachelor of Business at Toowoomba's Darling Downs Institute of Advanced Education.

Gerard had prospered under the watchful gaze of the fastidious headmaster and his future was looking bright. He left Toowoomba Grammar having made loyal friends who would be there for him in times of crisis many years later.

Accountant

1988 to 1994

There is a tendency for you as a young man starting out into life to feel that you are but one of a crowd, and so can drift along with the rest and you will be all right . . . Well, that is a rotten bad tendency. Remember, you are you, you have your own life to live, and if you want to be successful, if you want to be happy, it is you who has to gain it for yourself. Nobody else can do it for you. When I was a youngster a popular song was 'Paddle Your Own Canoe', with the refrain, 'never sit down with a tear or a frown, but paddle your own canoe'. This was meant to give guidance for going through life – and very good too.

Rovering for Success, Robert Baden-Powell, 1922

The Ruthven Rush was an infamous annual event in Toowoomba that demanded equal doses of stamina and stupidity. Cheered on by classmates, local university students sprinted from pub to pub along the city's major thoroughfare, Ruthven Street. At each venue they had to skol a beer before running to the next, until they either passed out or crossed the finish line or both. The rite of passage was a fixture of university life in the 1980s.

Gerard and his friends didn't buy into the heavy drinking culture. Alan Hockings went to school with Gerard and started at the Darling Downs Institute of Advanced Education at the same time. Later it became the University of Southern Queensland. When I contact Hockings ahead of the trial, he says he'd spend hours playing the card game 500 with Gerard to pass the time when they weren't in lectures or studying. 'We were pretty boring really,' says Hockings.

Their wildest escapade occurred in the uni refectory. They were having lunch one day when talk turned to sport and they challenged each other to a foot race. In a mad dash to prove they were the fastest, they barrelled over chairs, under tables and around other students. Years later, Gerard's CV included a footnote from his uni days: 'Winner, quadrangle race.' Was it an embellishment from his impromptu race with Hockings? Or a separate, formal, race? There weren't too many details on the CV.

Hockings told me he found out about Gerard being charged with murder when a friend at work in Brisbane pointed out the story in the papers. The charge didn't match the boy he knew from school, or the man from university. 'I remember saying to my workmate I didn't think he was hot-headed enough for a crime of passion and wouldn't be stupid enough to do anything premeditated,' Hockings said.

While at uni, Gerard signed up for officer training with the Australian Army Reserves, as did his Toowoomba Grammar School classmate Fletcher Sigley. Sigley recalled army trucks arriving at the Toowoomba campus to pick up 30 to 40 people on a chilly morning around March 1989. Gerard and the other recruits were taken on a bumpy ride to Gatton, where the Queensland Agricultural Training Unit was based, for paperwork. Later they went to Brisbane for medical and psychological testing. Gerard gave the impression he was signing up out of a sense of patriotic duty and to continue a family tradition of service.

Military theory was combined with field trips, sometimes lasting weeks. Gerard was seeing a young woman who had enlisted at the same time. It was Gerard's first serious relationship. When I phone her in London, she politely declines to talk about Gerard, but is willing to confirm there was nothing out of the ordinary about the relationship.

After three years of study, Gerard landed a coveted graduate job with chartered accounting firm KPMG Peat Marwick in

Brisbane in 1991. Years later, in a court affidavit, Gerard said he earned his business degree over five years, so was only part-way through when he started with the firm. Australians were struggling through Paul Keating's 'recession we had to have', and it was a major coup to gain a job with one of the big accounting firms, particularly before his degree was completed.

Gerard was hired alongside between 20 and 30 graduates that year and started his first real job in Central Plaza One, a newly opened high-rise office tower in the CBD, Brisbane's tallest building at the time. Though their salaries were low – somewhere in the $20,000s – they were filled with excitement at beating hordes of other applicants to the prestigious posts.

Gerard started in the company's audit division. Like everyone else, he was given the opportunity to complete further professional training to become accredited as a chartered accountant. While the other recruits in his year beavered away earning the qualifications, Gerard didn't.

One colleague recalls: 'It was unusual, so people knew he didn't enrol. I think in my year he was the only one who didn't. It's probably not so unusual these days. Back in the early '90s, it was. If you didn't do it your career opportunities were somewhat limited.'

Perhaps the reason he lagged behind the others in pursuing his professional qualifications was that he was still studying for his degree. Gerard kept his head down and gained his Bachelor of Business, majoring in accounting, in 1992. He walked out of his golden job at KPMG the following year. He felt it wasn't for him, and never became a chartered accountant or certified practising accountant.

Consciously or unwittingly, he was following the advice of his great-grandfather that a young man should not succumb to the temptation to drift with the crowd but should 'paddle your own canoe'.

After a year as an accountant for a workwear company, he became a travel agent with the burgeoning Flight Centre chain in 1994. The company was aggressively recruiting university graduates at a time when jobs were hard to come by. Gerard was living at Wavell Heights in Brisbane's north with his parents and brother, Adam.

The next year saw Gerard move into Flight Centre's George Street building in the city to head a new 24-hour telephone service. More than just his professional life was changing. In his new office, he met his future wife.

'Til death do us part

1996 to 2000

With the lights of the Eiffel Tower twinkling above them, Gerard Baden-Clay got down on bended knee to propose to Allison Dickie. Knowing Allison was a fan of all things Parisian, Gerard could barely think of a more perfect setting to ask for her hand in marriage. Except, of course, for the real Eiffel Tower.

At this Eiffel Tower there were no gardens to gaze out across. No Seine to stroll beside while they planned their life together. Instead, the couple was looking out at Park Road, a busy cafe strip in inner-city Brisbane – home to a Vegas-style replica Eiffel Tower perched over an Italian restaurant. It is a strange cultural clash, one that leaves many diners scratching their heads as they admire the glittering tower while perusing a menu of pasta and pizza. At one end of the road is Coronation Drive, one of the city's busiest arterial roads, at the other a rattling rail bridge ferries commuters west from the city.

The tower was built to celebrate Brisbane's World Expo in 1988, almost 100 years after the original was built as the entrance arch and centrepiece of Paris's 1889 World's Fair. The replica was placed in front of an apartment and dining precinct known as Savoir Faire, although ironically towers over Italian eatery La Dolce Vita. Gerard was not the first, nor will he be the last, to use it to woo a mate.

Gerard would say he chose the location because they were due to go to Paris later that year, and he couldn't bear for Allison to be dawdling on every street corner waiting for him to present a ring. In reality, Allison wasn't waiting for a ring at all. Instead of falling into his arms with a joyful 'Yes!', she asked for a week to think about it. For Gerard, always concerned about losing face, it must have been an awkward moment, but he said a week would be fine.

Some may say that anyone who has to ponder a marriage proposal for more than a few seconds should probably say no, but after a week, Allison said yes. The couple drove down to see Allison's parents, Geoff and Priscilla, who had moved from Redbank to Paradise Point on the Gold Coast in their retirement. Gerard dropped Allison at a shop on the ruse of getting some bread, then went on his own to ask Geoff for his daughter's hand in marriage. Gerard had asked his father, Nigel, for advice on whether he should talk to the Dickies before or after his proposal. Nigel had thought it best to ask Allison first, in case she said no. If he was nervous, the Dickies soon calmed him with warm congratulations. The couple went out and bought a sizeable diamond ring – Gerard hadn't risked splurging on one up until then.

Gerard liked to consult with his parents, particularly his father, before making decisions. So, after asking Nigel how to propose, Gerard asked his dad when he should get married. Nigel looked at a calendar for his own wedding anniversary and saw it was on a Saturday that year, 1997. Wouldn't it be lovely, Nigel suggested, to marry Allison on the same date he married Elaine? Gerard and Allison agreed it would be a nice touch. They could do worse than emulate Nigel and Elaine's long marriage.

With the wedding date set, Allison's friends organised a kitchen tea party. Over champagne and finger food, the guests made a fuss of the bride-to-be, recounting stories from her childhood and travels and using the occasion to shower her with praise. Her friends admired Allison, and told her to be proud of what she had achieved. Following her success in the Miss Brisbane awards she had been named Ipswich Young Business Woman of the Year. Her rise up the corporate ladder was continuing, with a promotion to Flight Centre's global human resources manager in 1995, at the age of 27.

Allison wasn't the type to brag of her achievements. Whenever her friends ever saw her, she'd ask what they were up to, rather than talk about herself. Her interest in others was genuine. It's what they loved about her, along with her quirky sense of humour and a contagious laugh. Always the last to get the punchline, then the one to laugh hardest. At the kitchen tea party, everyone let her know how much they appreciated her.

As Allison was flooded with attention on the eve of her wedding, Elaine Baden-Clay decided it was time to change the focus. 'So, enough about Allison. Let's talk about Gerard,' she said to the group.

Not long before the wedding day, Gerard and Allison met a professional photographer on the steps of Customs House in the city. Allison looked stunning that day. Her hair and makeup were faultless and she was smiling broadly. Gerard looked dashing in a dark suit. Allison told one of her cousins, Jodie Dann, it was funny the picture turned out so well, because she had argued with Gerard all that day.

Allison had put the bickering down to the stress of organising a big wedding. They swiftly patched up their differences. She loved that he took charge and had big plans to match her own. He thought she was beautiful, and a world beater.

Allison asked her sister, Vanessa, friends Kerry-Anne Walker and Linda Ebeling and Gerard's sister, Olivia, to be her bridesmaids. Olivia was marked for great things in the military. At the Australian Defence Force Academy, she had been Cadet Captain with 222 cadets in her year under her command. She graduated in 1995 after three years of study, the first woman Cadet Captain to do so. Excelling at the academy, she had scooped both the RSL's Sword of Honour for outstanding leadership and the prestigious Commander in Chief Medal. The latter was the highest award a cadet could be bestowed, taking into account all facets of military and academic achievement, and Olivia was presented the medal by Governor-General Bill Hayden. She had gone straight into the Royal Military College Duntroon and graduated a year later as a lieutenant, shortly before Gerard and Allison's wedding.

All five shared a room together in a city hotel the night before the ceremony. A Harley-Davidson roared through the high-rises to collect Allison from the hotel and take her to a restaurant for dinner with friends. Her Harley riding 'chauffeur', sporting a goatee and impressive mullet, helped her into a black leather jacket, black helmet and sunglasses before the ride. Later, back at the hotel, the women all huddled together in the same bed in their flannelette pyjamas for a photo, and Allison gave her bridesmaids earrings to wear the next day.

Gerard had asked his younger brother, Adam, and a school friend, Rob Cheesman, to be groomsmen. Adam had followed his sister into the military and was that year to graduate from Royal Military College Duntroon.

The wedding took place at St Mary's Anglican Church on Brisbane's Kangaroo Point cliffs on 23 August 1997. It was 28 years to the day since Gerard's parents married. The bride made a grand arrival: a chauffeur in a suit, tie and cap opened the back door of a classic car and she stepped out. Allison looked angelic in a white, off-the-shoulder gown with long trail, embroidered bodice and sweetheart neckline. Long white gloves, a flowing white veil, tiara and drop pearl earrings fit the part of a princess, which was how Gerard treated her. Her tiara was a Baden-Clay heirloom, sent from the UK for the occasion. The groom was in a traditional dark suit, with a white rose tucked into his lapel, his hair neatly trimmed and face clean-shaven.

About 100 guests witnessed Gerard and Allison take their vows, to be together in sickness and in health, 'til death did them part. The wedding party took a ferry across the Brisbane River for the reception, which was held in historic Customs House in the city. Allison threw her bouquet over her shoulder and the bride and groom cut a four-tier white cake. It was a wedding with all the trimmings, except – to the shock of attendees accustomed to enjoying a drink – alcohol. Gerard and Allison, who were both social drinkers, had inexplicably made it a dry occasion. Flight Centre thrived on regular, merry get-togethers, usually late into the night, and some of their work colleagues were horrified to discover there would be no booze provided.

In the lead-up to the wedding, Allison told close friends Gerard had decided there would be no alcohol. There was never a clear explanation about why, but her friends assumed it was to save money. There were more than a few muttered words about Gerard being too cheap to stump up for drinks. Thirsty guests got their wallets out and bought their own drinks at the bar.

Geoff Dickie, standing to make his speech as father of the bride, told of his love for his daughter, but also had a heartfelt message for Gerard. 'She's my princess, you look after her,' he told his new son-in-law.

Kerry-Anne Walker hadn't approved of Allison's new love interest when they started dating. She didn't think Gerard was good enough for her friend – didn't really think anyone could be good enough for Allison. Gerard, trying to win her over, took her out to coffee one day and remarked: 'You don't really like me much.' Kerry-Anne had to agree. Everything always seemed to be about him. His career. His travel plans. His family.

As maid of honour, she stood to say a few words. 'I never liked Gerard . . .' she began. Naturally, she didn't continue in that vein. If Allison loved him, Kerry-Anne would love him too. 'But you better take care of her, otherwise you'll have me to answer to,' she said.

Speeches were a Baden-Clay specialty, and when Gerard stood to address his guests he had a lot to say. In tears, he thanked his parents, calling them 'Mummy and Daddy'. What with all the other people from his distinguished family to thank and acknowledge, the speech went on and on. Sober guests would swear Gerard's speech alone went for an hour-and-a-half. As the night drew to a close, the newlyweds left in a little red car, which was decorated with multi-coloured streamers and yards of white cloth. Gerard was behind the wheel and a big white sign was stuck to the passenger's side door, which read, 'Under new management'.

Gerard and Allison's new life together started with an extravagant overseas honeymoon that morphed into a working holiday. Kerry-Anne and both sets of parents were at Brisbane airport to wave them off a week after they married. Like their wedding, the honeymoon had all the bells and whistles.

After a brief stopover in Kuala Lumpur they spent ten days at a romantic resort in the Maldives. It was a dream start to their life together, and their travels were only beginning.

The island stay was followed by a 16-day tour of Turkey, a couple of weeks in Jordan, a dash through Israel, a couple of weeks in Egypt, and then another two weeks in Spain, Portugal and Morocco. For a few weeks they travelled through north-west Europe, taking in the Netherlands, Germany and Switzerland.

Gerard was particularly pleased to take Allison to the International Scout Centre at Kandersteg, in the Swiss Alps. As a living link to the original Chief Scout, Gerard was a welcome addition around the chalets, lodges and campsites.

Moving on to the UK, and having decided to set up base there, Gerard and Allison stayed with his grandparents, Betty and Gervas, in Somerset before they found work in London.

Gerard gained a job at Blockbuster International as a financial systems consultant in January 1998 and became the main breadwinner. Allison, who had soared up the ranks at Flight Centre, found herself in a low-paid position at Dale Carnegie Training.

While in London, the couple sent off applications for voluntary summer jobs at the Kandersteg Scout Centre. Accepted, they had only been working for a couple of weeks when they had to briefly return to Brisbane. Gerard's groomsman, Robert Cheesman, was getting married on 4 July. There was another important event to attend a week later: Gerard's sister, Olivia, was marrying his friend Ian Walton. Olivia and Walton had met at Gerard and Allison's wedding.

Before heading back to Kandersteg, Gerard and Allison consulted a doctor about medication for an upcoming travel adventure. It would have long-lasting ramifications.

Honeymoon's over

1998

By now seasoned travellers, and always well organised, Gerard and Allison took advantage of being in Brisbane in July to drop in to a travellers' medical centre. The couple had a three-month trip across South America planned for the end of the year.

Little yellow medical passports contained records of Allison and Gerard's injections and vaccinations from their travels, but one of the things they'd never had to worry about previously was malaria. They were offered a choice of preventative medication. One had to be taken daily, and the other, Lariam, was a weekly dose. The doctor they saw warned the pair that Lariam was unsuitable for people with a history of mental illness. Gerard and Allison, looking at each other, said that wasn't an issue and chose Lariam for the convenience.

Lariam is the brand name for a drug containing mefloquine – a synthetic alternative to quinine. US Defense Department biomedical research unit, the Walter Reed Army Institute of Research, developed mefloquine in the 1970s for use on troops. With an eye on the burgeoning third-world travel market, a deal was struck to allow Swiss pharmaceutical giant Roche the rights to develop the drug. In 1989 it was approved by the US Food and Drug Administration (FDA) and was marketed to civilian travellers under the name Lariam. Considered at the time to be safer than equivalent drugs, it became the most popular anti-malarial on the US market.

Before long, however, worrying reports of reactions, including amnesia and vivid hallucinations, began to surface. Initially, some were put down to recreational drug use or travel stress.

But the number of reports began to be compelling – sufferers told of vivid, often terrifying nightmares; they could hear voices murmuring and mumbling; they were plagued by a sense of impending doom and morbid visual hallucinations. In the early 1990s, UN peacekeeping troops and UK-based flight crews were banned from taking the drug over concerns about its psychological effects. But it wasn't until the early 2000s – years after Allison's experience in 1998 – that the effect on the travelling public started really being taken seriously.

Although Lariam is no longer marketed as a brand in the United States, generic anti-malarials containing mefloquine are still available. The US FDA warns side effects can include anxiety, paranoia, hallucinations, depression, restlessness, unusual behaviour and confusion. The side effects can persist even after the medication is stopped.

Author David MacLean charted the effects of Lariam in his book *The Answer to the Riddle Is Me: A Memoir of Amnesia*. MacLean woke up on a train station platform in India with no idea who he was and ended up in a psychiatric hospital suffering bouts of severe hallucinations.

Australian John O'Callaghan took Lariam after contracting malaria on a surfing trip to Indonesia. Before taking his own life in 2000, O'Callaghan wrote a suicide note outlining the effect of the drug: 'Since [Lariam] first blew my brains apart . . . I've never been the same. Always dazed and confused, always physically sick. Sorry mum, dad,' he wrote.

After the two weddings in Brisbane, Allison and Gerard had returned to the Scout Centre at Kandersteg in the Swiss Alps to complete their three months of voluntary work. In September 1998, they flew via Washington to Rio de Janeiro, Brazil. They had started taking the Lariam pills a couple of weeks earlier in order for the drug to take effect.

They had chosen a challenging trip, a truck tour. Piled in the back of a truck, it was a long and bumpy ride going from the east to west coasts: through Bolivia, Argentina, Uruguay, Paraguay and Ecuador. It ended in Ecuador's capital, Quito. At times the group of 16 would rough it, camping on the way. At other times they would be in hotels. Often, they were visiting big, dangerous cities.

Allison was well travelled, but she didn't have her usual thirst for adventure. Her new husband thought he noticed her becoming nervous, anxious and withdrawn. It first came to a head in Potosi, Bolivia. They were in a hotel room and Allison could not get out of bed. They had plans for the day to go sightseeing at the silver mines, which had once made Potosi the largest and richest city in the Americas. Allison was curled up on the bed and didn't want to go out. She said it wasn't like a normal sick feeling and she didn't need a doctor. Gerard headed out with the rest of the group, leaving her in the hotel room. The next day, Allison was back on her feet, like nothing had happened. But Gerard thought Allison's mood continued fluctuating throughout the trip.

Gerard became aware that her distress wasn't confined to tough travel areas when the same low mood persisted in New York, on their way back to the UK.

When they returned to Gerard's grandparents' home in Somerset, Allison crashed. She later told of being catatonic, of 'freaking out' and suffering hallucinations. They went to the local Taunton hospital, where a doctor noticed Allison was on Lariam. The drug had to be taken for a couple of weeks before and after travel; Allison and Gerard were still taking their weekly dose. For the first time, Allison and Gerard realised that the pills they were taking to ward off malaria may have been playing havoc with Allison's mind. The doctor said the drug should soon work itself out of her system.

After Christmas 1998, they went back to Kandersteg, where they had new, nine-month contracts to work at the Scout Centre. Gerard was assistant director and, for a period, acting director. At times he would be supervising 50 staff. Allison was relegated to running the shop and doing administrative work.

The job would later look good on Gerard's CV, but both he and Allison were working at the centre in return for their accommodation and a nominal salary. They were paid enough to splash out on a monthly dinner in town and treat themselves to the occasional Toblerone.

Still, Gerard loved Kandersteg and didn't want to leave. He wanted to be director, which would put him on some real money. Allison saw no future for herself there. Reflecting on this period in her journal, she wrote that she'd wanted to stay in Australia when she married, 'to be famous'. Her ambitions, her prospects, everything, revolved around being in a major city somewhere, not in this Swiss town of 1200, no matter how beautiful it was.

Even though Allison would have preferred to be home, at the end of their contract, she and Gerard made plans to stay on. They went back to the United Kingdom in September 1999 to complete a training course so Gerard could apply for the director's position at the Scout Centre.

The role never eventuated for Gerard. A director hurt his back, leaving Gerard to fill the void for a while, but it was only temporary. The opportunity for Gerard to be promoted vanished. The couple returned to Australia at the end of 1999 to regroup and catch up with family.

Setback

Their trip to Brisbane had been meant to be brief. Allison and Gerard had intended to continue their overseas travels in the New Year and had left their belongings in a UK warehouse. But while they were home, Flight Centre sought out Allison to return to work. She met with the company's new HR manager in November 1999 and took a part-time job helping prepare the company's annual overseas conference.

A journalist and photographer from Ipswich's *Queensland Times* caught up with Allison in April 2000 for a profile on the child ballet star and former Miss Brisbane. The report that ran in the paper said she was 'filled with bright prospects when considering her future', but her own words made it clear she was at a crossroads.

'At the moment, I'm at a fairly transitional period in my life,' Allison told the paper. 'I've always had goals and this is the next big step. It's a strange time; it's been good to just sit back and have the time – and then be able to say which direction to go in.'

Once Allison was back on the Flight Centre payroll, Gerard started trying to get work in the company too. He applied for a manager's position but was unsuccessful. Eventually, he found a spot on a new venture. Keith Stanley, Flight Centre's marketing boss, was putting together a team to explore the growing power of the internet. The new division was called Global Online and in March 2000 – four months after Allison returned to Flight Centre – Stanley gave Gerard a 12-month contract to work on the offshoot.

Stanley remembers Allison glowingly from their work together in her HR role. 'She was very talented,' he tells me.

'She had . . . a really open, honest sort of personality and people naturally liked her. In a HR role, that's obviously an advantage. She was very, very highly regarded by everybody.'

Gerard, on the other hand, he found 'very posh'. Says Stanley, 'He was very self-confident. He was proud of his Baden-Powell heritage . . . When he came back it was just timing really. I was looking to pull a team together, I wanted someone who had retail experience in the Flight Centre model and he had that. We'd been given the budget to do this test and he was there and we had the job. It could have been him or someone else.'

Although internet travel would eventually explode, this pioneering foray into the field was a disaster for the company. Gerard and his team attempted to create a viable online travel business and failed. Like many early online start-ups, they burned through money without generating the revenue to justify their existence. In August 2000, the small division was axed and staff given their marching orders. Gerard was abruptly sacked with the rest of the team.

It was difficult for Gerard to accept that despite signing him up for 12 months, the company was letting him go after six. He felt the rug had been pulled from under him, that it had failed to honour its promise.

Gerard and his colleagues were the first Flight Centre redundancies. Word of the failed internet division's spending spread like wildfire through the company. The rumour mill went into overdrive and some put the division's churn in the millions of dollars, with nothing to show for it apart from a few desks. Stanley confirms that the operation was 'running a lot of cash' but can't recall an exact amount. No one in particular was responsible for the failure, he assures me. The timing simply wasn't quite right. 'The company wasn't really ready for it and the internet wasn't ready for it either.'

Others may have taken the dismissal on the chin and moved on, or lobbied for a different role. But Gerard came out swinging. He consulted a lawyer, and then sued the company for breach of contract. A statement of claim was lodged in the District Court in Brisbane five days before Christmas. In it, Gerard claimed the firing was 'without reason or adequate reason'. He asserted that he had been planning to return to live and work in the UK before being enticed to work at Flight Centre. Up until then he had been 'gainfully employed' in Switzerland and the UK. In all, he demanded Flight Centre pay him $59,500.

'He challenged the company, that's fair enough, that was his right,' says Stanley, 'but if I remember rightly it didn't go anywhere.'

Only two documents were ever filed – Gerard's claim and the company's notice of intention to defend the claim. The issue disappeared off the radar.

There must have been an element of panic in the Baden-Clay household as Christmas approached that year. Gerard and Allison were renting a three-bedroom townhouse in Gubberley Street, Kenmore. They were a stone's throw from his parents, Nigel and Elaine, who had moved to Kenmore from their previous home at Wavell Heights.

All around Brisbane, homes were decked out with fairy lights, tinsel and Christmas trees, and families were preparing for beach holidays. It should have been an exciting time for Gerard and Allison because by December 2000, three years after their wedding, Allison was three months pregnant with their first child. But excitement about the impending new arrival was tempered by the sacking.

With a baby on the way, Gerard had to figure out how to make a living and what to do with his life. They had some Flight Centre shares to tide them over for a while, and Gerard started doing some stockmarket trading from a makeshift office in their garage.

Allison and Gerard's first child was born on 3 July 2001. Allison had gone through a rough patch emotionally during the pregnancy. Her mother, Priscilla, drove up from the Gold

Coast to help out after the birth. Priscilla was surprised to find a baby monitor in the kitchen was rigged up with a connection to Gerard's garage office. Gerard could hear anything going on in the home. Priscilla told family that when she went to speak to Allison, her daughter put her finger to her lips for her to be quiet. Outside, Allison told her mum Gerard could hear everything. Gerard separately explained the monitor was there so Allison only needed to call his name and he would be by her side. Priscilla thought Allison was coping about as well as any new mum, and didn't like the idea of Gerard listening in all the time.

If adapting to parenthood wasn't smooth sailing, Gerard's working life seemed to be floundering. His stockmarket dabbling from home hit trouble when al-Qaeda launched terror attacks in the United States on 11 September 2001. The travel industry was in turmoil, and the couple's investments were at risk, so in a panic they sold their Flight Centre stocks that day.

Gerard was at a first-aid course to prepare for a new job when the terror attacks happened. He had been accepted to chaperone students from Brisbane Boys' College (BBC) on a trip to India and Nepal. After the hijacked planes were flown into the World Trade Center in New York, the parents at BBC baulked at sending their children overseas, and the job fell through.

Despite being the sole breadwinner, having a six-month-old baby, an anxious wife and no real job, Gerard decided to join his brother, Adam, on a holiday to Europe at the end of 2001. Allison was left to cope with the baby on her own; luckily, she had the support of her parents.

On his return, Gerard battled away in the home office for a while, trying to turn a dollar. He would soon become aware of exciting changes in Brisbane property. Suddenly, the previously sedate real estate market was turbocharged. Backyards were turning into goldmines and there were opportunities aplenty for those willing to paddle their own canoe.

Boom

Once upon a time – and not such a long time ago – the thought of anyone paying upwards of $250,000 for an average house in Brisbane drew gasps of surprise. 'Quuuarter-of-a-miiiillion dollars,' people would drawl, rolling the staggering figure around on their tongues. To understand how the Brisbane housing boom of the 2000s shook the city, it's helpful to have a sense of the calm that preceded it.

In 1990, the median house price in Brisbane was $118,000. Over the next decade it grew, steadily but unspectacularly, to hit $173,000 in 2000 – an increase of 46 per cent. By comparison, over the next seven years, from 2000 to 2007, the median house price jumped a jaw-dropping 160 per cent to reach $450,500. After a decade of growth averaging just below five per cent, the city's real estate market was suddenly clocking up annual increases of 25 per cent.

Interstate and overseas migration to the Sunshine State and a shortage of supply were cited as reasons for the frenzied buying. The federal government's First Home Owner Grant, introduced in 2000, also buoyed the market. Rather than putting buyers off, the rapid price rises seemed to trigger a wave of panic buying as the momentum built on itself. And it wasn't just prices that were up. The number of houses changing hands soared to record levels too. In 1998 fewer than 16,000 houses were sold in Brisbane, for a combined total price of $2.8 billion. In 2003 upwards of 23,000 homes sold for $8.2 billion. For those who got in on the ground floor, a real estate agent's licence was as good as a licence to print money.

Brian Mason would one day come to feature in the Baden-Clay investigation. Long before that, his timing was superb.

With a background in the building industry, he joined the ranks of real estate agents servicing Brisbane's western suburbs in 1996. In his first year, effectively an apprenticeship, he made only $16,000 in commissions. The following year, he'd found his feet and earnt a respectable $60,000. By the time the boom started to hit, he was well placed to ride the wave.

As someone who had worked through leaner times, Mason was agog. He kept expecting the incredible ride to come to an end, but the buyers kept on coming. Mason would hold four open houses on a Saturday and have contracts on three by the end of the day. The next day he'd be fielding calls from anxious buyers who missed out. He teamed up with another agent and between them, from 2001 to 2008, they wrote up to $900,000 in commissions a year. Not bad for a bloke with just a few years' experience up his sleeve.

The pickings were especially good in Brisbane's western suburbs, which boasted some of the city's most expensive real estate. In 2007, Brookfield topped a list of Brisbane's priciest suburbs – ahead of Ascot and Hamilton – with a median house price of $1.3 million.

Agents were living large. Mason bought a Mercedes – his boss a Bentley. If Mason wanted a Harley he bought it, with cash. He went to Europe for a month to see family. While he was away, he made $50,000 from sales without lifting a finger. Houses were virtually selling themselves.

The biggest jumps in the median Brisbane house value were in 2002 (26.5 per cent) and 2003 (27.3 per cent). Gerard Baden-Clay watched the growth in amazement and set his mind on a new career. He was late to the party, and far from alone.

For years, the number of real estate agents had remained static in Queensland. From 1995 to 2002 there was a nine per cent increase in the number of licensed agents, and a five per cent decrease in real estate salespeople. It was a different story in 2003, the year Gerard joined the industry. That year alone, there was a 29 per cent increase in the number of licensed real estate agents – from 4493 to 5795 – and a 92 per cent jump in the number of registered salespeople, as Gerard became – from 5533 to 10,628.

He was but one of a crowd of newcomers flocking to property to make the most of the incredible price hikes and frenzy of sales, like prospectors in a modern-day gold rush.

Keeping it in the family

2003

Ray Leech and Jason Arnott were hiring, and there was a lot to like about Gerard Baden-Clay when he first walked into their real estate business. The duo had launched their agency, Raine & Horne Kenmore, only the previous year at Shop 3/2105 Moggill Road. It was a no-frills brick building, a couple of doors down from a busy Coffee Club franchise.

For their launch, a Black Thunder van from FM radio station B105 had rolled into the car park, Nickelback dominating their airwaves with 'How You Remind Me'. Ads in the *Westside News* publicised the occasion as 'the biggest free barbecue Kenmore has ever seen'. Only in real estate could some humble sausages be promoted with such fanfare.

Leech had launched six real estate offices during his career and Arnott had been a popular local agent for 16 years. It was their first business together and the plan was to build it up fast and offload it for a premium.

In their search for staff they had run job ads in the bulging classifieds of the local newspapers, and in walked Gerard. He had no property experience but was well spoken and presented, university educated and had a background in sales from his previous job at Flight Centre. He ticked the boxes. So much so that the two partners had the distinct impression it was Gerard doing the interviewing.

There were two other agencies he was seriously considering, he told them. Gerard's confident pitch impressed the pair. Real estate was, after all, the ultimate confidence game. But there was a catch, and it was a big one: Gerard didn't come alone.

If Leech and Arnott wanted him, Gerard told the startled agents they would have to hire his parents too.

During their combined decades in the real estate game, the two partners had seen many curious things, but they had never known an agent to include his parents as a condition of employment. The new office had only a handful of staff. Bringing in three members of the same family could upset the balance. Then again, three heads were surely better than one. The partners decided to give the unconventional arrangement a shot; however, Leech had a firm condition of his own: 'That's fine. I don't mind paying you a retainer. But I'm not going to pay your mother and father. You have to subcontract them on your own,' he said.

It was three for the price of one. Gerard accepted. He had a foot in the real estate game, with his parents along to tie his laces.

From the day the Baden-Clays arrived, it was apparent to the rest of the staff the family was an exceptionally tight-knit unit. Gerard's open affection with his parents was the first surprise for workmates. Gerard, Nigel and Elaine would hug and kiss each other warmly and often, in the office and in public. Leech marvelled at the big bear hugs Gerard and Nigel would exchange whenever they saw each other.

'Genuinely close,' he thought, 'totally genuine.'

Equally conspicuously, Gerard addressed his parents as 'Mummy' and 'Daddy' around the office and in front of clients. Arnott noticed that Gerard seemed to consult his parents before any decision. It all took some getting used to.

While other agents slogged away on their own, Gerard had the unique benefit of having his parents to share the load. One of the toughest challenges in real estate is securing listings; that is, finding properties to sell. It is especially hard for novices, who need to build a client base from scratch with no word of mouth.

Gerard largely left this grinding, mundane side of his new job to his parents. Nigel and Elaine, who were not getting any younger, did most of the legwork. This included the hard yards of working the phones and venturing out into the Brisbane heat to put pamphlets in letterboxes and door-knock house-to-house looking for sellers. The lifeblood of a real estate business, any agent will tell you, is sellers not buyers. The more the merrier.

Nigel and Elaine would round up a prospective client, and Gerard would step in to close the deal. His role was to convert the leads – to get potential clients to sign on the dotted line with him, exclusively. Then he would take the properties to the market and get them sold.

Nigel and Elaine were both about to hit their 60s and should have been retiring somewhere, but they'd had a setback and needed money. Nigel had progressed, over the years, from working in life insurance sales to building up a financial planning business. However, his planning for his own financial future hadn't worked out well. He had sold his business as part of his retirement plan, but only ever received an initial payment; the rest never came through. Nigel and Elaine's retirement income and nest egg were non-existent. That was how Gerard and his parents came to be working together in real estate. They were all registered real estate salespeople, which required them to work under a licensed agent.

Nigel and Elaine were gladly doing all that grunt work. The couple put their eldest son on a pedestal. They predicted that Gerard would become a superb businessman. Gerard was lucky to have Nigel and Elaine with him. The efforts of the parents freed Gerard to spend more time networking and building his profile.

Raine & Horne Kenmore may have been a new business when the Baden-Clays arrived but it was already doing a bustling trade. Leech had signage rights to the building so swathes of commuters saw the Raine & Horne name as they moved in and out of the western suburbs along Moggill Road.

The Coffee Club franchise, two doors away, drew all important foot traffic past the office. Often café customers would pause to browse the properties in the window. Leech, Arnott and their team were making the most of their contacts, giving the business a flying start. Gerard, Nigel and Elaine were perfectly placed to learn the ropes.

While Gerard was making headway in a new career, Allison was working her way through her own issues. She had fallen pregnant again, with the couple's second daughter. She was thrilled to learn she was having another child, but felt a return of overwhelming feelings of anxiety. It had been a battle, on and off, for years. It was finally time to do something about it. In September 2003, at 26 weeks, she knew she needed help and went to see a psychiatrist, Dr Tom George, after a referral from a GP.

Working from rooms in Everton Park in Brisbane's north, Dr George had more than 30 years' experience. In this first consultation Allison detailed her increasing anxiety and low mood. Frequent panic attacks included a highly unsettling incident when she was driving with her daughter in a baby seat in the back. On that occasion behind the wheel she had managed to pull over before passing out, but had progressively avoided driving since. She was fearful further episodes might cause her to faint and harm her unborn baby. Her confidence level had dropped, she felt far less energetic than usual and was worried her pregnancy might not go as well as expected.

Allison told Dr George she had experienced the same symptoms during her first pregnancy. She told him of her history. The hallucinations from taking Lariam. The anxiety going back to childhood. Other family members battled anxiety, she added. A miscarriage the previous year had been tough. Gerard's presence at home – after he had been axed from Flight Centre – had been a source of reassurance. She was anxious about being alone.

Dr George realised on the spot that Allison was suffering from depression and panic attacks, which were basically a sudden spike in anxiety. He recommended Zoloft, a brand name for the antidepressant sertraline. Gerard, who had taken Allison to the appointment, had reservations about medication. He'd later admit he didn't believe in depression and thought it was all in Allison's head.

Allison went with Dr George's advice and began taking Zoloft at the usual starting dose of one 50mg tablet a day. Sertraline, from a class of drugs known as selective serotonin reuptake inhibitors, controls mood by increasing the amount of serotonin available in the brain. Multinational drug company Pfizer developed Zoloft in 1990 and by 2005 it would be the most popular antidepressant in the United States, with more than 30 million prescriptions written annually.

A weight lifted for Allison. Now she had a name for what was troubling her, and the means to bring it under control. Within four weeks of starting on the medication, Allison's condition improved in leaps and bounds. By the time she gave birth to her second daughter in December 2003, Dr George noted Allison was symptom-free. The medication had done exactly what it was designed to do. It had been so simple. She had battled through for so long when all she needed was the right help.

At times she had been in no position to seek help herself. With her recovery there was some resentment. Why hadn't Gerard seen that she needed help? If she had been physically ill or injured he would have sprung into action.

Sold

2004

Jane Jones – not her real name – was a bright, blonde mother of around Gerard's age who became one of his first clients. She was divorcing, which meant she also had to sell the family home at Pullenvale, west of Kenmore. Her phone call to Raine & Horne was put through to the business's freshly minted agent, Gerard.

She'd phoned around other agencies, but when Gerard arrived punctually at her home, where she was waiting with her two young sons, he quickly disarmed her with talk of his own young family. Every day, he explained, he would leave work early to be home for quality time with his children. He also spoke of his other family, the Scout movement.

Jane's estranged husband had been a Scout, a fact she mentioned, which may have been why Gerard talked so much about his great-grandfather, Baden-Powell. She was more impressed by the way he spoke about his family life and kids. He struck her as honest and genuine. There was no hesitation choosing him ahead of the rival agents competing for her business.

Gerard listed the home in May 2004 and it went to auction two months later. Raine & Horne co-owner Ray Leech would remember this as an auction when he had to have a quiet word with Gerard about how he addressed his parents in public. As Leech arrived for the big day, he had overheard Gerard call his father Daddy. Leech admired the close relationship between Gerard and his parents, but he also had to consider what was best for the business. 'Can you call them Elaine and Nigel?' he suggested to Gerard.

The auction went ahead without a hitch, with the home selling for $600,000 – a $220,000 jump on what Jane paid only two years earlier. Gerard was on his way in the real estate game.

The Baden-Clays made it their practice to celebrate sales. When the trio sold a home, buyers were showered with bouquets of flowers or bottles of wine to encourage repeat business. Jane went on to strike up a friendship with Gerard. She would call him for advice on property investment and renovations and he would drop by for coffee and a chat.

Often Gerard would ask Jane to come and work for him. She was studying for a commerce degree and Gerard wanted her to do the books. She always refused. A single mother, she was aware of her vulnerabilities when it came to charming men like Gerard. But if he was interested in her romantically, he never made a move. Always, he talked about his wife and kids.

Aware of Gerard's growing commitments outside the office, which included his role as president of the Kenmore and District Chamber of Commerce, she quizzed him about how he managed to juggle everything.

'The way I do it is I work in the evenings,' he confided.

Leech occasionally entrusted Gerard with the running of weekly sales meetings and training new staff. A few times, he also offered his recruit advice about his young family: 'Just make sure you look after them because you'll lose them,' he warned the hardworking Gerard.

Two divorces had made Leech as aware as anybody of the perils of the industry. Real estate was a hugely demanding game for anyone who wanted to be successful. When an agent was 'in the zone', wives or husbands at home never saw them. The phone would ring 24/7. The industry could own you. Plenty of salesmen ended up having affairs. Gerard seemed to be trying to strike a balance between work and home life. Leech thought he might one day even buy the business.

However, some of the possible pitfalls involved in hiring three family members started to surface. Elaine was clashing with other staff, who found her manner haughty.

By contrast, Leech got along well with the Baden-Clays. He noticed there was never a cross word between Nigel and Elaine, who seemed at peace with one another. But he did have his own run-ins with Elaine at times. Gerard's strong-willed mother once made the mistake of giving Leech unsolicited business advice.

'Elaine, don't ever tell me how to run my own business. If you think you know how to run a real estate company, go and open your own,' he fired back.

Gerard, Nigel and Elaine were already considering their future.

All's fair in love and real estate

2004

Raine & Horne Kenmore co-owner Ray Leech was sipping a coffee when Gerard and his parents asked to talk. Cutting to the chase, Gerard informed his boss he was opening his own real estate business with his parents. They would all be leaving. They had been at Raine & Horne for less than a year.

It wasn't out of the ordinary for an agent to switch franchises or start out on their own, but the Baden-Clays had more news.

'Where's your location?' Leech asked. He wasn't expecting the reply that followed.

'Right next to you,' said Gerard.

Not only had Gerard and his parents secretly leased the empty office next door, they had entered into a franchise agreement with the rival Century 21 group. Gerard and his parents were to open at Shop 2/2105 Moggill Road, wedged between their old Raine & Horne office and the Coffee Club. Within a couple of weeks they would be competitors sharing a thin wall. Gerard and his parents would be trying to poach clients from under the noses of their old bosses. To allow them to open up on their own, Gerard had secured a real estate agent's licence. Nigel later did as well.

Acquaintances unfamiliar with the industry would sometimes ask Leech if he had taken a swing at his former staff member when he heard the news. Leech always laughed off that suggestion. 'I've been in this industry too long. You've just got to put your head down and make more sales,' he'd reply.

Even so, Leech had an expression for what the Baden-Clays had done: 'raping your brain'. Someone would come in, take your ideas and your systems and open up down the road. He was used to it.

Jason Arnott didn't dwell on the Baden-Clays' behaviour either. He simply couldn't feel threatened by them. They lacked the experience to be a real and immediate threat.

After the move, the Raine & Horne owners and the Baden-Clays would smile and wave and exchange courteous greetings when they saw each other. There was no animosity. But other agents drew their own conclusions about Gerard's motives for working at Raine & Horne with his parents: 'It all suddenly made sense. He was training his parents to be partners in the business,' says one former colleague. 'You learn from somebody then you become their opposition right next door. In real estate, people do things like that all the time. I just felt it was not very ethical to the principals, who were always very, very good to them.'

At the start, Century 21 Westside was just Gerard, Nigel, Elaine and an administration assistant. The small group looked even smaller in the large office space, which was bigger and more expensive than the thriving real estate premises they had left next door. But Gerard fancied his own business abilities, and his parents backed him to the hilt. They had to start from scratch, from the fit-out to their client base.

Early on, Gerard showed a flair for ruthless competition when he tried to poach the building's signage rights. Boldly, he approached the landlord and demanded the all-important rights, so he could increase awareness of his new business. Raine & Horne had the full rights to splash their brand across the top of the building locked into their contract.

Leech swiftly put a stop to the manoeuvring. 'Forget that. It's included in our lease that we have the rights; that ain't going to change,' he told the landlord.

There were further signs of Gerard's cheek later, when Leech and Arnott were planning to sell.

'Can I have a look at your figures for the last three years? I might be interested in buying your business,' Gerard asked.

Leech assumed it was a thinly veiled attempt to steal more secrets, but shared his figures with Gerard anyway. Sure enough,

Gerard had a look at the inner workings of the opposition and took it no further: 'I've had a think about it, I'll just stay with Century 21,' he told Leech.

Happily for Leech and Arnott, they got the premium they were aiming for when they sold out. Proving there was no bad blood, Leech later auctioned some homes for Gerard. And Arnott later picked Gerard to sell his sister's home at Brookfield. But they were under no illusions about Gerard: the mummy and daddy's boy could be tough when it suited.

The gold standard

July 2005

Phillip Broom slipped on a dark olive suit, a pair of brown leather shoes and matching belt, and checked himself in the mirror of his parents' Brisbane home. The suit was one of his favourites: single breasted, well made and contemporary. He was ready for his job interview with Gerard Baden-Clay. Broom was visiting from Sydney, where for the past nine months he had been state manager with Musiclink, which sold musical equipment. Before that he had spent five years based in bustling Tokyo, living out of a suitcase as he spruiked high-end instruments and audio equipment for another firm, Vestax.

He'd grown up in Brisbane, playing drums in covers band Dog Boxer and originals outfit Kosher at local bars and nightclubs. His claim to fame in his youth was having one of his songs played on the TV show *Smash Hits*, wedged between the No. 2 and No. 1 songs in Australia that week. It was only padding out the countdown, but for a brief moment his friends believed he had a No. 1 hit.

Broom had studied business at the Queensland University of Technology, where he met his wife, Michelle. The couple wanted to start a family and was planning a return to Brisbane. Broom wanted to stick with his strengths in sales, but flip from records to real estate, where agents were making a killing. Gerard's Century 21 Westside office in Kenmore was at the top of a shortlist. The western suburbs were Broom's old stomping ground, so he knew the area's upmarket, family lifestyle was a valuable commodity. But first he had to meet Gerard.

A short, immaculately groomed woman greeted Broom at the reception desk of Century 21 Westside on Moggill Road, Kenmore. Elaine Baden-Clay had Margaret Thatcher's bouffant hair and appeared to share the former British PM's penchant for pearls and power dressing, too. Elaine led Broom inside, where Gerard Baden-Clay was waiting with his father, Nigel. Gerard, the agency's owner and principal, was wearing his Century 21 jacket, company tie and matching trousers.

Though it is actually mustard, within the company, the eye-catching jacket is referred to as being gold, and agents are encouraged to wear it whenever they can. Since leaving Raine & Horne, Gerard had enthusiastically embraced every aspect of his new franchise and wore the jacket everywhere: to the office, to clients' homes, at auctions, for functions, for awards, to his kids' school for sports days, to lunch and on any number of other occasions. Rival agents speculated he even wore the gold jacket to bed, and not just to sleep in.

Nigel, standing next to Gerard, was yet to be introduced to Broom but was the first to speak. Taking one look at the prospective new employee, Gerard's dad seemed to conclude that Broom wouldn't fit in:

'Brown shoes. Probably going to be too cool for us,' he said, turning to his son.

It wasn't exactly the welcome Broom was expecting but he put the remark down to an awkward attempt to break the ice and quickly moved on.

The conversation flowed freely. Staring out from a frame on the wall was a figure Broom, a former Scout, recognised instantly. Lord Robert Baden-Powell was pictured in uniform with his arms crossed. An inspirational spiel accompanied the image. Gerard introduced Broom to his great-grandfather.

Gerard's surname puzzled Broom, who couldn't figure out how the name Baden-Clay derived from Baden-Powell. It was one of the first things he mentioned to his wife, Michelle, when he returned home. Years later he raised the origins of the surname when he spoke to police.

The sparse display windows of Gerard's business premises nagged at Broom too. There didn't seem to be nearly enough homes on offer. And the office was clearly too big for the small workforce, who were spread out through an expansive space. One area was effectively being used as a junk room. Wasted space was expensive – not a good sign.

But of all the people in the industry he'd met so far, Gerard seemed to have the most proactive and professional approach. The Baden-Clays must have been equally satisfied, brown shoes or not. As Broom caught a flight back to Sydney, Gerard sent him an email offering him a job. Broom had no hesitation in accepting.

Gerard's new business was finding its feet and Allison felt she had her battle with depression and anxiety under control. But the couple were at loggerheads over a new issue – whether to extend their family. Allison yearned for another baby. Gerard resolutely did not want any more children. He felt overrun by the presence of two small children, and their finances were stretched.

There had also been huge shifts in his relationship with Allison. On deeper reflection, Gerard might have seen more reason to admire Allison for the way she handled her depression: it didn't bring out her weakness; quite the contrary. Her anxiety meant it was sometimes hard for her to go out, to socialise, yet somehow she pushed through. She was a fighter. Gerard didn't see it that way. He had just wanted her to *get over it*. His eyes were elsewhere.

He'd worked with Michelle Hammond at Raine & Horne when he was new to the real estate industry. Hammond, a blonde of about Gerard's age, worked in admin in the firm. It would later come out in court that not long after Gerard moved on from the business to open his own Century 21 franchise, the pair launched into an affair.

Gerard's new salesman, Phill Broom, had an odd encounter with Gerard involving Hammond. One day, Gerard commented from nowhere that Hammond had breast implants. Broom asked how he could know, and Gerard said Hammond had been talking to the girls in the office about it and had showed him. He kept his relationship with Hammond relatively discreet, discovering he had a knack for keeping secrets. The affair lasted at least a month. It was relatively easy for Gerard. He was doing long hours in the office and Allison was used to him working nights.

Allison was still insistent about having another baby. Eventually he gave in and they started trying to conceive. Allison found out in February 2006 that she was pregnant again.

After the initial elation, she suffered a bout of anxiety that she recognised from her earlier pregnancies. This time she was ahead of the game. She went straight to her psychiatrist, Dr Tom George, about resuming her medication. Now she understood the problem and how to treat it, she wanted to nip it in the bud.

Dr George put her back on Zoloft and she was rapidly back in control. Allison and Gerard's third daughter was born in September 2006.

Here's my card

Saturday 21 April 2012

8.30 am

Gerard Baden-Clay pulled open the glass door at Kenmore Clinics medical centre, the first patient to arrive for the day. The receptionist was expecting him after an earlier phone call and went in to flag his arrival with the doctor rostered on for the morning shift, Candice Beaven, in her consulting room. Beaven listened as the receptionist briefly outlined the unusual case. Gerard's wife was missing. He might need grief counselling.

The 32-year-old GP had been working at the busy private practice in Brisbane's west for 17 months but hadn't treated Gerard or his wife Allison. Taking a seat across from the doctor, Gerard motioned to the wounds on his face. He'd cut himself shaving the previous day, he explained, and wanted her to take a look. After the introduction from the receptionist, Beaven was expecting her patient to be upset. She was surprised by Gerard's composure. He seemed anxious to have the nasty scratches on his face examined, but there was nothing to indicate his emotions were getting the better of him. It was remarkable given the strain he must have been under. That morning, police and volunteers were frantically searching for Allison in bushland around the well-heeled and tight-knit suburb of Brookfield.

Immediately, Beaven had trouble accepting Gerard's explanation for the injuries. There were three vertical scratches on his right cheek. It looked, frankly, like someone had raked their nails across his face. It did not look like any shaving cut she had seen – not that shaving injuries were a common complaint in surgeries. Far from it.

At first Gerard told Beaven a single pass of his razor caused the three slashes. It seemed unlikely. The wounds were spaced apart. When she questioned Gerard, he changed his story. Perhaps he cut himself a few times, Gerard offered. As he had been in a rush, he couldn't be sure.

Beaven persisted with more questions. 'Why didn't you notice bleeding after one motion?' she asked.

He was in a hurry, Gerard replied.

He had an answer for everything, even if his responses were sometimes contradictory.

The appointment wasn't going well. Then Gerard told the doctor why he was really there. Police had told him to get a GP to document his injuries, he said. 'I don't know if you know, but my wife is missing at the moment,' he said. He'd need the doctor's notes. Police had already photographed the suspicious wounds, he added.

Beaven's suspicions grew by the minute. As she was wondering what had really happened, the conversation inexplicably lightened. How long had she been at the practice, Gerard asked. Did she live in the area? As it happened, Beaven was looking to move closer to the clinic.

Never one to miss an opportunity – even while police were searching for any trace of his wife – Gerard slipped his Century 21 business card across the desk to the attractive young GP. 'I might be able to help you with that,' he said brightly, standing to leave. He was jovial and friendly as he walked out.

His charm wasn't working, not today. With her office empty, Beaven placed the business card in her top drawer and reflected on the appointment. Alarm bells were sounding in her head. The encounter would still be bothering her days later, when it was all over the news that the missing mother of three was out there somewhere, likely in serious trouble. With the unsettling consultation fresh in her mind, Beaven picked up a phone and dialled the number for her medical insurer. They advised her to document everything. She did.

Gerard rushed off. There were important things to do. For a start, he needed a second opinion on those damned facial scratches.

Brookfield

Moggill Road, one of the main links between inner-city Brisbane and the west, begins outside the lush green sporting fields of a century-old private school in Toowong. Brisbane Boys' College is part of the GPS network. Parents pay more than $20,000 a year to send their children to some of the schools in the group. And the suburbs that fan out from Moggill Road as it snakes through Brisbane's west are packed with willing customers.

In other cities along Australia's east coast, the western suburbs are the battler belt – cheap real estate for those who can't afford to be near a cooling sea breeze. But in Brisbane, the west is a leafy, upmarket family zone. From BBC in Toowong, Moggill Road roughly follows the line of the Brisbane River as it winds south-west through Taringa, Indooroopilly, Chapel Hill and Kenmore. At the bustling Kenmore roundabout, Brookfield Road exits to the right, winding out to an exclusive, often eccentric, enclave. Standard house blocks and neat red-tile roofs slowly give way to expansive acreage lots – a legacy of the area's farming days and restrictions on subdivision. Sweeping drives snake off from the main road, leading to comfortable homes with tennis courts, pools and horse paddocks.

There is nothing gauche or showy about the wealth that resides at Brookfield. Expensive homes often lie hidden, discreetly, behind trees at the end of long drives. Despite the notable wealth, little import is placed on personal appearance. The bloke grabbing a pie at the local shop in his shorts and thongs is as likely as anyone to have a Porsche Cayenne in the garage.

Lucinda Brimblecombe, an early 19th-century resident, is credited with naming Brookfield after its creeks and gullies.

Loggers arrived in the 1840s to harvest red cedar and hoop pine and were followed, in the 1860s, by farmers. The book *Brookfield Stories* chronicles that land was cleared for cattle grazing and for cotton, fruit and vegetable farms. Bananas, paw paws and pineapples were just a few of the crops transported to the city markets. A cemetery, school and dam followed soon after. In the 1960s, farmers began dividing and offloading their properties to academics, environmentalists, doctors and business owners seeking a so-called tree change.

The suburb's current residents include judges, lawyers, chief executives and media identities. They are an eclectic mix of characters who can't, or don't want to, fit in to the standard blocks of suburbia. They are, in more than a few cases, net-workers, high-achievers, gossips and eccentrics. There is an element of the English village about Brookfield. It is both pretty and charming but, at times, a little too tight-knit for some.

Many have pondered the reasons for Brookfield's unusual character. The answer might lie in the unique location. It is geographically contained – bounded by swathes of state forest. Roads do not pass through Brookfield; they end there. And socially, it has an uncommon feature: there is just one school in the suburb – Brookfield state primary. Brisbane suburbs are usually serviced by multiple schools and criss-crossed by 'catch-ment' boundaries to dictate which state schools that residents may attend. In Brookfield, nearly all kids pass through the doors of the local primary. It means that most parents know each other, at least in passing. Gerard and Allison Baden-Clay moved into the house in Brookfield Road in 2006. Moments from their front door was the undeniable heart of Brookfield, a 50-metre hub that comprises all the elements of country life: the local shop, the showground, a community hall, hairdresser, real estate agent, cricket ground and pony ring.

With the primary school tucked in behind it, the Brookfield General Store – established in 1871 – is a frenzy of activity on weekday afternoons, with 4WDs jostling for parks, children picking up after-school-treats and parents catching up on local happenings. The shop-cum-café is something of a gathering point. On regular mornings, many of the local mums work out on a cricket oval then sit down together for coffee and a chat. And every Friday evening, a country bar at the showground opens its doors to serve burgers and beers to locals.

Each year, residents flock to the Brookfield Show, and the social event of the year, the Brookfield Ball. The farms may have gone, but village life remains.

Red lights, blue ribbons and idle banter

Ray Van Haven wasn't your average chamber of commerce hand pumper. In his native Holland, Van Haven had toiled for years in the construction of red light districts. After migrating to Australia he found work as a financial planner at a bank in Kenmore and became president of the local business chamber. He'd volunteered for the unpaid role out of a sense of community service and to connect with like-minded entrepreneurs. But not long into his tenure Van Haven seized an opportunity to return to his roots and bought a brothel, Oasis, in Sumner Park in Brisbane's west. It was all legal and above board, but Van Haven didn't want to be known as 'the brothel-owning chamber of commerce president'. He was aware too that not everyone in the conservative western suburbs would be thrilled with his new business venture, so Van Haven spared their blushes and stepped aside. Fresh-faced real estate agent Gerard Baden-Clay eagerly stepped up to the plate in late 2004.

Gerard's new role saddled him with extra responsibilities, but it also gave him a certain cachet and unrivalled opportunities to network. It was through the business group that Gerard met the newly elected local MP, Dr Bruce Flegg, a fascinating character worthy of a book himself.

A medical doctor and self-made millionaire, Flegg was by far the richest man in state parliament. Before entering politics, he had moved from working in doctors' surgeries to owning medical centres and had developed a knack for betting on the stockmarket. His mandatory entry in parliament's register of interests reads like the holdings of a Middle Eastern prince. A multi-million dollar home on 1 hectare in Brookfield, four investment properties on North Stradbroke Island, a 40-hectare rural property in northern New South Wales, holiday units at a Gold Coast resort, investment units at Noosa Heads and Spring Hill and a large body of shares made him the envy of many a colleague. In 2007, the state's annual *Sunday Mail* rich list estimated he was worth some $20 million. He was a blue ribbon Liberal to represent a blue ribbon Liberal electorate.

The seat of Moggill – representing the relatively well-to-do residents of Chapel Hill, Kenmore, Brookfield, Pullenvale, Moggill, Karana Downs and Mt Crosby – had almost always been a conservative stronghold. When Flegg was elected in 2004, Moggill was one of only five seats from 89 across the state to vote for a Liberal member. When the next election was called, in 2006, Flegg was leader and, therefore, in the firing line when the party again performed poorly, winning only eight of the state's 89 seats.

Things were going from bad to worse to farcical for Flegg in December 2007 when he sought Gerard's company for a night out. His party – such as it was with just eight parliamentarians – no longer wanted him to lead but could not decide on a successor. In ridiculous scenes, the MPs were split down the middle 4–4 on a vote for a new leader. They were in 'lockdown' at Brisbane's five-star Stamford Plaza Hotel until someone could be convinced to switch sides and break the impasse.

The situation went beyond absurd when Monty Python's Eric Idle intervened. The comedian happened to be staying at the same hotel ahead of a show in Brisbane and, spying the press pack outside, strolled over to hold his own press conference. 'I'll volunteer for it,' he said of the Liberal leadership.

Asked if he would call the situation 'Pythonesque', Idle replied: 'I think that's slightly insulting to Monty Python, don't you? I think we're slightly more successful.'

The media had a field day. *Courier-Mail* cartoonist Sean Leahy, with typical brilliance, depicted Flegg hanging on the cross, parodying a scene from *The Life of Brian*.

Amid the hoopla, Flegg seized the opportunity to escape the hotel stand-off. Pulling some strings, he procured two tickets to Idle's show that night. He cut the cartoon out of the paper and sent word to Idle that he would be in the audience and wouldn't mind an autograph.

With a spare ticket in hand, the MP invited Gerard to join him. 'I'll have to check with Allison,' Gerard said. There was something in Gerard's tone that suggested he was embarrassed at seeking permission from his wife. Flegg sensed all wasn't well with Gerard's home life. Gerard was soon back to Flegg. He would go.

Flegg drove, with Gerard beside him. On the way to the Queensland Performing Arts Centre, Flegg broached the subject of Gerard's discomfort about his call to Allison. Flegg, a father to four sons, had been married for 17 years before a painful divorce. His battles in politics were nothing compared to the torture of the slow end to his relationship. He thought he recognised in Gerard, a father of three young girls, someone who was going through similar pain. He also believed that men needed to look out for each other, and didn't do so enough. The trained doctor wanted to help. Flegg told Gerard he knew what it was like to have to get a 'leave pass' and asked how things were at home.

The MP knew Gerard as a man who was constantly concerned about his image. Whenever Flegg asked him about business, it was always booming, his agency never better. This time, for a brief moment, Gerard let down his guard: 'Not good, mate, not good,' he told Flegg.

When they arrived for the show, 'Not the Messiah', Idle acknowledged Flegg in the Lyric Theatre audience and made a joke at his expense. Afterwards, Gerard and Flegg met the comic and his entourage in the bar next to the theatre and they all had a beer together. Despite its occurrence in the midst of one of his worst experiences in politics, Flegg remembers it as one of the best nights of his life. Idle signed Sean Leahy's cartoon for him. Flegg still has it at home as a reminder of the whole extraordinary episode.

Gerard too appeared to enjoy the chance to unwind. His responsibilities at work and home were adding up.

The real estate expert

When Gerard opened his Century 21 real estate agency in 2004, the push to build the Baden-Clay brand was on. It began when he managed to secure the presidency of the Kenmore and District Chamber of Commerce that same year and went into overdrive when he launched his own blog, unabashedly called The Real Estate Expert, in 2007.

He seemed to revel in his role as self-appointed moral compass for the real estate industry and community in general. In a crowded market, Gerard used his great-grandfather to help sell his brand of honesty and integrity and promoted himself as a devoted husband, father and servant of the community.

'Gerard Baden-Clay operates at the forefront of long-overdue change in the business of real estate,' his blog read. 'Gerard's personal philosophies of ethical excellence and team loyalty, derived from his lineage as the great-grandson of international Scouts founder Baden-Powell, have found their perfect landing spot in the field of real estate.'

Gerard wrote that his interests were 'spending as much time as possible with my family' and also camping, travelling and Scouting. His blog listed mostly action movies as his favourite films, but ever the loving husband he added *Bridget Jones's Diary*. 'No, you're not imagining things – I really DO enjoy a good "chick flick" with my beautiful wife!' For his favourite books, he nominated several Wilbur Smith novels set in Africa, and his great-grandfather Baden-Powell's book *Rovering for Success*.

The blog became a vehicle for Gerard to impart his strong views about ethics, and to challenge those who didn't live up to his high standards. He found a slew of impressive sounding letters to sign off his blog: BBus (Bachelor of Business); AFAIM (Associate Fellow of the Australian Institute of Management); and LREA (Licensed Real Estate Agent). In one of his sermons on ethics, in September 2007 he wrote:

> We've come a long away as an industry but the legacy of years gone by lingers . . . Recently we've seen several tales in the media of agents buying under-priced properties under alias identities. It is appalling behaviour and, tellingly, such agents almost always come unstuck . . . and quickly. But it does us all a huge disservice. I was going to use this blog to take the moral high ground on behalf of our local industry, but only last week had cause to call into questions the ethics of a competitor. I did so not for the sake of market position but because we all suffer when someone lowers the bar. I'm sure the person in question knows exactly what I'm talking about. Ethics aren't just fash-ionable in real estate – they're mandatory. And governed by law. Until next week . . .
>
> Posted by Gerard Baden-Clay BBus, AFAIM, LREA.

Much of Gerard's moralising would come back to haunt him, but one lecture in particular stood out. As a local identity with an inflating profile, Gerard was asked to contribute to a weekly 'moral dilemmas' column in Brisbane's daily newspaper, *The Courier-Mail*, in February 2008. The question of the day was whether honesty was still important. Gerard wrote: 'In business, it's simple: never lie. For starters, it's the wrong thing to do, but secondly you will always get caught out and usually when you least expect it. There are just too many people, too many per-sonalities, too many trails . . . and too much to lose.'

Four days later, on a roll, Gerard made a speech at Kenmore State High School. He had been invited to address students because the Scouts movement was celebrating its 100th year. That same morning, prime minister Kevin Rudd had made a groundbreaking apology to the Stolen Generations – Indigenous

Australians forcibly removed from their families through much of the 20th century. Rudd spoke emotionally in parliament of the 'profound grief, suffering and loss' of Aboriginal and Torres Strait Islander people as a result of the actions of governments, churches and welfare groups. Now Gerard drew parallels between himself and the prime minister – both were 'making history' that day, he said.

'In our own small way we are making history today . . . we are contributing to the history of this esteemed school and, perhaps more importantly, to our own personal history.'

He went on: 'To me, the most fundamental element of good leadership is to lead by example. If you want to see a clean school ground – you should pick up rubbish . . . and then ask for help. If you want dress standards to be better – you should dress well first. If you want people to be on time for class and events – you should always be punctual yourself. If you lead by example, others will follow.' Not everyone was sold on brand Baden-Clay. At monthly meetings of the Kenmore chamber of commerce, president Gerard's self-promotion at the microphone could be a turn-off.

Peter Newing, a real estate agent in Brisbane's western suburbs for more than 20 years and principal of his own agency, found him insufferable. 'He was part of the reason I stopped going,' Newing tells me.

There were three things he used to always talk about. One was, naturally enough as you'd expect at a meeting like that, he'd brag . . . about his brand and his office. The second thing was he would always bring up the fact he was related to Baden-Powell. And the third thing which really used to make my skin crawl, not because he was talking about it, but the way he talked about it – it sounded forced and insincere – was his involvement with the local church. I just thought he comes across as a man of straw. He's got this big chest, puffed out, saying things like, 'I remember last Sunday when we were talking about Jesus and thinking about all you people out here struggling in the business world.' I just thought, 'I'm not wasting my morning listening to this phoney.' For him it was building up that trustworthy God-fearing, honourable, respectable image. It was smarmy. It made me want to vomit.

Gerard's agency was gradually taking on more staff but he had big plans; for example, he pictured that he could open seven real estate offices in the western suburbs. To expand, he'd need help from people other than his ageing parents, and in 2008 was grooming salesman Phill Broom to become a partner. That year, Gerard promoted Broom to a senior sales agent and gave him a set of personalised number plates, SETTLE.

As it happened, Century 21's number one Queensland agent, Jocelyn Frost, was looking to return to the western suburbs from Brisbane's bayside. Frost had started in real estate after a wildly successful career in Tupperware sales, in which she had 300 people working for her in her own franchise. She was a natural saleswoman and took to real estate like a duck to water. In 2007, Frost had earnt almost $800,000 in commissions from property sales, putting her in the top one per cent of Century 21 performers worldwide and earning her a 'Double Centurion' award. Gerard and Broom didn't fancy competing with Frost if she moved into their area. At a Century 21 conference on Hamilton Island, they sounded her out about joining them as a partner. Before long she was on board.

Broom and Frost each bought an equal, one-third stake in the business with Gerard, paving the way for his parents to retire. The two new partners paid only cursory attention to the underlying financial position of the business. They felt no need for caution – Gerard seemed to be made for success. His public profile had been growing. In 2005 and 2007 Century 21 Westside had won a Quest Business Achiever Award. An exuberant Gerard was photographed pumping his fists in the air in celebration at each of the events. In 2008 the business also made *Business Review Weekly*'s top 100 Fast Starters list and was a Real Estate Institute of Queensland Top Agency of the Year finalist.

Gerard, in his promotional material from around this time, was brimming with confidence: 'I'm very proud of what we've created here . . . Your reputation is everything in this business and we continue to receive wonderful testimonials each week from people who appreciate the professional integrity and personal ethics that define the way we do business here,' he wrote.

While he set the bar so high in public, privately Gerard was spectacularly failing to meet his own standards.

Toni McHugh

Things could have been so different if Toni McHugh and Robert Mackay-Wood had chosen a different agency to sell their block of land back in 2005 – if they had turned away the confident Century 21 salesman, Gerard Baden-Clay. But Gerard, as flash as a rat with a gold jacket, worked his charm and soon had McHugh hanging on his every word.

McHugh was born on 5 February 1971 – five months after Gerard – in the Sutherland Shire in Sydney. Her parents were upstanding Catholics, and McHugh was their wild child. At 16 she fell pregnant, had a son, and fell out with her parents.

'I was the only one they didn't bother to send to a private school because I was the rebel, not worth spending money on. Then I shamed the family by having a baby when I was still a teenager,' she would later say in a paid interview with *Australian Women's Weekly*.

Whatever relationship she had with the baby's father, it didn't last, because in her early 20s the attractive brunette fell for Mackay-Wood.

A decade older than McHugh, Mackay-Wood was a science graduate who had worked as a research assistant at Cornell University in New York, where his projects included alfalfa breeding. He became a University of Sydney teaching lab manager in biological sciences and, in his relationship with McHugh, became step-dad to her young son.

From the mid-1990s they lived together at Blaxland, in the Blue Mountains, across the road from the Glenbrook Lagoon. By then, the creative, fun-loving McHugh had a Bachelor of Visual Arts from the University of Sydney. After adding a graduate diploma in education to her credentials, she started work as a high school arts teacher.

She and Mackay-Wood had twin boys in the late '90s. A couple of years later, they bought a 'dream home' farther west in the Blue Mountains, in Shortland Street, Wentworth Falls. McHugh brought her artist's touch to the home, and it was in pristine condition when they put it on the market in 2003 in order to move to Queensland.

In the Sunshine State, they bought a 1.5-hectare block of land in Pullenvale on Brisbane's western fringe. Mackay-Wood got a job at the University of Queensland. McHugh left teaching to begin a career in property, managing homes for Rental Hotline in Toowong.

Deciding to sell their Pullenvale block in 2005, they contacted the relatively new Century 21 Westside and met Gerard and his parents, Nigel and Elaine. The Baden-Clays secured them as clients and sold the block.

Interestingly, Gerard's mother had her own instinct about McHugh. During a strange exchange with Century 21 colleague Phill Broom not long after that land sale, Elaine was disparaging about McHugh. Broom had a working relationship with McHugh through her Rental Hotline property management role. When he made a passing complimentary remark about McHugh one day, he was pulled up short by a surprisingly hostile Elaine.

'You can't trust that woman,' she told Broom, knowingly.

Broom didn't understand. McHugh seemed pleasant enough to him. A few days later, Elaine took it upon herself to warn Broom about predatory women: 'You need to be cautious, Phill. You're a good-looking man; you're going to go into single ladies' houses or houses where wives are getting divorced. They will make a play at you and you have to be strong and stand by your wife.'

Taken aback, Broom nodded in agreement. 'Okay, I didn't ask, but thanks,' he thought.

Elaine's instincts proved correct. In 2007, McHugh clicked onto the Century 21 Westside webpage and emailed an application for a sales job. Gerard hired her in April of that year. She had a crush on her new boss from the beginning.

Later, she would tell police: 'When I first started working with Gerard, there was definitely chemistry for me. I admired him and I was attracted to him. I don't know how he felt.'

Gerard, after hiring McHugh, continued to behave like a devoted family man. Every day except Sundays, he would open the business at 8.30 am and by 5 pm he would be heading home to be with his family. He explained to McHugh the agreement he and Allison had – that he would be home every afternoon for 'couch time': the couple wanted their daughters to see them together. McHugh saw Gerard as an inspiring leader and a good father; her attraction to her boss never wavered.

For the first year, they worked side by side without the relationship straying beyond the professional. It wouldn't last.

A highlight of Brisbane's calendar each year is the fireworks event Riverfire, when the city's residents combine two of their great loves: the waterway at the heart of life in the Queensland capital and colourful explosions. Brisbane's penchant for fireworks is almost unrivalled in Australia, from the big-ticket events of New Year's Eve and Australia Day to the tiniest school fairs.

Up until 2010, Riverfire culminated with a Royal Australian Air Force F-111 jet swooping over the CBD for a spectacular 'dump and burn' of fuel. The burst of flames and blast of heat would wash over the tens of thousands crammed into riverside vantage points.

Two days before the F-111s were to launch into action in August 2008, Gerard Baden-Clay enthusiastically embraced the event in a posting on his blog, The Real Estate Expert. The previous weekend had marked Gerard and Allison's 11th wedding anniversary.

Big bang! This weekend marks the end of winter and the start of spring, and as usual the event is marked by the fabulous RiverFestival . . . I usually like to take my young family up to

Mt Coot-tha where we can experience the spectacular display from a 'safe' distance, where the crowds are slightly smaller and the noise a little less threatening to young hearts and ears! Hopefully too, the F-111's will perform their customary 'dump and burn' again this year, which for me (as a frustrated fighter pilot!) is the highlight of the show! During the day, we have an equally impressive display of property for you to view!

In hindsight, the title of the jubilant blog – 'Big bang!' – seems loaded with hidden meaning. The day before that entry was published, Gerard and Toni McHugh began their fateful relationship.[1]

The pair were working back late in the office when it happened. 'He asked me to kiss him. I did,' McHugh would tell the police. Three years of pent-up sexual tension ignited into a passionate affair.

Among the newly listed homes featured in the 'Big bang!' blog was an acreage property on Grandview Road, Pullenvale. Gerard and Toni kept finding reasons to visit the area. Off Grandview Road is Mill Road, a secluded spot where the pair met for late-night trysts in the first, heady weeks of their affair.

Gerard drove the white Prado to meet up with McHugh. His family affectionately called the car 'Snowy', and it was usually used by his wife. Gerard would fold the seats down to create a makeshift bed. With cicadas screeching in the darkness around them, nothing disturbed the two 37-year-olds.

As well as hooking up on dark back roads, the pair used the office for after-hours sex. As McHugh put it more delicately when she spoke to police: 'We would then be intimate in the Century 21 Kenmore office.' Gerard would tell his wife he was going back to finish off some work.

The lovers would send steamy emails to each other about what they planned to do when they met. Gerard unleashed a stream of X-rated fantasies. When police later recovered some of the missives, there were blushes all around among seasoned investigators. The emails never saw the light of day, but reflected Gerard's well-concealed private desires. Along with their explicit sexual fantasies, the pair also exchanged tales of woe about their respective partners. Gerard was adamant that his marriage was effectively over.

'Gerard told me that he did not love Allison and they had not slept together for many years,' she said in a statement to the police.

On two occasions in the early stages of the affair, Toni rather self-consciously walked up the long driveway to Gerard's home on Brookfield Road. Both times, Allison was away with the girls at her parents' house on the Gold Coast.

This was at the start of the relationship. I never felt comfortable about going there. On both occasions Allison and the children were not at home. I think they were down the coast with Allison's parents. The first time I went to the house we slept in the spare room. I stayed the entire night on that occasion. The second time we pulled a mattress out into the lounge. I did not stay the night on this occasion, as Gerard was not well. I did not see any bedding, sheets or blankets to indicate to me that he did sleep on the couch. This, however, did not appear to be unusual. Gerard would not have wanted the girls to know. At least this is how I justified that to myself.

For McHugh, the affair was too much of a burden while she was still in a committed relationship. In November, three months after the affair began, McHugh broke up with Mackay-Wood to pursue a future with Gerard. She moved into a small unit at Jerdanefield Street at St Lucia and arranged shared custody of their twins. Gerard didn't follow her lead.

Gerard and Toni thought they had been careful about concealing their feelings from colleagues, but the spark between them had not gone unnoticed. Gerard's business partner Jocelyn Frost sensed there was something between Gerard and Toni almost as soon as she started at Century 21 Westside in 2008. Whether it was intuition, experience or keen powers of observation, Frost suspected the two were more than merely colleagues.

It was all but confirmed in an incident in late 2008. Frost was standing at Toni's desk. Toni was excitedly relaying a clairvoyant reading that told her she had a love interest in her life, but she didn't know who it was.

'It would be Gerard, wouldn't it, Toni?' Frost blurted out. Frost knew by Toni's shocked reaction she had hit the mark. Toni didn't know how to respond and disappeared from the office for a few hours. She had said nothing but her reaction spoke volumes.

Field signals

Two weeks after Gerard began his affair with Toni McHugh, business partner Phill Broom welcomed his first child into the world. Despite his own marriage unravelling, Gerard played the doting father in a blog announcing the arrival of Broom's son, Darcy.

'For those of you who have been fortunate enough to experience the miracle of bringing a new person into the world,' Gerard gushed, 'you will no doubt join me for a collective "aaahhh" at the thought of the joy that Phill and Michelle must be feeling right now, and at how fortunate Darcy is to have been born into such a loving home. When I was speaking with Phill earlier, I asked if he had enjoyed any "fast-asleep-on-your-chest" moments with Darcy, and when he replied in the affirmative, I nearly shed a tear at the memory of such simple pleasures! I don't think it matters who you have talked to or how many books you've read, nothing can prepare you for the roller coaster of emotions that the birth of your first child can evoke . . . We look forward to seeing Darcy in a gold jacket at an open home soon!'

Broom and Gerard were friends. Their business partnership had become official that month. But Broom was cautious about fatherly insights from Gerard. He may not have known much about parenting but he always felt Gerard had an overly controlling relationship with his wife and daughters, and kept them in their place. The most telling example was Gerard's extraordinary use of field signals to communicate with and command his children.

The first time Broom recalled noticing it was at a function at a park. Gerard had brought his daughters along, and at some point had wanted them to come to his side; rather than calling out, he simply raised his hand to his head. Like magic, the little girls came running. Broom couldn't be sure about what he was seeing initially, but on the rare occasions when the girls came into the office, he witnessed similar occurrences. The girls would drop in on odd afternoons or school holidays and quietly occupy themselves drawing in the boardroom. If they wanted their father, instead of calling out to him, they silently signalled.

If Gerard was having a conversation with someone, for instance, the girls would silently enter his office, touch his knee and wait until he gave the go-ahead to talk. Broom saw again that Gerard would touch his head when he wanted the girls and they would appear. After a while, Broom's curiosity got the better of him, and he quizzed Gerard about the interactions.

'It's a field signal in the military; it means, "Come here",' Gerard explained. It was important to set a framework for how children behaved in a social context, Gerard said. He'd taught his children that if they wanted his attention when he was talking to someone else, they should tap his knee and not say anything.

Broom's father had been in the RAAF for 20 years, and his mother was involved with Girl Guides. Even so, he'd never seen field signals used in daily life before, let alone with young children. It took the expression 'Children are to be seen and not heard' to a whole new level.

Gerard tried to impart some of his parenting wisdom on his younger colleague, the overall message being that a firm hand was needed. Whenever the girls did something wrong, Gerard explained, you sternly lectured them and waited for an acceptable reply. They had to respond with 'Yes, Daddy.' Not 'Okay' or sullen silence, but 'Yes, Daddy'. Gerard was controlling of his family in a way Broom vowed he would never be.

Jocelyn Frost had more to say about Gerard's strict parenting when she spoke to police: 'I believe that Gerard had a bad temper with his children,' said Frost. 'I remember on a couple of different times that he had told me that he had belted the children.'

Of course there was no hint of this in his blog. As usual, Gerard's post, while ostensibly about Broom's newborn son, was really about emphasising his own credentials as the sensitive family man.

Keen observers might have noticed also that while Gerard reflected on the emotions of cradling a newborn, there was no mention of the woman who had delivered all three of his children, Allison. His wife was a key omission in the post.

He was in the early throes of his affair; she seemed to have been cast aside like a used dishcloth.

Allison wasn't alone when she went to see her psychiatrist, Dr Tom George, on 3 June 2009. At this visit, she'd come with Gerard, to talk about the crisis in their marriage.

Their relationship had deteriorated and Allison felt they needed professional help. She wanted to get things back on track; she also knew nothing of the affair bubbling away in the background. Allison was aware she and Gerard had grown apart, but she put it down to the stresses and strains of having a young family.

At Dr George's, Gerard vented his frustrations about the relationship. He was tired of making all the decisions, plus he was under considerable pressure at work. Sales were now few and far between in his real estate business. He was upset that Allison had gone and bought an expensive treadmill when they were short on money.

The couple told Dr George they hadn't had sex for two years. Gerard said he felt isolated, unsupported and resentful. He was thinking of ending the marriage, but felt guilty about the impact on Allison and their daughters. He didn't mention his ongoing affair with employee Toni McHugh.

Allison told Dr George she did not want the marriage to end. She wanted to fight to stay together, just as she had always pushed through when times were tough. She had come through the other side on her depression and believed they could work their marriage problems out. Dr George recommended a marriage therapist.

The next month, Allison again went to see Dr George about her marriage. It was the last appointment she would ever have with the psychiatrist. She told Dr George her wedding anniversary was coming up. Allison, ever hopeful, had booked a room at a resort on the coast and let Gerard know he could join her if he chose. The ball was in his court.

Secret's out

2009

In a throwback to a bygone era, the Tattersall's Club in the Brisbane CBD accepted only men as members. However, the doors opened to the hoi polloi for functions, and one of Gerard's best young salesmen, John Bradley, was celebrating his engagement to girlfriend Stephanie Fisher. As waiters strolled the carpet with trays of champagne and seafood canapés, a strategic battle was playing out among the guests.

Phill Broom had noticed some awkwardness among his colleagues, and it had to do with Allison Baden-Clay. Gerard didn't always bring his wife to work events, and Broom had the impression some people were surprised to see her at the engagement party. He got the distinct impression that Toni McHugh ran a mile whenever Allison came near her.

Although she didn't mention anything to Broom that night, Jocelyn Frost noticed something too – Gerard was ignoring Allison and spending a lot of time with Toni.

Broom felt it was important to know what was going on within his business. Thinking he was onto something about Toni avoiding Allison, he decided to test his theory. Toni was chatting to Broom's wife, Michelle, while Broom was talking to Allison. Gradually he shifted position until Toni and Allison ended up side by side. Abruptly, Toni made her excuses and left the party. Broom was now certain she was avoiding Allison. Almost straight after Toni departed, Gerard said he had to go to the bathroom.

He'd been gone for ten minutes when a worried Allison approached Broom, concerned that her husband appeared to be missing: 'He's got this allergic reaction to shellfish. He could have had some prawns,' she said, then asked Broom to check the toilets.

Broom told Allison he was happy to oblige, but then Gerard reappeared and was his usual self. Later, when things were all out in the open, McHugh would confide to Frost that Gerard had indeed raced out of the party to see her off. When he rushed back inside, his heart must have been pounding from the effort, but he appeared impressively unruffled.

Back at the office in the days after the engagement party, Broom and Frost discussed the dynamics of their colleagues. 'It's all Michelle and I talked about on the way home,' he told Frost.

For the two business partners, the affair could have serious ramifications. Anything Gerard did with a staff member could impact the business. Getting to the bottom of the relationship between Gerard and Toni was vital to them.

Conscious that he had no proof of an ongoing affair, Broom resolved to find out for sure. The first thing he did was approach Gerard directly, in his office, and ask bluntly if he was having an affair with Toni. He hit a wall of denial.

'You're accusing me of cheating on my lovely wife,' an outraged Gerard replied.

For the next few weeks Broom kept probing. Eventually, it was McHugh who caved, not Gerard, and admitted to the affair.

Broom stormed back into Gerard's office: 'You've been lying to me. Toni has told us there's something going on. You told me there wasn't.'

Caught out, Gerard resorted to tears, breaking down crying. 'I'm going to end it,' he swore to Broom. 'It's over. I can't do this. I love my wife. I love my daughters.'

Dear diary

Be thankful for what you have; you'll end up having more. If
you concentrate on what you don't have, you will never, ever
have enough.

Oprah Winfrey

Allison was sitting outside Brookfield State School, waiting to
collect her daughters, when she turned to a new page in her
spiral-bound journal. It was a Friday afternoon in April 2010,
two years before she would vanish from her home down the
road. Seemingly convinced she could reshape her life by the sheer
force of her will and some celebrity advice, she had started a
gratitude journal. Allison loved self-help books and anything
with a positive bent. Her journal was all about taking stock of
the positive things in her own life, no matter how big or small.
Under the heading 'My gratitude list', she wrote the things she
was grateful for that day. Since taking Gerard to see her psychiatrist almost a year earlier, things had improved at home. Gerard
hadn't walked out; he'd been making an effort, and made the top
of her list.

'Today I am grateful for . . . The loving text I just received
from my husband; The fact I could afford to have my hair done
and buy a new top today; The school I am sitting outside where
my girls attend; For the relationship we have with the teachers
and principal; That we live in such a wonderful suburb – close
to some wonderful after school activities; For Paula Barrett
and the wonderful programme she has written that has helped
my family; Being associated with Pathways at this stage of its
growth; My wonderful parents and their tireless, unconditional
love; My education at IGGS [Ipswich Girls' Grammar School]

and all the friends I made; [and] AYBC [Australian Youth Ballet Company] and the places it took me.'

Allison had become involved in Pathways, a program that sought to promote resilience in children and families. Child psychologist Dr Paula Barrett designed it to help tackle the many young people who suffered in silence through anxiety and depression. For Allison, it was an issue close to her heart, and it was no surprise for it to be on her gratitude list. There were also some blasts from the past. Allison had loved Ipswich Girls' Grammar School and hoped to send her daughters there after primary school at Brookfield. And Allison still held the AYBC of her childhood dear – her experiences still fresh in her mind, and valued, all these years later. Her eldest daughter had inherited her enthusiasm for ballet, and once a week Allison would teach dance at Brookfield State School. As a sideline, to earn extra money, she was also selling Neways health and beauty products.

Her journal entries over the next fortnight reflected a woman doing her best to be positive. Thoughts of her daughters, parents and friends brought her happiness.

'[18 April 2010] I am grateful for 1. My ballet friends and the lovely breakfast I had this morning. 2. My parents who were committed to driving me to my ballet lessons. 3. My husband for booking in until 2 pm so I could enjoy my morning and for making dinner. 4. My 3 beautiful girls who continue to amaze me. 5. The wonderful pony club and park that we enjoyed this afternoon. 6. Midi – the 'flash' car I was able to drive today. 7. Anne and the kindness she showed to me and hopefully to G. 8. Tallebudgera and the wonderful time we have with friends.'

The following day's entry also listed eight points. '[19 April 2010] I am grateful for . . . 1. My husband taking the time and effort to make my morning smoothie. 2. My [eldest daughter] who tried to 'push thru' today and is so flexible and reasonable when she's sick. 3. My husband only working 5 mins away from school to pick up [the girls]. 4. My gift giving parents who love giving me things from their garage sale. 5. Mum and Dad's church – that they have found it and it has the perfect activities for them – like the garage sale. 6. The health of my Mum and Dad and that they still enjoy their little holidays together. 7. The park at Paradise Point with its lovely swing and close proximity to Mum and Dad. 8. The Health Food Shop at Para.'

Allison's family loyalty extended also to the Baden-Clays. '[Undated] I am grateful for . . . The beautiful weather – the sunshine; The cabins at Talle; The time I had to walk this morning; The time I had to shower this morning; G computer and technology; The fact G is a gadget person; Australia – the country I was born; My in-laws living so close; My sister-in-law for all she has done for me in the past, for her support with Neways, her support while I was sick; My friends sharing this weekend.'

'[1 June 2010] I am grateful for . . . My ability to afford Lesley and the gym; My ability to afford to be at home with [my youngest child]; Our house and its location to BSS; Deb – the cleaner; My little helper and making the quiche; Snowy – the Prado; Marcia and the help she is giving me; My parents looking after the girls so I could have some time off.'

Conference call

A hush fell over the packed auditorium as Sir Bob Geldof took to the stage for the Australian Real Estate Conference of May 2010. One of the biggest events of the year on the real estate calendar, the conference was being held at the Sydney Convention and Exhibition Centre at Darling Harbour. Geldof's keynote address, 'Reaching Your Dream. A World Icon's Insight on the Secret to Success', was exactly the kind of motivational fare the industry's leading lights had come from all around Australia to see. Lateral thinker Edward de Bono assured the assembled delegates, 'Your Success is Determined by How You Think'.

More than 2500 people signed up for the event, and among them were Century 21 Westside's three partners, Gerard Baden-Clay, Phill Broom and Jocelyn Frost, who had flown in from Brisbane. Gerard pulled Frost aside to let her know in advance another staff member would soon be arriving too. He was flying Toni McHugh to Sydney.

Frost knew McHugh wasn't coming for the conference. Despite Gerard's morning smoothies for his wife, his loving text messages and his reliable school runs, he was continuing his affair with McHugh. And his infidelity went way beyond that.

On his trip to Sydney, Gerard was taking full advantage of the time away from his family, and his Darling Harbour hotel room. Although Gerard had told Broom he would end the affair, he evidently had not. The couple spent three days together. It was time enough for Toni to imagine a normal relationship with Gerard, without constantly looking over her shoulder for Allison.

On one of the evenings, after the conference wrapped up for the day, Gerard, Toni, Broom and Frost went for dinner at a harbourside Chinese restaurant. Over steaming plates of fried rice and stir-fries, Gerard and Toni let their guard down and behaved like a couple on a night out with friends.

Broom had suspected for some time the affair was back on. But it was still a bold statement from Gerard and Toni. They were prepared to be together regardless of what their closest colleagues thought.

Something else stood out to Broom that night. Another real estate agent, Jackie Crane, came along for dinner. Crane was a blonde mum, about the same age as Gerard and Toni, and worked at a real estate agency on the Sunshine Coast. She had met Gerard at a training course and they'd become close. Broom once again picked up on some odd body language: it seemed as though Crane expected to be Gerard's special guest at dinner that night.

None of the other guests knew it – certainly not Toni McHugh – but Gerard had been a busy man. He'd later testify in court that he was back and forth with Crane by phone and email for weeks. He admitted that when Crane arrived at the start of the conference, he had a night with her.

The next day, Gerard coolly phoned Toni and urged her to fly down to Sydney. When Crane turned up at the Chinese restaurant for dinner, she found Gerard only had eyes for Toni McHugh.

Meanwhile Gerard, who had now cheated on his mistress as well as his wife, stayed in his marriage and made big promises to McHugh: he was going to leave his wife and marry her. They were going to live together, his kids and her kids, in one big, happy family.

Back in Brisbane, Frost and Broom found themselves colluding, uncomfortably, in Gerard's affair with Toni. Gerard told Broom he was in love with Toni and was planning a future with her. Once, while they were discussing Broom's plans to buy a new car, Gerard volunteered he'd need a bigger car to fit Toni's children as well as his own.

Whenever the two men went for a round of golf on the lush courses of the western suburbs, Gerard would constantly be texting. Gerard admitted some of the messages were for Toni, not Allison. Broom knew Gerard was going to Toni's unit late at night, at first during the weeks Toni didn't have her sons, but later Gerard would visit after she put the boys to bed.

At a real estate conference later in 2010, around the time of Gerard and Allison's 13th wedding anniversary in August, Broom implored his business partner to stop living a lie. Gerard said he didn't love his wife and was over his marriage.

Toni confided in Jocelyn Frost her plans to make a future with Gerard. Frost tried to convince Toni it wasn't going to work, that Gerard wouldn't leave his wife. Toni didn't want to hear it.

'I told Toni what type of man he was,' Frost would tell the police, 'and I would tell her to leave, however she would get angry and stop talking to me and being my friend. Toni would tell me that Gerard had promised her that he would marry her.'

The office

Two Century 21 Westside staff members came into the office one morning with a story to tell. They had been putting flyers in letterboxes the previous night when Gerard drove past and, realising he had been spotted, pulled over to say hello. They were around St Lucia, in Brisbane's inner west, a long way from Gerard's home. Gerard told the pair he was on his way to the St Lucia BP service station for fuel, but they didn't buy his story and one of them discussed it with business partner Phill Broom. Gerard was tight with money and usually bought his fuel from Shell service stations to use the 4-cents-a-litre off vouchers from Coles supermarkets. It seemed obvious he was going to Toni's home at St Lucia late at night.

The slip-ups started to accumulate. A fortnight or so before Century 21 Westside salesman John Bradley's 2010 wedding, Gerard said he would be there but that Allison wouldn't be able to make it because she had commitments with the girls. But Allison had sent a written RSVP saying they'd both be in attendance.

On another evening, Gerard, Broom and Frost went to the Gold Coast for a Century 21 retreat at the Crown Plaza Hotel. Broom's wife came along too, and Frost brought her husband, but Gerard didn't bring Allison.

The next morning, when Broom went to the reception desk to pay the bill, he asked the staff if his business partners had been down for breakfast yet and was told Gerard had checked out around midnight. Broom thought it odd, and later concluded Gerard had returned to Brisbane to spend the night with Toni.

'If there was a free breakfast Gerard would normally always be there,' he told police.

When Ben Bassingthwaighte found out about the affair, he was one of the last in the office to know. Bassingthwaighte joined Century 21 Westside in 2008 and had a quarter share of the property management, or rental, side of the business. Gerard, Broom and Frost held the remainder.

One day in late 2010, Gerard pulled Bassingthwaighte aside and revealed to him that he was having a relationship with Toni. Bassingthwaighte told Gerard he needed to do the right thing and come clean to Allison.

By that stage, Gerard and Toni had already been seeing each other for more than two years. Bassingthwaighte didn't want any part of it and was glad he hadn't known earlier.

He had met Toni before he started at Century 21 when both had worked for property management firm Rental Hotline, which became Run Property. At the previous business, they worked in separate offices. They became closer friends at Westside. Bassingthwaighte would come to have numerous conversations with both Gerard and Toni about the affair. He urged Toni to move on and find someone new. The advice fell on deaf ears. Toni said it was hard, because she loved her married boss. Likewise, Gerard openly pined for McHugh, telling Bassingthwaighte he stayed with his wife for his children's sake. In Gerard's mind, he was the one making the sacrifice by remaining in the marriage.

Gerard started telling others of his affair too. Since opening his own agency in 2004, Gerard had built a rapport with Century 21's Australasian chairman and owner, Charles Tarbey. The men would catch up at regular Century 21 functions. Tarbey would recall meeting Allison at least half a dozen times at these events.

Gerard trusted Tarbey enough by around late 2010 to share his big secret. Tarbey had flown Gerard to Shanghai with him to work with the business's IT developers. During the trip, when talk veered to Gerard's private life, he confided in Tarbey about his affair with Toni, but added it was over and he was trying to patch up his marriage.

Other staff started to feel Toni was getting preferential treatment. The arrangement in Century 21 Westside, at Gerard's insistence, was for phone calls to come through the main office number. Westside advertisements listed this landline rather than agents' mobile numbers. Officially, it was so calls were always answered and queries followed up and the work fairly divided. Callers would be directed to agents, supposedly in equal fashion. Unofficially, it was all about control. Gerard and the partners had the ultimate say on who was assigned properties.

Given that the call allocation system was open to abuse and the boss was locked in a steamy affair with a staff member, others started to feel they might be being short changed. Toni seemed to receive leads that the other partners were unaware of. She, of course, said the claims were nonsense. Toni was positive that she never crossed the line in the office, that she had always kept it professional. But there was growing resentment about her obviously close relationship with the boss.

The Westside office, which once had a good social atmosphere, would start to seize up. One saleswoman walked out after less than a year working there, after an argument involving Toni McHugh. A former staff member tells me: 'She had a stand-up fight with Gerard – "Well, of course you're going to support your girlfriend on this; you treat her like a princess."'

Happy anniversary

Traditionally, on a 13th wedding anniversary, a husband gives his wife a gift of lace. Gerard gave Allison one of the worst days of her life. Despite her efforts in her journal to see the best in her husband, they had become virtual strangers. Gerard was having an affair but had not left his wife, let alone told her about what was going on. Instead, he chose a much more hurtful path – he had simply withdrawn from the marriage. Despite having attended a few counselling sessions together, things between the couple were getting worse, not better.

Allison woke up that Monday 23 August 2010 and could bear no more. She steeled herself and asked Gerard a simple question: 'What's wrong with us?' On this rare occasion, Gerard gave an honest response: he didn't love her anymore.

A distraught Allison phoned her best friend, Kerry-Anne Walker, and tearfully relayed the conversation. Walker went straight around to Allison's place at Brookfield. Allison told her there was no explanation for Gerard's outburst. Worse still, he had delivered it so coldly. No tears or attempt to feign sadness.

Walker told Allison she needed to leave the relationship. No one wakes up one day and says they don't love someone anymore, unless there's something going on. He must be seeing someone else. Allison was adamant Gerard wasn't having an affair. She'd asked him, and he had looked her straight in the eye and denied it. Allison didn't think there was any way Gerard could pull off a lie like that.

Rather than turning the blame outward, she turned it inward: perhaps she was at fault. Consequently, Allison's first act in trying to mend her limping marriage was an attempt to fix herself.

To do this, she turned to someone else she trusted – Dr Phil McGraw, the TV psychologist who found fame on Oprah Winfrey's couch and went on to front his own show and publish many books for couples in crisis. On her grim 13th wedding anniversary, Allison fished out Dr Phil's book *Relationship Rescue* and began completing one of its exercises in her journal.

The exercise presented a series of half-sentences. Allison's role was to complete the sentences with the first thoughts that sprang to mind. Cursing herself for everything under the sun – from being overweight to failing to live up to Gerard's expectations of a mother – the thoughts that poured out were deeply sad.

1. I tend to deny . . . most things.
2. I am happiest when . . . I am with my family and friends.
3. Sometimes I . . . sabotage things.
4. What makes me angry is . . . when I feel I have been unfairly treated.
5. I wish . . . my marriage was like it was before the actual ceremony.
6. I hate it when . . . my weight bulges over my pants.
7. When I get angry I . . . sulk.
8. I would give anything if my partner would . . . make love to me.
9. Sometimes . . . I take the easy way.
10. I would be more loveable if . . . I loved back and was myself?
11. My mother and father . . . have struggled with their relationship.
12. If only I had . . . 1 million dollars, a size 10 body. Put more effort into my marriage.
13. My best quality is . . . my perception.
14. Sometimes at night . . . I stay up too late.
15. When I was a child . . . I was treated like a princess.
16. My worst trait is . . . my lack of communication.
17. My life really changed when . . . I got married and had kids.

18. If my relationship ends it will be because . . . G has had enough and doesn't love me anymore and of all the crap I have dished out to him over the past 13 yrs.
19. My partner hates it when I . . . sabotage our parenting and not do as I say I will.
20. When I am alone I . . . relax.

Desperate for the marriage to survive, Allison resolved to fix the problems. The young ballerina in her obviously still felt she could overcome any hurdle if she just worked a little harder.

Immediately after Gerard's anniversary attempt to end the marriage, she had consulted a new marriage counsellor, determined to salvage the relationship. The counsellor's response, which she relayed to Kerry-Anne Walker later, was not what Allison wanted to hear. Most times in this situation, the counsellor informed her, the marriage ended.

Allison was horrified. She didn't want to hear the marriage couldn't be salvaged. 'I'm here to fix my marriage and they're telling me it's not going to work,' she told Walker, who thought the advice made a lot of sense.

But Walker couldn't make Allison see she was fighting a losing battle, any more than the counsellor could. Allison resolved to get the relationship back to the way it was before they married, and continued furiously working through Dr Phil's exercises to make sense of it all, save her marriage and improve herself.

Unhappy with the counsellor's take on her marriage, Allison shopped around for some more palatable advice. She wound up in the office of Dr Laurie Lumsden at the Kenmore Village Shopping Centre on 9 December 2010. Lumsden had been a psychologist for 45 years. Allison told him of seeking help with someone else in the city but had decided to try a local. She was hoping Lumsden would talk to her husband, but wanted to see him first herself.

Lumsden did a test to see where Allison fit on the scale for stress, anxiety and depression, and found her levels completely normal. Allison had been open with the psychologist about her history of postnatal depression, and he was impressed by her recovery. Allison had been studying for a Master of Psychology when her first daughter was born. She hoped to one day complete it. Lumsden told her that when she did, he would love her to work for him.

Gerard did go to see Lumsden twice, in separate appointments later that month. He told the psychologist he was stuck between whether to stay in his marriage or leave, but chose not to mention his continuing affair with Toni McHugh.

By the end of the month, Allison was confident she could turn things around in her marriage. Her big family Christmas party went ahead, as usual, and Allison had a warm half-hour conversation with Mary Dann, her aunt. Mary would never forget the way she spoke that day about her three young daughters. Allison was intensely focused on raising courageous girls who would make their own decisions in life and above all, be free to be happy.

Bruce Overland

New Year's eve 2010

Hunched over a computer keyboard, careful to ensure neither his wife nor mistress could find any trace of his activities, Gerard quietly tapped out a new online profile. This one wasn't for his real estate agency, and he didn't use his real name – the name he had always been so proud of. On this day, he was Bruce Overland, an alter ego he had invented for his illicit activites. And the profile he was compiling was on Adult Friend Finder, a sex, dating and swingers website.

'Looking for discrete Sex,' he typed. Under the section headed 'Introduction', he added some more details.

'Married, but don't want to be – looking for some sex on the side!'

Bruce Overland was a name Gerard had been using as an alias in his business life for years. Although Gerard lectured others about ethics, he was secretly using Bruce Overland to keep tabs on his rivals and even bait them online. He would email other agents as Bruce Overland – a wealthy miner looking for prestige property in Brisbane's west – and get added to their databases. Once he was on their mailing lists he could track new properties as they came onto the market and keep up to date with their sales techniques.

But Gerard took it further. On one occasion he bragged to Phill Broom that he'd arranged for a former Century 21 agent, Ann-Louise Savage, to collect the fictitious Overland from the airport. Apparently Savage had done something to raise Gerard's hackles, so he decided to mess her around. Savage knew Bruce Overland as a WA-based miner and prospective client who had inquired about million-dollar plus homes.

The name was also convenient for pursuing affairs. As Bruce Overland on Adult Friend Finder, Gerard typed out a false date of birth, but other details rang true:

Sexual orientation: Straight.
Looking for: Women
Birthdate: January 1, 1970
Marital status: Married.
Height: 177–180cm
Body type: Average
Smoking: I'm a non smoker.
Drinking: I'm a light/social drinker
Drugs: I don't use drugs
Education: BA/BS (4 years college)
Race: Caucasian
Male endowment: Average/Average
Circumcised: Yes

Gerard was chasing the opposite sex in the real world, too. Incidents of inappropriate behaviour around women were racking up. Cheryl Kelly worked with Gerard in his real estate office and was taken aback when her boss asked if she had ever had a threesome. She wasn't comfortable with the question, or with Gerard's habit of hugging her when the agency sold a property.

Century 21 Westside partner Phill Broom would also tell police of being uneasy about the hugs Gerard dished out to staff. Broom thought it was a calculated ploy to cover the hugs he gave to Toni.

Gerard's pursuit of women at times went from the off-putting to the plain bizarre. Melissa Romano, a pretty, blonde real estate worker, was in touch with Gerard about a property deal on the Gold Coast in 2009. She spoke to Gerard on the phone a number of times and, characteristically, he asked her to come and work for him. When Romano turned down the offer, the conversation took a bizarre turn.

'Well, if you're not interested in doing that, then I've got another job to do,' Gerard volunteered.

'Well, what is that?' Romano asked.

'I'm looking for someone to kill my wife,' he said.

After Allison's disappearance, Romano went to the police, and later told her story to *60 Minutes*, claiming Gerard was deadly serious at the time. Detectives concluded Romano was an unlikely assassin, and suspected Gerard was trying to woo her with an appalling pick-up line.

Allison's cousin Jodie Dann had always had reservations about Gerard. They multiplied the day she saw Gerard and Toni McHugh at a coffee shop together at the Gailey Road Fiveways at Taringa. There was something about the way Gerard and Toni behaved when they were together that troubled Dann. She had a gut reaction and guessed their secret on sight. 'That's Gerard. He's having an affair with that woman,' she told the friend she was with.

Dann and Allison had been close when they were young. They used to spend hours playing on a wooden cubbyhouse Geoff Dickie had built in the bedroom Allison and her sister Vanessa shared at their childhood home in Redbank. Dann recalls Allison as being the sweetest girl, never in any trouble, and a perfectionist who strived to please her parents.

Later in life, Dann became a court advocate with the Ipswich Women's Centre Against Domestic Violence. Dann and Gerard did not get along. When Allison had been in a relationship with Ian Drayton, Dann saw her all the time. Allison and Drayton would drop around for dinner most weekends, and they'd share spaghetti bolognaise and a cheap bottle of wine. After Gerard came on the scene, Dann rarely saw Allison. Although the cousins lived on the same side of town, they never once had dinner together. Dann invited Allison to come around with the girls to use her pool, but the offer was never taken up.

Dann suspected there was more to Gerard than met the eye. At one point, Allison broke her ankle, and said she had fallen down some steps. Dann thought there might be another explanation and told her mum, Mary, she was worried Gerard may be hurting Allison. Her mum cautioned Dann, saying her work made her see everything through a prism of domestic abuse. Dann was not so sure and told Allison's mum, Priscilla, of her concerns.

In her job, Dann saw men like Gerard all the time. They would turn up to court in expensive suits and with impeccable manners, then the court would be told of the fear and control they inflicted on their wives. Usually in these cases, the women had been victimised for years before finally coming forward, after hanging on to false hope their husbands would treat them the same way they had when they first met. These were the men she worried about the most, because their abuse was more insidious, and hidden behind a veneer of wealth or respectability.

One of the few people independent of either Allison or Gerard's family to ever witness events inside the Baden-Clay home was their cleaner, Deb Metcalfe. Metcalfe, an office assistant, was cleaning part-time for extra cash. After registering with an agency, she was sent to Allison and Gerard's Brookfield home in early 2010. Metcalfe liked Allison from the start. Only 20 minutes after they met, Allison had to go out and was telling Metcalfe, a stranger, where she could find the spare key to let herself in if no one was home in future.

Metcalfe cleaned Allison and Gerard's home every Tuesday for the next two years. During that time, she saw Allison was a loving and relentlessly busy mum, always racing around to get her kids to school or pick them up and drop them off to extra-curricular activities such as dancing or swimming. Allison went out of her way to make Metcalfe feel comfortable, making her lunch if she was at home, or giving her a card and small gift of a candle and cupcake at Christmas.

It stood out to Metcalfe that Allison would never talk about her husband. Photos of Gerard lined the walls, but Allison only ever talked about her children and work. Metcalfe never met Gerard but tells me, in hindsight, she thought back to all those months working in the house and wondered what sort of husband Gerard must have been. Early on, Allison had asked Metcalfe to do some ironing if she had time and Metcalfe obliged. But Allison soon approached apologetically with a request: Gerard wasn't happy with the way Metcalfe was ironing the cuffs on his business shirts, Allison said, and showed her how he liked it done. Metcalfe duly took note, but after a while Allison asked her not to worry about ironing anymore. Metcalfe remembers thinking at the time that Gerard must be very particular.

Allison generally had the slow cooker going, preparing a meal for that night's dinner. She was particularly obsessive about her weight. Metcalfe sometimes saw Allison weighing her food before eating. A fitness fanatic herself, Metcalfe often chatted with Allison about weight-loss strategies. Whenever Metcalfe encouraged Allison and told her she looked great, the support would always be met with appreciation.

Storm brewing

Despite the turmoil in Gerard's private life, 2010 was the biggest year yet for Century 21 Westside. While the rest of the world was still being buffeted by fallout from the global financial crisis, in the leafy western suburbs, their business was doing a roaring trade. Phill Broom and Jocelyn Frost were dedicated to sales, and Gerard was managing the agency. Ben Bassingthwaighte was in charge of rentals. As fast as Gerard's partners could list houses, they were selling them. Gerard proudly told people his agency had become the number one Century 21 office in Queensland and ranked tenth nationally. Gerard's dreams of career success appeared to be within reach.

As the business progressed he abandoned his original plan for a series of branches throughout the western suburbs and set his mind on a single, giant office instead. The partners all agreed it was time to expand. Broom and Frost were riding high on their lofty commissions and were up for the challenge. By now, the business had outgrown its current office space in Kenmore. They discussed knocking out the walls and setting it up as a big open-plan space. But the lease was coming up for renewal fairly soon and in the end they decided to roll the dice – to move to bigger premises and go on a recruiting drive.

They found a space two suburbs closer to the city, at the corner of Swann Road and Moggill Road at Taringa. It sat between the western suburbs and the CBD, so thousands of commuters passed every day. They'd have the naming rights to the building, which they thought would give them significant exposure. There was double the space, which meant they could hire the new staff they needed to grow. Everything about their new super-office seemed perfect. They would be within reach of the entire west. They could tap into St Lucia, Indooroopilly, Chapel Hill, Kenmore, Brookfield, Pullenvale, Moggill and across the river to Sinnamon Park, Jindalee and beyond.

In their excitement, the three key partners glossed over the risks. They were uprooting their business from a location where they had a name and following. They were moving to a building that was isolated, with no surrounding businesses to draw foot traffic. And they were doing it at a time the market was unsteady. Yes, they had been doing remarkably well but in real estate, things could change dramatically, without warning. Their outgoings would multiply: the rent was enormous and until their old lease ran out, they would have to keep paying for the Kenmore office space. They would also have to pay for a new fit-out at Taringa and all the other expenses associated with relocating.

They leased three separate offices in the Taringa building to obtain the space they wanted, and Gerard oversaw the shop fit-out from November 2010. Internal walls were knocked down and rebuilt; the premises were painted, carpeted and wired. Gerard took charge of the hiring, selecting nine new salespeople and an extra support person. The additional staff would take the office head count to 27.

They moved around Christmas and planned an opening for 10 January 2011, when the new staff members were due to start. But the plans quickly derailed. In December, Broom would recall, he found out the business couldn't afford to pay the directors the fees they were owed. By then it was too late to back out of the move to their big new office. And the finances were much worse than Broom or Frost imagined. Almost as soon as they'd moved offices, Gerard called a meeting and broke the bad news to Frost and Broom. The finances were diabolical. They were severely in debt.

'Phill and I were in absolute shock. This was because 2010 was such a great year. We wondered where the money had gone,' recalled Frost.

Gerard would blame Broom and Frost, accusing them of dropping the ball with sales while he did everything to get them into the new office. Still puzzled, Broom and Frost tried to figure out how they had landed in so much trouble. Broom did the sums. In the final quarter of 2010, they'd raked in about $600,000 in commissions. There should have been plenty of money to tide them over.

'Given that the sales from the fourth quarter were massive, it was a question of where the money had gone,' Broom would tell police. 'It got to a point where we were robbing Peter to pay Paul. We were taking debt from the previous quarter and carrying it over. The back-pay to Jocelyn and myself was quite large. The reality was that there wasn't as much money as was supposed to be there.'

When Frost looked back, she realised how naive she'd been. She'd trusted Gerard to handle the finances and hadn't been firm enough in demanding information that might have revealed the true position of the business. 'Gerard always had reasons for not having his financials ready every week at management meetings,' Frost told police. 'We had some discussions about whether we could afford to move and afford to rent the larger place. I asked Gerard several times for the financial records to show we could afford it, but it never really showed us the data.'

Broom looked back at Gerard's performance. The partners had long ago agreed Gerard would run the office to free Broom and Frost to bring in business and income. Bassingthwaighte's job was to run the rentals side. Gerard, as principal and managing director, would look after training, recruitment and accounting. He was rewarded handsomely to do this but he had staff helping him. He had someone looking after the accounts plus he had a PA, bookkeeper and two front-of-house people. None of these people generated income.

As for Gerard's job of keeping the office running smoothly, that hadn't happened either. Between managing his complicated love life and joining every community association going, he'd failed to manage his own business.

There was also the matter of their expensive new office. Although all the partners agreed to the move, they'd leased a bigger space than Broom thought was wise. The rent, at $16,000 a month, was more than double what they had been paying at Kenmore. It was all very well Gerard thinking big but it was not sustainable.

Broom had suddenly woken up to reality, and he could have kicked himself. In the belief that all was rosy, he'd just bought an expensive sports car. His wife, Michelle, had recently given birth to their second baby, and they'd just returned from an expensive holiday. He also had a significant tax bill due in February 2011. His wife had asked him weeks earlier if relocating was a good idea, and he'd been sure there were enough sales in the bag to keep them going, even if things were quiet after the move.

While the business had seemingly been going well, privately Gerard had been treading water. To pay his credit card bill he'd borrowed money from his parents and had shuffled funds from his margin loan.

After Gerard revealed the dire state of the finances, the three sales partners agreed to talk again in a couple of days. One way or the other, his partners decided, things were going to have to change.

Flood

If Gerard Baden-Clay didn't have enough on his mind – with an impatient lover, anxious wife, three children, debts up to his eyeballs and business partners in revolt – Mother Nature was about to turn on him too.

Two intense thunderstorms crossed the south-east coast of Queensland on the morning of 10 January 2011 – the day the Century 21 Westside's grand new office was due to open. By 11 am they had formed a single monster storm cell. It swept south-west, crossing Wivenhoe and Somerset dams, which were designed to supply Brisbane and Ipswich with water and protect the state capital from flood. Intensifying as it went, the storm cell continued on to the Toowoomba range.

The previous month had been the wettest December in south-east Queensland since records began in 1900. Now the system was dumping vast quantities of rain on an already sodden catchment. Reports came into the weather bureau of up to 80 millimetres falling in some areas in around 30 minutes. The ground simply could not take any more, but rain was still falling heavily – and running off just as fast.

There was no warning before the flash flood hit Toowoomba, Gerard Baden-Clay's old home town, about 1.30 pm. It came in a brown, frothing torrent, breaking creek banks, sweeping through the streets, tossing cars around on the crest of its murky waves. The city was suddenly in chaos.

Into this drove Donna Rice in the family's white Mercedes. She was on her way to see her eldest son, Chris, and with her were his brothers Blake, 10, and Jordan, 13. When they reached the intersection of James and Kitchener streets, water was already coursing over the road. But they were in the city's

CBD and it didn't look too deep to Donna, who was being urged forward by an exuberant Jordan. As they drove across the intersection, water was not yet over the tyres, but the car's engine stalled, leaving them stranded. After phoning 000 on her mobile, shortly before 2 pm, Donna spoke with a police officer who, like many, had no idea what was unfolding on the ground and how quickly the water was rising around the family sedan.

Donna and her two sons had climbed onto the roof of their car as the water continued to rise around them. Horrified onlookers attempted a rescue, one man wading out with a rope tied around his waist. He grabbed Blake after Jordan – who could not swim and was terrified of water – urged him to save his younger brother first. Before Jordan and Donna could be rescued, they were both washed away by a torrent tearing down the main street of their home town. The pair managed momentarily to grasp a pole before Jordan lost his grip and Donna, a loving mother to the end, let go to pursue her son. Their bodies were found more than a kilometre away.

Throughout the morning, amateur weather buff Neil Pennell had been glued to his computer screen watching the cell on the Australian Bureau of Meteorology (BOM) radar. He was growing alarmed by what he saw and concerned that no flash flood warnings had been issued for townships that lay in valleys down the range from Toowoomba. There was going to be a hell of a lot of run-off coming their way. He posted a message on the Weatherzone online forum: 'Do you think BOM is on the case with that cell . . .? Those rain rates between Esk, Crows Nest and Toowoomba are truly frightening. I fear that there could be a dangerous flash flood very soon, particularly in Grantham. Am I overreacting?'

He wasn't. It was estimated as much as 200 millimetres of rain had fallen in one hour in some areas. Down the range, sedate creeks and brooks were turning into raging rivers as run-off washed downhill gathering speed, power and debris. Thick gum trees snapped like twigs and were carried away in a roaring mass of water. Boulders, earth, fences, sheds and the remnants of houses were caught up in the indiscriminate floodwaters.

At Murphy's Creek in the Upper Lockyer Valley, one resident would recall seeing a huge wave cascading down the valley around 1.47 pm. The creek rose about 12 metres in 12 minutes. Houses were torn from their stumps and residents swept to their deaths. Local Selwyn Schefe and his daughter, Katie, aged six, were trying to make it to higher ground when the flash flood engulfed their car. Katie's body was found 5 kilometres away. Selwyn's was carried 101 kilometres.

As the water rushed onwards, the BOM gauges began to record alarming rises in creek heights. At 2.20 pm, the creek at Helidon was at 4 metres, just 30 minutes later it was reading 12.66 metres. The figures seemed so fanciful they were dismissed as faulty readings, dooming residents of lower lying townships. Water raced down creeks and tributaries converging to feed a growing tidal wave.

Around 3.20 pm it hit Grantham hard. Resident Marty Warburton told police: 'Everything just went black, as if the sun had just disappeared. I realised that a massive wave of water was hitting the town and it was like someone had just turned out the lights . . . As I was standing there, I saw two human bodies floating past.'

The floods brought destruction and suffering. Families were torn apart, many washed away with their homes. Stacey Keep was six months pregnant and clinging to her 23-month-old daughter, Jessica, when the pair were dragged out of their Grantham home. When Stacey's leg became trapped under water, the torrent tore Jessica from her arms. 'I'll never forget that feeling of having your own child swept away from your arms and there's nothing you can do. A piece of my heart is missing and I'll never get it back,' she said in a *60 Minutes* interview. There were extraordinary stories of others who survived on the roofs of houses carried away by the flood.

In all, 21 people died in the Toowoomba and Lockyer Valley flash floods that day.

Less than an hour away in Brisbane, people watched news reports, horrified. They were shortly to learn the state's capital was facing a crisis of its own. Rainfall and run-off from the same weather system was still pouring into the two dams above the city, pushing them, literally, almost to breaking point.

The imposing Wivenhoe Dam was built in 1984. About 80 kilometres upriver from Brisbane, it performs a dual role of providing the city with both water storage and protection from floods, by holding back water which would otherwise stream down into the Brisbane River. Many believed Wivenhoe had 'flood-proofed' Brisbane in the wake of the devastating 1974 floods, when more than 8500 homes in Brisbane and Ipswich were inundated. However, flooding had been far from the public consciousness for many years leading up to the exceptional summer of 2010–11. For years the city had been in drought and living under strict water restrictions – it was illegal for residents to use sprinklers to water their gardens or hoses to wash their cars; egg timers were sent out to households to encourage shorter showers, and governments began planning for what seemed like an inevitable water crisis. Water levels in Wivenhoe fell to a woeful 16 per cent of its 1.15 million megalitre capacity. Some speculated it would never fill again and people began to think of Wivenhoe primarily as a water storage facility rather than a flood mitigation one.

In mid-2010, weather forecasters began to warn that the end of the year would see the emergence of a strong La Niña weather pattern, associated with huge rainfall in Australia. In fact, the indicators for an exceptionally wet summer had not been this strong since 1973–74. The BOM experts were spot-on with their predictions. It turned out to be a monsoon season the likes of which Queensland had not seen for a generation. Through December, the dams filled, and the exceptional storm that moved across the state on Monday 10 January pushed the system to the very brink.

On that Monday morning, Wivenhoe was at 148 per cent capacity. The dam has a total capacity of 2.6 million megalitres, which comprises 1.15 million ML for water storage and a 'flood compartment' designed to hold 1.45 million ML. At a capacity of 148 per cent, the storage is full and the flood compartment is about half full.

Dam operators urgently needed to get levels down to free up space in the flood compartment. But they were concerned large-scale releases would flood some crossings and low-lying areas. By Tuesday, with immense volumes of run-off pouring in and not enough being released, Wivenhoe had reached an alarming 190 per cent of capacity. Dam operators were forced to begin releasing enormous volumes of water. The nature of the emergency had changed: they were trying to prevent a possible structural failure as a result of overtopping.

At the same time as water was hurtling down from Wivenhoe into the Brisbane River, lesser flood waves – from the Lockyer Valley and Bremer River – were also flowing towards the capital. The 'floodproof' city was about to go under, catastrophically. The western suburbs, Gerard Baden-Clay's home and the centre of his business would be among the hardest hit.

Thursday 13 January 2011 was a picture-perfect day. The rain had stopped but floodwaters were still rising. So as the sun shone, brown, murky waters slowly engulfed Brisbane. In all, about 18,000 properties were inundated as the gentle river became a roaring beast. Boats were torn from their moorings – in some cases entire pontoons went careening down the river with boats sitting neatly atop before they were smashed to pieces against bridge pylons. The floating restaurant Drift broke free and collapsed against the William Jolly bridge in the heart of the city. The river was awash with debris – sinks, wheelie bins and furniture.

On Wednesday night, the 181-tonne floating Riverwalk, linking New Farm to the CBD, broke loose. Authorities revealed they had been considering using explosives to destroy the 250-metre concrete walkway before the flood moved too fast. If this new floating missile hit the supports of Brisbane's Gateway Bridge, it could do untold damage. Helicopters beamed live footage of a plucky tugboat captain determinedly nudging the mass of concrete safely under the bridge before pushing it aground at the river mouth.

The city's iconic sporting arena, Suncorp Stadium, became a giant swimming pool. As water treatment plants went under, Premier Anna Bligh warned Queenslanders raw sewage was being pumped into floodwaters. In some low-lying suburbs, stinking waters bubbled up through sewers and stormwater pipes then reached the streets.

When the water receded, the stench and the damage were overwhelming. But the city rallied. Brisbane City Council called on residents to pitch in for an unprecedented clean-up. For three days, authorities set up coordination centres across the city where volunteers with brooms and buckets were bused around to help flood victims with the sad task of throwing out ruined family heirlooms, furniture and mementoes. A fleet of rubbish trucks patrolled non-stop, carting away tonnes of sodden furniture, clothes, electrical equipment and memories. There were more than 25,000 official volunteers and thousands more unofficial helpers who joined what became known as the Mud Army.

For Gerard Baden-Clay's embattled business, it was a nail in the coffin. The list of flood-affected suburbs read like a roll-call of his prospecting grounds – Bellbowrie, St Lucia, Fig Tree Pocket, Kenmore and Moggill were among them.

The start of the year is usually a busy period for real estate agents, when people put Christmas and New Year celebrations behind them and get on with plans to buy or sell. No one was much was thinking about buying or selling on Brisbane's sodden Westside that year.

Flood

Right when Gerard was desperate for cash flow, the property market ground almost to a halt, courtesy of the biggest natural disaster of a generation. Recovery would be slow. Gerard could not take a trick.

Aftermath

January 2011

Nigel and Elaine's home in Durness Street, Kenmore, was inundated in the flood. The street rises in the middle and dips at both ends, so some homes were hit hard while others, narrowly, stayed bone dry. Unluckily for the Baden-Clay seniors, their home was a couple of houses the wrong side of the high-water mark. They'd sandbagged the property but the floodwaters gushed over the top. Neighbours who came to help would recall wading into the house with the muddy water at about knee height. Nigel and Elaine would have to move out for nine months while the house was repaired.

Century 21 Westside staff went to the house to help with the clean-up. Gerard and Toni McHugh went off together to get everyone lunch. They were gone for hours, according to one worker there that day.

With the market dead, the business partners had nothing else to do but continue to squabble. Frost was in a better financial position than Broom and agreed to buy his quarter share of the rental side of the business to help him out. Broom kept his separate one-third share in the sales side of the business with Frost and Gerard.

It wasn't long before there was another confrontation between the sales partners. Gerard went into Frost's office and called Broom in too. He couldn't run the business with the two of them demanding to authorise every payment. He felt they didn't trust him. 'I don't trust you,' Frost said bluntly.

A rattled Gerard told her he was going to buy her out. With the threat ringing in her ears, Frost left to visit a friend who ran another real estate agency. She wanted to know what the friend paid his staff and his costs at his highly successful business. Her meeting made her realise her own business was too top heavy, and Gerard was paying people to do what he should have been doing.

Frost and Broom decided they had three options: Gerard could buy them out, they could buy Gerard out or they could agree to change and stay together. They arranged another meeting. Bassingthwaighte was called in as moderator. Broom and Frost arrived with a list of demands – some shared, some individual – that Gerard would have to meet if the partnership was to continue. Gerard was to step down as managing director and return to sales immediately; retrench a staff member who was helping Gerard with the accounts; take three weeks off and get his private life in order; give the new staff notice that they would be on commission and not a retainer; stick to new rules on payments; and, last but not least, stop living a double life and choose Allison or Toni.

The meeting descended into a slanging match. Accusations flew. Gerard swore and cried. He was crumbling under the pressure. Broom recalled that when the subject of McHugh was raised, Gerard finally cracked.

'I only continue to fuck her for the sake of the business,' he blurted out.

The meeting went late into the night. When they left, they had resolved to meet again the following night to decide what they were going to do. Frost felt Toni needed to know what Gerard had said. But after talking to Frost, Toni went straight to Gerard, who managed to smooth it over.

When they met again, Gerard had regained his composure. Broom expected him to agree to their demands, return to sales and sort out his private life. But when Gerard faced them, he was defiant. He wasn't going to agree to any of their demands. His personal life was none of their business.

He didn't care if he went to the wall – he would not bow to his partners' demands. Gerard told them he had few assets to lose. He and his family were, after all, living in a cheap rental house. His counter offer was that he would buy Frost and Broom out of the sales side. Frost recalled that Gerard offered $25,000 to each of his partners. He said his friends would help him raise the money. His partners walked out in a daze. The meeting had not gone as they expected.

In the days that followed, Gerard changed the offer. He said his friends couldn't afford to pay them out. He said he'd take responsibility for the debt and buy them out for $1.

Gerard offered them a bonus as an incentive to stay on as sales agents. Frost and Broom signed over their shares of the business to Gerard. They felt they had no other option.

Frost didn't tell Gerard immediately, but she had no plans to stay on as an agent as he had suggested. A major factor in this decision was her chronic discomfort with the long-running affair being conducted in the office. Within weeks of signing over her share of the sales business, she was gone, though she retained her stake in the rental business.

Broom tried to battle on, staying at the business as a salesman. 'There was a massive shift in power,' he told police later. 'There was obvious animosity from other staff towards Toni. I was often asked questions by the staff about the relationship between Toni and Gerard. The relationship at this time between Gerard and myself was not particularly good. The relationship outside the business had completely stopped. I used to avoid Gerard.'

Meanwhile, Gerard's credit card debt was on the rise again. In March 2011, his brother and sister-in-law, Adam and Nicole Baden-Clay, transferred $20,000 to his account. Gerard almost immediately put all the money on his credit card. As soon as he paid it off, it rose again. From there, it climbed again until it maxed out in early 2012.

Gerard turned to his three closest friends too, asking them to bail him out. Robert Cheesman and Stuart Christ, who knew Gerard from their days together at Toowoomba Grammar, and

Peter Cranna, another long-term friend, came up with about $90,000 each to keep his business afloat. There were no formal loan contracts, merely a gentleman's agreement for the loans to be repaid with interest. Before lending Gerard the money, the men asked to see the business's books, and dubbed themselves his 'advisory group'. They discovered he had too many staff, and told him he had to downsize.

At first Gerard stuck to the deal, but before long the repayments stopped. His finances, after a temporary reprieve, were in dire straits, and his private life was about to be in even worse shape.

The last to know

Brookfield State School's annual trivia night always drew a good crowd. Gerard was usually front and centre, helping with an auction to raise money for the school. Getting into the spirit one year, he and Allison and the rest of their table had dressed as characters from the movie *Top Gun*. But on Friday 9 September 2011, he was late and Allison wasn't around either. No one seemed to know if he was going to turn up, and back-up plans were being made for the auction in case he didn't arrive.

Phill Broom was there with his friend Jeff Lock, who was on the school P & C with Gerard. Broom had quit Century 21 Westside on the previous Saturday. The day he left, Broom told Gerard he liked to think some day they would run into each other in a bar and have a drink together. Salesman John Bradley – whose engagement party had been instrumental in the affair being exposed in Gerard's office – quit the same day.

At the trivia night, Gerard arrived at the last minute and did the auction. He and Broom didn't cross paths. But another former Century 21 staff member was in the room and approached Broom.

'How long have you known about the affair?' she asked, in earshot of other parents. For so long, Gerard had managed to keep the affair from Allison. But now it was being discussed at the school trivia night.

The next week it was all over the school tuckshop too. Broom's friend Jeff Lock was on the tuckshop roster. Lock would remember one of the mums asking after the welfare of Broom, and replying that all may not have been as it seemed. Details are unclear but someone brought up Gerard's affair. In the afternoon, one of the mums ran into Wendy Mollah at school pick-up and told her about the affair too. She was Allison's friend, and her heart sank.

Mollah was a single mum of two and author of a book on how to get children through divorce and separation. She drove home and spent the night dwelling on the awful rumour. The next morning she knew what she had to do, and phoned Allison.

Gerard was in a staff meeting at the office when Allison rang his mobile. 'We've got to talk,' she said.

He knew instantly from her tone what the talk would be about. They agreed to meet at a McDonald's restaurant down the road, at Indooroopilly. He drove his Lexus – they called the car 'Midi', which Gerard liked to say stood for midlife crisis. Allison drove the Prado, 'Snowy'. Gerard arrived first and Allison parked behind him. He got out of the car and went and sat in the passenger seat beside her. She asked him straight out: 'Are you having an affair with Toni?'

He said, 'Yes', that he had been.

He'd later describe her reaction as disbelief. She got out of the car, in shock, and sat on the concrete kerb. She was shaking her head, saying, 'I can't believe this.' When she had asked him in the past if he was sleeping with anyone else, he had denied it, and she believed him. Her head was in her hands. Gerard thought she would vomit, but she didn't. When she regained her composure enough to speak again, she asked him, 'Do you love her?'

When he replied, 'No', Allison told him he had to make a choice – her or me. Instantly, he said he wanted to be with Allison and their girls. So she told him to end it: 'Now.'

Allison wanted McHugh out of the business from that moment on. He put his arm around her shoulders and she shrugged him off.

Straightaway, Gerard phoned McHugh and this time he was the one saying they needed to talk. They arranged to meet at her St Lucia apartment, where he told McHugh that Allison had found out and had given him an ultimatum. He said Allison had told him it 'wouldn't be pretty for him' if he made the wrong decision. The affair was over, he told her.

There was no discussion or bargaining; he was dumping McHugh and she didn't have a say in it. McHugh was as shocked as Allison, calling Gerard every name under the sun.

Gerard returned to Century 21 Westside at Taringa, sent out a group email saying McHugh wouldn't be returning, and set about calling his staff into his office, one at a time, to explain. It must have been an excruciating and embarrassing moment for his staff as Gerard told them he had been sleeping with McHugh and his wife had found out.

Gerard told receptionist Gabrielle Cadioli a different story to the one he had told his wife. 'He said it would be very difficult for him. He said [of McHugh], "I love her."'

When Ben Bassingthwaighte phoned McHugh to check on her, she was hysterical.

'Toni has said to me basically that Allison knows about the affair and was uncontrollably crying and upset. She was saying that Gerard had broken up the relationship and that he is gutless for breaking up with Toni and for not leaving Allison,' he said.

Gerard, separately, confided to Bassingthwaighte that McHugh took the split badly. 'Gerard told me that Toni had made a comment to him about their sexual relationship . . . Toni was berating him saying the sex was good but he is just an idiot.'

Jocelyn Frost, although no longer in the office, was informed about the dramatic turn of events and was immediately concerned. Having previously been close to McHugh, she knew perhaps better than anybody how badly Gerard's mistress would take being dumped, and was worried she would take her own life. 'Unfortunately, she can't manage without him. I was a support for her at that time and she was screaming and crying and had her two sons with her,' Frost told police.

A fuming McHugh went on a witch-hunt to find out exactly how Allison had learnt of the affair. Gerard said it came out because Phill Broom told Jeff Lock. McHugh phoned Broom and left a message on his voicemail: 'I can't believe Jeff would have told the tuckshop mums,' she wailed into the phone.

Broom was on a mini-break in Auckland with his wife, having flown out of Brisbane the previous day. Just when he thought he was free, he was dragged back in by McHugh's call. Gerard had tried to phone him too, but hadn't left a message.

Broom returned McHugh's call. 'She was not in a very good state. She was crying.'

About three weeks after learning of the affair, Allison made an appointment with Dr Nicholas Bourke at the Kenmore Clinics medical centre. She had previously consulted Bourke about her depression. Now, upset, she told the doctor of the turmoil in her marriage.

'Recent discovery of husband's infidelity. Obviously distressing. Has discussed with him relationship counselling and both are keen for this,' Bourke wrote in his notes from the appointment of 6 October 2011.

Allison asked Dr Bourke for tests for Hepatitis B and C, HIV, syphilis, chlamydia and gonorrhea. She didn't have any symptoms, but who knew what Gerard had been up to.

Although Allison would conceal the affair from some of her closest friends, in the privacy of the doctor's surgery she reached out for help. She was struggling to cope, she told the doctor.

Under the section in his medical notes to record the reason for the visit, Bourke wrote: 'Counselling relationship'. Bourke scrapped Allison's daily 50mg Zoloft tablet and wrote out a new prescription, doubling the dosage to help her through the crisis. Allison needed more than medication, so the doctor wrote a referral to counsellor Rosamond Nutting from the Bardon Counselling and Natural Therapy Centre.

Allison didn't accept Gerard's word that the affair was over. She began keeping tabs on her husband and monitoring his mobile phone. She told Gerard she wanted to see all his text messages and to know everyone he was calling. And from now on, she was going to work in the office too. Allison started at Century 21 Westside almost straightaway. It took a supreme effort to walk in to the office when everyone knew of Gerard's affair.

To reassure her, Gerard installed an app, Find My Friends, on both their phones. The app would allow her, through GPS tracking, to check his precise location at any time via his phone. The password Allison chose for the app, and shared with Gerard, was: 'ilovegwee'. It was a sad and girlish code for a program designed to track her cheating husband.

When she recovered from the initial shock, McHugh bombarded Gerard with phone calls and texts. He had chosen the wrong woman, she said, and pleaded with him to reconsider. He didn't respond. Eventually, McHugh stopped trying and accepted their relationship was over.

Frost tried to help her friend, getting her a new job in real estate. 'But she couldn't cope without Gerard,' said Frost. 'She was devastated that Gerard had cut it off.'

Amid all this turmoil, and with the wounds still fresh, the two women in Gerard's life inadvertently crossed paths. McHugh was with a personal trainer at Workout, a suburban gym on Witton Road, Indooroopilly. She looked up to see Allison and her youngest daughter at the front counter.

'I froze and tried to continue the conversation with the trainer as long as possible, hoping she would leave,' Toni said.

Afterwards, within minutes of each other, both women fired abusive text messages at Gerard.

Broke and broken

December 2011

Dr Bruce Flegg had long been a connoisseur of fine wines, and often he would select choice bottles as gifts for friends. In the lead-up to Christmas 2011, he had just such a present for Gerard Baden-Clay and phoned to let him know. Gerard invited Flegg to his office, saying he had something he needed to talk about.

Flegg had a sinking feeling when he parked in one of the visitor spaces at the front of Century 21 Westside at Taringa. It was the first time he had been to the new premises, and as he stepped out of his car and took in his surroundings, he thought it was a dreadful location for a real estate agency. Not only was it far removed from the loyal customers who frequented its original Kenmore home, there wasn't a single other attraction to draw people past the window, not even a café.

Inside, a far from festive Gerard accepted his gift, in its jolly Christmas paper. Flegg was taken aback by Gerard's tense, almost aggressive mood. It was a side to Gerard that he had not previously seen. They had barely exchanged the pleasantries of the season when Gerard asked for money.

Flegg asked Gerard how much he needed and his eyebrows arched at the response. Gerard wanted $400,000 to buy out his business partners. Flegg knew people sometimes looked at him and saw a man with deep pockets, but his money was invested wisely. Flegg was frugal and didn't take wild risks, which is exactly how the wealthy become wealthy and, more importantly, stay wealthy. He asked Gerard if he was looking for an equity partner. Gerard's answer was unequivocal: he wanted the money as an unsecured loan.

Strangely, for someone asking such a significant favour, Gerard wouldn't tell Flegg who his business partners were. Gerard's secrecy was a red flag.

It almost guaranteed Flegg wouldn't take the request seriously. Had it been a successful business, Flegg might have been able to find someone to invest. However, they would want to look at the books and that wasn't an option.

Over their years on the chamber of commerce together, Flegg had grown to know and like Gerard, but this request was out of left field. People always had deals on offer. This was different. It was like something you would ask of a family member.

Flegg knew Gerard was particularly close to his father, Nigel, and would be desperate not to let his parents down. Gerard's parents were proud of their successful son. A business failure would be devastating – Gerard would rather die than fail. But Flegg could see that was exactly what was on the cards.

Having already taken full ownership of the sales side of the business, Gerard was now desperate for the money to buy out Jocelyn Frost and Ben Bassingthwaighte from the rental side of the business. Frost had long since moved to a different agency and Bassingthwaighte was on his way out the door to become a police officer.

Frost and Bassingthwaighte agreed to sell Gerard their shares in the rental business for $200,000 and $100,000 respectively. Gerard had until 30 June 2012 to pay in full. If he failed to find the cash or to make agreed interest payments, the contract would be void.

Gerard viewed Flegg as his big hope for making the payment, but would have to settle for the Christmas wine. 'I really can't help you,' Flegg said, apologising.

The pressure on Gerard was piling up at work and at home. It had been an awful year. The flood had smashed his business, he'd parted ways with his business partners, Allison had found out about his affair, he'd cut loose his lover and staff had either walked out or been retrenched. Neither his business nor his personal affairs looked likely to improve.

Gerard had stayed with Allison, despite his earlier promises to McHugh. Keeping the marriage alive allowed him to live permanently with his daughters and to prevent what was left of his business being carved in two in a settlement. The trade-off was that he'd handed over control in the relationship to Allison.

He wanted to see Toni.

I'm yours

The Gailey Road Fiveways at Taringa is a little strip of shops
that was just down the road from Century 21 Westside. Close
enough for a quick trip without arousing suspicions, but out of
the way enough for it to be unlikely he would be spotted. In a
low-key café, alongside a chemist, bakery and butcher, Gerard
sat opposite Toni McHugh for the first time in three months.
After flatly ignoring all McHugh's attempts to make contact
since he unceremoniously cut her from his life, Gerard had a
change of heart and phoned her, out of the blue, in December
2011. Allison couldn't watch Gerard every hour of the day, and
he told McHugh he wanted to talk.

Over coffee, Gerard declared that he wasn't leaving his
wife but still loved McHugh. He wanted to say sorry, to patch
things up. McHugh could have told Gerard where to go. He
had humiliated her every bit as much as he had humiliated his
wife. But Toni loved him.

She was sold, and Gerard soon had what he wanted. The
affair, killed off so abruptly in September, reignited.

In the months that followed, the pair would talk frequently,
picking moments when Allison couldn't discover the affair had
resumed. Toni would call Gerard several times a week and,
taking the utmost care to be discreet, they would see each other.
Meeting at a coffee shop in Kelvin Grove in February, they discussed their future together. Gerard told Toni he was going to
leave Allison, and even set a date.

'Gerard told me that he was committed to our relationship
and stated that he would be out of his marriage by the 1st of
July 2012,' Toni later revealed to police.

Some may have found Gerard's self-imposed deadline less
than passionate – how businesslike to plan to leave his wife by

the start of the new financial year. But tax wasn't the only significance of that date. He had promised to begin a new life with his mistress on his wife's birthday.

Every couple of weeks Gerard and Toni would meet at a coffee shop, always during office hours. He told her he would come to her, unconditionally. After one of these meetings, they were unable to restrain themselves and retreated to a parked car for sex.

As part of her plan to both reconnect with her husband and keep an eye on him – and to help support the struggling business; it was, after all, the source of her family's livelihood – Allison had started working at the Century 21 office as general manager. Other staff had ensured, at Gerard's request, that any remnants of McHugh's time there were removed before Allison arrived. Allison set herself up, perhaps deliberately, at McHugh's old desk. And she had Gerard on a strict 5.30 pm curfew.

There was, however, a window of opportunity Gerard and Toni exploited. Allison would usually leave the office about 2.30 pm to collect the girls from school, so the lovers had a few hours for assignations and phone calls before Gerard had to be home. They didn't exchange texts because Allison demanded to see every message Gerard received. Email became the conduit for their passionate exchanges. For some time Gerard had been secretly using an email account under his alias, Bruce Overland. Toni would email 'Bruce' once or twice a day. They'd talk about how much they loved each other and when they could be with each other.

Toni may have appeared to have wholeheartedly taken Gerard back but she was now far less inclined to be pacified by his promises. In an email on 20 February 2012 to the Bruce Overland address, she spelt out her frustrations:

'Well you'll have to forgive me that I feel disappointed when this happens. I'm sick of hiding . . . I'm sick of being second best and having to take the back seat . . . all so she doesn't find out. Why should I believe things are going to be any different than the past. I shouldn't . . . that's the reality. She gave you an ultimatum and you honoured it ??? If I were to do the same tomorrow . . . I doubt you'd be able to pay me the same respect. Why should I accept anything less than she would? All I'm doing at the moment is pacifying your Fucked Relationship!! That's not fair G.'

Every now and again, Gerard said he wanted to put their physical intimacy on hold while he was still with his wife. McHugh would agree. Yet they kept ending up in each other's arms.

'These conversations would then lead to discussions about our future together,' Toni told police. 'Gerard had told me during a conversation that we had in March 2012 that he thought Allison was aware of his intentions to leave, however he did not elaborate any further.'

The last time the lovers would see each other alone, before everything changed, was in the middle of March. Gerard visited McHugh at her unit. They talked about how hard it was to stay in contact. Once again, they agreed they wouldn't have sex until they could be together like a normal couple.

Gerard was trying to save his business and needed to focus. 'Without that, he would not be able to provide anyone with a future,' Toni said.

Financially, Gerard and Allison were stretched to breaking point. One day in March 2012, their cleaner, Deb Metcalfe, arrived at their Brookfield home to find Allison upset.

'She said, "Deb, I need to talk to you. After today, I can't have you back any more. Gerard has told me I can't have any help any more."'

The weekly cleaning visits cost $100 for four hours and Allison explained to Metcalfe she and Gerard could no longer afford it. Allison became teary and kept apologising.

Metcalfe told her she understood and not to be worried.

Fifteen minutes

Allison was sitting in the Relationships Australia waiting room lost in her own thoughts when counsellor Carmel Ritchie called her in for her appointment. Ritchie, a former teacher with more than a decade's experience working with troubled couples, had a standard routine with new clients, where she would run through the ground rules and gather some basic information. She called it her 'housekeeping'. She went through these basic steps with Allison in their session at Spring Hill, central Brisbane, shortly after midday on Tuesday 27 March 2012.

Ritchie, wanting a snapshot of her new client in her own words, gave her 60 seconds to answer three questions: 'Who are you, what are your hobbies and what is something you're good at?'

Ritchie made notes as Allison mapped out that she was a mother of three girls aged ten and under; worked with her husband, Gerard, in a real estate agency four days a week; previously lived in the UK; was a ballet dancer, high achiever, spoke two languages (the others had dropped off over the years) and had studied psychology at university. Allison added that on her honeymoon, she'd suffered a severe reaction to Lariam anti-malarial tablets, which resulted in chronic depression and psychotic episodes and she had been on and off depression medication ever since. She had suffered panic attacks during pregnancy, and her husband's attitude was 'get over it'. During her second pregnancy, she saw psychiatrist Dr Tom George and started on Zoloft. For the past three years, she said, Gerard had been having an affair.

Quickly, Ritchie plotted this information on a genogram – a diagram showing Allison's family relationships and history.

Nodding, Allison told the counsellor that Gerard was a choleric personality, that he had high expectations of the children and of her. Her mum had a similar choleric personality type, she said. So too did Gerard's mistress, Toni McHugh, she added.

The session was coming to a close, and Ritchie had only scratched the surface. Although Allison had started the session saying she wanted to improve herself, it was clear her husband's affair was an open wound. Ritchie said if Allison wanted, she could bring Gerard along to a future consultation, where she would talk to him for the first half of the session and then see them both together. Allison told the counsellor she didn't think Gerard would agree but booked in another appointment for three weeks later before she left.

In her case notes, the counsellor summed up the conversation. Among the key points, she wrote that Gerard didn't understand Allison's depression. She highlighted the fact that he'd told Allison it was all in her mind and to 'get over it'. Allison felt unloved and unappreciated. Gerard told Allison she was not the girl he married. Allison too felt Gerard had changed, adopting a 'look after myself' attitude.

'Allison is a gentle conflict avoider who has said yes too many times in the relationship,' Ritchie wrote.

When Allison walked out of the session, she had a spring in her step. She liked Ritchie, plus now she had something to strive for. It might have been against the odds, but she was going to try to get Gerard to the next counselling session.

That same day, Toni McHugh fired off an email to Bruce Overland, Gerard's alias. She wanted the secrecy and games over. She wanted him to live with her.

'Have you thought about what you're going to do for a place? It would be so much easier,' she wrote, 'if you did just move in with me. She can get her own place and the week you have the children you move back to the house. Ie the kids don't move for the moment. She doesn't need to know where you're staying! Sorry it's up to you to work out and I shouldn't interfere. I'm sorry.'

Gerard reassured Toni in an email on 3 April 2012 – a week after Allison's counselling session – that he was sticking to his plan to leave his wife.

'I have given you a commitment,' he wrote, 'and I intend to stick to it – I will be separated by 1 July. In the mean time, it doesn't seem to be helping either of us to be snatching brief moments I love you.'

Toni, fiery as always, rolled her eyes privately; thought, believe it when I see it, and kept the pressure up.

On 11 April 2012, Gerard tried to calm his lover; they'd had a heated conversation. He swore that, this time, his marriage was over. He also used the special initials they had for each other – 'GG' for gorgeous girl, 'GM' for gorgeous man; 'This is agony for me too. I love you. I'm sorry you hung up on me. It sounded like you were getting very angry. I love you GG. Leave things to me now. I love you. GM.'

Meanwhile, on Monday 16 April – the final week of her life – Allison was back to see Carmel Ritchie. But this time she went to Ritchie's Kenmore office, and she wasn't alone.

'I think she was very pleased to introduce me to Gerard. She was smiling,' Ritchie later told a court.

Gerard followed Ritchie into the consultation room on his own, at the counsellor's request. Allison waited, barely believing she'd convinced Gerard to come along. Behind the closed door, Ritchie took the standard personal snapshot. Gerard said almost nothing about himself personally, preferring to define himself by his achievements. He outlined his roles in the school P & C and local chamber of commerce.

'For Gerard, his image in the community is very important. He believes he is a valuable member of society,' Ritchie wrote in her notes once the session had concluded.

Ritchie asked Gerard about his marriage, and scribbled down his response: 'Allison does not trust me. She questions me. She says yes when she means no.'

Gerard told the counsellor he was there because his wife wanted him to be there, but he didn't think it would help. He wanted to build a future with Allison but the past had to be left in the past. Discussing the affair was an unhelpful regression.

Ritchie roundly disagreed: 'He wants to get on with his life. Wipe it clean,' Ritchie wrote. 'He needs to accept that seven or eight months is very early days yet and to steel himself for the long haul.'

Ritchie put it to Gerard that ignoring his wife's feelings was no solution: 'I spoke about the fact he did have to sit and listen to Allison's feelings about the affair,' Ritchie said later. 'I told him that he can't put this in the past because for Allison the past is very much in the present.'

Gerard was convinced rehashing everything was a step backwards. 'Isn't that regression? Isn't that living in the past?'

Ritchie persisted, and eventually Gerard stopped arguing with her. It wasn't as if he had intended to put his cards on the table with the counsellor anyway. He hadn't mentioned that he had resumed his affair and promised to leave his wife by 1 July. And he didn't particularly want to be questioned closely either.

Now Ritchie presented him with a plan that would allow Allison to work through her feelings. Every second night, for 10 to 15 minutes at a time, Allison would be given free rein to vent to Gerard with all the things she was keeping bottled up. The talks had a time limit because emotions would be high. Gerard's role was simply to listen. This was Allison's time. And he absolutely must not be defensive. At the end of these short bursts, his response was to be limited to expressing remorse, if that was how he felt. Reluctantly, Gerard agreed.

Ritchie walked out of the room to get Allison. Her talk with Gerard had gone overtime, taking up most of the hour booking, and the counsellor was worried Allison would be upset.

Instead, Allison's face immediately lit up with a big smile. 'I'm over the moon you have spent this time with him,' Allison said.

The two women went back into the room. Out of the corner of her eye, Ritchie noticed something unspoken pass between Gerard and Allison. A look on his face. Moments later, Allison's smile was gone and she seemed on edge.

Ritchie explained what Gerard had agreed to. Fifteen minutes, where Allison could say and ask whatever she wanted.

Final hours

Thursday 19 April 2012

5 pm

Allison opened the door to the hair salon and silently took a seat in front of one of the mirrors. She had a cold she hadn't been able to shake for a week. Her nose was runny and eyes watery. But there was only one thing on her mind: Gerard.

For years he let her take the blame for their distance, yet he was at fault all along. To call it an affair was putting it too lightly. It had lasted longer than some marriages. When she finally found out, three years after it began, he blamed her depression. When she made tentative steps to resume a sexual relationship with Gerard he had laughed at her underwear. Told her she smelled. Whatever she had done, she didn't deserve this.

Now that the counsellor had given Allison a licence to grill Gerard about the affair for 15 minutes every second night, she was making the most of every session. The questions were jotted down in her journal so she wouldn't forget; it was as if she were a journalist preparing to crack a difficult interview.

Since seeing the counsellor on Monday, she had been interrogating Gerard and planning the questions to ask him in the future. When he took his lover, Toni McHugh, to the movies, did they travel separately? What did they see? Did they have dinner as well? Weren't they scared of being seen? Did they kiss and hug? Were the car seats down when they had sex or were they up? Did they lie in each other's arms afterwards? How many times?

Even though it sickened her, she couldn't stop. She needed to know every detail.

It had been seven months since she found out. Gerard immediately ended the affair. She'd put everything she had into saving

173

the marriage but inside she was furious. So often she'd copped criticism for shutting down instead of confronting a problem. Not this time. There was still so much more Gerard had to account for, and Allison had another barrage of questions ready for that night. As she ran through the list in her mind, she barely noticed stylist Monique Waymouth appear behind her.

'Okay, let's put in some foils,' Waymouth said, reaching for Allison's hair.

There was no response. Waymouth thought it was the afternoon peak-hour traffic streaming past the salon that was distracting her customer.

Gerard's phone was growing hot against his ear. Not long after Allison left the office for the hairdressers, he was on to Toni. He had to grab his moments when he could. But it wasn't just the overworked mobile phone that was beginning to hurt his ear. On the other end of the line, Toni was going ballistic.

He had been the bearer of bad news. His wife would be at the Real Estate Institute of Queensland's property management conference the next day. Gerard's problem – one of many – was that Toni was attending the same conference. The annual event was on at the Brisbane Convention and Exhibition Centre, and Allison was going with Kate Rankin from the office.

This was Toni's worst nightmare, and what made it all the more infuriating was that Gerard had left it until now – the day before – to tell her. Toni was apoplectic.

'When were you going to tell me this?' she demanded.

'I only just found out. I'm sorry,' he squirmed.

All of the disappointments Gerard had inflicted on her, too many to count, came flooding back to McHugh. He had done this to her too many times.

'I feel sick. How can you put us in this situation?' she gasped.

Both of them were married with children when it started. Toni had left her relationship. Left for him. In return, he gave her excuses, promises and stolen moments.

Gerard always said they would be together properly one day. He would come to her unconditionally. He just never delivered. He needed a push, Toni thought. So she gave it to him: What on earth is going on, she demanded? Would Allison still work at the real estate office when he left her?

'No. I intend to sell the business,' Gerard said.

Toni had heard it all before. She wanted specifics. 'What's going to come first? Do you sell the business or are you going to leave your wife?' she pressed.

'I'm going to leave my wife,' he said.

'Does Allison know about this?'

'No, she doesn't.'

The conference would be a disaster. Allison would be upset; she was already upset. Besides, Toni was always being told Gerard couldn't afford to leave his wife. So why was he wasting money on conferences? Toni insisted that Gerard tell Allison that she too would be at the conference in the morning. 'She deserves to know,' Toni said.

There was no reply.

As usual, Gerard was trying to live in two worlds at once. While on the phone to Toni, he drove to the shops and back to buy what was needed to make dinner for his daughters. Then he headed for his parents' home at Kenmore. When he arrived, the girls were in the pool.

On the other end of the line, Toni could hear one of Gerard's daughters trying to get his attention. Gerard's long-suffering mistress had listened to enough. She told him she'd call the next day and hung up. She wasn't backing out of the conference. Gerard was simply going to have to sort it out.

A long time had passed since Gerard had told Allison, on their wedding anniversary in 2010 that their marriage was as good as over. When he looked her in the eyes and said slowly and clearly: 'I don't love you any more.' It was not a hot flash of anger, but a clinical statement of fact. He was amazed when

Allison just didn't get it. The first thing she did was run off for yet more counselling.

Even the counsellor saw that the marriage was a lost cause. Somehow, Gerard had surrounded himself with ferociously determined women. Toni was being every bit as demanding. Both Allison and Toni were intent on exposing his every private thought.

Allison had turned the heat up on him a hundredfold since the counselling session. He knew she was going to interrogate him again tonight. Now he had the conference mess to clean up as well. Everywhere he turned, there was another fire to put out.

Allison had become an expert over the years at bottling up her emotions. Even with her closest friends, she was selective about what she revealed. She didn't want them to think less of her or, more likely, persuade her to leave her philandering husband. Some of her friends thought she and Gerard were a great couple. If only they knew.

Most people had no idea how she really felt. Outwardly, there were few signs anything was amiss. She worked hard to project an air of calm. But one thing gave her away. The small chink in her armour was her silence. When she was angry, she retreated into a mental cave to hide.

'A busy day?' asked Waymouth, wrapping foil around Allison's locks.

'Oh, yeah,' shrugged Allison, killing off the small talk.

Nothing seemed to be going her way. Even the salon couldn't get her hair right lately. This was her third time here in the past two weeks for a colour. She had been coming here for years, but her usual stylist was on holidays. Why now, when she had somewhere important to go?

Tomorrow was a big day. The property conference would put her in the same room as hundreds of Gerard's business colleagues. Some, maybe plenty, would know about the affair.

They would know his lover, Toni, too; she was, after all, in the same game. Allison wanted to hold her head high.

Long before she found out about the affair, she had tried everything to turn the marriage around. 'I don't want to be alone,' she had written in her journal. 'I am afraid of being alone and lonely. Maybe because I think I can't handle it. I am afraid of failing – failing in my marriage and what people will think.'

In the past, when Allison had set her mind on something, she would make it happen. Now, she wasn't sure what she wanted. The night before, when Allison turned to her journal, the penny had suddenly dropped: 'Had so many opportunities to tell me – let me believe it was all my fault. I was at your mercy. Forced me to bow to you. Think that's where you wanted me,' she wrote.

Apprentice Melissa Hayes, massaging two shampoos and then a conditioner into Allison's hair, didn't notice anything, save how quiet she was. Allison was miles away.

When she stood to leave the salon, it was night. Staff swept the floors and polished the counters in preparation for a 7 pm close. Walking to the door, Allison steeled herself for the confrontation ahead at home. Gerard was going to have to answer her questions. She had knelt before him for so long, but not any more.

As for her hair, this time she was happy with the colour. The next day, at least, she would be ready to take on the conference.

PART II – THE VANISHING

Allison Baden-Clay was propped up on the couch watching *The Footy Show*, her husband told police, the last time he saw her. It had been a relatively unremarkable night.

For others around Brookfield and beyond, the night had been punctuated by sounds and happenings that were far from usual. In some cases, the sounds in the night had made the hairs on the back of their neck stand to attention and sent them out into the darkness to investigate.

Tzvetkoffs

Thursday 19 April 2012

7 pm to 9 pm

Kim and Julie Tzvetkoff lived on the corner of Brookfield Road and Boscombe Road, opposite the Good Shepherd Anglican church, a childcare centre, and the little blue house where real estate agent Gerard Baden-Clay lived with his family. From high up on a hill on the left-hand side of Brookfield Road on the drive from the city, the Tzvetkoffs had noticed the Baden-Clays coming and going over the years, but the two families had never met.

On the evening of 19 April, Julie had been at a guitar lesson and arrived home at about seven. Her husband, Kim, turned up ten minutes later. He was unusually late home and would remember glancing at the clock on the wall as he walked in. It had been a long day for both of them, and they had a rest in the lounge before getting up to make something to eat. Both were in the kitchen when they heard the same sound, though they would recall it differently.

To Julie it was a sharp, hard yell. It lasted for a matter of seconds and no words were formed. She couldn't tell if it was a man or a woman, and put the time at between 8 pm and 9 pm. Kim was closer to the door. He would remember a startled or shocked yell. He was convinced it was a woman and felt she had been trying to shout something but had managed only to get a couple of words out. He put the time at between 7.30 pm and 9.30 pm. It was an atypical noise for the area, and for a few moments afterwards Kim kept an ear out for any further sounds, but there were none.

One thing the Tzvetkoffs agreed about was that the sound had come from opposite their kitchen – across the road, around the home of the Baden-Clays. They went to bed at 10.30 pm, with their windows and door shut.

Ironically, the Tzetkoffs had been caught up in their own legal drama a year earlier. Their adult son, Daniel, was at that moment under witness protection in the United States – the star witness in a billion-dollar money laundering case. An IT whiz kid, Daniel Tzvetkoff had developed software for the processing of online payments right when the online poker companies were looking for someone to handle their booming transactions. Most banks wouldn't go near it because of uncertainty about the legality of online gambling, so Tzvetkoff pretty much had the market to himself. Soon his company, Intabill, was boasting of 5000 clients in 70 countries and the money was rolling in. In 2008, at the tender age of 24, this unheralded kid had everyone scratching their heads when he began splashing his cash around. He was unmasked as the mystery buyer who had stumped up $28 million for a half-built Gold Coast mansion – the highest price ever paid for a Queensland house. He'd also splurged $7.5 million on a super yacht, $3 million on a Fortitude Valley nightclub and several hundred thousand on luxury cars, including a black Lamborghini Gallardo, which he drove with the personalised number plate BALLER. A relatively modest purchase in comparison to his others, in 2006 Tzvetkoff also paid $1 million for the house his parents now called home at Brookfield.

Perhaps predictably, the fall was as spectacular as the rise. Tzvetkoff's clients Full Tilt and PokerStars began to suspect they were being ripped off. They came calling for tens of millions of dollars they claimed the Brisbane boy genius owed them. At the same time, US authorities, separately investigating the booming poker industry, found gambling transactions were being disguised as payments for products such as golf balls to circumvent US laws. Intabill foundered. Tzvetkoff went to ground before inexplicably deciding to roll the dice and head to Vegas for a gambling convention. Dudded associates, pinching themselves that they weren't dreaming when he arrived, called authorities and he was arrested at gunpoint.

Facing 75 years in prison, Tzvetkoff turned informant, outlining the financial operations of major gaming websites to US authorities, eventually leading to an infamous poker shut-down dubbed Black Friday in April 2011. With his wife, Nicole, and son, Hugo, he went into witness protection.

He had cost a lot of people a lot of money, and placed the freedom of others at risk. It was lucky that the law got to him before some of the people chasing him for cash, a fact his parents were keenly aware of as they followed his plight from their Brookfield home.

Kim and Julie had purchased the house from Daniel in 2009, when things first started to go south. With all the bitter enemies Daniel had made, there must have been times when his parents were particularly nervous about sounds outside their home in the dead of night.

But it was the little house across the road, not their own, where the drama unfolded.

Shout, scream, thump, screech

Thursday 19 April 2012

10 pm

Climbing into her empty bed, Anne Rhodes stretched out and congratulated herself. Typically, when the Brookfield physiotherapist turned in for the night, her husband would have been there long before her. But tonight she had taken an early mark. Anne's face was well known to locals through her work at the small family medical practice run from a brick house on Brookfield Road. She looked at the clock. Ten o'clock. Normally, she wasn't in bed for another hour.

Minutes before, when Anne was brushing her teeth in the bathroom, she heard a disturbance from somewhere outside. There were raised, angry voices. She couldn't make out what they were saying or if they were men or women or a mix of both. As she picked up a book for a quick read before she turned out the lights, she hoped it was not the new neighbours. Anne had moved into the Deerhurst Road, Brookfield, home 22 years earlier. It was a peaceful area, most of the time anyway.

A couple of years earlier, there was a nasty dispute between the two neighbours across the road. One accused the other of working as a backyard mechanic on the acreage property. Spray-painting fumes were billowing across the fence and incessant banging on the cars was hardly adding to the ambience of the natural bush setting.

Surrounding residents took sides and fired off personal and legal letters to council and each other. Both neighbours ended up moving out, which was why Anne was worrying about the new residents across the road.

Now settled into her book, Anne heard another disturbing sound. A woman's scream, high-pitched and loud. In the silence of her room, she listened for the sound to repeat. It didn't. But soon, there came another noise. A thud, like a car hitting an embankment.

The windows from her bedroom faced out towards Brookfield Road, in the direction of the childcare centre. She had heard cars crash around the area before.

As she started to get up, she heard a screech of tyres and a car speed off towards Brookfield.

There must have been an accident, she decided.

Tangled web

Thursday 19 April 2012

10 pm

Stephanie Apps's teenage children were sorely testing her patience. Apps had taken her son, 13, and daughter, 15, with her to her mother's house for the evening and then they'd stopped at Nando's for dinner. On the drive back to their home on Boscombe Road, Brookfield, it was like World War III in the car with all the fighting between the two children.

When she finally pulled into the driveway at about 9.50 pm, she could barely wait until the car stopped to open her door and get away from them. No sooner were they all out of the car than all hell broke loose: her daughter and son were screaming at each other. Then Apps lost it too and shouted at them to cut it out. They paid no attention.

In the chaos, her daughter clumsily tripped on a ceramic pot plant at the front door, sending it tumbling. Smash. The pot lay in pieces. Knowing she was really in for it now, the 15-year-old ran off towards the driveway. In full flight, the girl ran smack bang into a spider's web. Tangled in the sticky web, and with the prospect of some eight-legged killer crawling on her in the darkness, Apps's daughter let out a piercing scream. It was the startled, high-pitched squeal of a frightened girl.

Her gobsmacked mum now had three reasons to be annoyed: the fighting in and out of the car; the broken pot; and disturbing the neighbourhood in the middle of the night. 'You're for it when I catch you,' she thought, then gave her daughter a mouthful.

Apps had previously helped orchestrate a 'grisly murder' in her suburb, albeit a fictional one, as executive producer of a gory revenge film. The movie, *Punishment*, was filmed predominantly around the hills and valleys of Brookfield in 2008. Apps was quite chuffed to see Brookfield on the big screen, even if the plot did involve a double murder and torture with a nail gun and electric saw. But it was nothing like the real crime that was about to throw a pall over the suburb she'd called home for 15 years.

Scraps

Thursday 19 April 2012

11 pm

Scraps the dog sprang out of the warm basket at the foot of the bed. Tearing out of the bedroom, he sprinted down three short steps and cut to the left. A quick dash across the tiled floor brought him to the front door. Spinning in circles, madly yapping and scratching to get out, he was not going to be ignored.

Eighty-year-old Voni Brumm, startled awake by the racket, pulled back the bedcovers. Swinging her feet to the floor, she rubbed the sleep from her eyes and followed, confused. Scraps, a 13-year-old toy poodle crossed with a silky terrier, had joined her household as a medical companion for Voni's late husband. Well trained, the faithful pet had never demanded to be let out in the middle of the night before.

It had been almost half a century since the foundation slab was laid for the Brumm house on Boscombe Road at Brookfield – while Voni was in hospital for the birth of her son Mark. Before Brookfield, Voni, her husband and their then 12-year-old daughter Kim were living in inner-city New Farm on the top floor of one of Brisbane's first high-rises. Raising a girl in a glass tower was one thing. Adding a boy to the mix was another prospect entirely, so they bought their own slice of rural heaven at Brookfield.

It was an expensive choice even all those years ago. For the price of the land, the Brumms could have bought a top-of-the-range house at nearby Kenmore. But then there wouldn't have been a 1-hectare block and wide-open spaces all around for the children to explore. Boscombe Road all those years ago was only a dirt track lined with pineapple farms and a handful of houses. Now the road was bitumen and branched off to dozens of homes.

When it came to change, the upstanding citizens of Brookfield could be a militant lot. When the Brookfield Road general store wanted a liquor licence, for example, residents blocked the move. When the Anglican hierarchy wanted to sell the Good Shepherd church on the corner of Boscombe Road and Brookfield Road to help pay for a cathedral development, a core group of parishioners – Voni among them – banded together and defeated the plan.

Brookfield residents might not have managed to stop time, but they had certainly slowed down the clock and the rate of so-called progress.

Voni's son grew up happily roaming the fields around Brookfield and became a photographer, but had died suddenly at 43, from a brain haemorrhage. A memorial garden on the church grounds was named in his honour. Voni's husband took the death hard. He had since passed away too. Voni stayed on in Boscombe Road with daughter Kim, her memories and Scraps.

Kangaroos and wild deer frequently came and went from the property during the night without a whimper from the pet. But on Thursday 19 April 2012, he was uncharacteristically bothered by something or someone in the darkness.

Kim heard the racket from her downstairs unit. She had arrived home at 10.45 pm and was getting ready for bed when the scurrying and barking started above her about 15 minutes later, putting the time at about 11 pm.

Flicking on the lights to the front porch, Voni had barely opened the front door a crack before Scraps squeezed through. In a flash, the little dog was off, disappearing into the pitch black near the fence line in the back paddock.

Neighbours to the right of Voni's home had lovingly groomed gardens, a tennis court and swimming pool. They were away at the Munna Point caravan park on the Sunshine Coast for a holiday, so at least Voni didn't have to worry about them being disturbed by the barking. Gerard and Allison Baden-Clay's home was just around the corner on Brookfield Road, a couple of houses away. Kim knew Allison from children's music lessons at the little Anglican church.

Voni didn't know what could be upsetting her dog. It was too late and too dark to follow Scraps into the paddock, so she went back to bed, leaving the pet out in the night.

Screams

11 pm
Bruce Flegg was sitting up in bed talking on his mobile phone when he heard the sound. Somewhere outside, a woman had screamed. It was a single, unbroken sound that went for about three seconds before tapering off. Even though he was engaged in his phone conversation, he heard it clearly. It was loud. High-pitched. Disturbing. Definitely a woman's scream. 'Did you hear that?' he said down the phone.

On the other end of the line was his friend Sue Heath, a customer service worker with Qantas at Brisbane International Airport. They had met almost 20 years earlier through the Liberal Party. Heath had her television on in the background while she was talking to Flegg. She hadn't heard anything, but she could sense his alarm.

It had been just under four weeks since the Liberal National Party stormed to power in the state election, ending the rival Labor Party's run of eight consecutive general election victories. Under the leadership of former Brisbane mayor Campbell Newman, they had decimated their opponents. The Liberal National Party now held 78 of the 89 seats in the state parliament. In his seat of Moggill, Flegg was easily returned with a large swing in his favour. In Opposition, Flegg had been shadow minister for education for two years. It was a portfolio he was passionate about. He had paid his own way to the UK and studied the school systems there. He'd written 20 or so education policies and had big plans for disabled and disadvantaged kids. Once in government, he was made Housing Minister instead of Education Minister and was bitterly disappointed.

He knew nothing about housing – not even who the former minister was. That was politics. Seniority, factions and party room support came into play. Still, the grind of the election campaign was behind him and he had a seat at the Cabinet table, the heart of power in the state.

Leaping out of bed after hearing the scream, Flegg padded across the soft carpet in his room to the hallway. Telling Heath he would call her back, he walked to the front door and stepped out into the darkness. It was the first time he'd ever felt compelled to go outside to investigate a noise in the night. Standing out the front of his home, he strained to hear anything that might explain the chilling sound. A party perhaps, or an argument. There was only silence.

Flegg had bought the Nioka Street home in 2004, forking out $1.45 million for the privilege of owning a mansion on a sprawling 10,000 square-metre block on a ridge overlooking Brookfield. The elevated position of the house meant he could hear almost anything that occurred below the property. His bedroom was at the front of the house, facing the Brookfield Showground, about a kilometre away as the crow flies. That was roughly where the sound was from, he thought. A bar opened at the showground every weekend, and when the wind was right, Flegg could make out entire conversations from revellers.

But it was Thursday and the bar was closed. Other sounds often travelled up to the house, seeming closer than they were. If possums ran across a roof seven or eight houses away, he would hear it. Along the rest of the street, residents were tucked away quietly in their million-dollar homes.

Out the front Flegg had a grass tennis court and a swimming pool, set in landscaped gardens, and the property then dropped down to a long street with a smattering of homes. He was convinced the scream had come from the front of the property, but with nothing to see, he went back inside.

His media adviser, Graeme Hallett, had only recently moved to Queensland from interstate and was staying in a back bedroom. Flegg knocked on his door. There was no response. Hallett was fast asleep and could not be roused.

While he was standing there he heard the second scream. It was softer, but still bloodcurdling, exactly like the first scream. The hairs on the back of his neck went up again. His unease grew. But there was nothing much he could do. There was no point calling police. He wouldn't know what to say.

He called Heath back then returned to bed. In the half hour or so before he drifted to sleep, there was only silence outside.

Tennis

11.30 pm

Susan Braun was tossing and turning in bed, unable to sleep, constantly looking at the clock. The minutes seemed to take forever to tick by. She remembers that the clock showed 11.30 pm before she finally drifted off. Very soon after, a noise woke her with a start from her shallow slumber. It was an unpleasant sound. Unsettling. Maybe a scream or a yell. A human sound, but impossible to say if it was a man or woman.

Her room was at the front left-hand side corner of her house on Brookfield Road, and she was used to the general noise from the traffic that flowed past her window. This was something else. It came from farther down the road, towards the Brookie store. She lay there listening out for more noises, before eventually nodding off once more. A second sound, much like the first, woke her again. She thought about getting up to see her husband, Greg, who was yet to come to bed.

The two of them ran the Brookfield Tennis Centre next to their house. Greg, for a time, had been a top-flight player. He'd made it all the way to the world's most prestigious tennis tournament, Wimbledon, only to be bundled out in the first round. Braun's singles appearance at the All England Club, in June 1973, ended swiftly with a 4–6, 4–6, 2–6 defeat to Allan McDonald from New South Wales. It was an unusual and ugly year in the championship's distinguished history. When Yugoslav star Nikola Pilic was banned from the tournament for refusing to play Davis Cup for his country, the newly formed Association of Tennis Professionals flexed its muscles and organised a boycott. A bloc of 81 players, including reigning champion Stan Smith and 16 men's seeds, sat out the tournament, Australian legends John Newcombe, Roy Emerson and Ken Rosewall among them. In their absence, Wimbledon officials filled the ranks with an assortment of grinders and hackers who might otherwise never have made it onto the hallowed courts. For Braun, the once-in-a-lifetime shot at the title was still exciting.

Braun's world ranking went on to peak at 269 in July 1978. Since then, his skills have been put to good use at the Brookfield Tennis Centre, established by his family way back in 1965, with its four synthetic grass courts. Braun became head coach and owner, alongside Susan, an accountant who works as the business manager. Private courts are scattered throughout the suburb's oversized backyards, but players need lessons and competition. Open seven days a week, it is a never-ending job. Even when the lights are switched off at 10 pm each weeknight, with their house next door, Greg and Susan rarely log off.

Susan lay in bed waiting for a third sound to follow the earlier disturbing noises. When there was silence, she decided against fetching Greg and fell back to sleep.

Kholo Creek

Friday 20 April 2012

Early hours

Fourteen kilometres to the west of Brookfield, Brian and Mary Mason were in bed in their house at Anstead. Mary, a Qantas flight attendant, was rostered to work on a return flight to Sydney on the Friday morning. She had gone to bed early and had to be at work at 5.15 am. Brian, a real estate agent at LJ Hooker at Kenmore, had a busy day ahead so he'd also had an early night.

Both were sound asleep when Brian's German shepherd, Sasha, started howling. Sasha was locked up in a large enclosed verandah at the back of the house at night for her own protection – Brian didn't want her swallowing a cane toad or coming off second best in a tangle with a taipan in the tall grass on the acreage property.

The Masons' home was up a rough dirt driveway off Mt Crosby Road, on top of a rise that dropped steeply to the Brisbane River. Big gum trees dotted the property, where the grass was dirt dry from a long pause between rains. Sasha's wolf-like howl echoed through the house, waking Brian. At first he stayed in bed, thinking the dog might settle. But the howling continued, waking Mary too from her slumber.

'I've got to get up in a few hours. Will you do something about that dog,' she said, rolling over.

Brian reluctantly got out of bed. He didn't look at a clock, but judging from what Mary had said about having to get up shortly, it must have been around 12.30 am to 1 am, he thought. Knowing the exceptional good senses of German shepherds, he guessed there was probably a stag outside disturbing the dog.

194

Sasha was still in full voice and looking out into the bush, in the direction of the small bridge where Mt Crosby Road crossed Kholo Creek, when Mason came up behind her. Grabbing her collar, he tapped an open palm on her snout and told her in no uncertain terms to be quiet. Finally, the howling came to an end. But in the newfound silence in the house, Mason could hear other dogs howling from surrounding properties plus some mumbling voices. Walking back to his bedroom, no sooner had he closed the door than Sasha too started howling again. Brian got back under the covers and apologised to his wife. 'Look, I don't know what's going on. Something's spooked those bloody dogs. They're all doing it. I can't shut it up. If they're all going, she won't stop.'

Ten more minutes of tossing and turning passed before the howling died down again and the couple was able to drift back to sleep. It felt like minutes before the alarm went off to wake Mary for work.

Pulling out of her driveway and turning right, her high beams lighting up Mt Crosby Road, Mary was still groggy after the disturbed sleep. About 500 metres up the road she blinked at the sight ahead.

Two cars were travelling towards her in the direction of Kholo Creek Bridge. It was a rarity to pass anyone at this hour, and the two cars heading towards her on the opposite side of the road stood out even more. The car in front was driving at speed. Immediately behind it was another car with its headlights off, driving so close they were not far from touching.

Mary had had such a peculiar night and start to the day already, and now here was one more bizarre occurrence. She frowned and concentrated on getting to work on time, but all these weird goings on stuck in her mind.

PART III – INVESTIGATION

Missing

Friday 20 April 2012

7.10 am

Brookfield dad Steve Womal was in the habit of paying close attention to cars and people around his suburb of a morning. Womal was a fly-in-fly-out worker at the Cannington silver and lead mine, 1300 kilometres north-west of Brisbane. Every second week, when he wasn't working, he would drive his son, 14, to the bus that would take him to Brisbane Boys' College in Toowong.

Since schoolboy Daniel Morcombe vanished from a Sunshine Coast bus stop in 2003, Womal had been extra vigilant around his neighbourhood. It had only taken a moment for a predator to lure Morcombe into a car, and Womal couldn't bear the thought of it happening to his own flesh and blood. Often he would make a mental note of the number plates of passing cars, peer into vehicles to see who was driving, and have a good look at anyone walking around. Early in the morning, there weren't usually many people out and about.

Womal's routine on school days was to drive his son from their acreage property in Upper Brookfield to the bus stop on Rafting Ground Road, just past Brookfield Produce, where residents stocked up on locally grown fruit and vegetables, pet supplies and hardware.

Generally, he would wait in his car until the bus approached, then loop around to the general store on Brookfield Road to grab the newspaper. He would be back at his car in time to see his son wave as he went past in the bus.

On Friday 20 April 2012, Womal looked at his watch as the bus passed with his son inside. It was 7.12 am, right on time. With the teen safely off to school, Womal started to drive home when he saw a friend, Phil Blair, near the showground, and stopped to say hello. Blair had been at a morning fitness session at the Brookfield State School oval.

Simultaneously, Olivia Walton was out scouring the streets of Brookfield. Olivia lived in Townsville but had been visiting parents Nigel and Elaine at Kenmore. It had been a busy morning in the household. Nigel and Elaine's younger son, Adam, had just become a dad to a baby boy in Canada and called them on Skype shortly before 6.30 am to show off the newborn. The video call was still going when Gerard phoned his parents at 6.46 am, and Nigel went out of the room to take the call.

Olivia would later say the first she knew of any trouble was when her mum came into her room and closed the door behind her. Gerard did not know where Allison was; she had not returned from a morning walk.

'I don't want to alarm you, but Al's missing,' Elaine said.

Olivia changed out of her pyjamas and drove off to search routes her brother said Allison might have taken. Olivia's in-laws had lent her a car to use while in Brisbane.

Driving up Boscombe Road, with Brookfield State School to her left, she saw a groundsman on a ride-on mower and stopped to ask if he had seen a woman out walking. He hadn't, so she continued on, turning left onto Brookfield Road. As she did, she glanced over to Gerard's home across the road, where her father's Holden Statesman was pulling into the driveway.

Olivia continued on, past the real estate agency, general store, hair salon and the showground, and turned right at the Brookfield Road roundabout onto Gold Creek Road. Allison sometimes walked to an aged care home about a kilometre from the roundabout. Olivia passed it, driving another kilometre before turning around and heading back. Seeing two women walking on Savages Road to her right, she stopped to talk to them, but they hadn't seen Allison either.

Heading back towards the Brookfield roundabout, Olivia slowed the car to a crawl, wound her window down and turned her hazard lights on. Peering into the bushes, she yelled Allison's name.

Olivia had run out of call credit on her phone, so she was limited to sending Gerard texts and he would ring back. She asked him some basic questions about what Allison would have been wearing. He thought Allison would be in three-quarter length pants and a black or white T-shirt and could have a cap on.

At 7.11 am, in a call of two-and-a-half minutes, Gerard asked Olivia if it was too early to call the police.

'No, not at all,' she said.

As Olivia hung up, she spotted two men near the showground – Steve Womal and his friend Phil Blair. She parked the car and approached them too. They hadn't seen a woman out walking, but Blair suggested Olivia should talk to personal trainer Daniel Crawford, who led the morning fitness class. She walked off to speak to him.

Olivia didn't name the person she was looking for. If she had, Womal would have known instantly who she was. Womal's younger son attended Brookfield State School in the same year as Allison and Gerard's eldest daughter.

The first time Womal met Gerard was at the 'burger bar', five or so years before Allison disappeared. The bar opened on the first Friday of every month at the Brookfield Showground. Parents would supply meat and bread for the evenings and volunteer as chefs. Money raised went to the Brookie school. Womal and Gerard were on snags and steaks duty and exchanged small talk. Womal would always remember Gerard making a big show of welcoming Allison and his daughters when they arrived, calling her 'angel', and the girls 'princess'. It all seemed a little over-the-top.

Over the years, Womal sometimes saw Gerard wandering around the Brookie school in his gold Century 21 jacket. Gerard was always talking to people, making connections. Allison would drop the kids to school and pick them up.

As a matter of fact, Womal had seen Gerard only the day before. The two dads had been watching the school's cross-country race. As usual, Gerard was mingling with other parents; he was under the shady trees around the school oval, where the event started and finished.

Womal recalled that Gerard looked immaculate in a business shirt, tie, black slacks and RM Williams boots. That was pretty much the way Gerard always looked when Womal saw him. Always dressed for success. Slick and professional.

On the Friday morning when the alarm was raised that Allison was missing, Womal only knew what Olivia told him – that a woman had gone for a morning walk and hadn't returned. Frankly, it struck him as strange. Why would someone be out looking so soon? It was only 7.20 am. Whoever was missing had probably stopped to chat to a friend or dropped in for a coffee somewhere. Surely it was a bit early to push the panic button. Shrugging, he made his way home. He had a paper to read.

This is all routine

Friday 20 April 2012

8.30 am

Senior Sergeant Narelle Curtis hung up the phone and spoke to the station's shift supervisor, Sergeant Andrew Jackson. There was a situation at Brookfield, and they needed to go there. Two officers responding to a call out were concerned that a man reporting his wife missing appeared to have scratches on his face. She set off from Indooroopilly Police Station, with Jackson behind the wheel. As they arrived at the Brookfield Road house, Jackson activated his digital voice recorder. It would capture Gerard talking about the injuries on his face almost before they'd had a chance to say hello.

'Cut myself shaving,' Gerard volunteered.

They went inside, where Curtis assured Gerard that the police would do their very best to find his wife.

First and foremost, Curtis wanted to know Allison's state of mind.

'Pretty good,' said Gerard, before adding she had a history of depression that had been managed by medication. 'We haven't really discussed it for a long time. It used to be a daily dose of Zoloft.'

'So, Gerard, basically you and your wife are estranged, are you?' asked Curtis.

'No. No, not at all.'

'All right. So there's no indication that the marriage is going to break up?'

'Um, I hope not,' replied Gerard.

After fruitlessly searching the streets of Brookfield, Olivia had taken her nieces to school and returned to find Gerard speaking to the police officers. He asked her to leave while he discussed some private issues with them, and she promised to be right outside if he needed her.

With his sister out of earshot, Gerard broached his cheating for the second time with police that morning: 'I had an affair that ended last year. Obviously that has put a, a strain on the relationship. But we've been working through it. And in fact we went and saw a counsellor on Monday.'

'Was there anything that came out of that session that would have upset your wife?' asked Curtis.

There wasn't, Gerard replied. 'Overall it was a pretty positive thing. There were some strategies. It's about rebuilding the trust and everything.'

The officers moved on to what Gerard knew of his wife's movements.

'What time do you think she got up?' asked Jackson.

'Did you sleep together last night?' added Curtis.

'I was saying before, I don't actually know. I'm a heavy sleeper and I snore and that sort of thing. I went to bed before she did last night,' Gerard answered.

'What time did you go to bed? Where was she when you last saw her?' asked Curtis.

'She was watching *The Footy Show*, on the couch.'

It wasn't unusual, maybe once every fortnight or so, for one of them to sleep on the couch watching the TV, he said. 'Whether she slept there or not, I don't know. She, um, does, um, go walking in the morning.'

Gerard's voice was hushed and the digital recorder at times barely picked up what he was saying. He was calm as he explained that Allison's walks were intermittent, but she would get up at 5 am to exercise two to three times a week. He and Allison were trying to lose weight before a planned holiday with friends over the Labour Day long weekend in a few weeks.

'Last night, she went and had her hair done,' he added. 'Well, for the third time. It was, you know, coloured, and they stuffed it up the first two.'

'What does she normally wear when she goes jogging?' asked Jackson.

Allison wore two outfits, Gerard said, for her exercise: either a black one or a grey tracksuit, which was missing. She also had a grey singlet top and sometimes wore a grey sloppy joe jumper. Her runners were not where she normally left them at the front door or anywhere else in the house. Her three-quarter-length pants, the 'daggy old ones', were missing too. 'She bought some new Lorna Jane ones in black, but they're here,' Gerard told the officers.

He obviously paid more attention to his wife's wardrobe than most husbands, surprising officers by deducing what Allison must be wearing based on what he noticed was missing from her clothes drawers.

There were two main routes Allison walked, Gerard said. One involved a journey to the Brookfield Village aged care home on Gold Creek Road. Olivia had already driven along there twice looking for Allison, he informed them. The second route involved doing a loop around the school to Brookfield Produce and back to their house. Neither was longer than a 2-kilometre round trip.

Curtis broached the topic of the painful-looking injuries on Gerard's face: 'Gerard I have to ask this question. Those two marks on your face could be consistent with having been scratched.'

'I was asked that this morning. I cut myself shaving.'

Ordinarily on a Friday, Gerard said, he would meet with his sales team at 8.30 am to go through the properties listed for the weekend. The plan was different that day because Allison and his property manager, Kate Rankin, were going to a seminar in the city. Gerard needed to look after the kids and do the school run. He was up just after 6 am.

'I do my usual, excuse me, shit, shower and shave in the morning,' he said, for the second time that day. 'This morning was no different. I check all my emails when I'm sitting on the toilet. I did that. Then I was rushing. I needed to get all the girls up. [My middle daughter] got up. And then I cut myself. She's always the first to get up but she was late this morning. They were tired. They all had cross-country.'

Curtis, returning to the couple's relationship, asked Gerard if Allison had ever run off before.

She hadn't. Nor had there been an incident the previous night that could have set her off, Gerard said. 'I mean, the counsellor on Monday suggested that we set aside 15 minutes a night, for Allison to be able to vent and grill me . . . and we did that.' But that wouldn't explain the day's events, he said.

Jackson asked if Allison, when she vented, screamed at Gerard.

'No. She's not like that. She had sworn at me in the past but she didn't swear at me.'

'How would you describe your general relationship at the moment?'

'It's been very good,' he said, but conceded that Allison had become suspicious of other women as a consequence of the affair.

Jackson reassured Gerard that the questions were routine: 'When someone goes missing, we've just got to check that everything is kosher. That's all.'

Curtis added, 'The reason why we're obviously questioning you in this depth, [is that] there doesn't seem to be a reason why she would have done this, this morning.'

'No. And that's what is bothering me. And that's why I called you,' said Gerard.

Keen to justify why he contacted the police so early, he said his wife was usually gone no longer than 20 to 40 minutes. 'But this morning is concerning me. And why I called you was because she had this seminar she was going to today with Kate and she's been excited about it . . . I knew she'd wanted to leave here at about seven.'

The couple had discussed their plans the previous night, he continued. His sister, Olivia, was down from Townsville with her three children and everyone was due to come over to the Brookfield Road home on Friday night for a sleepover.

'It's completely out of character, although there have been occasions when she's pissed off with me, where she hasn't responded to a text message or a phone call.' Gerard had sent two text messages to Allison and tried to call her, he explained.

Next, Curtis tried phoning Allison's number and left a voice message asking her to call Indooroopilly station.

There was something else, Gerard added. As a result of his infidelity and his wife's subsequent mistrust, the couple had put the Find My Friends tracking application on their iPhones. 'I didn't mention this to you before but, ah yeah, we, we have an, ah, ah, application on our phones, which really she sort of insisted upon, where you can look up and see where the other person is, based on GPS. So she can check up on me.'

Both officers instantly asked to use the application.

Gerard said he already tried but Allison's location had not come up. Location services on the phone would need to be turned on for the application to work: 'If you turn that off or, or whatever, you can hide from people who are following you or whatever.'

Senior Sergeant Curtis wanted to know more about how Allison learnt of Gerard's affair.

Gerard said he believed she found out from a friend at school after his former business partners blabbed. 'Allison wasn't working in the business at all. But she is now.'

'Okay. All right. That's where the trust issue is? So she's now decided to work in the business?' asked Curtis.

Gerard said there was a financial incentive for Allison to work in the business too: 'Things are pretty tight.'

'So there are personal issues and financial issues for you?'

Perhaps sensing where things were heading, Gerard tried to play down his marriage problems: 'We have a, generally, a pretty positive outlook on these sort of things.'

Curtis gave him another chance to come clean about any argument they might have had: 'Sometimes pressures make people act in different ways. Now, I'm only speaking, you know, from fairly extensive experience in this job. And people do act out of character. Now, you didn't get into a fight last night with her?'

'We've had some challenges, as I say.'

'So you've had some, some blues over this?'

'Yes. And, you know, there's this counsellor – One of the strategies that she recommended for us to work through things, and help with the building of trust and reconciliation and stuff was that we have a 15-minute session every day, each evening. That it be limited to 15 so it didn't drag on and, and that sort of thing. We had one you know, last night. There were some difficult things we talked about but, but it wasn't – we then finished. And then we, you know, talked about what was planned, what were the plans for today, you know, the kids' sleepover and that stuff.'

So, according to Gerard, there was a difficult discussion of 15 minutes the previous night as a result of his affair, then they had returned to more mundane, practical topics and he'd gone to bed.

Noticing a red mark on the inside of Gerard's hand, Jackson asked what had caused the injury.

'Um, helping my friend renovate his house.'

His school friend Robert Cheesman's house was due to be launched on to the property market that day. Gerard had repainted and recarpeted and was using a ratchet screwdriver to replace a bathroom light fitting the day before, on Thursday, when he cut himself, he said. His colleague, Jody, was with him when the accident happened but he hadn't mentioned anything to her at the time because they were rushing to finish the job so he could get back to a 3.45 pm parent–teacher interview at school.

The officers had seen and heard enough. Jackson told Gerard he didn't want to alarm him but he was probably going to have to call out the Criminal Investigation Branch (CIB): 'We probably just need to ramp it up; just to try and locate your wife as quickly as possible.'

Gerard, confused, asked what the officer meant when he said he didn't want to alarm him.

Jackson reassured him he only meant that there would be more police coming out.

Curtis added that the officers from the CIB would have a chat with him because the situation just wasn't what they normally expected in a missing persons case.

'At the end of the day,' said Jackson, reassuring Gerard once more, 'your wife might walk in in five minutes' time, and we stand everyone down. But in the meantime, we're better off dotting the Is, crossing the Ts, and getting the cars out there, having a look for her.'

'That's fine,' Gerard said. 'Like I said to the guys before, I'm happy to answer all the questions in the world, and that sort of thing, if it's going to help. But I want to jump back in my car and, you know, drive the streets or something. I'm, feeling like, "What are we doing?"'

Curtis went to the front porch and phoned the Indooroopilly CIB. Three detectives were soon on their way to the house. Outside, an officer noticed Gerard's father Nigel putting a vacuum cleaner in his car and stopped him.

Jackson spoke into his police radio: 'I'm just currently at this missing persons job at Brookfield. Could you just organise for all available Indooroopilly units to proceed out to this direction? We need to start our search for this person.'

Criminal Investigation Branch

Friday 20 April 2012

10 am

Detective Senior Constable Cameron McLeod, Plain Clothes Constable Cameron Simmons and Plain Clothes Constable Kellie Thomson added to the growing crowd of police at the house in Brookfield Road. Fewer than three hours had passed since Gerard made his emergency call. The three officers from the Indooroopilly CIB arrived at the house together at the request of Senior Sergeant Curtis. Generally, this was not how a missing persons case played out. If detectives got involved in every case where someone went missing, they'd never do anything else.

Sergeant Andrew Jackson walked the latest police arrivals up the front steps and introduced them to Gerard. Before leaving, Jackson passed his digital recorder to McLeod, a quietly spoken, diligent detective.

Gerard invited the officers to sit down at the dining table, where credit cards and paperwork were spread around a vase containing some ageing carnations. By now, it was becoming obvious police weren't simply going to take a standard missing persons report and clear out. Gerard was starting to struggle.

'Um, she was still up watching *The Footy Show*. Um, I wasn't feeling great so I, I just went to bed. Um, sorry I feel like I'm repeating everything for the third time. Um, oh my brain is just, ah I just, maybe you should just ask me questions.'

Gerard repeated some of the events of the morning, but he could feel the detectives staring at the raw, red wounds on his face.

'Um, I should clarify, yeah, I cut myself shaving this morning and everybody has said that looks suspicious.'

'Mmm, it does,' replied Constable Simmons, not mincing his words.

'And that's part of the reason I think that you're here,' continued Gerard.

Gerard went through mostly the same questions, and gave mostly the same answers. He repeated that before he had gone to bed, he and Allison had a 15-minute talk, as recommended by a counsellor: 'It's never much fun for me, to be honest.'

Gerard's energy was dropping. 'Sorry, I'm just exhausted now,' he said.

The detectives wanted to know what he'd discussed with Allison in their 15-minute debrief.

Gerard said Allison had a list of questions, but he didn't go into any detail.

As they spoke, the detectives were coming and going.

Constable Simmons interrupted to say there had been a breakthrough: 'Allison's phone's been triangulated.'

The phone was just out the back of the house somewhere, he said, and a search party was being formed.

The odd thing was, Gerard barely reacted. If he believed that his wife was about to walk back through the door with her phone in hand, or be found out the back somewhere, he seemed neither elated nor concerned. Others in his shoes may have leapt from the chair and rushed out to look. Gerard simply said, 'Okay'.

The detectives wanted to know if there would be any reason for Allison to be in any of the properties behind the house, and Gerard said no, it was residential. He added that a neighbour had previously complained when some free-range chickens the Baden-Clays had were eating her garden beds, and they weren't close.

Constable Simmons, looking at the scratches on Gerard's cheek, pointedly asked if Allison was left- or right-handed.

'Right-handed,' Gerard replied.

'I'm going to ask directly about the, the shaving. You've been to that many domestics. Ah, it doesn't look like a shaving cut. And having cut my face myself . . .'

Gerard said circumstances had been dire – presumably he was talking about his finances – and he hadn't bought new razors for about six months.

'Ordinarily in the morning I take a long time to shave, be as careful as I possibly can. And this morning I was rushing and I, um, you shave, you know, you shave. I shave down, I shave back, I'd go sideways as well, to try and make it as smooth as possible. I was rushing.'

Constable Simmons asked if he'd have any objection to the marks being photographed: 'Not that I'm, ah, alleging anything. But, um, if, you know, if that's your story, we'd like to um photograph them. Hopefully, Allison turns up, walks straight in the house, we can walk away.'

Legal advice

Friday 20 April 2012

As Detective Acting Inspector Mal Gundry drove to Brookfield, the plain-speaking cop had time to wonder what sort of home he would arrive to. It would have been easy to envisage a long driveway leading to a glass-and-steel mansion on a hilltop somewhere, with a lap pool next to a grass tennis court in the backyard. If he had known the illustrious history of Gerard Baden-Clay, and his position as principal of his own real estate agency, expectations would have been all the higher.

Gundry was officer in charge of the Indooroopilly CIB but was filling in as inspector for the Brisbane West police district, operating out of an administrative office on Station Road. When word filtered back of a situation developing with a missing woman at Brookfield, Gundry drove out to see for himself. With him was Detective Sergeant Chris Canniffe, who was relieving him as Indooroopilly CIB officer in charge.

When they pulled into the driveway, any thoughts of getting a glimpse into the lives of the rich and famous quickly evaporated. Gerard and Allison's home was as modest as they come, in Brookfield at least.

As soon as Gundry saw Gerard's face, he realised why everyone who arrived at the house that morning was concerned for Allison. The old-school detective couldn't accept the injuries on Gerard's cheek could have been from shaving.

Police needed to get a formal, signed statement from Gerard about Allison's disappearance. They also wanted to photograph and document his injuries. He was asked to go to Indooroopilly Police Station to do both, and agreed. Plain Clothes Constable Cameron Simmons drove him there.

Gundry soon fielded a call from Simmons, who said Gerard had allowed Scenes of Crime officer Sergeant Julian Dash to photograph him but had spoken to a lawyer and would not provide the statement. Gerard's unfettered cooperation with police was over.

Gundry was waiting when Gerard returned to his Brookfield Road house after 1 pm and went straight to the passenger side door where Gerard was seated.

'What are you doing?' the senior detective demanded. Gerard was within his rights to decline to give a statement, but in doing so was hoisting a giant red flag as far as Gundry was concerned.

Gerard said he was following the instructions of his lawyer, Gold Coast solicitor Darren Mahony.

'I want to talk to him,' said the detective.

Soon, Gundry and Mahony were in a row on the phone.

'Mate, what's going on here?' Gundry asked.

Mahony said he had instructed his client not to provide a statement. The lawyer told Gundry he had represented hundreds of people.

'And I've arrested hundreds of blokes,' said Gundry. He thought it was poor advice and told Mahony so.

Silence is generally the golden rule of defence lawyers, but it was up to Gerard whether he chose to follow any legal advice. By not doing whatever police asked of him, they would find it more difficult to rule him out as a suspect and move on.

Mahony was born in Toowoomba, where Gerard grew up after his family emigrated from Rhodesia. Though the two men had gone to different schools, they were the same age and had mutual friends.

On that first morning, Mahony asked Gundry what the next step would be for police. Gundry answered that it was none of his business.

Gerard looked remarkably cool amid the dramatic events around him. Gundry thought the real estate agent must be a good poker player.

Detective Sergeant Canniffe, a down-to-earth officer, smoothed things over with Gerard after the confrontation with Gundry. Later in the day, Gerard approached Canniffe and thanked him for his kind and calm manner.

Having been around the block a few times, Canniffe knew people reacted differently when they were under pressure. Some would keep asking police to repeat questions, to buy time to process the answers before responding. Canniffe would vividly remember Gerard's measured and deliberate speech. Gerard was thinking through his answers.

The detective gently tried to coax Gerard into making a formal statement: 'Mate, we're just trying to find your wife. We really need that statement.'

Gerard was apologetic. He was doing everything he could to help. But he wouldn't be providing the statement: 'Chris, I must take the advice I have been given.'

As they talked, Gerard's fingers kept shooting to his face to rub his injuries. Canniffe told Gerard the marks were one reason police were taking such an interest in the case, and asked why he kept touching them. Gerard said it was because the injuries were incredibly itchy.

With police starting to swarm the suburb to search for Allison, Gerard was thinking through the practicalities of finding himself under arrest.

'Chris, if I'm going to be arrested, I would like my sister, Olivia, to have custody of the children,' he said.

No one was talking about an arrest – police didn't even know if a crime had been committed – but it was playing on Gerard's mind.

Operation Kilo Intrigue

Friday 20 April 2012

Police had a decision to make. They could seal up Gerard's house as a crime scene and launch a major investigation or adopt more of a wait-and-see approach and give the missing mum time to turn up. There were competing factors. Allison's disappearance was suspicious, but to what extent? Gerard had lawyered up and was refusing to provide a formal statement, yet had spoken to police several times that morning. His shaving story didn't ring true, but perhaps his wife had run off after an argument and he was embarrassed.

Checking for any criminal history, detectives found Gerard was a cleanskin. No arrests. No complaints to police of domestic violence. The worst trouble Gerard had been in was for driving more than 30 kilometres an hour over the speed limit when he was a 17-year-old. He had a more recent traffic infringement for disobeying a 'no left turn' sign and a few others for speeding.

Mal Gundry went up the chain of command to Detective Acting Superintendent Bob Hytch, who was relieving as the Regional Crime Coordinator while the officer usually in the role, Detective Superintendent Mark Ainsworth, was on leave for a couple of weeks. Hytch was hours away from going on leave himself; Ainsworth was due back on deck the next day. Gundry and Hytch agreed it was time to establish a Major Incident Room (MIR) and bring in the Homicide Investigation Unit.

With that crucial decision made, Gundry took charge of the MIR, and set it up in the offices of the Indooroopilly CIB on the afternoon of Friday 20 April 2012. It would run separate

(Above) Allison and other members of the Australian Youth Ballet Company (AYBC) meeting Rolf Harris in Scotland. *Courtesy Inara Svalbe*

(Left) A proud new member of the AYBC. Allison at around 11 years of age. *Courtesy Inara Svalbe*

(Below) The ballerina on stage. Allison is on the far right. *Courtesy Inara Svalbe*

(Above) Exchange students. Allison, aged 17, pictured with Linda Drinnan. They both spent 1986 in Denmark and became close friends. *Courtesy Linda Ebeling*

(Right) A side trip during the exchange year. Linda, friend Philippa Mackenzie and Allison in Paris. *Courtesy Linda Ebeling*

(Below) In high spirits. Pictured with Austrian street performers, 1986. *Courtesy Linda Ebeling*

That's my husband in the turban. As newlyweds, Gerard and Allison travelled extensively. *Photo courtesy Linda Ebeling*

(Above) Beautiful bride, handsome groom. *Photo courtesy Linda Ebeling*

(Right) Heading off after a wedding with all the trimmings – except, to the surprise of some guests, alcohol. *Photo courtesy Linda Ebeling*

(Below) Gerard wore his gold jacket with pride, everywhere he went. *Jim Campey/Newspix*

(Above) The scratches that rang so many alarm bells. *Queensland Police Service*

(Right) Kholo Creek Bridge the day Allison's body was discovered on a bank below. *Glenn Barnes/Newspix*

(Below) Detective Superintendent Mark Ainsworth, the Regional Crime Coordinator, and Police Inspector Mark Laing, who coordinated the search, front media during the investigation. *Paul Guy/Newspix*

(Left) Allison's home, showing the carefully parked cars, on the day she was reported missing. *Queensland Police Service*

(Below left) The loungeroom. Gerard told police he went to bed before Allison and that the last time he saw her, she was watching TV. *Queensland Police Service*

(Above right) Leaf of *Dolichandra ungui-cati*, cat's claw creeper, that was entwined in Allison Baden-Clay's hair. Strands of her hair are still attached to the leaf. *Photo G.P. Guymer, Queensland Herbarium*

(Below left) Leaf parts (pinnae) of *Nephrolepis cordifolia*, fishbone fern. Plant material would play a pivotal role in the case. *Photo G.P. Guymer, Queensland Herbarium*

(Right) Allison's blood trailing down a side panel in her Holden Captiva, by the third row of seats. When police first examined the car, the seats had been folded down, and the boot was full of toys. *Queensland Police Service*

Left to pick up the pieces of her life, a shattered Toni McHugh – the 'other woman' – after giving evidence. She discovered during the investigation Gerard had dalliances during their affair. *Jack Tran/Newspix*

Gerard's parents, Nigel and Elaine Baden-Clay. An incredibly close family, the Baden-Clays' support for Gerard is unwavering. *Jack Tran/Newspix*

(Above) Leaving court after the verdict. Allison's parents, Geoff and Priscilla Dickie, with sister Vanessa and brother Ashley (immediately behind Geoff), are flanked by her best friend, Kerry-Anne Walker (left), and cousin Jodie Dann (right). *Jack Tran/Newspix*

(Right) Todd Fuller QC, Crown prosecutor. *News Ltd/Newspix*

(Below) Rally in King George Square, Brisbane, on 18 December 2015. Yellow, Allison's favourite colour, features prominently in fundraisers and events that commemorate her life. *David Murray*

to, but alongside, the search operation. The investigation into Allison's disappearance was assigned a randomly generated but fitting name, Operation Kilo Intrigue. Brisbane's leafy western suburbs weren't exactly a hotbed of violence, and it had been eight years since Indooroopilly CIB had a murder to investigate: the victim was 83-year-old grandmother Joan Pitt, who was strangled in her St Lucia apartment. The crime remained unsolved.

A formal process comes into effect as soon as an MIR is established. Officers are assigned roles; for instance, in charge of forensic evidence, intelligence, exhibits or door knocking. A 'reader' is responsible for carefully analysing every witness statement, in order to keep an overall picture of all the information coming in during the investigation. Detectives who obtain the bulk of the statements and run down leads, such as tips through Crime Stoppers, are known as 'trackers'. Sometimes officers have specialist backgrounds or interests and take responsibility for areas such as medical records or finances. An arrest team is appointed early on to make the arrest and lay charges, should that eventuate. Senior officers handle the media.

The effect of Allison's disappearance was that a range of officers dropped what they had been doing and put any plans on hold in order to join the search and investigation.

In the Homicide offices on level two of the Queensland Police Service (QPS) headquarters in Roma Street, Detective Sergeant Peter Roddick finally had some clear air. Roddick, a physically imposing man made more so by a shaved head and direct stare, was in a small team of detectives who had spent almost two years reviewing another prominent case, the 1991 murder of schoolgirl Leanne Holland, 12, at Goodna, west of Brisbane. The man convicted of Leanne's murder, Graham Stafford, had his conviction quashed in the Court of Appeal after 15 years in jail. A retrial had been ordered and police had taken another look at the evidence. The weighty report on the Leanne Holland case had only been finished that week, but any chance of some downtime evaporated when the Homicide Squad's Detective Inspector Damien Hansen briefed Roddick on Allison's disappearance about 3 pm Friday.

Roddick drove out to Brookfield with a cold case investigator, Detective Sergeant Mark Brand, that afternoon. Viewing photographs of Gerard's facial injuries, Roddick could only agree the case looked deeply suspicious. Other detectives from the squad would soon join them on Operation Kilo Intrigue.

Acting Inspector Ewen Taylor, the Metropolitan North police region forensic coordinator, was looking forward to some well-earned time off. Taylor and a colleague had been sharing the forensic coordinator's role for two years, after their predecessor took extended leave to work in the mines and didn't come back. It had been a relentless and brutal couple of years in the vast area he was responsible for north of the Brisbane River. Take the case of a mum who had killed her 14-year-old daughter, and then plunged to her death from Story Bridge. Or a husband who had bludgeoned his wife to death with a car tow ball. Long hours had grown into long weeks and long months as he was called from one horrific crime scene to the next, with only the rare break.

A man who enjoyed maintaining his fitness, Taylor relieved the pressure of his job, and stayed sane, by jumping on one of his mountain bikes and heading into the hills. Finally, that Friday, it looked like he would be able to get in a decent ride over the coming weekend. He was in the office at Alderley, north Brisbane, mentally mapping out his riding routes when Sergeant Julian Dash phoned at 1.25 pm Friday.

'You weren't hoping to have a weekend off, were you? Because you're not going to,' said Dash, who had just photographed the scratches on Gerard's face and uploaded them to the police Forensic Register.

The lauded register was developed in-house in the QPS and had been adopted in jurisdictions around the country. It allowed evidence to be uploaded from the field and stored in a central database for easy access to forensic officers and investigators. Taylor had personally photographed injuries in more than 600 cases and, as a supervisor, had viewed at least three times that many. When he logged on to the Forensic Register and brought up Dash's photographs of Gerard's face, the injuries were consistent with scratches he'd seen from assaults in the past.

With all thoughts of mountain biking gone, Taylor, the consummate professional, phoned to check in with Acting Inspector Gundry, who was at Gerard and Allison's house, and made sure there was a crime scene warrant; there was. Next Taylor called the head of the Scientific Section and said he would need some help on the new case, then contacted the Scenes of Crime officers at Indooroopilly and New Farm and asked them to meet him at Brookfield. Scientific officers specialise in advanced ballistics, bloodstain pattern analysis, document examination and fire and explosives investigations. Scenes of Crime officers are trained in the collection and recording of evidence, such as fingerprints, DNA, shoe sole impressions and tyre marks.

Heading out to Brookfield that Friday afternoon, Taylor's pivotal role overseeing forensic examinations on Operation Kilo Intrigue had begun. Numerous police were milling around the suburb when he arrived at four o'clock. His first action was to make sure the uniformed police guarding the scene kept a log of events, recording who was coming and going. He grabbed a roll of police crime scene tape and pulled it across the front driveway, blocking off the only entrance to the property. From then on, anyone who entered had to be in full Personal Protective Equipment – boots, a fluid-barrier suit, gloves and a facemask – to prevent contamination of the scene.

Forensics had advanced in leaps and bounds in the decade or so he had been working in the field. The era of waiting days or weeks for fingerprint matches was long gone. Scenes of Crime officers had at their disposal a mix of black, white and fluorescent powders to render prints visible on coloured surfaces. On a big job like this, fingerprints could be photographed, loaded onto his rugged Panasonic Toughbook laptop at the scene and sent wirelessly to the Fingerprint Bureau for searching, with a result in 20 to 30 minutes. DNA results could now come back within days or a couple of weeks, not months.

Initially, Taylor arranged for tetramethylbenzidine (TMB) tests for blood in sinks, on dirty clothes in the laundry, and on the vacuum cleaner that Gerard's father, Nigel, had loaded into the back of his car at the house that morning.

When he took in everything about the home, applying his customary logic and common sense, Taylor picked up on some details that seemed odd. One was that Gerard told police he went out looking for Allison in the couple's Holden Captiva, which was reversed into the side carport. To get it into this position, Gerard would have had to reverse awkwardly around his Prado, which was parked in a much more accessible spot in front of the house. Why hadn't Gerard taken the Prado?

When Taylor looked in the back of the Captiva, something didn't seem right with that either. The third row of seats was folded down to create a large boot area, where a pram for dolls and boxes of toys were all neatly arranged. If Gerard had been out driving the streets in the Captiva looking for Allison, why were the items still so ordered? The toys looked like they had been recently placed in the boot.

It was 10 pm when he packed up that night and briefed Gundry and Detective Superintendent Mark Ainsworth, who was returning from his leave the next day.

Forward command post

The mums arriving for the fitness class at the Brookfield State School oval thought Allison and Gerard's house must have been burgled. Police cars anywhere in Brookfield were an unusual sight. And these were impossible to miss. Gerard and Allison's home was on the main road into Brookfield – just before the turnoff to the primary school and only a couple of hundred metres from the general store, the commercial hub of the community.

The mums – and some dads – gathered at the school oval every Friday at 9.15 am for what they called their weekly torture session with Rocket Fitness trainer and former boxer, Daniel Crawford. At one stage, Allison had limbered up for the group fitness classes, but threw in the towel after two or three sessions, confessing 'hardcore' exercise wasn't for her. The other mums would occasionally see her out and about in the mornings, getting some more sedate exercise. She was a dawdler, not a power walker. Moseying along, it seemed she was out for fresh air rather than fitness.

As the exercise group went through their paces that morning, the police presence grew at Gerard and Allison's house. By the time the hour-long session was over it was evident that something was seriously amiss. Police cars and vans were now starting to assemble at the Brookfield Showground – there were uniforms everywhere. Someone told the group Allison was missing.

The two separate but equally important police operations revved into high gear at about the same time. While Gundry was frenetically formalising the criminal investigation, based at the Indooroopilly CIB office, resources were being skilfully mustered for the very public search, based at the showground.

Police Inspector Mark Laing was one of two men leading the search. Known universally as 'Sharky', Laing had held a variety of positions in his policing career. A former accident investigator and police prosecutor, he had spent a harrowing two-and-a-half years reviewing the long-running investigation into the murders of Neelma, Kunal and Sidhi Singh. The Singh siblings were found dead in a spa bath in their home at Bridgeman Downs, north Brisbane, in April 2003. Nine long years later, Neelma's former boyfriend, Max Sica, was being tried for the murders, and Laing had spent weeks assisting the prosecution.

On the morning Allison was reported missing, Laing was at the district office at Station Road, Indooroopilly. By early afternoon, when police at the scene phoned to say Allison hadn't returned and a forward command post had been set up at the Brookfield Showground, Laing phoned his colleague, Detective Acting Superintendent Shane Dall'osto, who was temporarily the officer in charge of the Brisbane West district, and the two arranged to meet in Brookfield.

Laing made it to the showground at about 1.30 pm; Dall'osto had arrived ahead of him. There were already 20 to 30 police in uniform gathered for a search, and Laing and Dall'osto got straight to work.

The two men coordinated the search for Allison from the showground, about 200 metres down the road from her house, for the next ten long, emotional days. Laing, a man with a soft heart and a huge capacity for work, was appointed the police forward commander.

Allison's large extended family was beginning to hear what was unfolding. Jodie Dann was at home in south-west Brisbane when her daughter Ashley noticed an alarming post on her Facebook feed at 6 pm.

'Mum, this is a photo of Allison. It says she's reported missing,' Ashley shouted out.

The QPS post said Allison Baden-Clay – Dann's cousin – was missing. Dann tried to keep calm and told herself it could be some sort of prank, but she was scared. When she phoned police, they confirmed that Allison was genuinely missing.

All her suspicions about Gerard over the years crystallised in her mind as she dialled the number for her mum, Mary Dann, Allison's aunt.

'He's done it Mum, he's done it. He's killed her,' she told Mary.

Dann's mum told her she couldn't know that yet. But Dann was certain.

'I'm phoning the police,' she told her mum. And she did. That night she phoned Crime Stoppers, and told them what she knew of Gerard's emotional and psychological abuse of his missing wife.

'He's killed her,' she told the operator. 'I'm Allison's cousin. You can verify that. I'm a domestic violence advocate, I've worked in the area for eight years, and he's killed her.'

Dann couldn't sleep. Her mind was racing. Where had he put her? Dann was thinking somewhere on Gold Creek Road. In a mine shaft somewhere. Maybe he'd made it look like suicide.

Meanwhile at Brookfield, police were working late into the night. In the afternoon one of the detectives, Plain Clothes Constable Kellie Thomson, had once more tried the Find My Friends application on Gerard's phone. The separate triangulation process had only shown Allison's phone was in a broad area spanning several kilometres. Previous attempts that day to use the tracking application had failed but Thomson seemed to strike it lucky: after a 10-second delay, a blue dot appeared on the screen. It was pinpointing Allison's phone to a home in Boscombe Road – it was the long backyard of Veronica Brumm, whose dog, Scraps, had demanded to be let out in the middle of the previous night. Police had searched the property throughout the day, and around 25 officers returned when darkness fell and fanned out in a line.

Laing and Dall'osto were among them, shoulder to shoulder, eyes straining in the dark as Allison's mobile was called. Their torchlights were off and there was complete silence. They were hoping against hope to see the glow of a display or perhaps hear a ringtone, or buzz. There was nothing.

When that failed, the Rescue 500 helicopter roared overhead, equipped with heat-sensing equipment, which should have picked up Allison's phone, provided it was still on. Nothing was revealed.

Laing got home at 11 pm. It was a disappointing end to a long day. Tomorrow, they would redouble their efforts in the search for Allison.

Test match

The hapless batsmen in the Brookfield United Cricket Club didn't know what hit them. It was 1994, and from the other end of the pitch, a medium-pacer came in and bowled them out, one after the other. By the end of the innings, he'd single-handedly knocked out the entire team, skittling them like bowling pins in a perfect strike. Detective Superintendent Mark Ainsworth's ten wickets for 26 runs on his home ground remains the best bowling spell in the 65-year history of the Stafford Cricket Club. It was an effort Gerard Baden-Clay, a cricket tragic, would have appreciated.

Ainsworth, born and bred on Brisbane's north side, was an all-rounder for Stafford from primary school until a simple slip on duty in 2000 almost claimed his life. A rising star with the QPS, he was doing the night shift in the job he loved when a phone call came in about a rape in the caves under Story Bridge. Clambering over a spiked fence in search of the offender, he lost his footing. At first he thought a spike had caught his pants, until he saw blood pouring down to his boots. He'd sliced the branches of the femoral artery in his thigh. Two police colleagues clamped the wound and rushed him to St Andrew's War Memorial Hospital at Spring Hill, saving his life and receiving commendations for their efforts. Ainsworth's cricketing days were cut short, but once recovered, his police career continued on its upward trajectory.

A natural leader, he'd joined the QPS in January 1980, fresh from graduation at Kedron State High. His uncle had been a policeman in Fingerprints and used to take him around on weekends to show him the job, sparking and nurturing his interest. In a career-defining moment, Ainsworth was seconded to Tony Fitzgerald QC's inquiry into entrenched corruption stretching to the top of the police service. Hand-picked for the role by Jim O'Sullivan – a future Queensland police commissioner – he was one of five surveillance operatives on the inquiry, tailing bookmakers and crime figures.

Roles followed in the former Criminal Justice Commission, as a detective in various CIBs, and secondments to the Australian Crime Commission and to the Queensland Floods Commission of Inquiry examining the devastating events of December 2010 and January 2011. But if Ainsworth thought he'd seen it all in his policing career, the Baden-Clay investigation was about to show him otherwise.

Ainsworth was at the end of a three-week holiday when he came into work a day early, on Friday 20 April 2012, to get on top of the workload he knew would be waiting for him as the Metropolitan North Regional Crime Coordinator. His role was to oversee investigations into major crimes, in an area spanning dozens of suburbs and hundreds of thousands of residents north of the Brisbane River. The phone tended to ring at all hours of the day or night, and he'd ensure the right resources were in place for the murders, sieges, sex assaults, armed hold-ups and missing persons cases that routinely occurred in a city of more than two million.

Acting Inspector Mal Gundry briefed Ainsworth on Allison's disappearance.

The next morning, Saturday April 21, was an early start. Gundry and Ainsworth led a 7.30 am briefing in the MIR at Indooroopilly Police Station, opposite the sprawling multi-level shopping centre, to detectives drawn from the local CIB, Homicide and surrounding stations. Officers from Forensics, Intelligence and other specialist areas filled the room.

Getting detectives to work on the investigation wouldn't be an issue – it was harder to get them to go home. A mum was missing and they wanted, desperately, to find her.

Ainsworth's next stop was the Brookfield Showground, where he checked in with officers at the search HQ. The showground was the home of the Brookfield United Cricket Club, trounced by Ainsworth in his cricketing days. The investigation would be more of a test match than a one-day event, and this time Brookfield was firmly on Ainsworth's side.

He would become the public face of the police search for Allison Baden-Clay.

It was midday when my partner, Catriona Mathewson, phoned to ask if I'd heard of anything happening at Brookfield. She was on her way to visit her sister on Friday 20 April 2012 and had gone past Allison and Gerard's house. At the time, I was working on investigations on *The Sunday Mail*.

'There are police everywhere,' she said.

A journalist, her curiosity had kicked in. Drug raids were being reported on the radio bulletins. She wondered if it was somehow connected. Her sister, who lives in a beautiful cul de sac beside a picturesque Brookfield creek, was trying to guess the reason for the unusual, and large, police presence. Within days police divers would be scouring that same creek and a waterhole in the massive search for Allison Baden-Clay. But that morning there was nothing being reported anywhere about Brookfield.

Catriona phoned again in the afternoon and told me even more police had arrived in Brookfield, including a forensics van. The Baden-Clay home had been cordoned off with blue and white police tape.

In the late afternoon, police issued a brief media statement about a missing mum. The few sentences gave no hint of the major investigation already unfolding. I realised that if forensics had been called in and the home sealed off, this was shaping up as more than just a missing persons case.

I Googled the name in the media release, Allison Baden-Clay. The search came back with profiles of her husband, Gerard, showing his great-grandfather was Scouts founder Robert Baden-Powell. That evening I phoned *Sunday Mail* news editor Sam Strutt on her mobile to let her know there might be a significant story developing. When I hung up, *The Australian*'s investigative journalist, Hedley Thomas – married to Catriona's sister Ruth – phoned from their Brookfield home and asked if I'd heard anything about the case. He knew the family involved.

Allison's disappearance hadn't made the Friday night news or the Saturday papers. Journalists on the police desk of *The Courier-Mail* had filed a story on the Friday, but missing persons cases were run of the mill and it was bypassed in the rush to get the paper out. I spoke to Strutt and editor Scott Thompson and they were both intrigued. An experienced news reporter, Suellen Hinde, was on the early morning shift and was already working on the story. She filed a couple of hundred words for the website – the first to be written on the case – and the media story came to life.

I found an address for Gerard's parents, Nigel and Elaine, and Hinde headed to Brookfield to try to speak to them. When she arrived, they didn't want to talk. Through the door, Elaine curtly ordered her to leave the property. In most missing person cases, relatives go to considerable lengths to get their loved one's face in the public eye and to keep it there as long as possible. Gerard's parents didn't want a bar of the media.

At Brookfield, Hinde talked to the top man, Detective Superintendent Ainsworth. While she was out, I'd been calling Gerard's friends and business associates. Picture editor Kevin Bull and photographer Jamie Hanson searched our archives and found a photo of Allison and Gerard together on their wedding day. By chance, staff photographer Steve Pohlner had photographed them for the popular *Sunday Mail* weddings pages 15 years earlier. They looked to be the perfect couple.

That night the story was on the TV news. The next day, the report of Allison's disappearance ran prominently in the *Sunday Mail*. The story of Allison and Gerard Baden-Clay would soon be dominating the media in Queensland. At our regular Tuesday news conference, where we discussed ideas for the coming weekend, Allison's disappearance was on the agenda for stories to pursue. Every news outlet in town was on the case.

I started making calls to anyone who may have had a connection to the couple. Among the first things I was told was Gerard had a mistress. There were suggestions he was in financial distress after the January 2011 floods, and had a major falling out with business partners. Those circumstances suggested there was more to the clean-cut well-spoken western suburbs real estate agent than met the eye.

Shithouse

Saturday 21 April 2012

Gerard and his sister, Olivia, arrived at the Brookfield Showground bright and early for the first full day of searching for Allison. Sergeant Greg Matthies, one of the Search and Rescue Management Coordinators (SARMACs), was setting up the forward police command post for the day. Matthies knew Gerard had called in a lawyer and was refusing to provide a formal statement, and was surprised to see him. He shepherded Gerard to a log near the cricket oval. Other officers milled about and one of them switched on a digital recorder as they sat down on the log to speak.

'How you feelin', Gerard?' Matthies asked.

'Shithouse,' Gerard replied.

Matthies said he'd need some information to help with the search, and asked Gerard to go back through events again.

Gerard repeated what he'd told the police the previous day: 'Um, I went to bed, ah, about ten o'clock last night. Oh sorry, the night before . . .' he started.

Matthies asked if Allison had gone to bed, and Gerard said he had started to think she had. When he had made the bed in the morning, he said, he had pulled the doona up on his side but Allison's was already up.

'So she must have done that when she got up.'

Allison had told him the night before of her plans to leave home by 7 am for the conference. She had been excited about attending it.

'So, um, I, I, I got up and started doing my usual routine, you know, sh–shit, shower and shave.'

There it was: that awkward phrase yet again.

He'd checked his emails on his phone while sitting on the toilet, Gerard continued. He was shaving as his middle daughter was waking up, and cut himself in the rush.

He had turned his wife's hair rollers on to warm, knowing she took about 45 minutes to an hour to get ready of a morning: 'And she'd had her hair done the night before. So I knew, you know, she would want to, and she was going to a seminar with, you know, two or three hundred people, so she'd want to be looking her best. And that takes longer, you know.'

He told Matthies about his wife's usual walking routes, and said his sister and father had driven to his house on the Friday morning when Allison hadn't returned. 'That's my dad's car that's parked there, which he's a bit frustrated about 'cause he needs it,' he said, motioning towards his house down the road. 'It's been held at the house.'

Matthies asked after Allison's mental state and whether she had been up or down.

'She's, she's been predominantly up, you know. We've had, had our ups and downs,' Gerard replied.

Asked if there was anyone Allison might contact or confide in, Gerard nominated her friends Kerry-Anne Walker and Wendy Mollah.

Matthies asked more questions about whether there had been any issues between them on the Thursday night, and whether Allison would harm herself.

'She, she had a history of depression and, um, that sort of thing. But that's, you know, pretty well managed by her medication and that sort of thing. But, um, but it never, never led to anything like that.'

When Matthies moved on to marital problems, Gerard bristled, asking him to keep his voice down. Even here, with his wife missing and his home a crime scene, Gerard was worrying about his reputation. Matthies apologised and didn't push the issue, no doubt wanting to try to keep Gerard onside.

The conversation was winding up, and Matthies thanked Gerard for being helpful. Shortly before they went their separate ways, the officer remembered to ask Gerard what Allison might be wearing.

'Ah, just grey three-quarter-length pants and, um, and a, and a sort of a singlet top, probably. And ah, a, and the day before, um no . . . must have been Wednesday, um, which was the last day she went for a walk, um, she wore a, a sloppy joe, ah top, 'cause it was, 'cause it's a bit cool.'

Asked what his plans were for the day, Gerard said he wanted to do whatever he could to help find Allison: 'Some of the guys yesterday said, you know, I said I wanted to go looking and that sort of thing, and they said not to.'

Matthies did not comment either way, and Gerard went off to find his sister. He had a morning medical appointment to get to, with Dr Candice Beaven, the Kenmore GP to whom he would offer his business card.

Search commander Mark Laing was disappointed to arrive just after Gerard left. There were many questions he wanted to ask.

Gerard never once returned to the search base.

Because of the rapport he established with Gerard on the Friday, the personable Indooroopilly detective Chris Canniffe became the Major Incident Room's family liaison officer. It was an unusual case, as normally the role involves dealing with a victim's family in one group as police search and investigate. In the Baden-Clay investigation, Canniffe became liaison officer for both Allison's family and Gerard's family separately.

As soon as Canniffe got into the Indooroopilly CIB on the Saturday morning, he phoned Gerard and asked for the name of the mistress he had mentioned to police the day before. At first Gerard didn't want to give him the name. When Canniffe said he would find out in a couple of calls anyway and was only asking as it would save him time, reluctantly, Gerard named Toni McHugh.

Canniffe wanted McHugh's phone number too. Gerard baulked at providing the number, telling the detective he would need to call him back.

Not long afterwards, Toni McHugh's phone rang – it was Gerard warning her police would want to talk to her.

Ewen Taylor, the methodical forensic coordinator, arrived at Allison and Gerard's Brookfield house early on Saturday, but someone had been there before him. Officers guarding the home told Taylor of a 5 am visit from Gerard's father, Nigel, who had wanted back his Holden Statesman and the vacuum cleaner. The car, however, was still in the driveway, where he had parked it the day before. The crime scene guards had strict instructions to turn away anyone other than a select group of police.

Nigel's Statesman was the first car police forensically examined at the scene. Officers found a Swiss army knife in the console, which was tested for blood with no result. With the day warming up, Taylor was concerned about the forensic officers sweating through their protective clothing and contaminating the cars. He arranged for Gerard and Allison's Prado and Captiva to be towed to a police vehicle examination facility, where the cars could be examined indoors in the cool.

Meanwhile, at Indooroopilly, police in the Major Incident Room were poring over the photographs of Gerard's facial injuries. At the MIR, the assembled detectives look at situations from every possible angle and everyone gets a hearing – anyone can throw up suggestions for debate. They realised they needed a ruler next to Gerard's marks to document their size to take the evidence to the next level. And looking at Gerard's Windsor knot and starched collar, they wondered what other injuries could be unseen beneath his neat shirt.

'Get him back here,' one said.

Taylor got a call from the MIR at about midday asking for new photographs. He asked a Scenes of Crime officer, Sergeant

Anthony Venardos, to meet Gerard at Indooroopilly Police Station to take the photographs. Gerard had given his consent.

This time, after taking photos with a ruler beside the scratch marks, Venardos asked Gerard to remove his shirt too. Until that moment, there had been considerable police speculation about the scratches plainly visible on his face. As Gerard unbuttoned his business shirt, he must have been nervous about what he was about to reveal.

On his chest, there was a painful looking mass of scratches or bruises. There were more scratches on the left side of his neck and near his right armpit. A caterpillar had bitten him at the school cross-country the day before, Gerard explained.

When Gerard had been photographed by police a day earlier he had, perhaps out of habit, smiled slightly for the camera. On this second occasion, he looked grim. His day had started badly and was getting worse.

Detectives gathered in the MIR to look at the latest photographs. There was a stunned reaction to the newly discovered injuries.

Back at Brookfield, as the examination of Gerard's home continued, Taylor saw a man wandering the grounds of the childcare centre next door, getting close to the crime scene. He went to investigate and discovered it was Allison's father, Geoff Dickie, forlornly searching for clues that could lead to his missing daughter, like any dad would do. Taylor tried to comfort him, telling him police were doing everything they could and gently directing him back to the forward command post at the showground.

Before Geoff left, Taylor asked his thoughts.

Geoff was prepared for the worst. Allison would never, ever willingly leave her daughters, he told Taylor.

Allison's cousin Jodie Dann, her nerves frayed from worry and lack of sleep, was at home with her husband, Jonathan. It was the morning of his birthday.

'I can't stay here any longer. I need to go out there,' she told him, and they drove to Brookfield, arriving well before lunchtime.

Initially, they thought they might not stop, but as soon as Dann got there, she knew she had to see Priscilla and Geoff. She found them waiting with one of Gerard's friends and hugged the couple. Geoff sobbed and sobbed.

Dann turned to Jonathan and asked him to please go home and get chairs and food: 'We need to stay here. This is where we need to be. I'm not leaving.'

Dann phoned her mum and dad, Mary and Noel Dann, who were in Hervey Bay. Noel was Priscilla's brother, the second eldest of the ten siblings. 'This is serious. You need to get here,' she said, and with that they were on their way.

The sun set on another frustrating day. Priscilla and Geoff were to stay at Jodie's south-side home, in her parents' granny flat.

As Dann and Geoff crossed the road together to leave the Brookfield search base, it was dark. A memory intruded into Dann's thoughts. When she and Allison were kids, Jodie would sleep beside her cousin on sleepovers and Allison would put her fingers in her mouth and rock back and forth to doze off because she was scared of the gloom. It seemed so poignant now.

Geoff looked as though every bit of vitality had been drained from him.

'Jodie, she is out there somewhere, in the dark,' he said.

Bloodstain

Sunday 22 April 2012

It was now two days since Gerard reported Allison missing. Police at the Central Exhibits Facility's vehicle examination area at West End were about to go over each of the couple's cars with the proverbial fine-tooth comb. Allison and Gerard had only had their Holden Captiva for eight weeks, after trading in a more expensive Lexus to save money. When the silver Captiva had rolled out of the showroom of the Village Motor Group at Petrie on 24 February, it was brand new with only 72 kilometres on the clock. The couple had named it Sparky. They'd had the white Prado, which they called Snowy, for years.

Senior Constable Michael Kelly, a forensic scientist from the Brisbane Scientific Section, was assigned the role of examining the Captiva. Nearby, another scientific officer examined the Prado.

In the Captiva's boot area, the neatly arranged doll's pram and other toys had moved around during the trip to the inspection site. Kelly and the police photographer assisting him, Sergeant Brett Schnitzerling, took out the toys and folded up the third row of seats. Kelly found himself staring at the plastic panel on the driver's side in the third-row seating area. A dark stain on the panel was dripping towards the floor. Schnitzerling thought it might have been spilt soft drink.

Kelly pushed a piece of blotting paper against the stain and a reddish blotch transferred to the paper with little effort. Next, he took a little of the chemical reagent TMB and applied it to the blotting paper stain. When blood is present, TMB reacts with haemoglobin and turns a blue–green colour. The test involves applying one to two drops of a TMB solution and one to two drops of a hydrogen peroxide solution to the blotting paper. Kelly watched as the paper turned blue–green. Blood.

His work wasn't over. Taking a swab head, he coated it with a 70 per cent ethanol solution then touched it against the Captiva bloodstain. Testing the swab with a HemaTrace kit, designed to detect human haemoglobin, he watched as a pink line appeared. It was human blood.

Kelly recognised the mark as a transfer stain, the term used when a wet, bloody surface contacts a second surface. The drips were flow stains, from the blood dripping with gravity or some other surface movement.

The discoveries continued. From the base area of the bloodstain, Kelly delicately retrieved a single strand of blonde hair. The hair and blood from the side panel would have to undergo DNA testing.

There was one more chemical to use but it was applied the following day. Luminol, a macabrely spectacular test that has become a staple of TV crime shows, glows a vivid blue in darkness when it comes in contact with blood residue. Kelly sprayed it throughout the Captiva, looking for any signs of a clean-up. When the lights of the vehicle examination area were turned off, the side panel lit up blue. There was a solid stain and two eerily glowing drips trailing towards the floor. There was no other blood found in the car.

At Brookfield, Ewen Taylor took a phone call just after 1 pm Sunday, informing him of the discovery of blood in the Captiva. He passed the news to detectives in the MIR. It was early days, but the significance was not lost on anyone. Concern for Allison's wellbeing heightened.

When vehicles have GPS navigation fitted, police can call in a forensic locksmith to unlock the data. Disappointingly, the Captiva didn't have GPS. Taylor, suspicious about the positioning of the toys in the boot, suggested detectives enquire into who put them there. The rush was on to identify the blood, so Taylor put in a priority request for testing and arranged for a Scenes of Crime officer to collect Allison's toothbrush and hairbrush for possible reference DNA. Next he called the police Fingerprint Bureau to the Brookfield house to check for prints inside and out.

In the days that followed, fingerprinting of the Captiva, including the toys in the back, returned only one print. It was on the service book in the glove box and matched a garage employee who had serviced the vehicle. It was not relevant to the investigation, but was an indication of how thorough the examination was. Prints weren't always left behind, so not much could be read from the absence of others.

While Taylor continued the painstaking search for clues at Brookfield, he received another call. There had been a car accident.

Crash

Sunday 22 April 2012

Detectives in the MIR at Indooroopilly police station stared at the latest photos of Gerard Baden-Clay's injuries. What had happened to his chest? Footballers among them would recognise the welts as the kind of marks you suffered when an opponent grabbed at your jersey and ripped at your chest hair in the process. But now that they had seen what lay beneath his shirt, they wanted to see more. Gerard still had his trousers on, and who knew what they concealed.

'Get him back again,' said a senior detective.

Driving to the station yet again to be photographed, with his lawyer not far behind him, Gerard gripped the steering wheel. So much pressure now. He had the police on his back. The media on his tail.

This time, detectives had a forensics expert waiting for him, and a magistrate had signed a Forensic Procedure Order, giving police the green light to conduct an intimate examination so they didn't need his consent.

As Gerard approached the Moggill Road police station at 3 pm, he could see photographers and TV crews crowding the front car park, waiting to capture his arrival. Rattled by the media throng, he kept driving. After doing a loop of the roundabout ahead, he doubled back on Moggill Road and took a left. He was in Musgrave Road, which is as straight as an arrow. One way. No oncoming cars. No big dips or bends. Just two, wide lanes running alongside the sprawling Indooroopilly Shopping Centre, the retail hub that had been there for more than 40 years. Like any other weekend, residents of the west filled the department stores, retail outlets and cinemas as Gerard passed. Entrances to multi-storey car parks flicked by on his left.

Gerard's world was closing in on him. He'd barely slept. On the passenger seat next to him, a copy of *The Sunday Mail* lay open on page five, where the story about his missing wife ran next to a photo of a beaming Gerard and Allison on their wedding day.

An overpass loomed ahead as he continued along Musgrave Road. Underneath, there was an exit to the left to a bus interchange. A large sign read, 'Buses only, No entrance'. Suddenly, Gerard rolled the steering wheel left, putting the car directly in line with one of the concrete pylons of the overpass. Mounting the footpath, the car drove straight into the massive column, instantly crumpling the bonnet and jolting Gerard violently in the driver's seat. Gerard Baden-Clay, pillar of the community, had idiotically slammed into a pillar on a perfectly straight road. Getting out of his car, he lay face down on the bitumen.

Paramedics and firefighters were alerted immediately and rushed over to him.

'I'm sorry, I'm sorry,' one of the fire fighters heard Gerard say.

Gerard told paramedics he must have looked down at his phone and crashed.

His lawyer, Darren Mahony, was on the scene before police. When detectives from the MIR arrived, Gerard was already on a stretcher and wouldn't talk to them. Raised into an ambulance, he was taken to hospital as a precaution.

Acting Inspector Mal Gundry and Detective Sergeant Chris Canniffe went to check out the scene of the crash. Orange traffic cones surrounded the car to prevent further accidents. There was no obvious reason why the blue hatchback – which Gerard had borrowed from his friend Rob Cheesman – had crashed into the concrete pylon. No other cars were involved. No skid marks were visible on Musgrave Road. Gerard hadn't braked, it seemed. The detectives and passers-by scratched their heads.

Back at Brookfield, Mark Ainsworth was briefing Allison's family and trying to ignore the incessant ringing of his mobile phone. Eventually, he excused himself and went off to take the call.

When he came back to the family, his face was bright red. 'Gerard has just crashed his car.'

Gerard had been wearing a seatbelt, and it was a relatively minor bingle.

If he was trying to harm himself, it didn't seem a serious attempt. Police had photographed his injuries twice. It seemed pointless to try to muddy the waters with new ones, if that were his intent.

Only 48 hours had passed since he reported his wife missing, and things were spiralling out of control.

7.15 pm
The Royal Brisbane and Women's Hospital emergency department was a constantly busy place. On any given night, its 18 beds were filled with drunks from the nearby Fortitude Valley nightclub precinct, injured children, patients in cardiac arrest or drivers and passengers pulled out of car wrecks. After crashing into the concrete pylon, an emotional Gerard Baden-Clay was occupying one of the beds. To be safe, emergency department doctors had put Gerard in a Philadelphia collar, commonly used for whiplash victims to stabilise the top vertebrae until X-rays can be taken.

Senior Constable Cameron McLeod, one of the first detectives to speak to Gerard at Brookfield two days earlier, raced to the hospital on the chance of a confession. McLeod found Gerard crying hysterically behind a curtain in the emergency department.

'I'm not answering your questions,' said Gerard, whose sister, Olivia Walton, and a legal representative were at his side.

Gerard may have been wondering what would become of the forensic examination he'd missed. The arrival of specialist forensic medical officer Dr Leslie Griffiths cleared that up: the accident had bought Gerard only a brief reprieve. In the doctor's possession was the Forensic Procedure Order to examine Gerard. Detectives wanted any injuries documented as soon as possible. Griffiths obliged by working the Sunday night. Police had briefed him on the car accident before he set to work.

The Queensland Health forensic medical officer was a highly experienced expert in his field. He held a Bachelor of Medicine, Bachelor of Surgery and a Master's degree in forensic medicine. He was a qualified pharmaceutical chemist and had given evidence at all levels of the justice system.

The medical collar prevented Griffiths from looking at Gerard's neck, until doctors confirmed there was no serious injury and approved its removal. Examining the injuries on Gerard's right cheek, Griffiths saw they were spaced apart and were several millimetres wide. They looked, to Griffiths, like fingernail scratches. There were already signs of healing, and Griffiths surmised the marks were at least 48 hours old.

On Gerard's right upper chest, Griffiths found the marks police had photographed the day before. Griffiths briefed police on his examination. Gerard had indeed suffered injuries well before his car crash, he confirmed. His later report made no mention of any examination or discoveries under Gerard's trousers.

Senior Constable McLeod secured an order keeping Gerard in hospital for a psychological assessment. Doctors gave his mental state a clean bill of health and he was released the next day.

Please help us

Having found no trace of Allison, police wanted Gerard to make a public appeal. Detective Sergeant Chris Canniffe approached Gerard's lawyer, Darren Mahony, and put in the request. Gerard said he would think about it, but he was worried. A trouble-making journalist could ask him about the scratches on his face. When it came to the crunch, Gerard refused to do it.

The next port of call for police, intent on a public appeal, was Allison's parents. Geoff and Priscilla Dickie said they'd do anything to help find their daughter. The couple went to police headquarters in Roma Street in the CBD on Monday 23 April 2012. Detective Superintendent Mark Ainsworth and Detective Acting Inspector Mal Gundry escorted them through a side door into a media room, where waiting journalists, photographers and camera crews fell silent.

Priscilla broke down as the cameras rolled. Through her tears she pleaded, 'As a mother, please, please help us to find our dear Allison. Our lives will never be the same. We must, we must, must find her. She's just so precious and she's so loving. We desperately need your support. Please, please help us.'

Geoff put his arm around his wife to comfort her. 'Please help us,' he urged, 'because there are three beautiful little girls of Allison's, wanting to see their mother.'

It was raw emotion and would hit a nerve when broadcast around the country on the TV news that evening.

Seated beside the Dickies, Ainsworth played down police investigations into Gerard. *The Courier-Mail* had that morning reported, for the first time, that police were treating the case as a 'crime investigation' and Gerard was a 'person of interest'.

To questions at the media conference about Gerard and the nature of the investigation, Ainsworth played a dead bat: 'Her husband was the person who reported Allison missing. There have been numerous inquiries with numerous people.'

But where was Gerard? His detour to hospital wasn't yet public knowledge, and his absence was glaring.

After Gerard had refused to make a public appeal, Olivia Walton contacted Detective Sergeant Canniffe. Walton told the detective she was ready and willing to front an appeal for her missing sister-in-law. But by then arrangements were in place; in Gerard's absence, Allison's parents were doing it.

Priscilla and Geoff's brave media appearance galvanised the community. Locals mobilised and joined the effort to find Allison. Police put out a call for residents to register dams and mine shafts and to check their properties; they were soon able to cross off their list homes all over Brookfield. Residents went out and searched on their own, trudging through the bush, shouting Allison's name. Was Allison still alive after almost four days? No one could know. But they pressed on.

Allison's family, caught up in a terrible waiting game, fell into a routine. Her uncles, aunts, cousins and friends would come from everywhere to the Brookfield Showground. They joined Priscilla and Geoff each morning and stayed until dark, then resumed their vigil the next day. At first, they sat out in the open, on seats overlooking the big oval used for happier community events, such as the annual show, cricket, horse-riding and fetes. After several days passed, the Brookfield Show Society threw open the doors of the country-style bar and an adjacent kitchen – where Gerard and Allison had once joined other parents at the Friday night burger bar. It gave Allison's family some privacy as they waited.

The peaceful little community came to resemble a disaster zone. It was as if a great flood or other calamity had struck the area. Searchers met en masse at the showground, rolled out maps and sketched plans on whiteboards. They set off on foot patrols, dirt bikes and horseback. The showground's oval became a landing-pad for helicopters, which roared in and out repeatedly in the search for Allison. From the air, searchers peered down at the rugged terrain below. There were acreage properties and bush tracks all over the place. Allison could be anywhere.

Everyone wanted to help. Stephanie Apps, whose kids caused such a ruckus on the night Allison went missing, feared the worst when she found disturbed earth on her property and noticed a terrible smell. She called the police, who delicately dug up the dirt, only to find rotting food buried there. It turned out that while Apps had been away recently, the power went out at her home and her mum had dug a hole to dispose of spoiled food from the fridge, not expecting to create a police incident.

Brookfield resident Will Truter visited the police command post to tell officers what he'd heard the night of Allison's disappearance. Truter lived in Winrock Street, 4 kilometres from Allison and Gerard. He'd been in front of the TV in his lounge room with family at 10 pm when two screams drove him out of his comfy chair and into the darkness outside to investigate.

His neighbour heard the same screams and yelled into the night that she was going to call the police, trying to scare off whoever may have been outside. The neighbour phoned Truter to check what he'd heard.

'While I was standing outside, we heard a third sound,' Truter told me later. 'It was like someone screaming and someone kept a hand over their mouth. That was the last we heard.'

Forward commander Mark Laing had seen plenty of missing persons investigations in which after a couple of days, the person sheepishly reappeared, having cleared their head. When Laing met Geoff and Priscilla and Kerry-Anne Walker at the search site on the Saturday morning, they told him straight that it was well outside Allison's character to go missing.

Laing didn't know what to make of Kerry-Anne at first – Allison's friend was so insistent the missing mum would never leave her daughters. The strength of her convictions soon convinced him that Allison was in dire trouble.

At first, Laing only had an old wedding photo of Allison, from almost 15 years earlier. He needed a more recent photo, but the man who was in the best position to provide one, Gerard, had been making himself scarce. Instead, Allison's sister, Vanessa, went to her parents' home on the Gold Coast and found a more recent photograph for Laing, who arranged for hundreds of flyers to be printed with Allison's photograph.

A priority for Laing was to find out everything he could about Allison to assist in the search. He had a long list of questions. He would have liked to have known more about Allison's mental state, her access to medication and money, whether she had any other relationships and precise details about her walking habits and outfits. Laing could never seem to get access to Gerard.

The search commander told Olivia Walton he would write the questions down for her brother, if he needed to clear them through lawyers.

By contrast, others were falling over themselves to help. A woman came to the search base and said she could round up 200 experienced horse riders if he said the word. State Emergency Service volunteers were turning up in droves – more than 400 would be involved. Recruits from the police academy were being sent out to help.

Reports of people hearing screams and other dramatic sounds on the night of 19 April kept coming in. There were so many screams, it was as if several people had been involved in foul play in Brookfield that night. Laing had to stay focused.

The primary search zone started at the house and moved outwards in an ever-increasing circle. Laing described the search pattern as like dropping a pebble in a pond – a splash in the middle, with ripples going outwards.

Until Allison was found, Laing, Shane Dall'osto and the SARMAC officers would presume she was alive. They were driving a search and rescue operation. Allison could have fallen down a hole and be waiting for them to put the right people in the right place. The searchers looked at cliff faces she could have dropped off. Police divers were brought in to wade through dams and swimming holes. Fire fighters rappelled down mine shafts.

Some nights, Laing would go to sleep worrying that only a handful of SES volunteers were confirmed for the next day. He'd get to Brookfield Showground the next day and find 60 volunteers there, ready to go. April 25, Anzac Day, fell on a Wednesday and was one of the biggest days of the search. People came from everywhere on the public holiday, asking to help.

Forensic coordinator Ewen Taylor used the Anzac Day public holiday to go mountain biking from one dirt track to the next on the outskirts of Brookfield in search of potential dumping points. He was riding home that afternoon when he got a call to say a hiker had found blood on Goanna Trail in the Mt Coot-tha Forest, which fringed the end of Boscombe Road. Taylor pedalled furiously all the way home, changed into his overalls and drove to the Gap Creek car park to meet the hiker. Using GPS coordinates, he found the trail of suspicious red dots, and performed tests at the scene, which confirmed the presence of blood. But when Taylor looked around further he noticed bloody gauze and a syringe. He phoned the Queensland Ambulance Service, who confirmed they had been at the site that morning to treat a seriously injured mountain biker.

Brookfield residents, trying to find any way to help, turned to baking and dropped off sweets and stews for the searchers with barely a word said. A local restaurant owner brought 400 bowls of food to searchers in two days. Allison's family went home each night and toiled in their kitchens, preparing sandwiches and scones and other simple food. They offered what they could to the searchers.

Sometimes simple gestures of support lifted the searchers just when they needed it. A Brookfield mum turned up at the showground with her daughter, who was no more than six or seven years of age. With the words, 'Thank you', the child handed Laing a drawing of police searching for Allison and also gave him a cupcake decorated with a face of icing and a cocktail umbrella. Laing took the treat home and kept it in his freezer for three months as a reminder of Brookfield's kindness.

Later, when the rain came, the Brookfield Show Society opened the doors to a hall alongside Brookfield Road. The society told Laing he had the run of the place for as long as he wanted – other events at the showground that might have conflicted or interfered had been cancelled.

Every couple of hours, Laing would go and talk to Allison's family and friends to fill them in on the latest developments. Priscilla's mother, Lily Dann – Allison's grandmother – turned up in a wheelchair and asked to meet 'Sharky Laing'. Lily, 91 years old, was tickled pink when Laing greeted her by remarking, 'Well, I know where Allison gets her looks from.'

Allison's family would ask Laing, 'Is this what you do for every missing person?' Laing, in turn, was impressed at how Allison's family stayed strong and never interfered. They never put pressure on him or the other searchers. Laing put the pressure on himself.

Privately, he was doing it tough. As the search dragged on, the mind played games from lack of sleep and the burden of responsibility.

There came a point when he felt he had to apologise to Geoff and Priscilla: 'I've let you down. I haven't found your daughter.'

Geoff reassured him the family had faith in the police: 'It's out of your control, mate.'

The pressure was being felt in the MIR too. Allison's disappearance was front-page news in *The Courier-Mail* every day and was leading TV news bulletins morning and night. Media crews pounced whenever anyone moved. Each new front-page story was put up on the walls of the MIR, a reminder of the intense public scrutiny of their work.

Even the ultra-experienced Detective Superintendent Mark Ainsworth was amazed at the public response. No single crime he'd worked on had ever garnered such attention or struck a chord with the community in the same way.

Back at the search post, Laing was struggling with a lack of detail and wondered time and again where Allison's husband was – the man who could have filled in most of the worrying gaps in knowledge.

Gerard was telling friends his focus was on making things normal for his daughters, and that officers had banned him from joining the search for Allison. Laing and other senior police knew of no such order, and there was certainly nothing preventing Gerard from visiting the forward command post at the showground.

Typically, during the search, Laing's day started with 5 am phone calls. He'd go straight out to the search base in the morning and stay there late into the night. His day would end when he crashed into bed around midnight. He and Dall'osto would be the last to leave the Brookfield Showground each night. He did not set eyes on Gerard once.

A little bit hurt

If Gerard Baden-Clay hadn't killed Allison, he was doing a fantastic job of convincing everyone he had. Absent from the search, refusing to speak publicly and dealing with police through his lawyers, Gerard behaved like a man with much to hide. He could have been the public face of the search. He *should* have been the public face of the search. He *should* have been a husband desperately hunting for his wife and the mother of his three children. He could have thrown his life open to police, whatever they might dig up and whatever the personal cost. But he didn't do any of those things.

During the search for Allison, there was only one occasion when Gerard spoke in public about his missing wife, and it went disastrously. Channel Nine crime reporter Alyshia Gates was waiting at the front of his parents' house at Kenmore on Tuesday 24 April. It was four days after Gerard reported his wife missing, and the day after Priscilla and Geoff Dickie made their emotional public appeal for help to find their daughter.

Gates started work around 5 am, and was the only journalist outside the Baden-Clay house early that morning. With the rest of the media pack elsewhere, Gates and cameraman Bill Heckelmann – a veteran with Nine for 40 years – got the scoop. Gerard and his sister emerged from the house, about to go for a drive, and the TV crew pounced, approaching Gerard on the driveway with the camera rolling. Instead of turning on his heel, Gerard strode over to the slim, blonde reporter and they started talking.

'I'm trying to look after my children at the moment,' Gerard said, his voice strained and high-pitched. 'We've got three young girls and we, we really trust that the police are doing everything they can to find my wife, and we really hope she will come home soon. And, um, I need to go now to an appointment. I'd just, we've got such great family support, my sister and family here, and they're looking after . . .'

He didn't quite finish the sentence, apparently unable to go on. But if he was fighting tears, they never came.

Olivia Walton, realising her brother was engaging with 'the enemy', rushed over and stood behind his left shoulder.

'There's been no contact, no contact at all?' the reporter asked, as Gerard went to leave.

'I've spoken to the police about everything,' replied Gerard, 'and I've had no contact from her at all.'

'Is there anything that may have, was she upset before she went away?' pressed Gates gently.

'No, and the police – I've tried to help the police as much as I can, we all have; everything we've got. So, thank you. I'm sorry,' said Gerard, wrapping up the conversation.

Gates, surprised she'd snared anything from Gerard, tried to keep him talking. 'Were you injured in a car crash a couple of days ago?'

'I was hurt a little bit but I'm okay. Okay. Thank you. Thank you very much,' Gerard said, and walked off.

'Thanks for your concern,' added Olivia, stepping in. As her brother retreated, she took the opportunity to enlist support for the search: 'We just appeal to the public to please help us in any way they can. We need to find her.'

Olivia couldn't negate the alienating effect Gerard had created; his worry had come across as forced at best. It wasn't as if he'd faced a grilling. Gates didn't ask, 'Did you kill your wife?' Gerard had been treated respectfully, yet he still couldn't get out of there fast enough, and had neglected to appeal for public assistance to find Allison.

Gates had been a journalist for 12 years, predominantly covering crime, and Allison's disappearance was easily the biggest story of her career in terms of public interest and the demand for stories from her office. Back at the Channel Nine studios at Mt Coot-tha, she watched the video over and over with colleagues. Gerard didn't come across as genuine.

Others reacted the same way. One of Gerard's former work-mates, who felt she knew him as well as anyone, watched the news that night and turned cold. When Allison went missing she didn't think there was a chance Gerard was involved, despite all the scuttlebutt. But that night, watching his performance on the evening news, she was taken aback and turned to a friend watching the news with her. They were both thinking the same thing: 'He's not telling the truth.'

Gerard's code of silence extended to his daughters. A school friend lived near Brookfield Showground, and there was an open invitation for the girls to drop around any time if they needed a break. On Thursday 26 April 2012, almost a week after Allison was reported missing, Olivia arrived at the friend's house with the girls.

While they were there, Allison's middle daughter made a comment about her missing mother then quickly hushed up: 'I'm sorry. I know I am not allowed to say anything until the debrief at night,' she said.

That morning, police equipped with a search warrant had conducted a raid on the Kenmore home of Nigel and Elaine Baden-Clay, where Gerard was staying. When Gerard eventually read through the warrant, he started wailing. The offence listed on the warrant was murder.

Detective Sergeant Chris Canniffe was at the back of the house and heard Gerard howl, 'I want to talk to Chris.' Canniffe went to the front of the house to see what was happening. He found Gerard visibly upset, though not in tears. The charge on the search warrant was 'preposterous', Gerard said.

That day, police interviewed Gerard's former business partners Phill Broom and Jocelyn Frost at Indooroopilly Police Station. Broom's lengthy police statement gave a withering assessment of Gerard.

'Gerard has a public face which is ethical, moral and upstanding,' he told detectives. 'He is involved in all the right groups, but it's always about what's in it for him. He would lecture staff about lying but would continue this long-term affair. I didn't appreciate how he could talk to me about being deceptive when he was living a lie.'

When Broom quizzed Gerard about his double standards and messy personal life, he was floored by his response: 'I asked him how he got into this situation and he said something like, "It's a lot like being a baby shaker. You don't think you're a baby shaker until you're caught shaking a baby."'

Broom added that Gerard had a 'unique' relationship with his family. 'They are a family where what you see isn't what you get. The family is very much about legacy.'

Nightmare

Sunday 29 April 2012

Taking his three daughters to the Ashgrove Baptist Church, Gerard was dressed in his Sunday best. He had a pink business shirt, black trousers, a black belt with silver buckle and shiny black shoes. The girls, in pretty dresses, emerged carrying colourful balloons with messages for their missing mum scrawled in black pen. Among the words was 'hope', and, peculiarly, 'forgiveness'.

It had been nine days since Gerard reported Allison missing and a beard now concealed the problematic scratches on his cheek. Allison was nowhere to be found, but the night before there had been a potential breakthrough on a big, empty farm block at Upper Brookfield, where women's running shoes and some silver tape had been found. Mark Laing, Ewen Taylor and other police were at the property until about 10 pm Saturday and did what they could with torches in the pouring rain. An officer guarded the scene until the morning, when police found more silver tape and a pair of gloves. The property was soon swarming with police, including officers on horseback and with cadaver dogs. Divers searched dams on the property.

Detectives had asked Gerard to attend Indooroopilly Police Station after the Sunday church service to view the shoes and tell them whether they were Allison's. On the way to the station, Gerard stopped at a park and dropped his sister and daughters off with Allison's parents, as had been arranged.

Since Allison had gone missing, Priscilla and Geoff Dickie had rarely spent time with their granddaughters, and only ever in the company of the Baden-Clays. The Dickies felt as though they were being watched by their daughter's in-laws. At one stage, Priscilla had to take one of the girls to the toilet, and Olivia joined them in the toilet block.

At Indooroopilly Police Station, while Elaine waited in the car, Gerard and Nigel were ushered into a room with Detective Sergeant Peter Roddick from Homicide and Senior Constable Cameron McLeod from the CIB. As soon as Gerard saw the shoes, he said they were not Allison's. So much for the discovery.

Never one to waste an opportunity, Roddick invited Gerard to change his mind and provide a formal statement. Roddick calmly but firmly told Gerard that the lack of detail provided to police on the day he reported Allison missing was hampering the investigation. Gerard's description of Allison's shoes was a case in point – he had told police they were white and blue, but not the brand or size or other information.

No such luck. Gerard flatly told Roddick he wasn't answering any more questions.

Police needed fingerprints from Gerard and Nigel, so Roddick and McLeod waited for the pair to phone lawyer Darren Mahony for approval. Eventually, they consented and McLeod went off to arrange the equipment.

Now Nigel grabbed the opportunity: he had a few things to get off his chest. Gerard's father said he had heard police weren't happy with the level of detail in his statement, and insisted he had told police all he remembered. There was something else too. A woman he knew – a good Christian, Nigel added – had woken from her sleep three times in a row with the same disturbing dream. In it, she was in Allison's body and was in a shed or some other dark place when a blanket was thrown over her head. Nigel told Roddick it was the first time he'd mentioned the dreams in front of Gerard, who was sitting silently beside him. His daughter, Olivia, however, had heard the story and was urging the family friend to call Crime Stoppers. Nigel wanted to know: had police been checking sheds in the area?

His suggestions for the investigation continued: Olivia had been getting a weird feeling when she went near a creek on Rafting Ground Road. And that wasn't the end of Nigel's advice. He told Roddick he had received an email from his younger brother, Crispin, in Namibia. Crispin wrote to remind Nigel about the case of a family friend who went missing in Africa 25 years earlier. In that case, the friend appeared months later, 1000 miles (1600km) away, outside a home he'd lived in more than a decade earlier. He was still wearing the same clothes he vanished in, and had no memory of anyone in his family. Nigel said the moral of the story was police should go back at least ten years in Allison's life.

The Homicide detective could only agree. But, while Nigel sat there suggesting police chase down dreams, 'weird feelings' and old haunts, Roddick pointedly remarked that the man best positioned to share a wealth of information about Allison was in the room with them, refusing to provide a formal statement.

Nigel retorted that when information was provided, police didn't use it. Gerard's father was particularly annoyed that a roadside mannequin police had erected to try to jog people's memories had been left bald. Allison had long, flowing auburn hair. No one was going to recognise her from that, he said.

Roddick explained that, in his experience, people remembered clothes before physical features.

Noisy sobs interrupted the exchange. It was Gerard. Through the sobs, he told the detective he was trying to look after his daughters and return some semblance of normality to their lives. He said he wanted his Captiva and his Prado back. In the room that day, he seemed intensely focused on what police were doing with the cars and was keen to know when they would be returned, despite telling Roddick he had been offered many loan vehicles.

Gerard also asked for a direct line to search commanders at Brookfield. He wanted more information but seemed oblivious of the fact that it was a two-way street. Detectives in the MIR and searchers at Brookfield were having no luck getting more information from him. The stalemate continued.

Gerard and Nigel gave their fingerprints and then went to leave. Through the windows, they could see the media pack outside. They expressed their deep unhappiness to police about being hounded. Elaine had the car engine going out the front. They phoned her to say they were on the way out, then rushed into the sunshine and took off without a word to the waiting journalists.

Roddick wasn't the only one fielding questions from Gerard and his family about the return of their possessions. Detective Sergeant Chris Canniffe had rarely heard from Allison's family in his role as the MIR's family liaison officer. However, he had provided his mobile number to Gerard and found himself constantly taking calls from Gerard and Nigel, asking for their cars and computers back or appealing for 'clarity' on when they would be back.

The search for Allison went on without Gerard. At the Brookfield Showground, Allison's family wondered how long police would keep up the intensity. So far there had been no let-up. The search had only grown and SES volunteers were still out in force. Deep down, everyone knew it could not go on forever.

Allison's family found themselves talking about murdered schoolboy Daniel Morcombe's inspirational parents, Bruce and Denise, and the immeasurable pain they must have suffered as they waited almost eight years to find him. How long could Allison's family keep up their own vigil? They had lives waiting for them – work to be done, children to care for. Now the family sorted out who could stay at the Brookfield Showground and who needed to leave.

To pass the time, they sat and discussed anything that could distract them from the awful circumstances that had brought them together. Mary Dann, Allison's aunt, taught some of the others how to knit and they made wool scarves.

Police had gradually been preparing them for the worst. Nothing was ever said directly. At first, search commanders had been updating them on how long a person could be expected to survive alone in the bush. Gradually, those briefings became less frequent and towards the end of April, they stopped altogether. By then, police had also started to mention eventually scaling back the search. The feeling was they were going to keep going at the same pace for at least a couple more days. Just a few more painstaking plans, grid patterns, helicopter flights and long days on foot, horseback and trail bike.

And then what?

Found

Professor Daryl Joyce would usually go kayaking on a weekend, but in April 2012 he had two weeks of leave. It was so good not to have to rush to get out on the water this morning. The University of Queensland horticulture researcher, who was in his 50s, had taken time off work to set up a vegetable garden on his 1-acre block in Karalee, Ipswich. The Monday was his first day of holidays, and after a weekend of rain it was gloriously sunny. He planned a relaxing paddle to clear his mind before getting stuck into the garden. Joyce kissed his wife goodbye as she went to work then loaded his fibreglass kayak onto the top of his car and drove five minutes down the road to the Riverside Park boat ramp.

It was about 8.30 am when he left home and he was soon bobbing in the Brisbane River, paddling upstream towards Ipswich. Joyce was a creature of habit; he always went against the tide on the journey out and cruised with the tide on the way back. Today was no different. Sticking to the left bank, he paddled for a couple of kilometres before crossing to the other side and turning back.

Kayaking had been an enjoyable weekend hobby for about six years. The dad of three grown-up children used it as a chance to get some exercise and fresh air.

On the days he paddled towards Ipswich, he liked to duck into Kholo Creek on his left on his return to the boat ramp. Years earlier, he'd found a beautiful, semi-tropical rainforest area where the tall trees formed a canopy overhead and the water became clear. He'd never seen anyone else on the waterway and felt he'd discovered an unspoilt secret. Since the floods of January 2011, a large tree had blocked access to the little creek at low tide. Today, his timing was spot on: the tide was high enough for him to cruise across the top of the fallen tree when he reached the creek mouth at close to 10 am.

He was paddling under the big water pipes that crossed the creek. Then he saw her. The woman lying on her side on the exposed, muddy bank under the bridge ahead on his right. For a moment, Joyce thought she might have been sleeping. As he drifted past, he realised who it was. Allison. The three-quarter-length pants and running shoes, like the mannequin dressed the same way on the news. He knew instantly. As he passed her, the breeze carried the scent. She was dead.

There was no way he could get out of his kayak onto the creek bank and he never took his mobile phone when he went to the river. Joyce paddled back to the boat ramp, drove home and phoned the Karana Downs Police Station.

Mark Laing had a grin on his face. He had just concluded a formal meeting with a visiting officer. Laing's colleague, a friend, had light-heartedly offered to take over the search because he couldn't find Allison. Laing's comeback was that the fellow officer couldn't run a toilet without it getting backed up. Light banter helped ease the stress; Laing had had plenty of practice.

Within half an hour the same colleague phoned Laing. 'Mate, you're not going to believe it,' he said, and told Laing a body had been discovered. This was no joke. Laing took in a lungful of air and listened intently.

Laing had never heard of Kholo Creek. It was at Anstead, on Brisbane's western fringe, well beyond the search zone. He got behind the wheel of his car and drove out there. Officers were on the scene and had cordoned off the bridge.

As he walked over to be briefed, it hit him. Allison was long gone. He could not have done any more. He could not have saved her. But he felt he had failed.

The search coordinator had started pondering how to temporarily keep the discovery from the media when a Channel Seven news helicopter appeared overhead. Allison's parents hadn't been informed yet. Laing had to move fast.

Priscilla Dickie had given him her mobile number. He called her. When she answered, Laing politely asked to speak to Geoff. He didn't know why, but he felt he needed to talk to Allison's dad first.

Geoff and Priscilla Dickie were at a lawyer's office in the city, getting advice on how they could have better access to their granddaughters. They had had enough of the irregular, brief visits with the girls and of being monitored by the Baden-Clays.

Laing had no intention of breaking the news over the phone but he had to ensure Allison's mum and dad didn't hear it from anyone else. 'I want you to come back. I need to talk to you, but I don't want you to listen to the radio,' Laing told him.

The man who had been the public face of the investigation, Detective Superintendent Mark Ainsworth, was in his office at Alderley when Assistant Commissioner Brett Pointing came in to tell him about the discovery of the body. Ainsworth got straight into his car. As he drove, it struck him what a long distance it was between the little creek he was heading to and Allison's home. The drive seemed to take an age before he reached the police roadblock on Mt Crosby Road, where officers waved him through.

He did the maths in his head. Walking that distance from Allison's home would have taken about three hours and involved navigating narrow road verges, possibly in the dark. No one had seen Allison walking.

The body had to be Allison, and he felt relief. Ainsworth had for some time suspected that the best police could do for Allison's family was find her body so she could be given a dignified farewell, and hopefully piece together how and why she died.

Allison's cousin Jodie Dann had left the search base for a day to go into work. She had more than 70 domestic violence cases waiting for her in Ipswich Magistrates Court as the court advocate. She'd just made it back to her office late in the morning when her daughter, Ashley, phoned: 'Dad says you've got to go straight to the search site.'

Dann burst into tears as soon as she heard about the body. Like Ainsworth, she felt relief. What made her feel guilty as well was that from the word go she had been certain Allison was not alive. She was equally certain that Gerard was responsible and that he had to be held to account for what he'd done.

Dann drove straight to Brookfield Showground, where an officer at the gate was under orders to keep everyone out.

'I'll run over you if you don't move,' she thought, and the officer must have seen the look in her eyes. Reluctantly he moved aside, but followed Dann down to where the rest of the family was gathered. Once he'd seen forward commander Mark Laing open her car door and give her a hug, the guard retreated to his post.

Priscilla and Geoff arrived soon after. Laing and Dall'osto solemnly took them aside and broke the news of the discovery of a woman's body. Allison's parents were told police were unable to make a visual identification, but more likely than not, it was Allison.

They sat together and cried. Laing told Allison's parents he had failed them. He told them he was sorry.

Geoff shook his head: 'Mate, there was nothing you could have done.'

Months after Allison's death, Jodie Dann was in the Brisbane CBD for a conference on intimate partner homicide. As she walked past King George Square, she saw a small crowd gathered for the annual coming together of the Queensland Homicide Victims' Support Group.

Denise and Bruce Morcombe were there, talking to people about the Daniel Morcombe Foundation, set up to help keep kids safe. Dann decided on the spot to thank them. Whether Bruce and Denise knew it or not, they had been a source of strength for Allison's family, who, during the hours and days of waiting at the search base, had talked about the Morcombe family's incredible grace and resolve.

'I'm Allison Baden-Clay's cousin,' said Dann, introducing herself to Denise. 'Your strength gave us a lot of strength through that awful wait. We don't know how you ever did it. Yours was years. Ours was days. I just wanted to let you know. Thank you.'

The two women cried together for what they had lost.

Bringing her home

Monday 30 April 2012

Forensic coordinator Ewen Taylor owed his start in the specialist policing field to a climbing accident. Back in 2000, when he was in general policing, Taylor had been a keen mountain climber. Venturing up a cliff face in the Glass House Mountains, in the Sunshine Coast hinterland, he made a rookie error and plunged 12 metres to the ground. He was lucky to survive. With that dislocated shoulder, he was told, he couldn't keep tackling drunks for a living. The near-death experience led him to make the change to forensics. When Allison's body was discovered under Kholo Creek Bridge, Taylor's climbing and abseiling experience came to the fore.

Taylor's endurance had been tested as the investigation into Allison's disappearance added to months of relentless work. Despite the taxing workload, he was committed to the case. On that Monday morning, he reluctantly tore himself away from the investigation to attend a forensic coordinator's conference at police headquarters in the city. Colleagues looked at the dark shadows under his eyes and sympathised.

The meeting was interrupted by a phone call from Detective Inspector Mal Gundry at 11.30 am. Gundry said a body had been found, and Taylor excused himself immediately. Before leaving headquarters, he dropped in to the Scientific Section and Photographic Section to pass the word on. He was at Kholo Creek in less than an hour.

Studying a map of the area, Taylor noticed Kholo Creek ran through the Tyamolum Scout Campsite further upstream. Unbidden, Gerard Baden-Clay's proud family connection to the

Scouts came to mind. He shook his head. But right now he needed to concentrate on the job he was there to do. Taylor was determined to get it right.

Uniformed police had been the first on the scene after the call from kayaker Daryl Joyce. They had spotted a steep path that led to a flat ledge under the bridge. From the ledge there was a vertical 2-metre drop to the creek bank and Allison's body. Scenes of Crime officers followed the same route under the bridge to take some preliminary photographs; again, they didn't get too close. One Scenes of Crime officer, Tony Venardos, was making his way to the body clad in full personal protection equipment – including plastic boot covers that covered the tread on his boots – when he slipped and fell awkwardly in the thick mud. Water Police and the Dive Squad came to Venardos's rescue, and an ambulance took him to hospital with a dislocated shoulder.

Gaining workable access to the body was going to be a challenge for the forensics personnel. Low tide was at 1 pm, so water would soon start rising in Kholo Creek. No one knew how long the body had been there or whether the rising tide would engulf her. It was a race against time to do their job – and do it thoroughly – before the water level peaked. Taylor, after discussions with detectives from the MIR at the scene, judged the safest and quickest way to get to the body was to rappel down from the bridge. Normally, a forensic coordinator might have stayed on the bridge to call the shots from above. But Taylor knew how to work the ropes and took the chance to handle the job personally. He'd worked the case from the start and felt a responsibility to Allison.

Before he went down, Taylor phoned pathologist Dr Nathan Milne and asked him to come to the bridge. Milne reminded Taylor to make sure he took samples of the creek water to test later for diatoms – microscopic algae – which could indicate whether the victim had drowned.

Scenes of Crime officers dusted for fingerprints before the ropes were hooked up. Senior Constable Ashley Huth from the

Scientific Section was lowered down first, with the help of fire-fighters. Taylor followed. When they reached the creek bank, their gumboots sank deep into the thick mud, and without the support of the ropes, they would have gone face first. They were only a couple of metres from Allison but had to think carefully about how they would reach her.

Leaning against their ropes, the two officers collected and bagged samples of water, plants, soil and insects. Neither Taylor nor Huth had ever experienced anything like the extremely difficult and dangerous working conditions they encountered that day.

Initially the plan was to place bags on Allison's hands to preserve potential evidence beneath her fingernails. When they got to the body, they found Allison's inside-out, tangled up jumper was covering her hands and head. As the hands were already protected, the officers decided to leave them as they were. Taylor was glad to be under the bridge to make those decisions on the spot.

When the pair had carefully completed all the preliminaries, it was time to remove Allison from that cold place where she had lain. A stretcher and a fresh, sealed blue tarpaulin were lowered down. Taylor and Huth carefully placed Allison inside the tarp on the stretcher. It was almost 5 pm. When she was secured, a team of officers on the bridge, including detectives from the MIR, heaved on the ropes to pull her up. Back into the light of day.

Real estate agent and Mt Crosby Road resident Brian Mason had been following the search since the start. Sometimes he'd listen to an SES friend's radio scanner. Mostly, the talk on the radio was dull, but that day it crackled with a real development – the discovery of a body.

Mason's friend phoned at 11.45 am to let him know. Washed up at the weir at Mt Crosby, his friend said, mistakenly, as it turned out. Mason told his wife, Mary, and phoned his boss,

Julie Crittenden, who knew Gerard through the local business community. A news helicopter roared over the top of his property and hovered nearby, and Mason could see a cameraman hanging out one of the doors.

A second helicopter appeared, around Kholo Creek Bridge. Mary had gone off to check the mail and came running back with news police had closed off Mt Crosby Road. Mason went to look and found that two police officers had parked a vehicle across the road from his driveway, another police car was down at the bridge and two officers were peering over the railing. A journalist arrived with a photographer who was carrying a long lens, and a police vehicle drove past towing a boat.

Mason realised his friend's tip was not quite right. The body wasn't at the weir; it was under the bridge up the road from his home.

'She's under the bridge,' Mason said to an officer at the roadblock, seeking confirmation.

The officer replied that he didn't know.

Gerard's affair with Toni McHugh wasn't yet public knowledge, but Mason had already heard the worst kept secret in real estate. 'Well, I might know more than you do. This is what happens when you have an affair with one of your staff members, the wife finds out, they have a squabble, she gets herself done in and ends up under that bridge,' he told the startled officer.

As he retraced his steps up his driveway, it dawned on him: his dog Sasha's out-of-character barking had happened on the night Allison disappeared.

Back inside his home, he told Mary the search was over. Then he asked his wife to recount the story she had told him about her drive to work in the early hours of the morning on Friday 20 April, when Gerard would report Allison missing. Mary told him she had seen a car with its headlights off, tailgating another car.

'You've got to talk to the police about this,' he said.

Mary was going to Perth that afternoon. She phoned Crime Stoppers when she got back days later.

Meanwhile, other things came to mind for Brian Mason, like Sasha's odd behaviour in the days after Allison disappeared. The dog had sat at the front of the property, looking out into the bush in the direction of the bridge. She barely moved for days.

After Dr Nathan Milne, senior specialist forensic pathologist with Queensland Health, received the call from police forensic coordinator Ewen Taylor, he hurried to the scene. With him were a forensic pathologist and senior forensic pathology registrar. He leant cautiously over the bridge to catch a glimpse of the body, and could just make out Allison's head and upper torso.

When Allison was winched to the bridge, the indent left behind in the mud indicated she was there for some time. Milne noted that the officers moved the body without significantly disturbing the position of the limbs or clothing.

Under a marquee and lights from the fire service, Milne could see the woman wore what appeared to be a jacket – caught up around her head and neck and entangling her arms – and a singlet with a built-in bra, three-quarter-length pants and sneakers. The significant decomposition was consistent with death occurring at the time Allison went missing. Insects and insect larvae had attacked the soft tissue of the face, head, forearms and left lower leg. Part of the skull was exposed.

Police anxiously awaited a determination about how she died. Milne couldn't tell them on the spot from what he'd seen, and left the bridge at 6 pm.

The body was taken to the government mortuary, and by eight o'clock was undergoing a CT scan. There were no obvious fractures. The horseshoe-shaped hyoid bone in the neck was intact, providing no evidence of strangulation, though not excluding it either. Milne told Mal Gundry there was no obvious cause of death, and they would have to see what came of a post mortem the next day.

Detectives Chris Canniffe and Cameron McLeod went to the Century 21 Westside offices at Taringa to tell Gerard a woman's body had been discovered. They were too late. When the officers arrived, Gerard told them he had found out online.

His father, Nigel, was with him at the office and volunteered to formally identify the body.

Allison was not in a state to be identified by sight, and the detectives said it would not be necessary.

At the Brookfield Showground, the thoughts of Allison's grief-stricken mother turned quickly to her granddaughters. The three girls were the only living link Priscilla Dickie had to her daughter. She felt a powerful need to see them, to drink in the signs of Allison she recognised in them, to connect with and console them.

Geoff said he simply couldn't call Gerard, not even to ask to see the girls. Desperate for the contact, Priscilla decided to ask herself. Leaning against a fence outside in the late afternoon, she phoned Gerard.

'Can I just come around and see the girls?' she asked her son-in-law.

Gerard said no. He hadn't told the girls anything yet. He was going to wait until there was confirmation from police that it was Allison.

Priscilla was prepared to do things his way: 'Okay, well I won't tell them. I just need to see them. I just need to give them a hug.'

Gerard wasn't budging. He said it wasn't appropriate and they should talk about it the next day. There was media everywhere and he didn't want to add to the circus.

'Please, Gerard. I just need to hug the girls. I just need to see them. I can come to the house. They don't even need to come outside. What if it was just for five or ten minutes?' She was begging him now.

'No,' he said, and hung up.

Death puzzle

She was still wearing her rings. The gold wedding band was engraved: 'G&A 23:8:97'. Her engagement ring, set with an 8-millimetre diamond, was on the same finger. For police, it was another layer of identification. It also meant that whatever had happened to Allison, she hadn't been robbed of her jewellery.

Dr Nathan Milne passed the two rings to detectives observing his post mortem examination at the John Tonge Centre at Coopers Plains, in Brisbane's south, on Tuesday 1 May 2012. Officers were in place beside him in the examination room, and in a separate viewing room where there were rows of bench seating. The officers were from a multitude of units within the QPS, reflecting the size and strength of the team investigating Allison's death: Detective Sergeant Rhys Breust from Homicide; detectives Cameron McLeod and Cameron Simmons from Indooroopilly CIB; forensic coordinator Ewen Taylor; Sergeant Nicole Tysoe from the Scientific Section; Senior Constable Kylie O'Sullivan from Scenes of Crime; and Constable Jackie Lucas from the Coronial Support Unit.

The tags on her body bag read 'Unknown Unknown'. When its seal was first broken, Milne had peeled back the blue tarpaulin wrapped around the body. Leaves and bark peppered Allison's hair and body, and Milne set them aside, along with dirt and mud samples, for later examination. On closer inspection, Milne could see the tangled clothing he thought was a jacket the day before was actually a light-coloured Bonds jumper.

He detailed his findings in a report compiled in the months following the autopsy: 'The unusual position of the jumper may have occurred after death with movement of the body. It cannot be excluded that it was used as a ligature [cord],' Milne wrote.

He examined the clothes in more detail. She was wearing a purple size 12 Short Stories singlet with inbuilt bra, dark Katies pants, light-coloured underpants, white and blue Lynx size 9 sneakers and short white socks. It all closely resembled the clothes Gerard described when police arrived at Brookfield that first day, when he said Allison's 'daggy' old pants were missing and that she wore a singlet and sometimes a jumper on her morning walks.

As Milne examined the jumper, the fingertip of a cream-coloured rubber glove fell out. He knew it wasn't from the mortuary but couldn't say where it came from. Officers who retrieved Allison from beneath the bridge wore gloves. In the difficult process of pulling her body to the top of the bridge, it was possible one of the gloves tore. Milne would later tell a court it was more likely the glove tip got there during the recovery of the body, rather than being deposited by a killer.

Pink nail polish on her fingers was worn and absent in areas. Her height was 170 centimetres and weight was 72 kilograms. Decomposition had reduced her body weight. Discolouration of the skin, areas of skin slippage and mummification – accelerated loss of moisture – all matched the position the body was found in: signs Allison had been under the bridge all along.

'This is suggestive of the body coming to be in the position in which it was found within a relatively short period of time after death,' Milne wrote.

Soft tissue decomposition meant Milne could not examine the eyes, ears, nose, lips and tongue. In the exhaustive examination that followed, hampered by the decomposed state of the body, he could only identify three possible injuries. The first was a possible subdural haemorrhage. From granular brown material found between the left side of the brain and the dura – the tough, outermost membrane covering the brain – Milne surmised there might have been an impact to the head with a moderate degree of force.

'If death was the result of a subdural haemorrhage, it could have taken hours to occur after the time of impact,' Milne wrote.

Secondly, there was a chipped tooth, which could indicate a blow to the mouth region, 'probably of a mild or moderate degree of force'. But there was no evidence of when the chip occurred. Thirdly, there was a bruise, or possible haemorrhage, on the left inner chest wall, which indicated there might have been an impact of a probably mild force to the chest area.

Milne noted the significant soft tissue loss, particularly from the face, forearms and lower left leg, could indicate injuries in those areas that were now impossible to detect. It was speculative. Allison had been exposed to the elements too long for certainty.

There were no fractures to the skull, nasal bone or ribs. There was no evidence of sexual assault. The lungs did not have the appearance of drowning.

Milne examined Allison's history. She had suffered from asthma and had been prescribed Ventolin and Seretide inhalers, but her condition did not appear to be severe. He noted she had been prescribed Zoloft, or sertraline, for depression.

'This had been a long term condition,' wrote Milne, 'being present after the birth of her first child in 2001.'

Allison had a history of high blood pressure and diabetes associated with pregnancy, and as a child had probable low thyroid function.

Levels of the antidepressant sertraline and its metabolite desmethylsertraline would be found in the blood. Sertraline overdose could cause vomiting, lethargy, difficulty walking, seizures, a rapid heart rate and death, Milne noted. Reaching conclusions on the amount of the drug was difficult, not least because decomposition could have altered the levels in the blood. Only blood from the liver was available, which wasn't ideal. Normally, Milne would have taken a specimen from the blood vessels in the legs. And the sertraline could have been expected to move around the body after death, so he could have been seeing a distorted level. Milne found that as a consequence of the effects of decomposition, there was 'insufficient evidence' to say sertraline overdose was the cause of death. Her blood-alcohol concentration of 0.095 could be attributed to processes in the body after death.

'In my opinion the cause of death cannot be determined,' Milne concluded. 'The degree of decomposition was significant and this limited interpretation of all facets of the post mortem examination. It is most likely the effects of decomposition destroyed or concealed evidence of the cause of death.'

At about 3 pm on the day of the autopsy, forensic odontologist Dr Alexander Forrest, examining the body and using dental records, confirmed the woman was Allison.

Police kept a lid on the results of the post mortem. For all anyone knew throughout the remainder of the investigation, police knew exactly how Allison died.

Gerard was in the money, or at least stood to be. Allison had three life insurance and superannuation policies and Gerard wasted no time in trying to claim them. Life insurance companies generally ask to be told as soon as possible when a policyholder dies. Gerard took the advice to the extreme end of the range. On the day the body was found under Kholo Creek Bridge, he advised insurers of the discovery. The following day – autopsy day – he further advised insurers he planned to claim on her policies. Pathologist Nathan Milne had not yet confirmed the body was Allison when the insurers were contacted. Subsequently, Gerard sought a death certificate as a matter of urgency. When he received it, he lodged claims on each of Allison's policies and asked they be expedited. Altogether, the policies provided for a $975,000 payout upon her death.

In the months leading to her disappearance, Allison and Gerard had been frequently in touch with their financial adviser, Tommy Laskaris, about reducing their life insurance cover. One of Gerard's policies, a Whole of Life Plan with AMP, dated all the way back to 1981 when, at ten, he first moved to Toowoomba and his father worked as a life insurance salesman. Gerard took on other policies over the years, which added up to a total payout of $3 million if he was to die. Allison followed his lead and took out a policy with TAL in April 2000. She took out a separate Asteron Life Policy in March 2008. A third, separate superannuation policy included death cover.

Allison and Gerard had only just discovered they both had an extra level of death cover through their superannuation funds. Amid the couple's other financial challenges, their insurance premiums were overdue and they started trying to reduce the payments. On 17 April, just three days before Allison was reported missing, she emailed Laskaris asking what he'd found out about reducing her policies. The same day, Laskaris inquired with insurers about scaling back Allison and Gerard's cover by $200,000 each. When Allison died, her cover had not yet been reduced.

Gerard – the sole beneficiary of Allison's will – stood to pocket the payout as long as he was not found to be involved in her death.

Police went to speak to Gerard on the day of the post mortem and found him in the office of Peter Davis SC, a heavy-hitting barrister of more than 20 years' experience. Gerard was calling in extra legal firepower.

Courier-Mail photographer Nathan Richter had followed Gerard to Davis's office too, tailing the real estate agent all the way from his parents' Kenmore home to the city in a white-knuckle ride with graduate journalist Kris Crane beside him. Richter, who lived in Kenmore, had been assigned to Allison's disappearance since the beginning and had become a thorn in the side of Gerard and his family.

Seeing Gerard get dropped off in the city, the photographer double-parked his car and sprinted through the crowds of city office workers to catch up. He got a photo of Gerard walking in front of a Pie Face store, phone to his right ear, covering the scratch marks on his cheek.

On returning to his car, Richter discovered his pursuit of Gerard hadn't gone unnoticed when a car pulled up alongside him and the irate driver unleashed a barrage of abuse. The penny dropped. Richter must have inadvertently put himself between Gerard and a police surveillance team covertly tracking him.

That afternoon, solicitor Darren Mahony confirmed Gerard had sought additional legal advice from Davis.

'My client is devastated by the loss of his wife,' Mahony said in a statement. 'His family is devastated. His primary concern is the welfare of his three very young daughters and attempting to provide some stability and normality to them given the tragic news and the unrelenting media barrage. Given the intense public interest in the matter, no doubt prudent people would understand the reasonableness of seeking such advice.'

With the discovery of the body, the police forward command post moved from Brookfield Showground to the Tyamolum Scout Campsite near Kholo Creek Bridge. Mark Ainsworth told media the search area extended more than 500 metres from the bridge, and a team of 25 detectives was working on the investigation.

'Obviously there's been a deal of rain on the Friday night and Saturday, so we've got to examine all that as well . . . if the body has washed down to its final resting place or something else happened,' he said.

Even with the breakthrough of locating Allison's body, the police had an overwhelming number of questions. They now knew where she'd been the whole time they were searching, but how did she end up there? And who was responsible?

Pandora's box

A growing tide of public opinion against Gerard Baden-Clay had compelled Brookfield resident Hedley Thomas to act. Thomas, a leading journalist, had lived in Brookfield for 13 years. There weren't many people in the little community he didn't know. Gerard was not a close friend, but certainly an acquaintance. Thomas had chatted to him and had no problem with him. Surely the man he knew from shared shifts barbecuing burgers and sausages for school fundraisers couldn't have killed the mother of his three children.

Based at *The Australian*'s Brisbane office, Thomas had built a career and formidable reputation from being unafraid to take a contrarian view. Everyone seemed to think Gerard had killed his wife. Thomas had told friends at a party within days of Allison's disappearance that Gerard was the top suspect and it didn't look good for him, but the journalist also wanted to believe differently. It bothered him that people seemed to be lining up to knock Gerard down, yet no one he knew openly bagged the real estate agent before Allison went missing.

Police seemed focused on Gerard, and Thomas knew better than most that a rush to judgment could lead to a miscarriage of justice. He earnt a Gold Walkley, one of the highest awards in Australian journalism, for stories exposing the Australian Federal Police's flawed pursuit of Mohamed Haneef, a Gold Coast doctor wrongly accused of terrorism in 2007 and made to look guilty by misleading police leaks to the media. Thomas was concerned some of the media stories and public sentiment about Gerard were starting to take on a similar negative tone, perhaps encouraged by police.

Thomas thought Gerard might be getting bad advice. Everyone suspected the real estate agent had murdered his wife. If he wanted to stop looking guilty, he had to stop acting guilty. Stop running and start standing up for his wife. Show his face at the command centre at the Brookfield Showground. Make an appeal and help find Allison. He needed to speak up, not remain silent.

With police and public suspicions soaring, Thomas paid him a visit at the Kenmore home of his parents, Nigel and Elaine, on the morning of Monday 30 April 2012. They'd exchanged texts and Gerard had invited him over. Thomas was conscious police had turned the place upside down and that it was probably bugged. Inside, the two men suspiciously eyed the vase of flowers on the kitchen table. They went out into the back garden to talk.

Thomas wasn't covering the story and didn't intend to. But if Gerard wanted to end his frustrating silence and go public, he was willing to get involved. It would have to be no holds barred.

Their chat was off the record, so what Gerard said to the journalist is unknown. Gerard's three daughters played around them as they spoke. The girls were all over their father, whom they obviously loved. One climbed onto Gerard's lap and reached out with both hands to touch his new beard.

'Daddy, when are you going to shave?' she asked, interrupting the chat with Thomas.

'I'm growing it for Mummy, until we find her,' he replied.

As Thomas drove away from the Baden-Clay seniors' house, leaving Gerard to weigh his options, he heard a breaking news story on the radio. While he had been talking to Gerard at Kenmore, a kayaker had discovered a woman's body under Kholo Creek Bridge. Thomas knew it had to be Allison. He pulled his car over and, at 12.41 pm, sent a text to Gerard.

'Gerard, brace the children for bad news. There are reports of a body being found.' Gerard never replied.

Thomas arrived home feeling sick about the discovery of the body and believing police were too quick to judge Gerard. He said as much to his wife, Ruth, before they went to bed that night. He drifted off to sleep with the meeting, and tragic news, turning over in his mind.

That night he had a dark dream that would long unsettle him. He was back at Nigel and Elaine's house, sitting opposite Gerard in the autumn sunshine. Only this time, as they spoke, Gerard's hand casually reached over to a small box on the table between them, lifting the lid. First one, then dozens, then hundreds of angry wasps swarmed from the box and massed around Gerard's face in a thick black cloud. Thomas frantically tried to swipe them away, unable to see Gerard's face through the veil of wasps hanging over him. Gerard carried on talking, oblivious. Thomas woke with a start.

The journalist wanted to react with logic, rather than emotion, but he couldn't shake the feeling his dream was significant. He asked his wife, Ruth, a fellow journalist and always a reliable sounding board, what she thought. It's simple, she replied. His subconscious was telling him what his conscious mind had resisted – Gerard's story didn't ring true. The dream, she offered, symbolised Gerard opening Pandora's box and spreading a stream of lies over their small community.

Ruth, like Hedley, had known Gerard and Allison. She felt heartbroken for Allison's family and friends. The search had weighed heavily on the entire suburb. Brookfield was a small place and the Thomas's daughter went to Brookfield State School with the Baden-Clay girls. Everyone at the school knew Allison and Gerard. Allison was always helping out with reading or maths, while Gerard, vice-president of the P & C, seemed a permanent fixture too in his eye-catching gold Century 21 jacket.

The school organised counselling sessions for students, but the intensive search had been inescapable: there were traces of it all over Brookfield. The main road in and out of the suburb led past both the Baden-Clays' home and the police command post. Police had based themselves at the Brookfield Showground, just metres from the school and next door to the local shop. Uniformed officers and orange-clad SES workers seemed to be everywhere, day after day, searching, organising, asking questions. Children saw police divers combing the creeks and waterholes where they spent their summers swimming and larking about. And with vast tracts of uninhabited bushland to check, authorities called on residents to help by either searching their own large blocks or the swathes of state forest bounding the suburb.

Ruth and her daughter spent hours walking through the bush calling Allison's name. Countless others had done the same. Overhead, helicopters circled endlessly, like the foreboding wasps in Hedley Thomas's dream.

Still curious about his nightmare, and more than a little spooked, Thomas Googled 'dream analysis' and 'wasps'. The results heightened his unease.

'Wasps stand for "low" instincts, desires and feelings, especially rage, blind aggressiveness, hate or revenge,' one site read.

Families divided

The mistrust was mutual when Gerard Baden-Clay sat across a picnic table from Allison's father, Geoff Dickie, to discuss funeral arrangements. They were meeting at Rafting Ground Reserve, a popular park with a children's playground on Moggill Road in Brookfield. Heavily treed and next to a winding creek, it's normally a peaceful pit stop from the busy road beside it, but the meeting turned into a showdown.

Before they started talking, Gerard held up a digital recorder and asked Geoff if he would mind if he recorded the conversation. It came across more as a statement of intent than a request. Geoff – according to friends who recounted the conversation – had a rare flash of anger. He was there to talk about his daughter's funeral. Why would Gerard want to record that?

Gerard said it was so he didn't forget anything. The explanation was hard for Geoff to accept. It seemed more likely that Gerard was protecting his back, with the implication that he suspected Geoff might twist their chat, misreport it.

Showing no hint of being perturbed by his father-in-law's anger, Gerard placed the recorder in a breast pocket. Not once had Gerard asked the Dickies how they were. Not once did he say he was sorry for their loss. Crows cawed in the background as they continued their tense discussion.

In the days leading up to the funeral, Gerard sent through a list of demands. He wanted a Scouts emblem printed on the front of the service notes. He wanted to see all the speeches in advance. He wanted to give his own speech at the funeral. And he wanted to be the last to speak. Allison's family did not want Gerard to speak at all, but he had a bargaining chip. If he didn't get his way, he warned the Dickies, he would not bring his daughters. The thought of the girls missing out on their mother's funeral terrified Geoff and Priscilla.

Meanwhile, Gerard's family and friends knew who to blame for the mounting tide of opinion against them: the media. The Baden-Clays adopted a 'them and us' approach, laid bare in a Facebook post from Olivia Walton's husband. Ian Walton had left his Flight Centre career behind him and was a pastor at the Northreach Baptist Church in Townsville. Walton wrote, soon after Allison's body was discovered that the family was 'struck down but not destroyed', quoting the Bible, and proceeded to rail against the reporting of the case. He said that the media was: 'glorying in the most revolting and salacious gossip. They seem determined to do all possible to damage and destroy. They have virtually imprisoned us in the house! They have NO regard for Allison or her family – despite their "crocodile tears".' He added that there may be more and worse to come, and urged supporters not put their trust in what they read.

Dr Bruce Flegg was starting to have some serious concerns about his friendship with Gerard. When Allison first went missing, murder was the last thing on Flegg's mind. He knew, through Gerard, that Allison battled depression and assumed she had simply run off. The newly appointed Housing Minister had even offered Gerard accommodation at his own hilltop Brookfield home.

Several days into the search, Flegg still did not suspect foul play and visited Gerard at his parents' home in Kenmore. 'What happened to you?' the MP asked when he saw the scratches on Gerard's face for the first time.

'I crashed the car,' Gerard replied, somewhat disingenuously.

Another theory started to form in his mind. Gerard had asked him twice in recent months for hundreds of thousands of dollars. Flegg started to suspect loan sharks could be behind Allison's sudden disappearance.

'Mate, you haven't borrowed money off the wrong people, have you?' he asked. Gerard quashed the theory.

One thing that did stand out to Flegg was Gerard's reluctance to speak about his wife at all – you'd think he'd want to talk about nothing else.

After Allison's body was discovered, a phone call from Gerard rang alarm bells. Reports had just appeared in the media of a traffic camera at the Kenmore roundabout, where the road branches off to Brookfield. Afterwards, Gerard phoned Flegg and wanted to know all about the camera. He asked Flegg if he knew whether the camera recorded all the time. The request for information about the camera was a bit like Gerard's request for loans – blunt, and a touch demanding. It was couched in terms of it being useful to help catch the killer, but Flegg couldn't help but feel suspicious. He told Gerard he'd have to get back to him, but never did.

A couple of days later, police wanted to speak to Flegg. Detective Sergeant Gavin Pascoe, from Homicide, asked Flegg about his contact with Gerard. In particular, Pascoe wanted to know what phones Flegg had and whether he had given anything to Gerard. Flegg gave Pascoe a statement saying he hadn't given Gerard a phone, car, money or anything else other than moral support, and to the best of his knowledge no one else had. It turned out that Flegg's friend Sue Heath had taken the phone around to Gerard.

Flegg asked Gerard to return it, but he kept stalling and wouldn't give it back. The key person of interest in a murder probe was running around with a Cabinet minister's phone.

Flowers for Allison

Every question about Allison's death remained unanswered. Police knew her funeral would be charged with emotion. As the date approached, detectives in the Major Incident Room were throwing around ideas. During this brainstorming, they hit upon a unique trap to catch a killer. A magistrate granted warrants approving their plan: hours before the funeral, a tiny recording device was hidden among the dozens of flowers draped over Allison's rosewood coffin.

The plan was to close St Paul's Anglican Church at Ipswich to all except immediate family before the service. Gerard was told he had time to visit Allison alone, as she lay on a bed of satin. Perhaps, in the solitude, he would tearfully apologise. Perhaps he would confess. It was a long shot, but modern policing is as much about lateral thinking as it is old-fashioned legwork.

On the day of the funeral, all the detectives investigating the case joined mourners gathering outside the 153-year-old, brick, Gothic Revival church, the oldest in Queensland's Anglican network. But their bold plan was brought unstuck when someone from the church, unaware of the arrangements, opened the doors early and mourners started respectfully shuffling inside. Gerard would not have a moment alone with his wife after all. The misunderstanding barely mattered, as Gerard was running concerningly late. So late that Allison's family began to wonder if he was going to turn up at all.

His demands to speak last at the funeral had been denied and, minutes before the 11 am service was to begin, he hadn't arrived. Priscilla Dickie nervously turned to family and said he wasn't going to come. Allison's cousin Jodie Dann, sitting one row behind search commander Mark Laing, was feeling sick. Would Gerard really carry through on his threat and keep his daughters away from their mother's funeral?

'I think I'm going to throw up,' Dann whispered.

'Use this,' Laing replied, handing over his police cap.

Dann took the hat. But it wasn't needed. With three minutes to spare, Gerard strolled into the church with the girls. Allison's three devastated daughters sat in the front left pew with their father and aunt, Olivia Walton. Priscilla, seated in the front row on the opposite side, couldn't take her eyes off the girls, seated in front of the coffin and a large framed portrait of their mother.

Her heart on the verge of breaking, Priscilla stood up, walked to the front row and wedged herself next to the girls, sending Olivia to join her husband, Ian, in the row behind. For most of the rest of the service, Priscilla cuddled the youngest of the girls.

Laing couldn't take his eyes off Gerard. Several times, Laing's partner nudged him to try to stop him staring, but he was lost in a cloud of grief. On the front of service booklet was a photo of Allison – taken on the steps of Customs House, to mark her engagement to Gerard – and the message, 'Celebrating the life of Allison Baden-Clay'. The Dickies had refused to put a Scouts emblem on the booklet. Allison might have carried the Baden-Clay name, but her links with Baden-Powell and the Scout movement ended there.

Allison's sister, Vanessa Fowler, and brother, Ashley Dickie, delivered the eulogy between them. Ashley told the service he was just two weeks old when Allison, in grade one, took him into her class as a living, breathing show-and-tell. Later, he had to grin and bear it when Allison and Vanessa used him as their very own doll.

Vanessa spoke of Allison's achievements, the most important of which were her daughters. Allison was the reading volunteer at school, the tuckshop lady and the mum who took her girls to ballet, music, choir and netball. She was the one constantly striving to improve herself, while always putting the needs of others before her own.

'She could laugh for herself, by herself and at herself, long after the punch line had been delivered,' said Vanessa.

The eulogy had not been shown to Gerard in advance and it became rather pointed as it went on. Allison – found 14 kilometres from home – had a 'love of chocolate and loathing of exercise' and would sit on the bed with a diet book in one hand and a sweet in the other, Vanessa told her fellow mourners. '[At school] she was always the last one out of the change rooms and the first one in, dragging her feet around the oval and making any excuse to get out of PE. Exercise and going to the gym were just not her thing.'

Vanessa kept her composure until the end. She had a promise to make to her sister: 'Allison, there are many questions that are unanswered, many pieces of the puzzle that need to be put together, and we, your family, pledge to you that we will have these questions answered. We will bring you justice because you deserve nothing less. "Why then, why there, why now?" we cry. "Why did she die?" The heavens are silent.

'What she is remembered for depends on us. How we choose to live will decide its meaning . . . She will be remembered for her acts of kindness and love. Allison, your loss has been felt throughout the country, by people who do not know you. Your passing has heightened the need for all of us to provide a safe and peaceful community and world for our children. You have been taken from us far too early but you will never be forgotten by all those who knew you and loved you.'

Allison was loved, and sorely missed. More than 600 people gathered at the funeral to pay their respects. There were too many to fit in the church, so some stood outside. Two guards of honour formed. Students from Ipswich Girls' Grammar, Allison's old school, and members of the Queensland Fire and Rescue Service, Geoff's former workplace, lined up on each side of the sloping bitumen road to the church for the coffin to be carried to the waiting hearse.

Afterwards, mourners approached Gerard to shake his hand or hug him tight. His eyes were red and misted. Others were waiting for their turn to console Gerard when a man in a dark suit moved purposefully through the milling crowd. Detective Sergeant Peter Roddick, from Homicide, stopped only when he came face to face with Gerard. Everyone else would have to wait. Roddick leant in close and they shook hands.

Those standing nearby thought Roddick sounded sincere as he offered his condolences. But there was something else about the approach. The detective was right up in Gerard's face. The unspoken message for Gerard was there was nowhere to hide. Even at his wife's funeral, he wasn't safe from the detectives on his tail. Wherever he went they would be watching him. Gerard looked shocked to have been approached.

'I just hope you find who did this,' he said.

'Don't worry, Gerard, we will,' Roddick replied, gripping Gerard's arm firmly.

When Roddick walked off, Mark Ainsworth made his way through the crowd until he was in front of Gerard. Ainsworth had been at the forefront of Operation Kilo Intrigue for three weeks, but it was the first time he had met Gerard. The senior cop went to introduce himself but it wasn't necessary.

'I recognise you from the TV,' Gerard said.

'I'm sorry about the death of your wife,' Ainsworth said as they shook hands.

Gerard repeated that he hoped police found the person who did this. Ainsworth assured Gerard they would.

The bug hidden on Allison's coffin had been part of a highly secretive operation, but the cluey funeral director had put two and two together. As the service ended he had some concerns. If the covert recording device had batteries, they could explode in the cremation process. It was a potential workplace health and safety concern.

After the funeral, he warned a detective there wasn't much time to remove any objects that may have been left with the coffin.

Detectives didn't reveal much, but the expensive device had already been spirited away. It was a shame it hadn't worked but they were undeterred. They were determined to solve this case.

No stone unturned

As pressure was mounting on Gerard, it was also being felt by police. With the search and rescue parts of the operation wound up, the investigation had gone from the background to the forefront of the case. The public, and family, wanted answers.

The test results on the bloodstain in the rear of Allison's Captiva were coming back in stages. First, when they were lacking a reference sample, police could only confirm it was female blood. Next, after Priscilla and Geoff Dickie provided DNA samples, police confirmed it was from a female offspring of the couple. Finally, after the discovery of Allison's body, police had a definitive DNA reference sample. The blood in the car came back a match to Allison. The only other person who had driven that vehicle was Gerard.

Other incriminating evidence emerged in a forensic examination of Gerard's iPhone. Downloading the contents of the phone had shown it was used to Google the words 'taking the fifth' just after 10 pm Wednesday 18 April, two days before he reported Allison missing. The American term, referring to the Fifth Amendment in the US Bill of Rights, is invoked when a person refuses to speak to police or in court because their testimony could be used against them. At 7.09 am on 20 April, six minutes before he phoned police to report Allison missing, Gerard also appeared to have searched the term 'self-incrimination'. Ironically, the search itself seemed incriminating from a man whose wife had vanished.

The police Electronic Evidence Examination Unit also discovered an inconsistency in Gerard's story: his iPhone was connected to a charger at 1.48 am on the day Allison vanished. Connecting an iPhone to a charger leaves a little-known electronic trail. Gerard had told police he went to bed at 10 pm and slept until after 6 am.

Although a case seemed to be slowly building against the high-profile estate agent, police had to keep an open mind. The detectives in the Major Incident Room at Indooroopilly set about checking every angle. And for every productive lead they chased down, there were hundreds of dead ends. Prominent cases, such as this, generated myriad tips and lines of inquiry. Often it was the work no one saw – that came to nothing – which was the hardest and most time-consuming.

Detective Senior Constable Grant Linwood from Homicide returned from leave on Monday 23 April 2012 and went straight into Operation Kilo Intrigue. Linwood had spent a good deal of the previous two years working on the investigation into Daniel Morcombe's murder as it moved into the covert operation phase.

In the Morcombe case, undercover detectives used a Canadian technique known as the 'Mr Big' sting to convince serial child sex offender Brett Peter Cowan he was being recruited into a criminal gang. Cowan fell hook, line and sinker for the story 'the gang' was involved in drugs, guns, black market crayfish, prostitution and even blood diamonds. Before letting him in on the big stuff, they told him, the gang needed to be sure he wasn't linked to any major crimes which could come back to haunt them. Thinking he was about to score a huge payday, Cowan confessed to abducting Daniel and murdering him on an isolated macadamia farm in the Sunshine Coast hinterland. Later, when he led the undercover operatives to Daniel's remains in August 2011, he ended a long and painful search.

On the Baden-Clay investigation, Linwood would prepare a table of all the 'person of interest and vehicle of interest' sightings around Brookfield and Kholo Creek. It ran for pages and pages, ranging from men loitering on the street to mysterious vans and other vehicles. They all had to be ruled out as being connected to Allison's disappearance.

The MIR went through the process of identifying known sex offenders in the western suburbs and checking their locations on the night. They looked back at other sex offences in the previous three months, such as random attacks on bikeways or peeping Tom incidents.

Any person stopped by police for suspicious behaviour – or street-checked – in the Brisbane West police district in the lead-up to Allison's disappearance was reviewed as a potential suspect. Assaults in the Brisbane West police district were examined for parallels. Two teenagers fighting over a skateboard, a road rage attack and drunks at a local train station were among the cases scrutinised.

The high-profile nature of the case also brought out everyone from the well-meaning to the misguided to the downright bonkers. One caller to Crime Stoppers reported seeing a deer running across a Brookfield road on the night Allison disappeared and thought it should be reported. Another provided details of a man supposedly having an affair with Allison – when police checked they found it was untrue and malicious.

On another occasion, detectives were in the MIR when Nigel Baden-Clay called to report a stranger – and a very strange one, at that – was in front of his Kenmore home talking about Allison. When the detectives arrived, they found colleagues in uniform had already put the man in the back of their police car. He was swinging a pendulum back and forth and insisted he was communicating with Allison before dramatically announcing she had revealed her killer.

'And he lives there,' he shouted, pointing to the Baden-Clay home.

Police found the man had also been harassing Scotland Yard about the disappearance of Madeleine McCann in Portugal.

Separately, a Crime Stoppers caller urged police to take account of the Cosmic Pendulum. Nigel himself passed on details of dreams for detectives to follow up.

Gerard too was fielding prank calls at his home and business. One caller rang the real estate agent saying he wanted to sell his home in Brisbane's west. When Gerard inquired as to where the home was, the caller said it was at the corner of Murder Drive and Homicide Avenue.

On top of the information flowing to police, tips and rumours were flooding in to newsrooms. One persistent suggestion was that Nigel had taken his life in a park near his home. After the 50th tip within a few days about Nigel's supposed demise, *Courier-Mail* investigative journalist Josh Robertson called Nigel's Kenmore home.

'Hello,' Nigel answered. Robertson made his excuses and quickly hung up.

Another early focus of investigations was the vacuum cleaner Nigel loaded into his car at Brookfield on the morning Allison was reported missing. Aside from a ball of matted hair and fluff inside, police found tantalising pieces of a shredded document. Specialist document examiners spent weeks painstakingly reassembling the pieces like a jigsaw. When they were finished they discovered it was nothing more than an entirely blank piece of paper. Tests did not find any traces of blood on the inside or exterior of the vacuum.

In the search for Allison's missing mobile phone, the police checks extended to rooftops and septic tanks. A Brookfield resident found a screw had been taken out of her septic tank and called police, who came out and checked it but found nothing to link it to Allison.

Scientific officers went over Gerard and Allison's house in minute detail, checking for blood or other evidence. The entry and exit points, manhole, floor, furniture, kitchen knives, camping gear, keys, roof, drainpipes, carport, patio and a camping trailer in the carport were closely examined. Plants were growing over the septic system so it was clear it hadn't been opened. Any stains were tested, including one on a kitchen scissors block and another in the carpet in the main bedroom.

Hope was pinned on the traffic camera at the Kenmore roundabout that Gerard had asked Dr Bruce Flegg about. On the night Allison went missing, it had recorded grainy vision of what could have been Allison and Gerard's Holden Captiva. One of the Homicide detectives had a background in auto theft investigations and knew more about cars than anyone his colleagues had ever met. To the amazement of the other police on the case, the detective put together a 'line-up' of cars to compare with the blurry CCTV images from the roundabout and other witness statements.

Detectives borrowed a Holden Captiva from a car dealership and drove it to the roundabout at about the same time of night to see if it matched the vehicle in the footage, but nothing conclusive was revealed.

An officer of similar size to Allison volunteered to be a 'body', and they loaded her into various parts of the Captiva and confirmed she could fit.

Detectives conducted other experiments. Allison had been found wearing running shoes, and investigators wondered if laces looked different if tied by someone else. So the investigators tried tying each other's shoelaces. They found the exercise was pointless because, even in the office, everyone tied their laces differently. One detective routinely tied his own laces differently on each shoe.

Any fragment that could possibly have been a piece of Allison's chipped tooth was sent to forensic odontologist Dr Alexander Forrest to examine. Hundreds of tiny objects from the vacuum, cars and Brookfield home were dispatched to Forrest, but the missing tooth chip was never found. Most of the items turned out to be stones. Police liked to say no stone was left unturned.

Almost 1500 lines of inquiry were run out during Operation Kilo Intrigue, three times as many as the average murder investigation.

'Net detectives

Among all the outlandish tips and spooky dreams that peppered the Baden-Clay investigation, there was one 'eerie feeling' that would truly send a shiver down the spine of many. On 28 April 2012, a Brisbane resident using the cybername 'Alicat' logged on to the popular Websleuths crime site to contribute to a free-wheeling discussion about the search for Allison Baden-Clay: 'I'm out this way,' she wrote, 'and I keep getting eerie feelings around Kholo Creek overpass. I know it probably sounds silly, but it's the "what if".'

Two days later, Allison's body was found under that exact overpass. It shocked many and fuelled a feeling on the message board, however misguided, that ordinary citizens could help contribute to the investigation.

The amateur sleuth has long been a staple in crime fiction. The idea that average Joes and Joesephines can crack cases that have stumped the professionals appeals to armchair detectives the world over. The internet has taken this fascination to a new level. About ten years ago, websites began springing up which allowed crime buffs to read about and debate high-profile crimes – Justice Quest, Official Cold Case Investigations, Porchlight International and Websleuths among them.

In the main, they focused on missing persons and cold cases. There have been instances where users have actually solved cases by linking unidentified bodies with missing persons reports. But police around the world are split on the merits of citizen detectives. Some jurisdictions in the United States upload details of crimes and missing persons cases to public websites, while others regard keen amateurs as a hindrance.

Allison Baden-Clay's mysterious disappearance would become one of the first Australian cases to make a big impact on international crime forums. The first posting on the US-based Websleuths appeared on the day Allison was reported missing.

'This lady is missing less than 1 kilometre from my house,' wrote Brookfield resident 'Kiwijayne', who added a link to the initial police press release.

Soon more people, local and otherwise, were commenting and 'Allison Baden-Clay of Australia', as it was listed, appeared on the website's list of 'hot cases'. *The Guardian* reported in 2010 that the site attracted 25,000 interactive users a day. Unrestrained by laws governing mainstream media, Websleuths became the 'go-to' site for the latest theories and rumours – some spot on, and some wildly off beam.

It's worth noting that before things went online, Brookfield residents were already serviced by a well-oiled, well-staffed and well-resourced rumour mill. The advent of an online forum where people could anonymously share information, opinions and theories turned it into a gossipy village on steroids. For every person commenting, more watched from the sidelines.

Speculation about the identities of some of the more prolific posters became a source of local gossip in itself. According to the grapevine, as well as your average curtain-twitchers, lawyers, doctors and other professionals were joining the fray. Brookfield lore has it that a well-regarded local, familiar with the justice system, was the person who photographed hundreds of pages of court documents on a smartphone and posted them online. Every witness statement would mysteriously appear on the internet, and the pages clearly weren't official copies, which were available from the court registry for a hefty fee.

People weren't merely observing the Baden-Clay investigation, they were actively seeking to participate in it, to help solve the crime or at least to satisfy their own curiosity about some of the perplexing rumours.

One rumour that had locals transfixed revolved around a chain that reportedly vanished from the Kenmore Village shopping centre car park around the time of the murder. Sleuthers became convinced it was used to either move or dispose of Allison's body. One mum started quizzing shopping centre staff and was told security guards had indeed been searching for the chain. A local lawyer followed it up, inspecting the replacement chain and concluding it would be very easy to remove should anyone wish to pinch it in the dead of night.

Gerard's affair with Toni McHugh was all over the internet long before it was being reported by news outlets. Over on Aussie Criminals and Crooks, blogger Robbo put McHugh's photo online in the week after Allison's body was discovered. With the online debate in overdrive, one Brookfield resident logged in as 'Keyboredom' and tried to hose things down.

'I live very near the missing lady's house too, so would just like to point out that living in the area doesn't make me an expert, and local gossip in Brisbane's "leafy western suburbs" is one of its biggest problems. People take an inch and create a mile. I can guarantee the husband would not be the only local to be carrying on a "common knowledge" affair . . . Everyone is so nosey he'd have to have a network of tunnels to escape the Flying Monkeys of Brookfield.'

Keyboredom was trying to stop a runaway train.

Allison's case was truly a murder of the modern age. People were logging on to get the latest news or gossip unfiltered and uncensored. But, with no gatekeepers or fact-checkers, there were predictably some shocking stuff-ups. A series of Chinese whispers ended with real estate agent Jocelyn Frost being wrongly identified on Websleuths as Gerard's mistress.

On 6 June 2012, Websleuths member CaseClosed compiled a 'rumour list' to track tips discussed online but not in mainstream media. With its references to cause of death (COD) and domestic violence (DV), it's fascinating reading and, in hindsight, demonstrates the jumble of fact and fiction that both confused and fuelled online discussion:

Police were at the family home the night before her disappearance; Lawyer present when police arrived at family home; Children were home and said something odd to police; Victim was on medication for depression; Victim could not cope at some stage due to depression/needed GBC's help daily; DV/ broken arm/fallen down stairs, etc; COD is strangulation/bath water in her lung; Body found with missing limbs/chains, etc; Fight at a restaurant; Chains missing from Coles/construction site; Murder for hire by triads/bikies/loan sharks, etc; NBC sitting at bus stop in the middle of the night; NBC looking frail/could have dementia; Second or more mistresses; Pregnant mistress who is no longer pregnant; Blood found in one of the family cars; Scratches on GBC's chest/bruises on chest, etc; NBC/GBC washing cars Friday morning; Family home with windows boarded up; Prado damaged prior to her disappearance; Evidence of Google searches in computers about masking DNA/accessing Life insurance; Tattooed man with a white van, with long blond hair, wearing gardening gloves seen near Kholo bridge. THE ABOVE ARE ALL RUMOURS!

Elsewhere online, Ipswich councillor Paul Tully was in no doubt about who killed Allison Baden-Clay. Police had yet to make an arrest, but Tully was ready to point the finger in his regular blog – only, everyone missed it. Tully, as always skating close to the line, used a secret code in writing about the case: the first letter of each sentence spelled out a message.

May 5 2012

The noose is slowly tightening around the killer of Brookfield mother-of-three Allison Baden-Clay.

Hopes of ever finding her alive faded quickly as the search for her body dragged on for over a week after her bizarre disappearance last month.

Even from day 1, with the rapid deployment of police and SES volunteers, the entire situation looked very grim for Allison's family.

Her disappearance was said to have occurred during a late night walk through the suburb, with even old gold mine shafts thoroughly checked to see if she had met some accident or possibly foul play.

Until the weekend rain of 28-29 April, her body could have remained concealed forever in Kholo Creek near Mt Crosby to be long forgotten by the general public while her family grieved for decades.

So it was a remarkable twist of fate with the unseasonal April showers which finally switched the police enquiries from a missing person investigation to a murder investigation.

Brookfield residents who were stunned by Mrs Baden-Clay's disappearance were shocked by the fact this well-respected, cheerful local mum had been brutally killed in the middle of the night in, or near, their quiet piece of Brisbane suburbia.

And the leafy, tranquil suburb of Brookfield was changed forever in the twinkling of an eye.

No one dared to speak too openly of their individual speculation as to the possible identity of the killer but the community's private thoughts and feelings became part of the grieving process not only for the family but the wider Brookfield community.

During the 10 days preceding the discovery of Allison's body, the local tight-knit community had hoped and prayed for a miracle.

During that time, the community worked, searched and prayed together in the belief Allison might eventually come home – but that was not to be.

In Brisbane's western suburbs, the possibility of finding her alive kept the community spirit intact but it was all crushed with that terrible discovery by a canoeist at Kholo Creek near the Brisbane River, opposite Karalee.

During that time, the love for Allison by her family and the broader community was readily apparent.

In the police media conference which followed soon after her disappearance, Allison's parents Geoff and Priscilla Dickie made an emotional appeal for her return, with their grief almost overwhelming, but in the end their heartfelt appeal was to count for nothing.

The final conclusion to this shocking crime is still to be played out but the family and the community can only hope and pray the killer is quickly caught.

Although Tully was rather more outspoken than most members of the community, he was spot-on in his last sentence.

Truth to tell

Toni McHugh scanned the room. She couldn't see Allison Baden-Clay among the crowd at the Real Estate Institute of Queensland conference. McHugh had been braced for an uncomfortable encounter with her lover's wife since the day before, when Gerard told her Allison was going. Toni had really given him a piece of her mind about it on the phone. But as she looked around at the crowd gathered at the Brisbane Convention and Exhibition Centre that Friday 20 April 2012, she could see neither Allison nor Kate Rankin, the Century 21 Westside staffer who was supposed to go with her.

McHugh had started a new job in property management at Blocksidge & Ferguson the week before and had been looking forward to the event – until Gerard yet again pulled the rug from under her. Since being forced out of Century 21 Westside in 2011, when Allison found out about the affair and demanded her immediate departure, McHugh had drifted from one job to the next. The stress had got to her so much that she experienced a panic attack one day at work. McHugh had hoped catching up with colleagues at the property management conference would give her a boost. The last thing she wanted was to run into her rival.

With Allison nowhere to be seen, McHugh was buoyed by the brief hope her lover had finally found some courage and told his wife the truth.

In the lunch break, McHugh phoned Gerard to find out what had happened. As soon as he answered, she could hear his distress. Allison was missing, he said.

'She went for a walk and didn't come back.'

'Did you argue?' McHugh thought back to her tense phone call with Gerard the day before.

'No, we didn't argue,' he replied. He said he couldn't think of any trigger for Allison to take off.

'Where are you now?'

'I'm at home now. The police are searching the place for clues.'

'You can't talk now, obviously.'

'It's not a good idea for us to talk. We should lay low,' replied Gerard.

Immediately, McHugh's thoughts turned to how this dramatic turn of events would change things for her. Allison had probably stormed off to get Gerard's attention. When she inevitably turned up, he would no doubt be shocked into staying with her, yet again. McHugh had been waiting three years for Gerard to end what he claimed was a loveless marriage. After countless promises, he'd finally given a date for his departure – July 1. Now it was all bound to come to nothing, once more.

'See you later. For all it's worth, I love you,' McHugh said, ending the call.

That night, as word filtered out about Allison's disappearance, a friend sent a text to McHugh just after midnight.

'Hey Toni! I know it's late but a friend just shared a link on Facebook about police searching for Allison Baden-Clay. Isn't that G's wife? Hope I haven't woken you. Sorry if I did. Bek xo.'

'Yes it is,' replied McHugh. 'I didn't know what the latest was. I'm extremely worried.'

'Shit Toni, too weird! I just got woken up by Leo & happened to check Facebook while I was up & nearly choked when I saw her name. Fingers crossed she's found safe & sound. Try to get some sleep, I'll talk to you tomorrow.'

The next day, at 9.30 am, McHugh and her twin sons were having a quiet Saturday morning at home when she had a call from a blocked number. It was Gerard, warning McHugh that police knew of their affair and would want to talk to her.

Shortly afterwards, a detective arrived at her apartment

complex, asking her to attend Indooroopilly station. She did as requested, providing the first of her police statements.

'Gerard stated that police will want to speak with me today and stated the police feared the worst and that Allison had met with foul play,' McHugh told detectives that day. 'He also mentioned that the police were aware of our affair. I then asked him what I should do, to which he replied I should tell the truth.'

McHugh gave police the basics of their relationship. How it had started years earlier. Its ups and downs. That it was ongoing and they were planning a life together. That Gerard had promised to come to her, unconditionally.

McHugh was still with police at the station when Gerard phoned her mobile.

'Can you talk?' he asked.

'No, I can't. I'm with the police,' she said.

'Just answer yes or no. Do they know we are back together?' he said.

'Yes,' she answered.

Gerard had told the police the day before that his relationship with McHugh was over.

Over the following weeks, McHugh made further formal statements to police. Police wanted to know if McHugh had an alibi for the period Allison went missing. McHugh was home with her 14-year-old sons. The boys shared a bedroom and went to bed between 8.30 pm and 9 pm each night.

'I remained at home with my boys all night that night,' McHugh said.

Realising that the police investigation was growing more focused, McHugh started dwelling on all the messages she had exchanged with Gerard by text and email over the years. Some were intensely private. McHugh went into her iPhone and deleted exchanges with Gerard. She did the same with her emails.

Seriously spooked, McHugh was reluctant to set foot outside her St Lucia unit, but her mum called and said she needed to come out. McHugh's parents lived in a suburb past Anstead in

Brisbane's west. On the morning of Monday 30 April, McHugh left her apartment and went to her parents' house. To get there, she drove along Mt Crosby Road and over Kholo Creek Bridge, over the very spot where Allison's body lay abandoned on the creek bank. Just hours later McHugh heard the news. A body had been discovered under the bridge and the road was now closed.

Gerard was back in touch with McHugh in mid-May, calling her at work. 'I love you,' he said. 'I don't know what's gone wrong here. I know you haven't done anything as you must know in your heart that I haven't done anything.'

'I know and I know you can't talk to me or anyone else as that was the advice given to you by your lawyer.'

'That's right.'

'How are you coping?'

'Not well.'

'I guess the next I see you will be in court?'

'No, no,' replied Gerard.

'I love you and stay strong,' McHugh said.

As the police investigation continued, McHugh talked to her former partner, Robert Mackay-Wood. Her theory, she told him, was that whoever did kill Allison would have driven out of Brookfield by the back way, along Rafting Ground Road.

'There would have been less likelihood that they would have been seen,' she later told police.

Police kept returning to McHugh, gleaning more details about Gerard with every contact. The affair had become central to the investigation. It was a possible motive for Gerard to murder his wife, along with the insurance payout of almost $1 million he would receive on her death.

Since Allison's disappearance, I too had been finding out more about Gerard's relationship with McHugh. In her photo on Century 21 Westside's website, McHugh was well groomed. She looked dignified. She appeared to be around Gerard's age, brunette and was wearing the company's gold jacket.

I first phoned McHugh on Friday 27 April 2012, a week after Allison was reported missing.

'I've got nothing to say to you,' she said, and hung up.

Over time, I spoke to multiple sources about the affair. The accuracy and relevance of the information was all too apparent.

Before publication, I phoned Gerard and told him what the story would say. I'd been trying since the start to get Gerard to open up to me, but he had rebuffed my every approach. This time he listened quietly until I finished speaking. But he wasn't going to break his silence.

'I'm with my daughters right now,' he said softly, and hung up.

While he had sounded calm on the phone, the conversation was a watershed moment for Gerard because he immediately set about informing family and friends that he had been cheating on Allison for years. It was about to appear in the paper, he told them.

I also phoned McHugh again, left a detailed message on her voicemail outlining the story, then sent her a text message too. There was no reply. In one last effort to ensure she was forewarned, with a chance to respond in case she missed the messages, I phoned one of the people closest to her and asked him to pass it on.

The story about Gerard and Toni's affair ran across two pages in *The Sunday Mail* on 20 May 2012. It was the first time the affair was aired in the mainstream media. It broke the news that the relationship had not ended, but was ongoing at the time of Allison's disappearance, and was being closely examined by police.

Once the news report was out, detectives in the Major Incident Room seized the opportunity to change tack with Gerard's mistress. It was time to show some of their hand. A pile of salacious emails between McHugh and Gerard had been recovered from their computers. And police knew McHugh was far from the only woman Gerard had been sleeping with behind his wife's back.

Detective Sergeant Peter Roddick and Detective Acting Inspector Mal Gundry went to McHugh's unit early in Monday morning. Roddick pressed the buzzer and held it until McHugh eventually came out. She said they'd woken her and asked them to come back in half an hour, and they obliged. When they returned, the officers assured McHugh that police were not behind the media report about the affair; it wasn't a leak, and must have come from someone else. They sympathised with her. But, the detectives said, there was no hiding from the affair any more and they wanted to work with her.

They asked if she had a lawyer – there were things they needed to discuss. She confirmed she did. The lawyer was Marek Reardon and the detectives arranged a meeting in his office, where they handed him examples of the recovered emails between Gerard and McHugh. In the days that followed, police would continually return to McHugh. On one occasion, they showed her photographs of Gerard's face from the day he reported Allison missing, with the scratches trailing down his cheek. McHugh also became aware of some other important information about Gerard.

On Sunday 27 May 2012, McHugh's mobile lit up with an unknown number. She answered and heard a familiar voice: 'It's me.' But an icy reception awaited Gerard. Someone from the police – it wasn't clear who or how – had let McHugh know she was not the only 'other woman' in his life.

McHugh laid straight into him: 'I know what you've been doing. How could you do that to me?'

Even after Allison had been found dead, McHugh had stayed loyal to Gerard, thinking she was his true love. Now she knew she wasn't his only lover on the side, and that he had been lying to her too.

McHugh knew one of the other women, Jackie Crane, who had been hanging around at the Australian Real Estate

Conference in Sydney in 2010 and had left her husband not long after. Century 21 Westside partners Jocelyn Frost and business partner Phill Broom had noticed unusual chemistry between Gerard and Crane. Frost told McHugh she suspected something might be going on between Gerard and Crane. McHugh had even asked Gerard, and he had denied it. Gerard had always told McHugh he had never been with any woman besides Allison. Blinded by love, she once believed him.

McHugh also knew of Michelle Hammond – another woman Gerard had an affair with – from real estate circles. Hammond had worked with Gerard at Raine & Horne years earlier. McHugh wanted to hear Gerard confirm it himself, then demanded to know if the suggestion of yet more affairs was true.

Gerard admitted it was. Scrambling, he reminded McHugh of a conversation in late 2011 when their affair had reignited. At the time, Gerard cryptically said he would need to sit down and be honest and frank with her in the future if they were going to be in a normal relationship. They'd never had that frank and honest discussion, and McHugh never suspected he was hinting at other affairs. Gerard didn't want to talk further on the phone. He wanted to meet.

'I basically asked him why I should give him any time to explain,' she later told police. 'Gerard then told me that he loved me. He again said that he did not know what went wrong there and that he believed the police would find the killer and bring them to justice. Gerard told me that he would ring me at work the next day. On Monday. Gerard did not call me.'

In the days that followed the call, McHugh went back to see the detectives at Indooroopilly Police Station to complete her fourth statement.

'I can expand on the following . . .' she said, before elaborating on intimate details about their long-running affair.

Roddick, from Homicide, showed McHugh a hand-drawn map in Allison's journal that she had asked Gerard to sketch during a 15-minute venting session. McHugh was stunned to recognise the floorplan of her unit – a regular rendezvous point with Gerard. The same journal was filled with Allison's questions about Gerard's affair with McHugh, penned in the days before she went missing.

'Gerard always writes in capital letters,' McHugh said, confirming the map was in his handwriting. A handwriting expert would confirm the same.

One day in June, Gerard phoned McHugh at work from a blocked number. He was outside her office, in a cab. 'I need to talk to you,' he said.

When McHugh slid in next to him in the taxi, a paranoid Gerard asked her if she was wearing a wire.

'No! Of course not,' she said.

The pair went to a Fortitude Valley rental unit. In her later interview with the *Australian Women's Weekly*, McHugh would explain that they both knew their phones were being tapped and Gerard wanted to stop anyone listening in. Once they were inside the unit, he told McHugh that he had sex with other women to make sure what he had with her was real.

Arrest

The senior ranks of the Metropolitan North police region and the state's Homicide squad gathered in a conference room at Alderley on 12 June 2012 to discuss the progress of Operation Kilo Intrigue. Mark Ainsworth and Mal Gundry joined Detective Superintendent Brian Wilkins, the head of Homicide, Detective Inspector Damien Hansen, also from Homicide, and Detective Inspector Bob Hytch. They had more than a century of policing experience between them.

Ainsworth spoke about the operation for a couple of minutes and then handed over to Gundry to outline the investigation into Allison's disappearance and death. Gundry went through it from start to finish.

Gundry talked through everything police had done to exclude the possibility that Allison had been randomly abducted. He had a long list of investigations into known offenders and reported sightings of people and vehicles of interest. The team in the MIR had taken 500 witness statements. Among them were people who were at locations all over Brookfield, where Allison vanished, and around Kholo Creek, where she was found. He added that although no one saw the body being dumped under the bridge, no one saw Allison out walking either.

He concluded by saying that police were ready to charge Gerard with murder. The group agreed. Gerard Baden-Clay would be charged with murder the next day. Gundry started setting a plan in motion for the arrest.

Chris Canniffe and Cameron McLeod, from Indooroopilly CIB, had been appointed to the arrest team at the start of the investigation. When the decision was being made to make the arrest,

Canniffe and McLeod had already been sent north in a government jet to have a chat with Gerard's sister, Olivia Walton, at her home in Townsville. It wasn't as glamorous as it might sound. They shared the cramped jet with prisoners being transferred to correctional centres through the state's north. Commercial flights to Townsville took two hours. The bunny-hopping government jet, stopping at a range of towns all along the way, took more than five hours but saved the QPS some money.

A decision had been made in the Major Incident Room to share selected snippets of the evidence against Gerard with his family. If Gerard's family knew more about what happened to Allison, perhaps an insight into the police case would encourage them to talk to the detectives. Canniffe and McLeod told Olivia, among other things, about the electronic evidence showing Gerard's iPhone was connected to a charger at 1.48 am when he said he was sound asleep. The detectives didn't give away that they had found Allison's blood in the Holden Captiva.

Walton didn't add anything of great value in the conversation. At the end of their talk, she asked if police considered her a suspect too. Police had no evidence linking anyone other than Gerard to Allison's disappearance.

Simultaneously, detectives were talking to Gerard's parents, Nigel and Elaine, in Brisbane.

That night, Canniffe and McLeod were told of the arrest plans and took the first commercial flight back to Brisbane the next morning.

It was a day of the year no one expected an arrest. Game two of the State of Origin was on in Sydney that night. One of the great rivalries in Australian sport, the annual rugby league grudge match between Queensland and New South Wales was akin to a religious event. Workers would be knocking off early to gather for barbecues and get-togethers with friends. Gerard would not be thinking an arrest could be ahead, making it the perfect day for police to make their move. McLeod was wearing his maroon State of Origin jersey when he arrived at Indooroopilly Police Station to meet up with his colleagues, but changed into the more appropriate arrest attire of a dark suit and tie.

In the early afternoon, police quietly took up positions all around the Toowong Village shopping centre. Gerard's business had all but collapsed after Allison went missing. He'd been forced to move out of his big Taringa office, where he once dreamt of dominating real estate in the western suburbs. Retaining a handful of staff and with about the same number of properties for sale, he was working from a small office space on level three, above the shopping centre. Memorably, when he moved into the new office he had told lurking *Courier-Mail* police reporter Brooke Baskin it was 'business as usual'.

The plan was for the detectives to go up to Gerard's office and ask him to accompany them to Indooroopilly station, where he would be arrested and charged with murder. If he refused, they would arrest him on the spot. Police wanted the arrest to go down with as little fuss as possible. In particular, police wanted to ensure there was no confrontation near his children. Gerard was due to pick up the girls from school.

As McLeod, Canniffe and Detective Senior Constable Grant Linwood waited for a lift to take them up to Gerard's office at around 2.40 pm, the plans went out the window. Colleagues had seen Gerard come down to the car park and get into his silver Toyota Corolla hire car. Alerted to the unexpected turn of events, the three detectives sprinted to Gerard's car. Linwood, getting there first, opened the driver's side door and pulled the startled real estate agent from the car. Gerard instinctively threw his hands in the air, offering no resistance, and Linwood released his grip. Canniffe asked Gerard to come with them to Indooroopilly station.

Gerard started making excuses. He had to collect his children. He needed to call his parents.

'Gerard, you're under arrest for murder,' Canniffe told him.

As he was escorted to the back of an unmarked police car, Gerard's overriding emotion was anger. He glared at the detectives, silently and sullenly. McLeod took the wheel, with Linwood a front passenger and Canniffe in the back seat with Gerard. Canniffe told Gerard he had a number of questions. Did Gerard have an explanation for the presence of Allison's blood in her car? It was the first time Gerard had been told of the evidence. Canniffe also asked Gerard if he had an explanation for the Google searches on his phone? Further, did he have an explanation for his phone being plugged into a charger at 1.48 am?

Gerard quietly gave the same response to every question: 'I want to speak to my lawyer.'

Other police were waiting at Brookfield and moved in to collect Gerard's three daughters from school as soon as the arrest was made. They were taken to Ferny Grove Police Station to keep them away from all the fuss that would surround their father. Allison's parents, Priscilla and Geoff Dickie, would take care of them from then on.

There were no TV news crew or photographs to record the arrest – it was successfully kept under the radar. Only after Gerard was taken into Indooroopilly Police Station and put in one of the two small cells behind the front counter, did word start to spread. Then, media descended on the station from everywhere.

Gerard's solicitor, Darren Mahony, visited him at the station. Mahony asked police if there was any reason the arrest had to be that night. Perhaps he had Origin plans.

Detective Sergeant Peter Roddick had been one of the officers sent to the girls' school, and when he returned to Indooroopilly Police Station he went to see Gerard in the cells. Gerard was staring blankly at the wall. Roddick asked what his daughters' favourite toys were, and Gerard didn't reply. Roddick had to repeat the question, and this time Gerard listed a toy for each of the girls for police to collect from his house.

It was almost unheard of: the football was playing on a TV in the station's meal room, but few people were paying attention. New South Wales won, levelling the best-of-three series 1–1, but that wasn't the reason for the lack of interest. The detectives had just taken a decisive step towards getting justice for Allison.

Chris Canniffe and Cameron McLeod started working on the objection-to-bail documents. There was still much work to be done.

PART IV – TRIAL

Phone a friend

Gerard Baden-Clay spent his first night behind bars in the company of drunks and State of Origin rabble-rousers. From Indooroopilly Police Station, detectives had driven him to the Brisbane Watchhouse in the city. He was, by far, the highest profile prisoner in the cells that year. Around 9.30 am the next day, he was taken to the adjoining Brisbane Magistrates Court in the rumpled work clothes he was wearing when arrested.

Journalists crowded the courtroom but, as he took his seat in the dock, Gerard managed to turn his body around to deny all assembled a glimpse of his face. Court artists were reduced to sketching the back of his head. In any case, it was to be the briefest of appearances: the proceedings – to set a new court date – lasted less than a minute.

Outside court, Darren Mahony said simply: 'Mr Baden-Clay maintains his innocence.'

If Gerard had hopes to make bail and return to his daughters, he would have been disappointed. Magistrates do not have the power to grant bail on murder charges, and Gerard's legal team would need to wait for a date in the Supreme Court to make an application.

Once the initial hearing was over, Gerard was led to a holding cell but was soon brought back to Court 3 for another matter. Police, who wanted to shave the beard he had been growing since Allison disappeared, had applied for a Forensic Procedure

Order to do it. The magistrate swiftly granted the application, allowing police to see what was disguised by the new growth. Forensic medical officer Dr Leslie Griffiths – who had examined Gerard in hospital after his car crash almost two months earlier – was called to the watchhouse to carry out the order. Shaving Gerard's right cheek, Griffiths found his injuries were fading but still clearly visible and had scarred. Superficial shaving cuts would not have been expected to form scars.

When the examination was over, Gerard was driven in a prison van to his new home, the high-security Arthur Gorrie Correctional Centre, at Wacol in Brisbane's south-west, which sat behind row after row of razor-wire fencing. Prior to joining the 865 inmates on remand there, Gerard went through a strip search, interview and shower. He changed into a green prison-issue T-shirt and was photographed, his eyes red from crying: prisoner E00477.

Because of his high profile, he was kept under observation in the jail's medical centre. Brett Peter Cowan, charged with the abduction and murder of Daniel Morcombe, was also being housed there. Beef stroganoff and penne pasta were on the menu on his first night in the prison. It was a long way from the rolling hills of Brookfield.

Gerard's family was already working overtime to get him out on bail. Dr Bruce Flegg was a wealthy man, but even for him the request was extraordinary. Not long after Gerard was arrested, Flegg answered a phone call. It was Gerard's sister, Olivia. She cut to the chase. Would Flegg stump up $1 million as a surety for Gerard's bail?

The bold request took him by surprise. It was wildly out of touch with reality. All it would take would be for Gerard to skip bail and Flegg would be out of pocket. Not to mention how it would look for the MP. He was a man who prided himself on his loyalty, and his friendship with Gerard had already led him into some tricky situations. This request was going too far.

He told Walton straightaway he couldn't help, and in an instant the phone call was over.

Walton and Gerard's parents were still able to put together a sizeable $500,000 surety, putting their own homes on the line and getting some help from other friends. Gerard would live with his parents if he was bailed. His hearing was scheduled for Thursday 21 July. Two days beforehand, Olivia emailed friends to say they had enough surety but urgently needed $30,000 for legal bills.

Gerard, looking at his clean criminal record and the fact that there was only circumstantial evidence against him, thought he was a good chance of bail.

Bombed out

Chief Justice Paul de Jersey was livid. Standing on the footpath on George Street in the city, he had been evacuated along with everyone else in Brisbane's Supreme and District courts. An anonymous caller had phoned in a bomb threat against Gerard's bail hearing just minutes after it got underway, forcing the entire Law Courts Complex to be cleared.

'It is absolutely disgraceful, if this is a hoax, that proceedings of the state's highest court can be disrupted in this way,' de Jersey told reporters, as sirens echoed through the buildings behind him.

Gerard, still in Arthur Gorrie's medical unit, missed all the hullaballoo. He'd chosen to stay at the jail to await the result of the Supreme Court bail hearing. Given it became even more of a circus than usual, it was a wise choice.

Justice John Byrne, the judge in Max Sica's trial for murdering Sidhi, Kunal and Neelma Singh, had just begun his summing up when the alarm bells rang from the Baden-Clay bomb threat. Justice Byrne, one of the state's most senior judges, would later preside over Gerard's trial. He cleared the court and Sica was ushered outside to the rear of the building and handcuffed to a set of bike racks until the threat subsided. Two weeks later Sica would be convicted of the triple murder and sentenced to life in prison with a record non-parole period of 35 years. Other judges were clearing courts throughout the ageing complex; a new courts building was only months from opening on a separate site on George Street. Security staff ushered hundreds of court staff members, lawyers and jurors into lifts and down fire escapes. Following the bomb threat, court proceedings were cancelled for the rest of the day to allow the police dog squad to search the building. They found nothing. Gerard's bail hearing was adjourned until the next day.

Police would trace the threatening call to a public phone box in Western Australia before the trail went cold. Drama seemed to follow Gerard wherever he went.

The extra time would prove useful to police, who thought they had made a major breakthrough that morning. In the Electronic Evidence Examination Unit at police headquarters, investigative computer analyst Neil Robertson was re-examining data retrieved from Gerard's iPhone.

When Allison had first gone missing, Robertson had used a forensic tool called the Cellebrite Universal Forensic Extraction Device (UFED) to download data from Gerard's seized phone. He used a separate application called Cellebrite Physical Analyser to make the data readable. As luck would have it, a new version of Physical Analyser had just been released.

At 8.30 am on the day of the hearing, Robertson used the new version to review the data from Gerard's phone, hoping to pick up something he had missed before. Spectacularly, he did. It was showing Gerard had made a previously unknown FaceTime call to his father, Nigel, not long after midnight on the night Allison went missing. FaceTime is an Apple product that allows video calls between devices such as iPhones and iPads. FaceTime calls are made over the internet and do not appear on standard call records. The pivotal call appeared to have lasted 1 minute and 23 seconds at 12.30 am on Friday 20 April. Gerard had told police he was asleep from 10 pm onwards. The call was showing as a deleted entry, suggesting Gerard tried to conceal it.

Robertson fired off an email to Detective Sergeant Peter Roddick from Homicide, at 11.53 am – less than three hours before Gerard's bail hearing was to start. Roddick hastily typed up a new affidavit to add to the police bail objection, detailing the last-minute advice from the computer analyst.

That afternoon – while the courts complex was shut down – police conducted a raid on the home of Nigel and Elaine Baden-Clay. Detectives from the Major Incident Room arrived at the Kenmore home just after 5 pm with a warrant to search and seize any Apple products. Gerard's parents had been out for a walk with their dog and returned to find the police on their doorstep. Elaine curtly asked the detectives to remove their shoes before entering. They left empty-handed. The couple did not own an iPhone or iPad.

Later, Elaine would recount handing police the fruit bowl from the dining room table as the only apple product in the house.

Gerard's new bail hearing started afresh at 10 am on Friday 22 June 2012. Justice David Boddice stepped in as a replacement for Justice Martin, who had other commitments. The new hearing began with Gerard's barrister Peter Davis again seeking to portray the case as weak.

Davis said there was no known cause of death, no time or even date of death, no real evidence of the place of death, no sightings of Gerard at the bridge where Allison was found, and no sightings of him outside the family home at all that night.

'This is one of the strongest applications one will ever see for bail where there's a murder charge,' Davis told the court.

Davis added Gerard had three children, a real estate business, had not tried to flee during the high-profile investigation and faced a likely two- to three-year delay before trial.

'For a period of some two months, my client is pursued and pursued and pursued and pursued by the media, and it's constantly reinforced to him that he is the prime suspect, he's the person who everybody thinks has done it. He doesn't take off. He doesn't leave over that period.'

Crown prosecutor Danny Boyle conceded some of the evidence might not make it to trial, but said for a bail hearing the judge needed to be informed of the full circumstances.

'The case against him, in the combination of circumstances, is quite compelling,' Boyle said.

Justice Boddice adjourned the hearing until 1 pm for his decision. Bail on murder charges was rare.

When court resumed, Justice Boddice began by saying it was particularly difficult to assess the strength of circumstantial cases because ultimately it would be up to a jury to interpret the evidence. But he said the case was far from weak: 'Whilst it is circumstantial, there are a number of factors which, if accepted by a jury, would represent a strong case.'

The judge went on to outline the key points of the Crown case for the first time. Avid court watchers goggled as the evidence was spelt out: the scratches on Gerard's face; the iPhone being plugged into a charger at 1.48 am; Allison's blood in the Captiva; Gerard's affair with Toni McHugh; his promises to leave his wife by 1 July; the financial pressures and the haste to claim his wife's life insurance of almost $1 million. Then there was the looming clash between Allison and McHugh at the real estate conference the next day.

Things did not look like they were swinging Gerard's way as the judge worked towards his conclusion. The murder charge and the mandatory life sentence it carried were powerful incentives for Gerard to flee, Justice Boddice said. And although he had concerns about holding someone in custody at length without a conviction, the possibility Gerard would run was too great. Boddice ruled Gerard would have to stay in prison.

Devastated at being denied bail, Gerard was considering ditching his defence team. In the quest for new advice, a flurry of calls and text messages were exchanged between Olivia Walton and some of Queensland's top lawyers. Solicitors Michael Bosscher and Tim Meehan from Bosscher Lawyers drove out to Arthur Gorrie Correctional Centre to visit Gerard on 2 July 2012. The pair were representing Daniel Morcombe's accused murderer, Brett Peter Cowan.

Something about Allison's story had always galvanised friends, and often complete strangers, to act. Roni Johnson had never met Allison but both had three children and both lived in Brookfield. Allison's disappearance had resonated with Johnson immediately. She had known Allison's cousin Jodie Dann growing up and they had mutual friends. At Allison's funeral, Johnson ran into Brookfield United Cricket Club president Mike Kaye, who said a few club members were trying to arrange a fundraising match against firefighters and SES volunteers involved in the search. Johnson said she might be able to help.

She envisaged a low-key event with a raffle. Before she knew it, there was a media frenzy and she was bombarded with donations. Posters had to be constantly updated with the new attractions and prizes on offer. The match was held at the Brookfield Showground on 24 June 2012, less than a fortnight after Gerard's arrest. It had turned into a family fun day, with a jumping castle, face painting and animal petting zoo. Everything was donated. The little cricket match raised $50,000 for Allison's daughters and became an annual event.

Herbarium

June 2012

The Queensland Herbarium at the Brisbane Botanic Gardens offers a remarkable, free, public service. Bring in a sample from a plant – any plant – and the Herbarium's experts will identify it. An assortment of amateur botanists, green thumbs and gardening retirees regularly make their way to the front counter with leaves, branches and fruit in hand for help in solving botanical mysteries. Sometimes frantic parents arrive to check on plant life swallowed by their adventurous children. At other times it's developers, who pay corporate rates for checks on their land. Around 4000 identifications are conducted a year. In mid-2012, the Herbarium had high-priority clients calling – police investigating the death of Allison Baden-Clay.

Acting Inspector Ewen Taylor, the Metropolitan North police region forensic coordinator, arrived at the Herbarium with an armful of botanical exhibits on 27 June 2012, five days after Gerard was denied bail. They were the very last forensic items Taylor had to drop off for examination from Operation Kilo Intrigue. Almost two months had passed since the discovery of Allison's body on the banks of Kholo Creek. Taylor wanted the Herbarium to examine plant material from clothing, shoes and various cars. At the top of his list of priorities was an examination of plant material recovered from the Captiva, which police believed Gerard had used to transport Allison's body. Leaves and grass recovered from tyres, the undercarriage and inside could have yielded valuable clues linking the vehicle to Kholo Creek. There were also three jars containing leaves and bark retrieved from Allison's body during the post mortem, but

Taylor hadn't given them much thought. Later, he would reflect on how easily he could have missed one of the most important breakthroughs in the investigation.

With other staff away or unavailable, Herbarium director Dr Gordon Guymer volunteered to personally handle the request. The short, sprightly 58-year-old Herbarium boss was the son of potato farmers from northern New South Wales. After earning a scholarship to university he excelled in botany, perhaps because of his upbringing on the farm. Impressively credentialled, he had been a botanist with the Queensland government since 1980. Before he stopped counting, he had identified more than 100 new species of plant. It was the kind of job you could never get away from. Once, in Brazil for a seminar, he was at the base of the Christ the Redeemer statue and glanced down to recognise weeds abundant in Queensland. His work was always all around him.

Guymer had worked with the police before and was fully aware that, internationally, botany has long played a significant role in criminal investigations. One of the most notable early cases was the 1930s trial of Bruno Richard Hauptmann for the kidnapping of aviator Charles Lindbergh's 20-month-old son, Charles Junior. A US wood expert, Dr Arthur Koehler, provided intricate evidence linking a homemade ladder used in the kidnapping to wood taken from Hauptmann's attic.

The highly professional Guymer put aside his normal tasks and began examining the Baden-Clay material. In a small laboratory on the Herbarium's second floor, wearing his white lab coat and with the acrid smell of chemicals in the air, he methodically moved through the police exhibits. Guymer noted there was plant material from Adidas and Asics shoes, a hiking boot, and vacuum cleaner bag. More plant material was recovered from a car's suspension system, driver's side step bracket, tyre tread, a hose near the rear passenger's side wheel and foot wells.

The process extended over days. Towards the end of it, Guymer picked up the three 500-millilitre bottles containing leaves and bark. Emptying the first of them, he found a tangle of hair, plant material and maggots, preserved in alcohol. Looking at snippets of the material through a stereomicroscope, Guymer could identify some of the plant species as soon as he saw them. For those he was unsure of, he had an enormous reference library at his fingertips. Below the lab, the Herbarium's first floor housed a collection of 820,000 botanical specimens. The eminent botanist shuttled between the collection and his laboratory upstairs, identifying the species from Allison's hair and body.

From the plant evidence, delivered to him almost as an afterthought, Guymer was building towards a powerful deduction. But as new lines of investigation were emerging, others were disintegrating.

Glitches

The walls of boutique Gold Coast firm Jacobson Mahony Lawyers are lined with images of bushranger Ned Kelly. An armour-plated villain, Kelly was sentenced to death in 1880 for the murder of Constable Thomas Lonigan. A crowd of 5000 people descended on Melbourne Gaol for his execution. The legal firm chose Kelly as a decorating theme not because he was one of Australia's most famous criminals, but because he was a man who could have done with a good lawyer. At his trial, it was reported, Kelly had a heated exchange with the presiding judge, Redmond Barry, about whether he would have been acquitted if his inexperienced and underprepared lawyer had argued self-defence.

'I wish I had insisted on being allowed to examine the witnesses myself. If I had examined them, I am confident I would have thrown a different light on the case,' Kelly reportedly said before being sentenced to hang.

Outlining 'Our Philosophy' on their website, Jacobson Mahony Lawyers explained: 'Our offices are adorned with Ned Kelly prints to remind us that every person is entitled to skilled representation, a fair and just hearing, and above all, is innocent until proven guilty.'

On 4 July 2012, almost two weeks after Gerard was denied bail, a fax arrived at these very offices. Crown prosecutor Danny Boyle was advising Gerard's lawyers of a significant mistake in information provided to the court during the bail hearing. Boyle wrote he was sending as an attachment a new affidavit from police computer analyst Neil Robertson with the details: 'The information in the new affidavit confirms that there is no evidence of a "FaceTime" call between the phone of Gerard

Baden-Clay and the phone of Nigel Baden-Clay on the morning of 20 April 2012.'

Robertson explained in his affidavit how the new version of the Physical Analyser software used to examine the contents of Gerard's phone had misinterpreted a deleted call. In simple terms, the FaceTime call between Gerard and his father was a furphy – the result of a glitch in the system used to extract data from Gerard's iPhone. The apparently incriminating call had never happened – and had never been possible in the first place. Gerard had an older model iPhone 3GS, which did not have a forward-facing camera and did not allow FaceTime calls – something police had not taken into account when initially analysing the data. And Nigel did not have an iPhone at all. In the rush to add material to the bail documents, the wrong information had been presented to the court and reported in the media.

Boyle proposed going back to Justice Boddice to correct the error. Gerard now had some ammunition to attack the police investigation. It was an embarrassing misstep and it was not the only piece of seemingly incriminating evidence that was about to fall apart.

His lawyers were working to refute another significant piece of the electronic evidence, which also related to Gerard's iPhone. Police said he had Googled 'self incrimination' minutes before phoning police to report Allison missing on Friday 20 April 2012. It didn't look good, particularly as Gerard had called in a lawyer and refused to give a formal statement that same day. However, since being arrested Gerard had said there was an innocent explanation – he had looked up the information days earlier while watching TV legal drama *The Good Wife*.

Jacobson Mahony Lawyers' clerk Kurt Fechner found a TV guide from *The Courier-Mail* that listed the programs aired on Wednesday 18 April – two days before Allison was reported missing. The guide confirmed *The Good Wife* started at 9.30 pm on Channel 10. Fechner found a DVD of the series and went to that night's episode, *Another Ham Sandwich*. Watching it to the end, he counted three references to 'taking the fifth'. Gerard told his lawyers he was watching the show at his Brookfield home with his parents when one asked, 'What does that mean – taking the fifth?' He used his iPhone to search for a definition of the term at 10.08 pm. One result from a Google search of 'taking the fifth' is a Wikipedia page on self-incrimination – the term apparently searched on Gerard's phone shortly before he reported Allison missing.

Fechner was convinced there was an explanation for the apparent two-day disparity between searches for 'taking the fifth' and 'self incrimination'. He began researching Apple forums online and found iPhone searches automatically reloaded pages when the browser is opened, after previously being closed. Bingo! When Gerard had used his phone to search for the Queensland Police Service website on the morning Allison went missing, there had been an automatic reload of his innocuous search days earlier. This one, it seemed, would have to be filed under 'truth can be stranger than fiction'.

Buoyed by the defeat of two planks of the police case – the FaceTime call and suspicious searches on his iPhone – Gerard started gearing up for another run at bail.

Herbarium II

Dr Gordon Guymer separated the specimens before him by their species. He'd quickly identified all of the botanical material police had recovered from Allison's hair and body. Many home gardeners would have been familiar with the species Guymer identified, though few could reel off their scientific names, as he could. He tallied the contents of the first bottle – seven large, intact leaves of crepe myrtle (*Lagerstroemia indica*); three leaflets, and a tendril with claw, of cat's claw creeper (*Dolichandra unguis-cati*); seven frond parts, or pinnae, of fishbone fern (*Nephrolepis Cordifolia*); bark and leaves of eucalyptus; a leaf from a Chinese elm (*Celtis sinesis*) and a leaf from a lilly pilly (*Acmena smithii*). In the second and third bottles, Guymer identified more fishbone fern fronds and woody plant stems.

The identification process was only the first phase of Guymer's work on the case. Now that he knew *what* they were, he had to work out *where* the leaves had likely come from. On Friday 13 July 2012, a fortnight after dropping off the exhibits, police forensic coordinator Ewen Taylor returned to the Queensland Herbarium, picked Guymer up and drove him to Kholo Creek Bridge. Indooroopilly CIB officer in charge Mal Gundry and Homicide squad detective Gavin Pascoe met them there.

Guymer was looking for the six species of plant he identified in the lab. Crepe myrtle, growing up to 6 metres tall, was a favourite of suburban gardeners for its attractive displays of red, white and lavender flowers in summer. In autumn, the leaves dropped off and the trunk shed its bark to produce a smooth, twisting surface with its own shades of pink, grey and brown. Lilly pilly plants were another suburban favourite, often used to create hedges. Fishbone fern, native to Australia, needed little encouragement to develop into dense clumps and was common around Brisbane homes. Cat's claw creeper, popular in older-style gardens, was an American vine so aggressive that it had been declared a weed of national significance in Australia and banned from sale. It produced pretty yellow bell-shaped flowers but smothered native vegetation. Chinese elm was another declared pest in Queensland that rapidly spread through backyards, along creeks and in bushland. Eucalypts, the great Aussie gum trees, were an integral part of the landscape in both backyards and bush.

Taking his time, Guymer searched 50 metres either side of the bridge. From his years of working with south-east Queensland flora, he instantly recognised most of the plants growing in this area: lantana, one of Australia's worst weeds; billygoat weed, a garden escapee; the castor oil shrub, whose seeds and large leaves contain toxic ricin; the edible common raspberry; native sandpaper fig, named for its coarse leaves; and brown kurrajong, which once provided bark fibre for Aboriginal people to make nets for fishing and hunting. Of the six plants Guymer identified in the lab, he could find only Chinese elm and eucalypts in the vicinity. Crepe myrtle, cat's claw creeper, fishbone fern and lilly pilly were nowhere to be seen. Guymer and Taylor went around the corner to Little Ugly Creek off Wirrabara Road, and then to the Scout campsite in Bunya Street, and again could not find any of the missing four plant species.

Next stop was Brookfield. At the home of Allison and Gerard Baden-Clay, Guymer stared into the garden. There, swaying in the gentle breeze, was the same array of plants he had identified in his lab. He could see a Chinese elm and a small-leaved lilly pilly. Crepe myrtle trees were growing along the edge of the concrete apron at the front of the house, along the edge of the carport and along the paving edge at the back of the house. Fishbone ferns were growing under the crepe myrtles at the back of the house. And cat's claw creeper was climbing vigorously over the crepe myrtles and carport.

That afternoon, Guymer conducted a more detailed examination of the home, with detectives watching on. In the rear patio area, he confirmed there were four crepe myrtle trees, which were bare after dumping their multi-coloured leaves in a thick layer through the back yard. Police collected about 100 leaves from the patio and bagged, sealed and labelled them. Separately, the botanist supervised the collection of five fallen fern pinnae from among the fallen leaves on the patio. Clumps of fishbone fern ran for 8 metres under the crepe myrtles, and several small cat's claw creepers were entangled in the crepe myrtles. A Chinese elm was growing near the back patio.

In the carport area, Guymer identified five more leafless crepe myrtle trees and collected fallen leaves from the ground. Cat's claw creepers grew along the carport floor and scaled support posts to the roof.

Back at the laboratory, Guymer confirmed the bagged material contained crepe myrtle leaves, two small fishbone fern pinnae, a cat's claw creeper leaflet, a tipuana leaflet and three eucalypt leaves.

The following week, on Wednesday 18 July 2012, Guymer joined some of the core investigating team – Mark Ainsworth, Cameron McLeod, Mal Gundry, Gavin Pascoe and Ewen Taylor – at Indooroopilly station to brief them on his findings. The detectives digested the information and its ramifications. Allison's hair had been washed and coloured at the hairdresser's the night before she vanished. Somehow, her clean locks had become matted with leaves – seemingly from her own garden – around the time of her death.

Taylor picked Guymer up from the Herbarium again the next day and they drove to Gerard and Allison's home. This time, Guymer oversaw the collection of cuttings from crepe myrtle trees around the back patio area and adjacent to the carport. The cuttings would be planted in the Herbarium's greenhouse. Regardless of what happened to the trees at Brookfield Road, police would have access to the crepe myrtle cuttings at the Herbarium for future analysis.

Guymer, Taylor and detectives McLeod and Gundry returned to Kholo Creek Bridge for a more detailed search of the area. Walking along the eastern side of the creek bank, using binoculars to see across to the other side, the Herbarium boss identified and listed 37 separate plant species. In addition to the species he had located in his initial visit, he jotted down plants including dill, wild radish, stinging nettle, slender celery and hedge mustard. Critically, there was no crepe myrtle, cat's claw creeper, fishbone fern or lilly pilly. Nor could he locate any of these four plants in a new and rigorous search of nearby Little Ugly Creek at Wirrabara Road. Guymer and Taylor went back to Brookfield. Driving along Brookfield Road towards Kenmore, the first crepe myrtle tree he spotted was 600 metres from Gerard and Allison's home and there were others at two more properties further away – but none of the five other key plant species were found with them. It was a unique combination – the botanical fingerprint of the Brookfield Road residence.

In the weeks and months ahead, Guymer set about proving beyond doubt that Allison and Gerard's home was the only location in the vicinity where all six species could be found growing together. Thanks to his thoroughness, police had powerful new evidence indicating Allison had been assaulted or killed on her own property, and her body dragged through the leaf litter.

Forensic coordinator Ewen Taylor was in awe of Guymer's efforts and attention to detail. While some people simply did their jobs, others, like Guymer, went above and beyond what was asked of them. Police colleagues thought the same of Taylor, who had found a kindred spirit in Guymer.

Suicide theory

For more than a decade, Allison and her brother, Ashley Dickie, had owned a cute beach shack at Paradise Point on the Gold Coast. The investment property was right next door to their parents' home. The siblings had bought it jointly with their respective spouses for $165,000 in 2001. They had been renting it out for $340 a week. It was registered, however, only in the name of Gerard and Allison's company, World of Top Step Pty Ltd. Manoeuvring from behind bars at Arthur Gorrie, Gerard wrote to the Australian Securities and Investments Commission informing them his wife had died and he had become sole director and secretary of the company. He then put the Gold Coast property on the market. 'Renovate, detonate or land bank for the future,' read the marketing slogan. An auction was planned for 16 September 2012.

Allison's family discovered the plan and was horrified. They wanted any money in their daughter's estate to go to her children, not be swallowed up funding Gerard's defence. They had to move fast if they wanted to stop Gerard spending the money. Lawyers for Geoff Dickie appeared in the Supreme Court on 5 September to argue his daughter's assets should not be sold or the proceeds divided before Gerard's trial. Dickie filed an affidavit saying he was 'concerned that the advertising of the property for sale by auction indicates Gerard is taking steps to dispose of an asset in which Allison's estate may have an interest'.

Justice Glenn Martin – with the consent of all the parties – gave Geoff Dickie interim control of Allison's estate until a verdict was reached in Gerard's trial. It was too late to prevent the sale of the Gold Coast property. A pre-auction offer of $440,000 had already been accepted. Most of the money would go to the bank – there was a $335,000 loan against the property. Justice Martin ordered any money left over from the sale be put in a trust account.

Gerard's legal bills were mounting, and were about to rise again with another attempt at bail. His second and final bid for bail was held in the new $570 million Queen Elizabeth II Courts of Law building on 14 December 2012. He would either be home for Christmas, or face at least another 18 months behind bars awaiting trial. In documents filed ahead of the hearing, he had promised to have no contact with Crown witnesses, but a note at the bottom of the paperwork specified that would not encompass his three daughters. He wanted to be back with the girls.

Once again, Gerard awaited the result from Arthur Gorrie Correctional Centre. His sister and some of Allison's family took seats in the packed public gallery ahead of the 2.30 pm hearing. Allison's uncle Don Moore and cousin Jodie Dann had committed to attending every court hearing to relay information to her family. Justice Peter Applegarth would bring a new set of eyes to Gerard's bid for bail.

Gerard's defence team had been provided with the police brief of evidence, and his barrister Peter Davis SC came out with all guns blazing. He told the court there was a compelling alternative theory Allison was not murdered at all.

'An examination of the Crown brief showed there is as good, if not better, case for suicide of Ms Baden-Clay as there is for murder,' he said.

Davis said toxicology results showed there was a 'real possibility that she died of an overdose' of Zoloft. Notes in Allison's journal fitted with the suicide theory, he added.

'She's speaking about not wanting to be alone, and being afraid of being alone,' he said.

Meanwhile, Gerard's affair – cited as a motive for murder – was equally consistent with a motive for Allison taking her own life. He added an empty Zoloft packet had been found in the couple's Holden Captiva. Davis said the police had held evidence back from the previous bail hearing of a witness seeing a woman walking on Boscombe Road at Brookfield at 5.30 am on the day Allison went missing. Local resident Trent Cowie told police in a statement dated 22 April that the woman was wearing a purple or pink T-shirt and bike pants with dark-coloured shorts over the top. Cowie thought she might have been in some difficulty. Allison was found in a purple singlet, sports shoes and sports pants. Since the previous bail hearing, Gerard had also provided an innocent explanation for looking up 'taking the fifth' and 'self-incrimination' on his iPhone, Davis said. Police had also admitted there was no FaceTime call between Gerard and his father Nigel on the night Allison went missing. Delving into Gerard's finances, Davis said police had submitted at the previous bail hearing that he had debts in excess of $1 million. But they had not canvassed assets. A financial analysis by police showed that taking into account assets – including the value of the rent roll, the investment property on the Gold Coast, and shares – Gerard was only in a slight negative financial position of less than $60,000. Davis submitted that the Crown case had weakened, reducing the flight risk.

Prosecutor Danny Boyle argued Gerard had never indicated to police that Allison was suicidal, and the autopsy report did not support Davis's claim she died from an overdose. Boyle also had the significant new botanical evidence from the Queensland Herbarium's Dr Gordon Guymer, which he told the court was consistent with Allison's death at the house and her body being moved to Kholo Creek. In more detailed written submissions, Boyle also outlined four forensics experts had found the marks on Gerard's face were typical of fingernail scratches. And investigations by civil engineer Martin Giles had found water levels in Kholo Creek would not have moved Allison's body to where it was found, suggesting she had been on the creek bank all along.

Justice Applegarth adjourned to consider his decision and the public gallery spilled out of court, abuzz with the new 'suicide theory'. Applegarth returned to court in the late afternoon. His findings were that Allison had not made any threats to take her own life, and there was nothing in her journal to indicate she was contemplating suicide. While the autopsy had not established a cause of death, there was little evidence to support the suicide theory – the defence could put it no higher than a possibility. Applegarth placed little weight on the sighting of a woman walking at Brookfield. He added that Gerard believed he was in a desperate financial state.

Applegarth concluded the Crown case had not significantly changed. It was 'reasonably strong' and was 'certainly not a weak one'. He refused to grant Gerard bail, slamming shut the prison gates until trial.

Committal

Gerard quietly slipped into the dock and took a seat out of line of sight from the gallery, in the far back corner. It was day one of his committal hearing, but almost no one saw him enter. Only when solicitor Darren Mahony approached for instructions did Gerard pop his head forward. Wearing a dark suit and dark-rimmed glasses, observers noted that he was clean shaven – no longer sporting the beard he had grown after Allison vanished. The only other difference in his appearance was a bad prison barbershop haircut.

The six-day committal hearing before Chief Magistrate Brendan Butler SC was an opportunity for the defence to cross-examine witnesses and test the Crown case. At the end of the hearing, Butler would decide if there was enough evidence for Gerard to face trial.

Prosecutor Danny Boyle was back for the committal and told the court there would be 330 statements tendered and 42 witnesses called, starting with Allison's best friend, Kerry-Anne Walker.

Signalling the suicide theory was still high on the defence agenda, Peter Davis SC was soon firing questions about Allison's depression at Walker. Afterwards, Walker would dwell on the things she wished she had said to stop the defence inflating her friend's mental battles. Allison had depression, yes, but had successfully sought treatment and was a capable, busy and devoted mother and wife. Walker resolved to be firmer when the case went to trial.

A defining moment emerged early in the committal. Queensland Health forensics expert Dr Leslie Griffiths was giving evidence about Gerard's facial injuries, which he believed were from finger-nails. As he spoke, a close-up colour photograph of Gerard's wounded cheek appeared on screens in the court for the first time. A collective gasp from the packed public gallery reflected the impact of seeing the red marks trailing down his face.

Court 17 was the biggest in the Brisbane Magistrates Courts building in George Street. The 90 seats in the public gallery were full or close to full each day as a succession of headline-grabbing witnesses took their turn in the witness box. Dr Bruce Flegg told the court Gerard's requests for large sums of money were 'highly unusual'. Gerard's former business partners told of their falling out. Phill Broom told how it was impossible to keep up with Gerard's messy love life. Jocelyn Frost said she was 'very naive and trusting' and had been left out of pocket when she left the business.

One of Allison's friends, Helen Wilson, noticed that during the breaks, Olivia Walton would step up to the glass screen of the dock, and brother and sister would have intense whispered conversations. As a witness, Walton wasn't allowed in the court during evidence and would disappear before proceedings started. The serious, hushed chats seemed to be more about tactics than support, and Wilson felt her blood boiling. It seemed off, to her. Geoff and Priscilla had stayed away from the hearing because they were witnesses. The next time Walton approached the dock, Wilson went and stood next to her.

'Can't I just have a minute to tell my brother I love him?' Walton said.

'I don't love you, Gerard, I hate you,' blurted Wilson, surprising even herself with the outburst.

Olivia's eyes opened wide, and a member of the defence team yelled to no one in particular, 'Get that woman out of here.' Right then, Magistrate Brendan Butler entered and Wilson shot back to her seat.

The confrontation had the desired effect, however. Security stopped Walton from approaching the dock after that.

The most anticipated witness was Toni McHugh. Protecting her from the media pack, police drove McHugh into an underground car park and escorted her up to court in a private lift. Looking nervous as she entered the witness box, she brushed her long, dark hair back from her face and took a deep breath. Dressed in a conservative black suit, McHugh detailed her three-year relationship with Gerard – the broken promises and stolen moments. She began crying when asked about her angry conversation with Gerard the day before Allison was reported missing. McHugh was shocked, she said, when Gerard had told her both she and Allison would be attending the same real estate conference the next day.

'[I said] "I feel sick. How can you put us in this situation? I think you should tell Allison."'

She told the court she had last seen Gerard a week before his arrest when the pair met to discuss his other extramarital affairs. The former lovers had not seen each other for nearly a year leading up to this court appearance, and McHugh couldn't help shooting nervous glances at Gerard throughout her testimony.

Allison's cousin Jodie Dann, watching in the public gallery, got the impression that McHugh was still in love with Gerard.

At the end of her evidence, police led McHugh out of court through the magistrate's side door, allowing her to avoid the waiting photographers. The front page of the next day's paper would have to make do with a sketch of Gerard's 'other woman'.

Police scientific officers gave evidence about the blood in the Captiva, and Queensland Health forensic scientist Amanda Reeves said it matched Allison's DNA.

Gerard's barrister, Peter Davis SC, is renowned as one of the legal community's gentlemen outside court, but few people would want to face him from the witness box. Police investigative accountant Kelly Beckett was one witness who felt Davis's selective wrath. He said bitingly, 'You have spent, I suggest, a huge amount of time studying these accounts. And the only thing you can point to by way of default is his credit card is overdue.'

Some handled the defence barrister's interrogation better than others. School teacher Christine Skrzeczynski had come forward to say she was the woman spotted walking on Boscombe Road at Brookfield on the morning Allison disappeared. A blonde, she would have closely resembled Allison in the dark. Davis sought to crack her story on day five of the committal, but Skrzeczynski was steadfast, saying she walked that route at that time on every work day, and provided evidence she went to work on 20 April. Davis could have been an errant young student. She left little doubt she was the mystery walker that morning.

Professor Myron Zalucki, an entomologist and insect ecologist, arrived at court looking suitably eccentric – wearing a broad-brimmed bush hat and twirling an umbrella. Zalucki had gone to the Brookfield State School oval with police to search for caterpillars – after Gerard claimed the injuries on his chest had been caused by a caterpillar during the school's cross-country. Zalucki said he did not find any caterpillar nests in the acacia trees at the school oval, and could not find any evidence of stinging caterpillars in the Brookfield area. Davis asked if he thought Gerard could have been bitten.

'Can we not use the term bite?' replied Zalucki, who said there could be painful envenomation from some caterpillars if they deposited their hairs under a person's skin – it was nothing to do with being bitten. Zalucki was non-committal on the subject of whether Gerard's injuries could have been caused by a caterpillar, saying it was hard to judge.

Toxicologist Professor Olaf Drummer dealt a blow to the defence's suicide theory on the sixth and final day of the committal hearing. Drummer told Davis the level of medication in Allison's blood was relatively normal and was not enough to kill her.

Indooroopilly CIB detectives Cameron McLeod and Chris Canniffe and Homicide detectives Peter Roddick and Gavin Pascoe were the final witnesses at the committal hearing. The detectives, under cross-examination, variously weren't able to shed any light on who told Toni McHugh of Gerard's affairs with other women. They were also unaware of any police telling Gerard he could not participate in the search for Allison, as he had claimed.

The public gallery was packed to the rafters for Chief Magistrate Brendan Butler's decision. In the end, it was a mere formality. But before Butler could hand down his ruling, Gerard's barrister Peter Davis stood to announce that although his client 'vehemently denies' the charges, he consented to being committed to trial. It was all theatrics. Butler hardly needed Gerard's consent.

For six days, Gerard had stayed in the far back corner of the dock to remain out of view of those in the court. When Butler asked him to stand for his decision, Gerard again hung back in the rear corner. Butler ordered him to step forward into plain view before continuing: 'I'm of the opinion the evidence is sufficient to put the defendant on trial on the offences charged.'

Asked if he had anything to say, Gerard replied: 'I am not guilty, Your Honour.'

At the front of the court building, Olivia Walton was fighting in her brother's corner, reading a prepared statement in front of TV cameras: 'I still believe that my brother Gerard is an innocent man. I will continue to support him throughout this process. One day the truth will be revealed. Gerard is an innocent man.'

There was still time for Gerard to reconsider his story. People in situations like his are usually advised to consider pleading guilty to a lesser charge of manslaughter. He might argue, for example, that Allison had died accidentally in a fight – perhaps they had a heated argument. There was certainly plenty for the couple to clash over. It would then be hard for the Crown to prove murder, an offence that requires an intent to kill. A guilty plea to manslaughter would likely see him out on parole in eight years. A murder conviction, on the other hand, would carry a minimum 15-year non-parole sentence.

Gerard's story wasn't changing. He was, however, thinking about changing his legal team. Having been lawyer-shopping via Olivia immediately following his arrest, he now dropped solicitor Darren Mahony, who had been advising him since the day Allison was reported missing. He would be replaced by solicitor Peter Shields, a former detective who had spent 14 years in the Queensland Police Service, including three in Homicide, before changing teams. Shields had never shied from a good fight – in his legal career and on the field as a former first-grade rugby league player. In the 1990 Brisbane Winfield Cup grand final, as a winger for Valleys, he scored the first try but was also at the centre of a brawl described as the worst in a decade of finals. Dark-haired with a light, salt-and-pepper beard, Shields had convinced Gerard he could take the fight up to the prosecution.

Barrister Peter Davis SC was also off the case. Gerard decided to go to trial with Michael Byrne QC, who regularly worked with Shields. Byrne had been a barrister since 1977 and was formerly Queensland's Deputy Director of Public Prosecutions. He was the state's most experienced prosecutor when he quit in 2001. The grey-haired silk had a calm and dignified presence and air of authority in court.

A tale of two husbands

A few weeks before Gerard-Baden Clay was to stand trial, I found myself watching a YouTube clip of his only TV interview. Alyshia Gates, the journalist who waited outside his parents' Kenmore home early one morning and managed to catch Gerard and his sister leaving the house, had put herself in the right place at the right time. She ended up in the running for a Logie Award for Best News Report for the snatched interview.

My gut was telling me Gerard deserved an award of his own for his performance that day. His quavering voice didn't ring true, and he seemed anxious to wind up the interview. I wondered what a body language expert would make of it all. On a whim I decided to ask one.

Joe Navarro is a former FBI agent, lecturer and author. He spent 25 years at the Bureau, and helped set up the elite Behavioural Analysis Program, made famous by a host of fictional works such as blockbuster movie *Silence of the Lambs* and the TV series *Criminal Minds*. A specialist in non-verbal communication, or body language, Navarro retired from the FBI in 2003 and has since been teaching, writing and consulting. A chance meeting in 2005 led to an unusual sideline coaching poker players. Professional poker has become a lucrative and competitive field, and players are always looking for something to give them an edge.

There are a couple of well-known 'tells', or signals you may be lying, in poker, and players have found ways to counter them. Pupils dilate during lies, so many players have taken to wearing sunglasses. A hard swallow indicates discomfort, so players have taken to wearing scarves. Navarro offers tips on 'reading' less obvious tells in his books, *Read 'Em and Reap:*

A Career FBI Agent's Guide to Decoding Poker Tells and *200 Poker Tells*. He has also written guides for police on conducting interviews and spotting signs of deception. At 61, the prolific author was still very much in demand.

Without expecting too much, I dashed off an email to the address listed on Navarro's website. I briefly outlined the case and asked if he perhaps had time to take a look at the news clip. Just 13 minutes later, a reply pinged into my inbox from the other side of the world. It was 7 pm at Navarro's home in Tampa, Florida, but he had replied almost immediately, agreeing to take a look.

Later, at night in Brisbane, another message from Navarro popped up in my inbox: 'Are you on Skype?'

I rushed to the computer, began downloading and installing the program, raced to the bedroom to throw on a fresh work shirt and sat down in front of the computer screen in my smart shirt and rumpled pyjama bottoms.

I needn't have worried too much. Navarro was doing up his tie as we spoke, the living embodiment of the saying: 'If you want something done, ask a busy man.' He explained he initially watches clips such as Gerard's interview with the sound off, to pick up on non-verbal cues only. If anything looks odd or indicates discomfort, he returns to that section of the clip and turns the volume up to see what was being discussed at that point.

In Gerard's case, Navarro noted a 'hard swallow', indicating discomfort, after Gerard said he trusted police were 'doing everything they can to find my wife' and just before saying, 'We just hope she will come home soon.'

The lack of tears, Navarro said, was not an issue. 'There are behaviours that we demonstrate when we're devastated that go beyond tears.' Touching the neck and biting the top lip are two of these – neither of which Gerard did.

Navarro was also concerned by Gerard's apparent anxiety to end the interview – he walked away after a few minutes, leaving Olivia to make a short plea for public information to find Allison: 'She's there pleading for assistance to find her sister-in-law and he just walks away. We call that distancing. It's not like he was being hammered [by media]. That walking away, that just reeked. People that are genuine are running into the house grabbing one more photograph to show to the public to say, "This is how she looks with her hair coloured; this is when it's clean; this is when it's dirty; this is one after work. It's everything they can do to help find this person."'

While nothing definitive could be read into such a short clip, Navarro explained it thus: 'When I look at cases like this, I say, does their presentation put things to rest for me or does it make me want to dig deeper. This one, definitely I want to dig deeper.'

After the conversation with Navarro ended, I pondered his remark that the genuinely devastated often bit their upper lips. Biting the bottom lip displayed anxiety. Biting the top lip was devastation.

I went back to YouTube and searched for clips of Tom Meagher. It seemed an obvious comparison and revealed a tale of two husbands. Meagher's wife, Jill, vanished after a night out with friends in Melbourne in September 2012. It occurred just three months after Gerard Baden-Clay had been charged with murdering the wife *he* reported missing. As initial reports about Jill's disappearance became public, a few cynics eyed her husband with suspicion. But Tom was an open book, throwing himself in front of the media in a constant push to keep his wife's face on TV and in the newspapers. Five days after she disappeared, serial rapist Adrian Ernest Bayley led police to her body. He was sentenced to life imprisonment in June 2013.

The many clips of Tom's constant pleas for help to find his wife contrasted jarringly with Gerard's single, reluctant media appearance. The videos showed Tom constantly biting his top lip as he answered question after question about Jill. Like a punch-drunk boxer, he stood in front of the media pack until they ran out of questions. He never took a backward step, never tried to end an interview early. Asked by one journalist what his plans were, he replied: 'Well, we're still doing loads of postering, a Facebook campaign and Twittering – all that stuff. But I'm doing loads and loads of interviews and media stuff. I just want to get as much out there as possible.'

Keeping the media spotlight on his missing wife and pleading for information was just about the only thing Tom Meagher could do and he did it zealously. It fitted with Navarro's assessment that relatives of the missing were generally media-hungry, not media-shy as Gerard had been – even turning down a police request to front a public appeal for information when Allison was missing.

Trial begins

A month out from Gerard's trial, prosecutors invited Allison's family to a private meeting to brief them on what to expect. The family had been getting to know Consultant Crown Prosecutor Danny Boyle, who had been on the case since the start. Boyle had launched his legal career 25 years earlier. Tall, with a distinctive shaved head, he had an easygoing and friendly manner, perhaps best described by the adage, 'You catch more flies with honey.' For the trial, he would be working side-by-side with Todd Fuller QC, a bookish, tactical prosecutor who held the third most senior role in the Office of the Director of Public Prosecutions. One rung above Fuller was the Deputy Director, Michael Byrne QC, who had prosecuted Brett Cowan for Daniel Morcombe's murder earlier that year. It was fortunate, for clarity more than anything else, that Byrne was not involved in the Baden-Clay trial. Had he been, it would have resulted in the confusing scenario of having three Byrnes in court – Michael Byrne for the prosecution, Michael Byrne for the defence, and John Byrne as judge.

Only on the biggest of cases would two senior prosecutors be assigned, and both were present for the meeting with Allison's inner circle – Priscilla, Geoff and Ashley Dickie, Don Moore, Jodie Dann, Kerry-Anne Walker and a Queensland Homicide Victims' Support Group representative. Fuller outlined the game plan. He would start with the discovery of Allison's body at Kholo Creek Bridge, then go backwards in time to explain how she got there. The most recent high-profile murder prosecution in Queensland was that of Daniel Morcombe's killer, Brett Peter Cowan. In that instance, Daniel's parents, Bruce and Denise, were called as the first witnesses, to allow them to sit in court for the remainder of the trial. Fuller explained he would be taking a different tack. His first witnesses would be the people who found Allison. He told Allison's parents his strategy was to keep the case as simple as possible. He did not want the trial sidetracked, or jury confused by tales of Gerard's behaviour in the distant past, no matter how appalling. The evidence he presented had to be narrowly focused. It was going to be difficult for the family, who knew much more than Fuller planned to present to a jury at trial.

Gerard's trial finally got underway at the Queen Elizabeth II Courts of Law on Tuesday 10 June 2014, after the Queen's Birthday long weekend. The court on level three fell silent as Justice John Byrne entered at 10 am. White haired with a matching beard, the 65-year-old judge had a presence that commanded authority. Justice Byrne's associate formally called the case for trial, announcing 'the Queen against Gerard Robert Baden-Clay'. Asked to enter his plea to the single charge of the murder of his wife, he answered in a firm, clear voice, 'Not guilty, Your Honour.'

The next big question for Gerard's trial was how long it would take to select a jury. In rare cases of immense publicity, jurors could be asked about their impartiality. Justice Byrne had ruled the jury would be asked three questions: Whether they or relatives lived in various areas in the western suburbs, including Brookfield, at the time of Allison's disappearance; if they had attended a fundraiser or donated to any fund set up in connection to the case; and whether they had ever expressed an opinion about Gerard's guilt or innocence. Answering yes to any of these did not automatically exclude potential jurors, which was just as well, as some observers wondered whether the court could ever find 12 jurors and three reserves who hadn't expressed a view on Gerard's guilt or innocence.

One by one, potential jurors were called into court. If they made it to the witness box and the bailiff started reading the affirmation or oath, they were through to the jury. About a dozen people had to turn and walk out again when the defence called 'challenge' or prosecution called 'stand by'. But in less than an hour, a jury of 15 had been chosen. Prosecutor Danny Boyle read aloud the names of 77 witnesses to be called, and the jury was asked if there was any reason they could not serve impartially. None raised their hands, and they were sent out to answer the three questions.

Two women admitted they had expressed views on Gerard's guilt or innocence. Defence barrister Byrne wanted to ask the jurors what their views were, however Justice Byrne said the important thing was whether the jurors believed they could be impartial – the mere fact they had expressed a view was 'scarcely surprising'. Both jurors were brought back individually, and each asked if they could reach a verdict with an open mind. Both said they could.

'I don't think I would've sat here this long so far and been through what the judge has said this morning if I didn't think I could,' one replied. 'Also, the nature of my job – I am a scientist. So I would prefer with any hypothesis to actually see it proven first.'

Byrne said the defence would not challenge the women, and the jury selection was complete. Seven men and five women would decide Gerard's fate, with three women reserves. Justice Byrne's instructions had a modern flavour, with warnings for the jury to stay off Twitter, Facebook, YouTube, blogs and the internet in general when it came to the case. He told the jury to 'pay careful attention to the evidence and ignore anything you may hear or read about the case out of court' including the inevitable barrage of media reports.

'Such reports tend to be confined to some matter thought to be newsworthy. Such a matter may well be of little or no significance in the light of the whole of the evidence,' he said.

With the jury selection formalities complete before lunch, Allison's family released a brief statement requesting privacy.

'As a family we would like to thank the Australian media for the respect you have shown us over the past two years during what has been the most devastating period of our lives . . . We ask that you respect our privacy and our decision not to grant interviews and refrain from photographing or filming the children.'

Solicitor Peter Shields had been trying to cultivate some goodwill for the Baden-Clays since taking over the case. At a pre-trial Justice Department media briefing, Shields asked journalists to leave Gerard's family alone during the trial. He added: 'These are good people.'

Outside court in the lunch break, Nigel and Elaine Baden-Clay and Olivia and Ian Walton gathered behind Shields as he read out a prepared statement: 'The defence and my client's family will not be making any statement to the media or answering any questions asked by the media until after the verdict. I also ask the media to respect my client's family as they attend court in support of Gerard.'

After lunch, the trial moved to floor 5, Court 11, where it would remain for the rest of the proceedings. To cater for the expected public interest, live footage of the trial was also being beamed onto screens in Court 17, one floor above, and to a media room on floor 10. In the main court, there was some jostling for the 48 public seats. Allison's family and friends took out the group of 15 seats on the right and also some of the 33 seats on the left. Geoff and Priscilla Dickie were staying away until they gave evidence, and would rely on family to update them at the start of the trial. Don and Julie Moore and Jodie Dann took a seat in the front row. Helen Wilson, Allison's friend who had been at the front of the line every day at the committal, took a seat in the second row. The Baden-Clays set up camp in the front row on the left, behind the dock, where they could be closest to Gerard.

Nicest guy in the world

Allison was lying on her side, as though asleep. A closer inspection revealed the reality. Todd Fuller was describing kayaker Daryl Joyce's grim discovery on his gentle paddle along Kholo Creek. Police rappelled from the bridge. Hoisted her up. It was just how Fuller told Allison's family he would start, but it was still impossible to prepare for the graphic photographs that flashed up on the screens in the court as he gave his opening address. Tragic images of Allison on the muddy creek bank, which lodged in your memory and reappeared when you closed your eyes. An eerily unnatural pose, with her jumper caught up around her arms and pulled over her head. There was no escaping from them in the courtroom. Television screens hung from the walls on either side of the court and sat on the desks in front of the jury and on the bar table. There were even small screens at Gerard's feet in the dock.

Gerard showed no sign of being rattled by the succession of harrowing images of his dead wife, glancing nonchalantly towards the biggest screen on the right of the court.

Fuller's words tumbled out rapidly at the start, rushing jurors into the trial. He slowed to tell the jury 'a little bit about her' – her marriage, children and home on Brookfield Road. How Allison had a normal day, and then was gone.

'The Crown case, ladies and gentlemen, is a circumstantial one, and the Crown says that Allison Baden-Clay did not die of natural causes, that she in fact died at the hands of her husband.'

Fuller went through the story. There was a lot to take in, but it all built up to the scratches on Gerard's face: 'Allison Baden-Clay's mark upon him,' he finished.

The trial's first witness was Ewen Taylor, the tireless police forensic coordinator, who talked the jury through the process of gathering evidence and described the solemn day he lowered himself down from Kholo Creek Bridge. Photographs of Allison's body reappeared on the screen. Still, there was no change to Gerard's blank stare in the dock.

Next up was Sergeant Murray Watson from Indooroopilly Police Station. Watson had helped Gerard evict tenants from a property in Chalcot Road at Anstead in 2010. A 'cult' in the house was feared to have stockpiled weapons, and Watson had met Gerard there at least three times. It was around the corner from the Kholo Creek bridge, and his testimony was intended to demonstrate Gerard was familiar with the area. But when defence barrister Michael Byrne stood, he had a card up his sleeve. Watson had known Gerard for years through organisations such as the chamber of commerce and Rotary.

'And you regarded him as being "one of the nicest guys in the world", didn't you?' asked Byrne.

'Yes. I would say that's true,' replied Watson.

The words hung in the air. It had inadvertently turned into a glowing character reference for the accused.

The Crown's theory was Gerard had taken Allison's body down an embankment on the right-hand side of the bridge. Underneath the bridge, he simply rolled her over a ledge to the muddy creek bank below. She lay there until she was found. It would explain the lack of footprints or any other disturbance in the mud around her.

Senior Constable Ashley Huth described the treacherous conditions on the muddy bank when he rappelled from Kholo Creek Bridge with Taylor. He said he had also conducted a thorough search for blood around Gerard's home and didn't find any.

The first day of the trial had moved faster than almost anyone expected. A few things stood out. There had been no mention of Allison's $1 million in life insurance. In earlier court hearings, the payout had been cited as a motive for the cash-strapped Gerard to murder his wife. And absent from the witness list read out to the jury were Gerard's former business partners Phill Broom and Jocelyn Frost. Fuller had told Allison's family he wanted to keep things simple and clearly he meant it.

Day two of the trial began with more grim evidence about the discovery and examination of Allison's badly decomposed body. Again, Gerard sat through it passively. Justice Byrne had ruled in a pre-trial hearing the prosecution could not present evidence that granular brown material found on Allison's brain may have been a subdural haemorrhage.

At trial, pathologist Nathan Milne said Allison's only injuries were a probable bruise on the internal lining of the chest wall, perhaps from a mild blunt force, and a chip from her lower left eye tooth. Milne suspected the body was under the bridge in the position it was found within hours of death because of features including hypostasis – the settling of blood with gravity on her right side – and other changes he observed on different parts of the body. He found nothing to suggest Allison drowned, overdosed or fell from the bridge, but conceded in cross-examination he couldn't rule these out.

Simpler murder trials had gunshot or knife wounds to present to the jury. This wasn't one of those cases.

Last song

The repeated refrain from the next set of witnesses was that Allison had seemed normal – happy in fact – on her last day alive. Fiona Christ had a pleasant 20-minute chat with Allison at Brookfield State School when they were dropping their children off at prep at 8.30 am on Thursday 19 April 2012. Allison was excited about the birth of her nephew the previous day and mentioned picking up Olivia Walton from hospital after she had suffered a crippling headache. They spoke about the school cross-country ahead that day and finalised sleepover plans – some of their children were to stay at the Christs' and some at the Baden-Clays' on the Friday night. The Mother's Day stall was coming up and they put their names down to help with the morning set-up. There was nothing out of the ordinary.

'She seemed fine and she seemed happy,' said Christ.

Michael Byrne, in cross-examination, wanted details of Allison's depression. Christ said Allison first told her of being depressed after her eldest daughter was born in 2001 and that she had spent a lot of the time on the couch around that period. Gerard stayed home to support her.

Asked about other incidents, Christ answered that Allison was unable to drive their children to a camp in late 2011 because her antidepressants made her nauseous and dizzy.

Raising the birth of Allison's nephew, Byrne made a statement of his question: 'Were you aware that Allison had desperately wanted a male child?'

Christ, who had just told the court of Allison's happiness at the birth of her nephew, said she wasn't aware.

Anne Swalwell also ran into Allison outside the prep class-room about nine that morning. Swalwell's daughter took jazz ballet lessons with Allison at the school. The two women discussed the upcoming Mother's Day stall. Swalwell was organising it, and Allison said she would 'have to get time off from the boss' to make it.

'It was all just, you know, banter. Friendly banter. She seemed happy that morning, actually,' Swalwell said.

Karen Nielsen, an owner of real-estate training firm PRET Australia, had a four-hour meeting with Allison at Century 21 Westside that day. Allison wanted to grow the business and they discussed strategies. Nielsen thought Allison was 'extremely positive' and they arranged to meet again.

As they were finishing, Allison wanted to take Nielsen to meet Gerard. He was on the phone when they first went into the room and Allison picked up a photograph of their three children and showed it to Nielsen. When he hung up the phone, Allison introduced Gerard. Nielsen left about 1.30 pm.

'She was extremely involved and engrossed in what we were discussing the whole time I was there and we left on a positive note,' Nielsen said.

Under cross-examination, Nielsen confirmed Allison had discussed being on a protein diet and exercise program. Allison had given her a piece of cake at lunch but wouldn't have any herself.

Former Century 21 Westside receptionist Gabrielle Cadioli also remembered Allison being happy and engaged in her work that day. Cadioli said she and office manager Elizabeth Scully had told Allison to leave early for her hairdressing appointment that afternoon because there had been an accident on the freeway and it was clogging up Moggill Road. Allison said goodbye in the afternoon and added she had the real estate conference the next day and wouldn't be back until Tuesday.

'She was in a really good mood. Allison enjoyed training and she'd vocalised that to me before. She was having a bit of a joke and was laughing with us that afternoon as well,' Cadioli said.

In cross-examination, Cadioli agreed Gerard was a good boss who put her through a business administration course.

Byrne then took Cadioli to a topic that was already becoming a familiar source of his questions – depression. On previous occasions, Cadioli admitted, Allison had spoken to her in general conversation about suffering anxiety and depression; Allison had wondered whether she had passed the illness on to her daughters.

Allison's happy mood appeared to have vanished by the time she reached the hair salon on the afternoon of 19 April. Hairdresser Monique Waymouth said Allison was there for her third appointment in just over a week because she was unhappy with her hair colour.

'She seemed a little bit stressed when she came in, and then she was fairly quiet,' Waymouth said.

This may have simply reflected Allison's frustration at returning to the salon to have a colour redone.

The next witness called was one of the few people Allison confided in during the last months of her life. Wendy Mollah had tipped her off to Gerard's affair with Toni McHugh after hearing the talk around Brookfield State School. Mollah told the court she met Allison through the school, where they had children in the same grade: 'She was a wonderful mother. Most of her time was spent doing things for them.'

The two friends had signed up to a course called 'Real Estate Options' about a year to 18 months before Allison's death, with the hope of trying to make some money. It was more evidence of Allison making plans for the future, but this particular element had a twist: Allison didn't want Gerard to know about the course. Mollah didn't broach it at the trial, but some friends thought Allison was starting to make contingency plans for a future without Gerard.

Mollah told the court Allison had been around for dinner three weeks before she died, and seemed fine but was struggling to deal with the affair.

Gerard got in touch with Mollah through the school on the day he reported Allison missing: 'He sounded very casual. I was surprised. If your wife is missing . . . He just said she'd gone for a walk and she hadn't come back.'

On the day Allison vanished, her three daughters were taken to Indooroopilly Police Station to speak to detectives. Videos of the little girls talking to police one-by-one were now shown to the court. As soon as the eldest daughter appeared on court screens, Gerard's face crumpled. Impassive and dry-eyed through the images of his wife's body, he was instantly in tears at the sight of his daughter. Aged ten at the time, she was in her school uniform, with her hair pulled back in a ponytail, sitting on a wide brown couch with a fluffy toy orangutan perched beside her and a red box filled with toys at her feet. The two female detectives interviewing her were gentle but she dabbed at her face with a tissue and burst into sobs.

'It was really just normal like every other night. She just put us to bed. She just comes in and says goodnight and gives us a pat,' she said.

Shortly after going to bed at about seven o'clock, she got up for a drink of water and her mum was on the couch and her dad was coming up the front stairs in pyjamas and shoes. He said he was going to do the ironing. In the morning her mum was gone. Her dad was 'trying to keep calm for us' but she said she didn't know what was going on in his head.

When police asked if her parents ever argued, she said: 'If they do fight, it's only little arguments that go for a couple of seconds and then they stop.'

When the second video was played, it showed Allison and Gerard's middle daughter struggling to speak through deep sobs in a different interview room. Her mum had put the then eight-year-old to bed exactly as she did every other night: 'She sings a song to me.'

Her mum checked on her again before going to bed, she said. The detectives asked her how she knew.

'Because she told me she would,' she answered.

They were just little girls, scared and missing their mum.

Thursday 12 June, day three of the trial, continued with police videos of the Baden-Clay girls. This time it was the youngest daughter. Just five years old, she was cradling a Teletubbies doll and tucked into the corner of the big couch under the orang-utan toy. She kicked her legs up and down as she tried to answer questions from two detectives.

Three more videos were shown to the court from police interviews with each of the girls at Surfers Paradise station on 27 June 2012, a fortnight after their father's arrest. The girls had not heard anything on the night their mum disappeared, they said. Detectives asked the girls about the toys found stacked in the back of the Captiva. The eldest said they had recently gathered up their old toys to give to charity. She hadn't seen them in the boot of the Captiva before.

The trial moved on to witnesses from around the western suburbs who reported hearing screams, thuds, barking and other mysterious sounds at various times and places on the night Allison disappeared. Fiona White heard two high-pitched screams at around 9 pm or 10 pm that were like 'someone falling off a cliff'. White, who lived in Clarkson Place at Kenmore Hills, couldn't be certain of the day but knew it was around the time of Allison's disappearance.

Brookfield residents Susan Braun, Anne Rhodes and Julie and Kim Tzvetkoff told of hearing various sounds between 8 pm and midnight. David Jenkinson, who lived at Karalee, about 500 metres from Kholo Creek Bridge, where Allison's body was found, woke to the sound of barking dogs, then heard two thuds 'like a cement bag or something heavy being thrown onto the ground' and a car door close about 10.30 pm. Real estate agent Brian Mason told of the cacophony of barking dogs at homes near Kholo Creek after midnight.

Battle lines

Elaine Baden-Clay was making a statement without words. It took a while to register, what with everything else going on in the trial, but soon it was impossible to miss: every day, Gerard's mother was arriving at court in the same loud purple jacket. Elaine had ditched her former sophisticated, feminine look and now sported severely cropped grey hair. And she seemed fixated with purple. Elaine wore a purple scarf and sipped from a purple water bottle. Olivia Walton donned a purple scarf too.

People started speculating about the significance of the colour. Like most things connected to the Baden-Clays, it seemed to have a Scouting link. Purple was the colour of the World Scout Emblem, as chosen by founder Baden-Powell. It is also the direct opposite of yellow on the colour wheel. Allison's family had publicly adopted yellow, but they were banned from wearing the colour as a symbol in court because of the risk it could prejudice the jury – the committal hearing had been a sea of yellow.

Unmistakably, the two families were on a collision course. They were already distant before Allison's disappearance. Now, they were bitterly divided by fierce, competing loyalties. At Gerard's trial, testifying one after the other, the two sides would tell two vastly different stories. One shone a light on the positive in Allison, and the other vividly highlighted the negative.

Nigel Baden-Clay was the first family member to testify, and started on the front foot by pulling up prosecutor Todd Fuller for pronouncing his son's name 'Ger-rard', lengthening the second syllable.

'Slight correction. We christened him Gerard [Ger-red],' Nigel said crisply.

Nigel told the court of taking an anxious early-morning call out of the blue from his elder son: Allison hadn't returned from a walk. Nigel drove to Gerard's Brookfield home shortly after.

'I noticed that he had cuts on his cheek and a bit of bandaid sort of coming off. He said, "I cut myself shaving this morning."'

Fuller asked if Gerard and Allison discussed their relationship with him.

'No they didn't,' Nigel replied. 'They were a very private couple, and we were unaware of the depression that Allison was suffering until probably four or five years into their marriage.'

The answer was telling – Fuller hadn't asked about Allison's depression. It seemed Nigel couldn't wait to throw it before the jury. Interestingly, he didn't volunteer information about Gerard's affairs when asked about the couple's relationship – just Allison's depression. In cross-examination, Byrne provided plenty of other opportunities, asking Nigel how he first learnt of Allison's depression. Nigel said Allison had phoned Elaine one day and asked to see her.

'Elaine explained to me that Allison had broken down in tears and told her that she was suffering from some illness, and she didn't know what was wrong with her, and could Elaine advise her on who she might seek to help.'

Elaine put Allison onto her own GP, who referred her to a specialist psychiatrist. Asked for any manifestations of the illness, Nigel said the curtains and blinds would be drawn and the house in semi-darkness.

With that evidence and Nigel still in the witness box, the first week of the trial was over. Evidence wasn't being taken on Fridays, and he would have to return on Monday. He had been the 23rd witness. At this rate the whole thing could be wrapped up in three weeks.

Allison's parents and Kerry-Anne Walker were told they would be among the next to give evidence, and faced an agonising wait over the weekend. Allison's cousin Jodie Dann found doubts creeping in. Was the prosecution rushing? Were they getting everything they could out of the witnesses as one after another was checked off?

On Thursday night I received an email from a friend of Gerard's who had been following the case through media coverage.

'I am starting to think the prosecution don't quite have enough,' the person wrote. 'I keep thinking they must have more – something up their sleeve – but it's not looking great at this point (albeit with many witnesses to go). All those contra-dictory reports from neighbours today about times and dates and directions of noises did little for the prosecution's cause in my opinion, especially in light of the girls' statements that they slept through and heard nothing. Am I reading this wrong?'

Back in the *Courier-Mail* office, sentiment was similar, with colleagues already predicting a 'not guilty' verdict. As Gerard knew, in real estate and in life, first impressions counted. People took mere minutes to make up their minds. What had the jurors made of the first week? There was a lot of evidence to come, but so far there was a feeling things were going Gerard's way.

The story of Allison and Gerard had been big news from the start, but the trial took the public's interest to a new level. Crowds of court watchers were flocking to the trial. Their numbers were growing bigger and they were arriving earlier each day. By the time the glass doors to the building opened at 8.30 am, there would already be a long line. From there, it was a dash through security, a race to the lifts, then a new line would form outside Court 11. The courtroom door would be unlocked shortly before the start of proceedings at 10 am. Family members were allowed in first, then those in line took whatever seats remained.

On Monday 16 June, the court was due to hear from those central to the case. Nigel Baden-Clay was to finish his testi-mony and would be followed by Gerard's sister, Olivia Walton.

Next were Allison's parents, Geoff and Priscilla Dickie, and her close friend, Kerry-Anne Walker. After Walker, star witness Toni McHugh was scheduled to face questioning.

It was a momentous day and the Dickie family's large contingent of supporters turned out in force. When the courtroom doors opened, 35 relatives and friends of Allison and eight relatives and friends of Gerard took their seats, leaving only five for the public. In a show of kindness rarely reserved for the media, the members of the public who were next in line stood aside to let me and *Courier-Mail* colleague Kate Kyriacou, along with Channel 9's Chris Allen, into court.

Those who didn't make the cut, many of whom had been lining up for hours, politely went to the overflow court upstairs, which was itself overflowing. In this court, people were crammed into every available seat including the dock, jury area and at the bench, ready to study the live video feed.

That morning, Gerard's barrister, Michael Byrne, resumed his questioning. Nigel was at pains to point out that two things Gerard did which had drawn heavy criticism in the media – namely, calling in lawyers on day one and trying to lodge an insurance claim with unseemly haste – were both down to him. Gerard's father told the court he suggested his son contact a lawyer after hearing that 15 police officers and nine police vehicles were at his son's home on the Friday.

'I found that alarming news and I immediately telephoned my son. I said to him, "It's probably time that you had a lawyer. Would you like me to organise that for you?" And he said, "Yes, please."'

Nigel turned to Gerard's friends Rob Cheesman and Stuart Christ for advice on a lawyer and 'both of them named the same person'. Nigel phoned the lawyer that morning, setting off a chain of events. The lawyer phoned Gerard and told him not to do anything until he heard from Gold Coast criminal defence lawyer Darren Mahony, who called a short time later. Nigel also testified he raised the issue of Allison's insurance with Gerard after the body was discovered at Kholo Creek.

'I said, "One of your obligations is to notify the insurance company as soon as it is obvious that the person is deceased." And understandably, [me] having been an insurance agent, he asked me to take care of the paperwork and he would duly sign it. So this is what I did.'

Fuller, in re-examination, asked Nigel if he saw any manifestations of Allison's depression in 2012, rather than the distant past. Here, Nigel offered his opinion about Allison's dress sense: 'One of the things that we came to realise was that Allison's dress was always of a dull nature. It was black or brown or possibly cream. There was nothing bright in her wardrobe at all, and I think that was a sort of an indication that she was a depressed person.'

Outside court, this comment had everyone talking. The whole of Melbourne would be depressed by his rule of thumb, someone groaned. The defence's tactic of highlighting Allison's depression was in danger of backfiring through heavy-handedness.

When Olivia Walton took the stand she described Allison's depression with an even greater level of detail. Olivia told the jury she graduated from the Australian Defence Force Academy and Royal Military College at Duntroon. She had been posted to Townsville, but was medically discharged with a back injury before returning to Brisbane in 1999. In lengthy evidence, Olivia told the court Gerard treated Allison like a princess – even calling her Princess when they first met.

'They were very much in love and it was very obvious. I loved seeing them together and I enjoyed their company,' she said.

However, she and husband, Ian Walton, noticed strain between the couple after they had their first child. They clashed over parenting styles and seemed less affectionate. Olivia said Gerard would drive Allison everywhere. Her brother would also visit frequently with their daughter while Allison remained home to rest, she said. After being diagnosed with depression during her second pregnancy, Allison asked Olivia to help with childcare once a week. Sometime around 2010, Allison came over one day, lay on the couch and began crying. 'I asked her what was wrong and I remember her telling me that their finances were – they were really struggling,' Olivia said.

Olivia and her family moved back to Townsville in June 2011 and had very little contact with Gerard and Allison in the year leading up to her death. Olivia was in Brisbane on holiday when Allison disappeared and had driven to her brother's home that morning to help search and settle the girls.

Fuller asked if Olivia remembered anything about her brother's physical appearance the morning he reported Allison missing.

'I really didn't, at the time, notice anything,' she said.

It seemed extraordinary. Others who encountered Gerard that morning noticed his scratches immediately. It was the reason police were on alert. It was one of the major reasons they were in court now. Yet the Duntroon-trained Walton – a former Intelligence Corps officer, no less – told the court she had not noticed anything remarkable about her brother's appearance that morning.

Fuller finished his questioning and defence barrister Michael Byrne rose. Mystifyingly, he began by calling Olivia 'Mrs Baden Walton'. Byrne wanted to know more about Allison withdrawing socially.

Olivia said she first noticed it when Allison and Gerard returned to Australia after their extended honeymoon: 'I perceived Allison's behaviour as quite odd and quite withdrawn, and whenever we visited their home it was always very dark and the curtains were always drawn. She didn't engage in social activities as much as I remembered.'

The worrying behaviour continued after the birth of their eldest daughter, Olivia continued, then related an incident in graphic detail. Olivia had picked up Allison and her daughter to go to playgroup. She strapped Allison's daughter into the car seat 'because she wasn't confident to do that'. In the three- to five-minute drive to the playgroup venue, Allison became increasingly anxious.

'We arrived at the playgroup, she opened the car door and vomited into the gutter and I noticed, as she got out of the car that she had lost control of her bladder as well,' Olivia told the court.

She took Allison home and helped her into bed, only realising later the incident was anxiety-related.

Some of the jurors looked distressed.

Walton, at Byrne's request, went on to detail how Allison wouldn't go to social events, leaving Gerard to take the children on his own. Another time, Allison broke her ankle and spent six weeks at Olivia's house and 'lay on the couch every day'. Olivia would do their washing and give them a meal. 'And sometimes that would happen even after Allison's ankle was healed, and before that too,' she added.

Olivia told of her surprise when Gerard started working from home for a period, 'but we realised that it was because he was wanting to be at home with Allison'. For a couple of years her brother rarely went out in case Allison needed him. The 'pressures of life seemed to be too much' for Allison and she struggled to stick to the parenting routines she and Gerard had agreed on.

Allison would ask Olivia to teach her how to cook and make meal plans. Gerard liked to have a routine where the children put themselves to sleep in their own bed without being coaxed or cuddled and 'that was something that was just very difficult for Allison'.

Byrne's questioning about Allison's depression went on. Allison's family and friends were angry about the portrayal of Allison that emerged. As the defence QC emphasised the point about Allison's struggles, some of the jurors shifted uncomfortably on their seats. One woman crossed her arms and shook her head as it continued.

Fuller, in re-examination, asked Olivia to go through Allison's employment. The answers highlighted Allison's capability. She had been teaching resilience to children, was holding parties to sell Neways health products and was working in the real estate business. The busy schedule didn't seem to leave much time for lying on couches, as had been portrayed. Asked if there was anything about Allison's mental state that concerned her when she disappeared, Olivia said the only thing that stood out was the possible effect of Gerard's brother having a son.

'She always had wanted a boy,' Olivia told the court.

Olivia left the stand, and it was Allison's family's turn. Priscilla Dickie got to her feet, bristling with nervous energy. She received unmistakable warm looks and sympathetic half-smiles from the jury as she confirmed she was the mother of Allison, born on 1 July 1968, a 'very cold morning'. Priscilla recalled that when Allison herself had children, she turned to her for help and advice. After the birth of her first daughter, Priscilla stayed with Allison and Gerard for a while but was wary of upsetting her son-in-law.

'I might've overstepped the mark at one or two times, because I was told by her husband, in no uncertain terms, that he was to bring up the children and not me; not to interfere, Grandma.'

There was only one direction this testimony was going. Priscilla's palpable anger towards Gerard was barely contained as she described arriving at Brookfield on 20 April and seeing the startling injuries on his face. Gerard was 'calm as a cucumber' and smartly dressed, Dickie remembered. Entering the house, she felt it looked sterile – much neater than normal. It struck her as strange that there were two teacups and saucers on the bench instead of the usual mugs, she said.

Fuller, at pains to ensure the evidence didn't spiral out of control, pulled Priscilla up short with a quick 'all right' when he felt she was going off track. The prosecutor inexplicably cut her off when Priscilla was about to tell the court how on the morning Allison vanished, as police milled around the house, Gerard had ushered the Dickies and Kerry-Anne Walker into the master bedroom and said he expected to be arrested. Priscilla twice tried to tell the story, only to be interrupted and redirected by Fuller. The jury would never hear the story.

Michael Byrne's first question for Priscilla was about Allison's depression. Byrne asked Priscilla if she knew if Allison was diagnosed with a major depressive illness. Priscilla said no, Allison never complained, but added her daughter wasn't able to talk in her former home at Kenmore because Gerard was always listening in: 'The baby monitor was in the kitchen and Gerard was working in the garage. I couldn't talk to Allison properly in the Gubberley Street kitchen because he, Gerard, could hear us in the garage. What sort of a life is that?'

Byrne said at Christmas 2011, Kerry-Anne Walker had called Priscilla because she was worried about Allison. Priscilla rang Allison to check on her.

'She told us that Gerard no longer loved her. I said, "Well come and live with us at the coast if you want to." She said, "No way." She wasn't going to leave him. No, she loved him, and those girls of hers. She would never leave those girls.'

Priscilla went to visit Allison and found her on the couch, dressed all in white. She made a point – perhaps for Nigel's benefit – of mentioning twice that Allison was wearing white from head to toe: 'I thought, my goodness what have you got all this white on you?' Priscilla asked her daughter what was wrong, and Allison said she wanted to be a better person. 'Now why would she want to be a better person?' Priscilla wondered aloud.

Byrne prompted Priscilla to recall that Allison had vials of liquid in the fridge door and had been injecting the concoction into her arm to get rid of fat.

'Yes, because she wanted to be what Gerard wanted her to be. That's what she wanted to be. And she tried everything she could for that man,' Priscilla said.

If she had been allowed to, Priscilla would no doubt have stood up in court and pointed to 'that man', Gerard, declaring him a killer. She didn't go that far but those in court were left in no doubt who Priscilla Dickie held responsible for the death of her daughter.

She did go so far as to point out during her testimony that even in life, he had failed to provide for Allison. 'I was always very disappointed,' Priscilla said of the fact the couple did not own their own home. 'She had rented homes ever since they first got married. Never got a house of her own.'

Priscilla had stood before the court determined to speak up for her daughter and she had done her very best. Her direct manner and staccato speech underlined the fact that – as the eldest of ten children – she was well used to getting her point across.

In the overflow court upstairs, there was an extraordinary scene – at the end of her testimony, Allison's mum was given a spontaneous standing ovation. She had been a circuit-breaker after days of heavy testimony about decomposition and depression.

Geoff Dickie entered the witness box immediately after her and, in a deep, clear voice, told the court he noticed scratches on Gerard's face as soon as he arrived at Brookfield on Friday 20 April. Geoff too tried to relay the conversation inside the master bedroom at the house, but Fuller stopped him. Geoff spoke only for a matter of minutes, saying lastly that Allison had been happy and 'wonderful' before she disappeared.

After completing their evidence Allison's parents were able to join friends and family in the public gallery, where they had seats waiting for them, as Kerry-Anne Walker was called to the stand.

Byrne suggested Allison was a private person who kept things to herself, noting she had never told her friend of Gerard's affair. Walker said she used to suggest Gerard may be having an affair but Allison dismissed it, saying she had asked her husband and he denied it: 'I think she never told me about the affair because she knew that I would jump straight in and pull her straight out of there, and she didn't want that. She wanted to work on her marriage. She loved her husband and adored her children.'

Byrne asked if Walker knew Allison suffered depression over a lengthy period. Walker said Allison was open about it but more recently was not depressed. They had lots of discussions in the final months about how Allison was standing up for herself more, was becoming more assertive in the marriage and was positive and in control.

Walker was not going to let Allison's name be dragged through the mud unchallenged. Her friend was simply not the woman she was being painted as – dressed in black, lying around all day.

To add to a day already filled with high drama, Toni McHugh was about to be questioned.

Mistress

Toni McHugh's love for Gerard Baden-Clay had ruined her life. Her name was mud, so she'd had to take a new one. She had been living under an assumed name in a beachside town north of Brisbane, watching the minutes tick by to the trial that would expose her once again to a flood of condemnation, anger, even rage. More than just 'the other woman', McHugh was now also a motive for murder. Memories of the shame of her teenage years, when the girl from a strict Catholic family fell pregnant at 16, came flooding back. But this time a national audience was feeding on her shame. To add insult to injury, the man who had cost her everything had been sleeping around behind her back. A fool to boot. Everything had been lost or damaged – her comfy pad on the Brisbane River, her decent well-paying job in the state's capital and her relationships with family and friends.

McHugh had come to the uneasy conclusion Gerard must have killed Allison. She couldn't see another explanation.

As at the committal hearing, police had helped McHugh slip into Gerard's trial without the abundant media setting eyes on her. The last witness on Monday 16 June, day four of the trial, she was wearing a striking blue silk oriental jacket over a white top, and her black hair was pulled back loosely.

At times it appeared to take a supreme effort for her to answer the prosecutor's questions. Her flat, carefully considered responses were often complimentary to her former lover. She had enjoyed her job at Century 21 Westside, and Gerard was a source of positive energy in the office. He was 'excellent at motivating people, excellent at enhancing a team atmosphere'.

There was more praise: 'I admired him. I admired his drive. I admired his ability to really make people feel that they had something to contribute and that they were going to do well. He was an excellent teacher and I, you, know, felt that I had a fabulous basis to learn real estate.'

In the dock, Gerard's blank expression held no warmth for his former lover as she detailed the course of their passionate affair: the years of secret meetings and circuitous discussions about their future.

'It was up and down all the time, year after year. He was adamant that he didn't have a relationship with his wife . . . didn't love his wife. But at the same time, he was never, ever disrespectful or callous or spiteful or hurtful. He was very fearful of Allison not being able to manage a separation or a divorce. He had voiced concerns about her mental strength. I was very aware of Allison's depression from day one when Gerard told us all about her illness.'

The 'rollercoaster' continued until Allison discovered the affair. McHugh became emotional in court when she recalled the moment Gerard dumped her. Clearly, it still hurt. Of her efforts to get him to reconsider, she said, 'It was pointless. He just would say, "I'm sorry."'

Despite everything, she was 'really very happy to see him' after he contacted her shortly before Christmas 2011. Once the affair resumed, they were more careful with contacting each other but: 'We'd try every day. It wasn't always possible.'

The last time they met before Allison's death was at a Kelvin Grove coffee shop before McHugh had an interview for yet another job. Gerard said it was too hard for them to keep meeting, prompting a round of probing questions from McHugh about his plans. He said he was going to leave his wife by 1 July.

Fuller showed the court emails between McHugh and Gerard, including one repeating the promise to leave his wife by 1 July.

'I thought he's just pulling a number out of thin air. In actual fact, I just didn't believe it. I didn't believe it at all,' McHugh said.

The prosecutor couldn't have been happy when McHugh played down her expectations. But he moved on to Thursday 19 April, where McHugh's testimony would be more damning for Gerard. McHugh was talking to Gerard on the phone about looking forward to the real estate conference the next day when he said, 'Two of my staff are going.' She knew Allison would be one of those 'staff'.

'I lost it,' she said, going on to detail the heated conversation. She had demanded Gerard tell his wife about the clash. She had demanded to meet to talk about how he was going to change things. He said he was going to sell the business.

It was the pivotal moment for the prosecution. Fuller was building a case that Gerard, under pressure from his mistress and his wife, erupted into violence that night. In the dock, Gerard never seemed to flinch or look away during McHugh's personal testimony. He faced her, watching impassively as she struggled through a tumult of emotions.

When Michael Byrne began his cross-examination, he went back to Allison's discovery of the affair. When it came to making a choice, he pointed out, Gerard chose his wife. Nothing had ever come of his many promises. Gerard's defence was minimising his emotional connection to McHugh. They planned to portray her as merely one of Gerard's many lovers – hardly a motive to kill his wife.

Byrne asked about the period when Gerard resumed contact with McHugh. She agreed Gerard had talked about options for her to work in Dubai, South-East Asia, Japan and the United Kingdom. The inference was Gerard was trying to rid himself of her.

The day was drawing to a close, but the defence was not finished with McHugh. She would have to return.

As McHugh prepared to leave court for the day, she had no idea of the mad scramble going on outside. After yet again missing a photograph of McHugh, *The Courier-Mail*'s picture editors sent every available photographer down to the court complex that afternoon. Two photographers from the paper staked out every exit in the building. Television crews pooled resources. When detectives drove McHugh out of an underground car park in an unmarked police car, she was greeted by an eruption of camera flashes. Her photo would be on the front page the next day, when she resumed giving evidence.

The defence continued to downplay Gerard's commitment to her. Byrne said Gerard had never encouraged McHugh to leave her de facto partner. Their relationship followed a pattern for years of Gerard 'talking the talk' but never following through. He said McHugh would become angry and frustrated.

'Can I suggest to you that what happened on the 19th of April 2012 was precisely what had been going on with the affair for the last three-and-a-half odd years, Ms McHugh,' Byrne said.

Critically, McHugh disagreed. This time it was different because she was taking a stand. She wasn't going to let it keep happening.

Byrne said that when Allison went missing, Gerard told McHugh to tell the truth when she spoke to the police. The QC then brought up McHugh's last meeting with Gerard in a Fortitude Valley unit after Allison's disappearance. He said the context of the meeting was that police had told McHugh Gerard had been in relationships with other women and she was angry and upset.

It was the first time the jury heard of Gerard's serial philandering.

In the witness box, McHugh became teary remembering the meeting and apologised.

With the other affairs now on the table, Fuller, on re-examination, asked for more details. McHugh said one of the other affairs occurred before they were together 'but the second, yes, we were definitely together when that happened'. It was when Gerard had talked her into joining him at the Australian Real Estate Conference in Sydney. She flew down on the second day.

'It's my understanding that it happened the day before,' she said of his other dalliance.

On that note, McHugh's time in the witness box was over. As she walked out, one of the reserve jurors crossed her arms, shot a withering glare at Gerard and shook her head.

Building the case

The Crown case was not a complicated one. Ultimately it boiled down to a handful of key points: Gerard's scratches weren't razor cuts, they were inflicted by Allison; the leaves in her hair were from the garden, becoming entangled when Gerard dragged her body to the car; the blood in the car got there when Gerard transported Allison's body to the creek; and the affair with Toni McHugh, combined with Gerard's personal financial crisis, put him under pressure. These were the planks Crown Prosecutors Todd Fuller and Danny Boyle laid down for the trial as they set about arguing Gerard's guilt was beyond reasonable doubt.

First the Crown had to deal with the suicide theory. Michael Byrne and solicitor Peter Shields for the defence were running hard on Allison's depression, implying she took her own life. Anticipating more to come, the Crown called a succession of witnesses who testified Allison's depression was well managed. She seemed in control and knew when to seek help. Medical practitioners and counsellors who had had appointments with Allison over a decade were called and gave evidence they had no concerns she could take her own life.

Among them was Dr Nicholas Bourke from Kenmore Clinics, who saw Allison four times, all in 2011. In May, he prescribed Zoloft to treat the teariness and other symptoms of depression that had returned as a result of relationship and financial stress. In October, when Allison consulted Bourke, she was struggling after discovering Gerard's affair with Toni McHugh. She also reported premenstrual mood swings, but never said anything to suggest she was suicidal.

Allison also saw psychologist Dr Laurie Lumsden in December 2010, after Gerard told Allison on their wedding anniversary he didn't love her. Lumsden told the court he found Allison's stress and anxiety levels completely normal. Prosecutor Danny Boyle asked about Allison's risk of taking her own life, and Lumsden's response dealt another blow to the defence suicide theory.

'At that time, absolutely zero. She discussed her depression as being in the past,' Lumsden said.

Psychologist Rosamond Nutting, from the Bardon Counselling Centre, saw Allison and Gerard three times between October and December 2011. The discovery of Gerard's affair had traumatised Allison. She was having flashbacks to seeing Toni McHugh's car at the gym and was blaming herself for being a bad wife.

'She was sad. She knew that the marriage hadn't been good, but she really wanted to pick up the marriage and get it going again,' Nutting said.

There was nothing in the sessions to indicate Allison was suicidal, otherwise Nutting would have contacted her patient's doctor.

Relationships Australia counsellor Carmel Ritchie had tried to avoid giving evidence. In pre-trial hearings, her lawyers argued her sessions with Allison and Gerard were confidential. But she had been ordered to testify, and took the stand.

Ritchie had seen the Baden-Clays together on the Monday before Allison's disappearance. Now she found herself in the uncomfortable position of having both the prosecution and defence cite the 15-minute venting sessions she had recommended Allison and Gerard schedule as being linked to Allison's death. On the Crown case, the venting sessions contributed to the pressure on Gerard before he murdered Allison. To the defence, Allison was dealing with powerful emotions that could have led her to storm off into the night, possibly taking her own life. Ritchie described to the court how hard she had had to work on Gerard to accept the 15-minute sessions.

Byrne, grilling Ritchie, said Ritchie had recommended the venting sessions without knowing what medication Allison was on or the status of her depression. He said Ritchie had given no restrictions or instructions on how to go about the sessions. Ritchie defended herself, saying the instructions were for Gerard to listen: 'I did not say he had to answer her questions.'

That was the problem with a lack of instruction, Byrne said. If Allison was asking questions, Gerard couldn't remain silent.

'And he may not be saying things that Allison wants to hear,' added Byrne.

Next, police appeared to talk about their dealings with Gerard on the day he reported his wife missing. Constable Kieron Ash, first officer on the scene, ignited the entire investigation with his concerned phone call to senior officers. 'When I first saw him, I noticed that he had scratches on the right-hand side of his face,' Ash said. He told the court he suspected domestic violence.

Sergeant Andrew Jackson told a similar story: 'As soon as he looked at me straight on, I saw a couple of large lacerations to the right side of his face.'

Constable Liam Braunberger brought Gerard's dire finances into focus. Braunberger was working at the front desk of Indooroopilly Police Station when Gerard came in briefly on Friday 20 April 2012. Braunberger had started a missing person file on Allison on the police QPRIME computer database and asked Gerard if she had access to any money.

'He stated that she had about $20 available to her, and after that he made a statement that they were on the bones of their arse,' Braunberger told the court.

Wednesday 18 June 2014
Dr Margaret Stark was the first of a series of experts to state that the injuries to Gerard's face had the hallmarks of fingernail

scratches. Stark was director of the NSW Police Force Clinical Forensic Medicine Unit and had been a forensic physician for 25 years. Stark examined photographs of Gerard's face. She said there appeared to be two separate sets of injuries caused at different times. Prosecutor Danny Boyle asked Stark about the wider injuries.

'These particular injuries are typical of fingernail scratches,' Stark said, adding they were not typical of a razor but that was as far as she could go.

Stark based her opinion on examining thousands of victims of assault and injured suspects. She added that if you nicked yourself, 'you'd probably stop and wouldn't go on and cause a second injury'. Smaller, redder marks on Gerard's cheek were more consistent with a razor, she said.

The Crown hoped the jury would draw the conclusion Allison had scratched Gerard's face, then he had tried to muddy the waters by adding razor cuts.

When Scenes of Crime officer Sergeant Anthony Venardos gave evidence, he introduced the jury to the injuries to other parts of Gerard's body. Venardos testified he took photographs of Gerard with his shirt off at Indooroopilly Police Station.

When the jury was shown the photos of Gerard's injured chest, neck and armpit, they leant in close to their screens and turned to each other. Their wide-eyed expressions no doubt mirrored the reaction of detectives when they first saw the same images.

Thursday 19 June 2014
The Crown had a bevy of highly experienced forensic experts to attack Gerard's claim he cut himself shaving, and rolled them out. Dr Robert Hoskins, a former Queensland Health forensic medical officer, had an extensive collection of scratch photographs. He examined photographs of Gerard's face and compiled a report.

'The first thing that springs to my mind is that those injuries are characteristic of fingernail scratches,' Hoskins told the court. 'They are ragged, roughly the right size, in the same direction and very approximately parallel with one another.'

Asked if the injuries could be from a razor, Hoskins said: 'I find it extremely implausible.' It was possible the other, smaller injuries on Gerard's face were from a razor and were more recent due to the appearance of fresher blood, he added.

Again, the evidence raised the spectre of Gerard attempting to conceal fingernail scratches with razor cuts. In further evidence, Hoskins said that Gerard's chest, neck and armpit injuries could be from fingernail scratches.

Queensland Health forensic medical officer Dr Leslie Griffiths had personally examined Gerard. Griffiths told the court Gerard's facial injuries 'resemble scratch marks' and it was 'highly improbable' they were from his razor. Griffiths thought the injury near Gerard's armpit was 'strap-like' and could have been from a backpack. He formed no conclusions on what had caused the separate injury on Gerard's chest, but it could have been from clothing being forced against the skin.

The final expert witness on Gerard's injuries was Professor David Wells, from the Victorian Institute of Forensic Medicine. Wells, head of the institute's Clinical Forensic Medicine Unit from 1985 until 2013, told the court he examined photographs of Gerard's face. He couldn't reconcile a razor causing the main injuries, but it may have caused the smaller ones.

Defence barrister Byrne cross-examined the expert witnesses at length, doing his best to sow the seeds of doubt. All the experts conceded they could not definitively say Gerard's injuries were fingernail scratches – but crucially, all believed they were.

Gerard had claimed the injuries to his neck and chest were self-inflicted scratches after a caterpillar fell on him. There was one witness who tended to back Gerard's version of events. Cameron Early was at the Brookfield State School cross-country event on 19 April 2012. Early knew Gerard through the school

P & C and Kenmore Chamber of Commerce. The two men were talking business underneath some trees near the school oval.

'He started, all of a sudden, pulling towards his left neck. He was standing to my left and he said words to the effect of: "Oh shit, what was that? Oh God, bloody hell, that hurt."'

A welt appeared on Gerard's neck, about an inch and a half long and as thick as a finger. Early presumed 'a grub of some description' fell from the tree and bit him.

It was common at the trial for issues to be dealt with over a number of days. The evidence moved from injuries to finances to personal pressures and back again. Sue Heath testified Gerard made a desperate request for $300,000 from her friend Dr Bruce Flegg in March 2012. Gerard said he would go bankrupt without it.

'He was distressed,' Heath told the court. 'You could just tell in his voice. He was normally very confident and he was genuinely really quite distressed. I felt really quite sad for him. I think he was under a lot of pressure.'

Psychiatrist Dr Tom George brought the attention back to Allison's state of mind. George told the court Allison came to see him with depression in September 2003 while pregnant with her second daughter. Allison was 'symptom free' within a few months, after starting on Zoloft. She had 31 consultations and eight or nine phone calls with George over the next six years.

'Her condition resolved and remained resolved for the vast majority of the time that she was under my care,' George said.

Prosecutor Danny Boyle asked if Allison talked about her children, and George said it was 'one of the main reasons she came to see me'. He said, 'All the conversations she had about the children indicated to me that she was extremely attached to them, extremely fond of them.'

Maternal attachment had a protective effect from suicide, George added. He had no concerns 'at all' about the risk of Allison taking her own life.

'Beyond that first one or two consultations, she was never depressed. She was functioning well. She had plans for herself. She had plans for her children. She was living an active, interesting social life.'

The evidence from Allison's GP, two psychologists, a counsellor and now her psychiatrist that Allison was not a suicide risk added up to a powerful strike on the defence theory that Allison may have taken her own life.

But Gerard's barrister Michael Byrne wasn't giving up on the angle. He asked George about a phone call from Gerard when Allison was pregnant with their third daughter in 2006. Gerard had found out they were having a girl, and worried Allison would react badly as she wanted a son. He kept the information to himself: Allison only found out the baby's sex at birth.

It was a theme the defence kept returning to. Two days before Allison was reported missing, Gerard's brother welcomed a baby boy. The defence lawyers were building a case that Allison took the news badly. The suicide theory was unspoken but always implied at the trial.

George, before his evidence was over, shot a hole through it: 'She was disappointed initially but very rapidly recovered,' he said. 'She felt a little sad for her husband, who she thought was very keen on having a boy.'

The second week of the trial was about to wrap up when Todd Fuller announced he had a brief witness. It was 4.27 pm, just three minutes before the scheduled end of the day's evidence. Usually there would not have been any new witnesses called at the late hour, but Fuller said Stephanie Apps was relevant to the view planned for the Monday. Apps was the resident of Boscombe Road at Brookfield whose children had been fighting on the night Allison was last seen alive. Apps testified that her daughter, 15, and son, 13, were arguing in the back of her car as they drove home from dinner. When they reached home shortly before 10 pm, her daughter had knocked over a pot, run into a spider web and screamed.

Apps went to the Brookfield Showground and told police at the temporary command post there about what had occurred on Thursday 19 April. She thought police should know that reports of screams in Brookfield that night could have an innocent explanation. She would have hated for anyone to connect the sounds from her driveway to Allison Baden-Clay's disappearance. A piercing female scream around the corner from Allison's home on the night she went missing could easily be misconstrued.

Surprisingly, despite the painstaking attention of their investigation, none of the police followed up with Apps. She had not been due to testify at the trial and was only in court because a private detective had approached her the previous Sunday and the defence asked her to make a statement.

Her testimony was over in less than ten minutes but effectively countered the significance of previous evidence about screams in the night. After Apps emerged, police scrambled back to their records to see how she could have been overlooked. Detectives could only find a reference to Apps being routinely door-knocked – there was nothing in the job logs about her approaching the police.

Outside court Allison's family wanted to know what it meant for the Crown case, telling Fuller it didn't look good for the evidence to emerge at the last minute. Fuller wasn't thrilled but didn't think the screams were central to the case.

Monday 23 June 2014
Gerard's defence team made quite an entrance when the trial moved out of the court to Kholo Creek Bridge at the start of the third week. The jury was to be shown key locations, and Peter Shields and Michael Byrne arrived at the bridge in a silver two-door Audi TT convertible. By contrast, prosecutors Todd Fuller and Danny Boyle arrived in a sensible family Mazda CX5, voted best SUV under $40,000 for the second year running. It said much about the comparative styles and pay packets of criminal defence lawyers and Crown prosecutors.

The jury arrived at Kholo Creek Bridge in a bus. Police had set up roadblocks on Mt Crosby Road on either side of the bridge. All traffic was stopped to allow the jurors to view the area unrestricted. It is against the law to identify jurors, so photographers and TV cameras kept their distance.

Much had changed at the bridge since the discovery of Allison's body. The verge on one side had been cleared of undergrowth and widened to create space for parking, and Allison's family had erected a large stone memorial. The prosecution and defence had discussed covering the memorial as it was potentially prejudicial to the case, but decided any attempt to conceal it would only draw attention. However, jurors were told they would have no reason to approach it.

A dirt track allowed jurors to get underneath the bridge if they wished. They spent almost an hour at the site before boarding the bus to be taken to Allison and Gerard's former Brookfield home. There were significant changes here too. The home's owners, who also owned the childcare centre next door, had tried renting it after Gerard's arrest but had no takers. It was being used as an office and training room for the childcare centre. When the jury arrived, they found the house had been repainted yellow – coincidentally Allison's favourite colour – and trees had been cleared from throughout the property. A new building was being erected between the home and the childcare centre.

The jury briefly walked around and through the house. The 'view' was over before lunch, but the trial was running well ahead of schedule and adjourned for the day.

Tuesday 24 June 2014

Gerard had a new supporter in court – his younger brother, Adam, who lived in Canada, had arrived. The first evidence Adam heard was about Gerard's requests for money from friends. The Crown sought to show financial desperation, while the defence painted a brighter picture of Gerard having friends in high places and a business on the mend.

Dr Bruce Flegg was up first, testifying about Gerard's requests for loans as well as the screams he heard on the night Allison disappeared.

Then came three of Gerard's closest friends – Robert Cheesman, Stuart Christ and Peter Cranna – the ones who had dubbed themselves his financial 'advisory group'. They were variously in each other's bridal parties, went on family holidays together and met up for dinners and social gatherings. In February 2011, with his business partners wanting out and real estate in the doldrums after the floods, Gerard turned to his best friends for a loan. They met up and delved into the company books.

After satisfying themselves it was viable, Cheesman and Christ reached deep into their pockets to each loan him $90,000. Cranna had been lending money to Gerard for years, adding up to an outstanding loan of $96,000. All three men gave evidence at the trial that the loans were sealed with a handshake. There was no documentation and no security.

'We spent maybe a month going through the figures,' said Cheesman, an accountant who owned a computer consulting business. 'We wanted to know how he got into that problem. We wanted to see some forecasts for the future. And then we lent him some money. The business was clearly in trouble, but I could see a way out.'

Cheesman said Gerard's business was blowing too much money on rent and staff. Gerard agreed to cut his expenses, and for a while Cheesman reviewed all outgoing payments. When Allison stepped into the business later in the year, his friends were comforted by her presence and took a step back. Cheesman thought he was going to get 10 per cent interest. Christ thought he was ultimately going to be repaid the principal sum of $90,000 plus $90,000 interest. Gerard kept up with interest repayments for a few months then stopped paying. Christ told the court Gerard later asked for more money at various times, but he didn't give him any.

In cross-examination, Cheesman and Christ confirmed Gerard's father, Nigel, phoned them looking for a lawyer the day Allison vanished.

'He was concerned that there was a lot of police,' Cheesman said. 'They were surrounding Gerard. They were asking him a lot of tough questions. [Nigel] suggested he contact a lawyer and I blew him off. I said it wasn't necessary and the focus was on finding Allison.'

Christ added that Nigel was distraught when he phoned in the morning and sounded 'very concerned about the line of questioning from police'.

'In his words, "They're going after him." I said something like, "Look, Nigel, just worry about finding Allison."'

Christ said Nigel persisted, so he gave him the number for Craig Thompson, a partner in Toowoomba law firm Wonderley & Hall Solicitors.

On the subject of Allison's depression, Christ told the court that sometimes Allison was quiet and reclusive and at other times she was great fun.

None of the three friends knew about Gerard's affair with Toni McHugh.

Experts from a range of disciplines were the next to be called as the Crown sought to show Allison was dumped where she was found and to exclude other possible causes of death, such as drowning or an overdose. Some of the evidence involved gruesome descriptions relating to Allison's body. The prosecution had arranged to signal Allison's family before difficult evidence, giving Geoff, Priscilla and other relatives time to leave if they wanted.

Professor James Wallman, a forensic entomologist, said insects recovered from around Allison's body could be consistent with death around the time she went missing. At a minimum, there would be an interval of three or four days between the death and the gathering of those insects around the body. He was unable to conclude if Allison had been submerged.

Dr Jacob John was a retired Curtin University professor involved in pioneering research into diatoms – microscopic algae – for 35 years. He told the court diatoms were present in all types of water body. Typically, when a person drowned, water rushed into the lungs and spread through the lymphatic system to other internal organs, depositing diatoms that could remain in the body for years. John found blooms of diatoms in almost all of the Kholo Creek water samples collected at the time Allison's body was discovered.

Examining bone marrow and liver tissue samples from Allison's body, John found no diatoms. 'The subject concerned did not drown in Kholo Creek or anywhere. There was no evidence of drowning at all,' he testified.

Professor Olaf Drummer, who had given evidence at the committal, was called to give evidence about the levels of antidepressants and alcohol in Allison's body. Drummer was a toxicologist, pharmacologist and head of Forensic Scientific Services at the Victorian Institute of Forensic Medicine. He told the court that patients who were new to the medication sertraline (Zoloft) could experience headaches, dizziness, sedation, drowsiness, difficulty sleeping and excitability. But side effects reduced with time, and the drug was relatively non-toxic. Sertraline overdoses were very rare and usually occurred in combination with other toxic drugs. Victorian and other records he examined did not have any cases of death from sertraline overdose alone.

Drummer didn't think Allison overdosed on sertraline: 'The levels themselves, in my view, do not lead me to think that the drug had any contribution to her death.'

Allison had a blood-alcohol reading of .095, but Drummer said alcohol was commonly produced in the body after death through fermentation.

In cross-examination, Michael Byrne asked Drummer to explain serotonin syndrome. Drummer said excessive increases in serotonin could cause confusion, anxiety, agitation and, in severe cases, delirium. Drummer agreed sertraline overdoses could cause serotonin syndrome.

Martin Giles, a senior hydraulic and environmental engineer at environmental and engineering services company Cardno, concluded Allison's body could not have washed up on the creek bank. Giles used Brisbane River gauges at Moggill and College's Crossing to determine Kholo Creek water levels. He said there had been 80 to 100 millimetres of rain in the days before Allison's body was found so he developed a rainfall run-off model of the catchment to take it into account. The end result was that it was 'impossible to imagine' the flow of water would have been enough to move Allison's body into the location it was found, Giles told the court.

No one had expected a botanist to be one of the star witnesses in a murder trial. But Dr Gordon Guymer was. And when he arrived at court in the third week of testimony, Guymer, in typical fashion, was exhaustively prepared for his testimony about the six plant species he identified from Allison's hair and body.

A month beforehand, the Queensland Herbarium director had arranged for colleagues to cross-examine him in a mock trial at work. Masters in their field, they were tougher on Guymer in a technical sense than any defence lawyer could have been. One colleague stumped him with a particularly incisive observation.

'Dr Guymer,' she said formally, addressing an imaginary courtroom at the Herbarium. 'You don't have any data about the likelihood of these six species being found in the one place, do you?'

Guymer realised she was right and set about compiling some. He put coordinate points from around Brisbane into a random number generator. Five suburbs were selected at random: Mitchelton, Durack, Salisbury, Taringa and Jamboree Heights. Guymer then went out and conducted plant surveys at 100 houses in each suburb – 500 in total – looking for the six species of plant he discovered in Allison's hair and body. Residents had no idea of the unusual mission of the man examining their front yards and peering over their fences. It was all in Guymer's own time and took him two full weekends.

In the end, out of the 500 residential properties he visited, he discovered one house at Taringa with five of the six species specified. The house was still missing the lilly pilly, which Guymer hadn't seen at any of the houses he checked. To find all six would have required an exponential increase on the 1 in 500 chance of finding five.

The senior botanist now had data to confirm what he had always suspected. There was only a remote possibility of all six species being found growing together – as they were at the Baden-Clay house – if a property was selected at random.

Guymer's persistence and dedication stemmed from a desire to be fully across the evidence he was presenting. In other cases, botany was on the periphery. He knew from early on that in this case, the Herbarium's work was crucial to the case and he didn't want any mistakes or surprises.

At trial, Guymer rattled off the scientific names and then the common names of the species he would be discussing. The crepe myrtle, cat's claw creeper, fishbone fern and eucalyptus were entwined in Allison's hair. The Chinese elm and lilly pilly were loose.

Each of the seven crepe myrtle leaves had been on the ground when they got mixed up in Allison's hair, Guymer stated. To be certain, he had taken cuttings from the trees at Gerard and Allison's home and grown them to observe their leaves over time. One of the cat's claw creeper leaves in Allison's hair had been pulled from a live plant. The fishbone fern leaflets were likely a mix of some fallen and some fresh. The eucalypt and Chinese elm leaves were fallen. The lilly pilly leaf was live or recently fallen.

Guymer talked in detail about finding the six species around the Baden-Clays' former home, and finding only two of the species around Kholo Creek Bridge. He told the court he carried out a plant survey all the way from Brookfield to Kholo Creek Bridge and only rarely found some of the key plant species.

The day drew to an end. The defence would cross-examine Guymer the next day.

Wednesday 25 June 2014

Guymer does not look like a particularly frightening man. But the greying, neatly dressed boss of the Queensland Herbarium seemed to have Gerard's defence team slightly rattled. At 9.20 am, less than an hour before he was to be cross-examined, Guymer met Michael Byrne and Peter Shields in a side room outside court. Gerard's lawyers had asked to speak to him. Byrne told Guymer he wasn't sure the defence had given his statements the attention they possibly deserved, and the two lawyers fired off 20 questions to gauge his responses. The grilling from colleagues in the mock trial had prepared him well; Guymer was not concerned by the defence questions.

Guymer had done additional research not referenced on the stand and now detailed it to Byrne and Shields. On his own initiative, he had conducted an experiment on crepe myrtle leaves to assess the effect of soaking them in creek water for up to ten days: he observed little effect. Guymer, of course, ensured the water precisely matched the salinity in Kholo Creek.

The defence weren't leaving anything to chance: They had sent another botanist to Kholo Creek to conduct plant surveys and check his work. Unsurprisingly, nothing had been found to contradict Guymer.

Byrne's cross-examination of Guymer was short when the trial resumed. Guymer agreed his plant survey between Brookfield and Kholo Creek bridge was along the roadside and did not venture into private backyards. He agreed cat's claw creeper was relatively common and ranked 23rd in a list of Australia's worst weeds. Byrne pointed out that plant debris could float down creeks and rivers.

In the end, the defence seemed happy to see the back of Guymer.

Police witnesses testified about the discovery of blood in the car, before Queensland Health senior forensic scientist Amanda Reeves gave evidence it matched Allison's DNA. Statistically, there was a 1 in 5600 billion chance of the blood being from someone other than and unrelated to Allison, Reeves said. Nobody could argue against such overwhelming odds.

Reeves also had some other evidence of interest from DNA tests of Allison's fingernails. Under one fingernail on Allison's left hand, there were 'very low level indications of the possible presence of DNA from a second contributor'. Frustratingly, Reeves said the levels were too low for comparison.

The Crown case was wrapping up and after a subdued start, they had built to a strong finish. The last witnesses to be called were the arresting officers, Detective Senior Constable Cameron McLeod and Detective Sergeant Chris Canniffe. The quietly spoken McLeod read aloud some excerpts from Allison's journal, where in the days before she died she had jotted down questions for Gerard about his affair with Toni McHugh.

'Movies/drive together – how many times; what see; dinner; scared of being seen; kiss/hug? Snowy – drive together; seats down; lie there afterwards; how many times; do afterwards; drive home?'

The rest of the courtroom was silent as McLeod continued to read Allison's questions probing every intimate detail of his affair. Allison had crossed some of them off. Others, about Gerard's treatment of Allison, were still waiting to be asked.

'Afterwards, why so mean? Laughed at undies. Told me I smelled. 40th birthday. Four weeks later, started. Dirty. Find whole thing dirty. Still get sick to the stomach.'

Allison's own words had given the jury an insight into how bruising and confronting the 15-minute sessions must have been.

Prosecutor Todd Fuller tendered some final documents. One was a life insurance schedule for Allison and Gerard, but Fuller did not read the amounts aloud. He went on to read 27 'admissions', or facts the defence had accepted. Among them, Gerard accepted his iPhone was connected to a charger at 1.48 am on Friday 20 April. He also agreed he called Asteron Life Insurance the day after Allison's body was discovered to ask about claiming on her policy.

'That is the Crown case, thank you, Your Honour,' Fuller announced when he was through the admissions.

At this point, Gerard's barrister, Michael Byrne, announced he had a matter to discuss with the judge so the jury left the court. As always when the jury wasn't there, a cone of silence fell over proceedings. The jury would know nothing of the events that followed until after the trial, but Gerard was launching a legal assault to take the murder charge off the table. Michael Copley QC had been brought in to bolster the already high-powered defence team. Copley told Justice Byrne the defence contended there was no case to answer on murder. His argument was there was no evidence to prove intent to kill or cause grievous bodily harm, an essential element of the charge.

If the tactic succeeded, Gerard would only face the alternative charge of manslaughter. Justice Byrne showed early signs of being unimpressed, interrupting Copley with his troubles about the submission: 'The first, and by far the most important, relates to the scratches.'

It was notable that in the absence of the jury, whereas previously there had been delicate references to 'injuries', this now went out the window – they were simply scratches. Byrne, who had been appointed a judge of the Supreme Court in 1989, said he was inclined to think the jury could conclude Allison scratched her husband's face while 'fighting for her life'.

An odd legal exchange followed. Copley argued that at best, all the Crown could show was there was a violent struggle and Allison died unintentionally. Justice Byrne observed it was hard to reconcile Gerard's behaviour afterwards if Allison's death was accidental.

'What he did involved disposing of a body in an undignified way and in a manner calculated to prevent its timely discovery. He then engages in serious subterfuge. He lies about the scratches and does more than that; he uses the razor blade to create the appearance some hours later of scratches on the face in the redder area. Now, he then lies to the police about these things and maintains the deception and has never departed from it.'

Justice Byrne had more to say: 'The jury might think that the pressure of it all, especially as he was most resistant to the idea that he should be subjected to hearing how his wife felt about the affair, led to a state of affairs where violence erupted and, for whatever reason, he felt then compelled to end his wife's life. Now, some of the jurors might think he was motivated by the insurance proceeds. Others might think that he was motivated by an anxiety to be with Ms McHugh. Others might think . . . he was simply so incensed by the exercise that Ms Ritchie had recommended that he lost his composure and attacked her.'

Watching from the dock, Gerard shook his head almost imperceptibly in disagreement as Justice Byrne spoke. Allison's family held their breath, but yet another decision went against Gerard. The murder charge stood.

Death of a salesman

Thursday 26 June 2014

No one really thought Gerard would take the stand. Well, almost no one. Among the few exceptions were a couple of detectives who had spent time with him. They had a bet with colleagues that Gerard, so convinced of his own charm, would testify. Allison's cousin Jodie Dann shared their certainty. Dann knew prosecutor Todd Fuller's view was that Gerard's lawyers simply wouldn't allow it – it was too big a risk. But while his reasoning made sense, Fuller didn't know Gerard. Dann was sure his arrogance would get the better of him.

Michael Byrne had requested the court start later than usual, to give the defence time to talk to their client about his decision. Proceedings were scheduled to start after 11 am.

As Gerard talked to his lawyers, lines were forming outside Court 11 and the overflow court upstairs. Crowds had built steadily throughout the three weeks of the trial and, since an early stoush over seats, court staff had introduced a numbered ticketing system. The Baden-Clay and Dickie families each had eight reserved seats. Everyone else lined up and was given a ticket according to their order in the queue. It was unprecedented. There hadn't been this level of public interest in a trial in living memory. The ticket colours changed each day to stop people reusing old numbers. Priscilla's nine siblings alone exceeded the number of allocated seats, so Allison's huge extended family and close friends joined members of the public and media in the chilly early-morning queue for tickets. On this day, it felt like a waste of time. If Gerard declined to give evidence, as expected, the trial would be adjourned until Monday.

For the first time since the trial began, the charismatic Detective Superintendent Mark Ainsworth arrived outside Court 11. Jodie Dann gave him a big hug before other members of Allison's family made their way over to greet him. Ainsworth, who was on leave, didn't want to take anyone's seat, so he went upstairs to the overflow court. When he found it was full too, he went to the media room where he found some space.

Outside the courtroom, friend Helen Wilson spoke fondly of Allison's habit of always turning the conversation away from herself to ask about others. Allison would have been shocked so much of her private life had become public property.

The trial resumed at 11.27 am and Michael Byrne rose to drop a bombshell: 'Your Honour, Gerard Baden-Clay will give evidence, will call evidence and will produce evidence in the trial.' Gerard was rolling the dice and betting on his ability as a salesman to convince the jury of his innocence.

It was an extraordinary development. As word spread through the court complex, the media conducted a quick straw poll with legal eagles. No one could remember the last time an accused in a high-profile murder case had testified. It would expose Gerard to many uncomfortable questions on cross-examination, but he knew the jury wanted to hear him say he didn't kill Allison and he wanted to be heard.

There was also a feeling in the wind that, despite presenting the bones of a strong case, the prosecution had failed to land any knockout blows. So much so, that when news broke Gerard would give evidence, those following the case on crime forum Websleuths congratulated prosecutors for luring Gerard to the stand.

'Represent weakness to induce a bluff – perfect poker,' wrote one. 'Well done . . . It's not every prosecutor who can get a defendant on a murder charge to strut on to the witness stand.'

It wasn't quite what the prosecutors were aiming for. Now Gerard had upped the stakes. He was not going down without a fight.

At 2.53 pm Brisbane's most infamous former real estate agent moved from the dock to the witness box and was sworn in. For most of those present, it was the first time they'd heard his voice, the rounded vowels a remnant of his African childhood. Everyone in court realised they were witnessing dramatic events. After two years of maintaining a steadfast silence Gerard was about to tell all.

Unfortunately for him, he got off to a faltering start. His defence counsel, Byrne, asked how long he had been married to Allison, and Gerard replied they were coming up to their 14th wedding anniversary. Byrne took a breath then launched into the question everyone was waiting for: 'Mr Baden-Clay, did you kill –'.

'Sorry. It would have been coming up to our 15th wedding anniversary,' Gerard cut in. Scriptwriters couldn't have matched it for black comedy.

Regrouping, Byrne repeated the question and this time the answer was a firm, 'No I did not.'

'Did you fight with her on the evening of the 19th?' Byrne continued, batting short, rehearsed questions to his client.

'No, I did not,' Gerard responded, on cue.

'Did you, at that time, leave your children alone in the house to go to the Kholo Creek bridge?'

'Definitely not. Never.'

'Did you ever take any steps to dispose or conceal Allison's body?'

'No.'

'Did you ever do any clean-ups of the house?'

'No.'

'Or the cars?'

'No.'

'Or the surrounds of the house?'

'No.'

'The patio?'

'No.'

393

'The carport?'

'No.'

'Were you ever scratched by your wife?'

'Never.'

He told the jury he and Allison 'were planning to spend the rest of our lives together'. He was in contact with Toni McHugh, 'but in my mind we did not have a relationship'.

With the big ticket items out of the way, the pace slowed and the tone softened. It was time for the defence to introduce Gerard Baden-Clay as a loving husband and father.

Byrne asked Gerard to recount how he and Allison had met. They had both worked at Flight Centre, he explained, before becoming momentarily side-tracked by business.

'I fell in love,' he said, 'with the company, if you like, as well, and I did very well. I was regularly a top performer.'

He fell in love, too, with the company's beautiful HR manager. They met when Allison had computer problems and he came to her rescue, he said, 'And she got more and more problems with her computer.'

But he had competition. 'Probably one of the most eligible bachelors within the organisation was my friend Ian Walton . . . In Flight Centre and indeed in the travel industry there aren't too many straight, male eligible bachelors around.'

Gerard, of course, won out, and Ian went on to marry Olivia Baden-Clay.

'I fell in love with her,' he said of Allison. 'I fell in love with her pretty well straightaway . . . I knew that she was the one,' he said, breaking down in the witness box for the first time. It was about 15 minutes into Gerard's testimony. There were many tears ahead.

He detailed their early years together.

'I actually proposed to her underneath the Eiffel Tower at Park Road. That was . . .' When Gerard paused, struggling to recall something, his barrister Michael Byrne prompted, 'Close to Paris?', obviously forgetting Gerard had popped the question at a replica tower just a kilometre or so down the road from the court house.

The more Gerard talked, the more relaxed and confident he became. He was warming to his task and those who had attended his wedding may have been put in mind of his epic 90-minute wedding speech. He also had a habit of digressing to strange details, such as where he and Allison were when Kieren Perkins won gold.

'I remember clearly that we were at a caravan park . . . because we both loved swimming and watching swimming and tennis and that sort of thing, and that's where we saw it, and people remember where they were when certain things happened and we were somewhere on a caravan park in the North Island of New Zealand.'

After they married, the couple planned a lavish extended trip around the world, but enjoyed a more traditional tropical getaway first. Here again, Gerard seemed focused on odd details, such as whether or not the resort had a television.

'So the "honeymoon" honeymoon – [the] stereotypical part – was about 10 days at an exclusive island resort called Vabbinfaru in the Maldives, which was just wonderful. They had a theme of no – no shoes, no news. There were no newspapers, no televisions. It was just a wonderful idyllic sort of a setting. We did find whilst we were there, that there was a television at the place, because, in fact, the day we left Australia on our honeymoon, which was a week after we got married, was the day Princess Diana died, and we learnt that news after we'd cleared customs and my parents and Allison's parents called down to us from the Brisbane Airport – through the observation deck, 'Princess Diana's just died,' and we couldn't believe it. We couldn't comprehend it, really, I suppose. We had no knowledge. And the staff had a little television up above the bar at this resort and we watched the funeral there.'

Perhaps a more romantic memory from their first holiday as husband and wife would have helped Gerard's case. But he was just getting warmed up; there were many more honeymoon tales to come.

He explained, in detail, the newlyweds' stay at the International Scout Centre in Kandersteg, Switzerland, including a glowing account of how his illustrious forebear had founded it: '. . . a place where all the Scouts from all over the world could come at any time of the year to meet with each other and enjoy each other's fellowship and that sort of thing, and also the alpine activities that were on hand there. It's just the most magical place in the world.'

His enthusiastic storytelling was beginning to seem surreal. He started to resemble a guest of honour on *This is Your Life*, rather than a man on trial for murder.

He had no qualms about paying the occasional backhanded compliment to his late wife. Gerard's job at Blockbuster International in London 'paid very, very well'. Allison's job with Dale Carnegie Training 'hardly paid anything', although it was 'great experience for her', he added. After London, they returned to Kandersteg and 'it was fabulous, it was a wonderful, amazing experience'.

Life for the newlyweds took a turn for the worse, Gerard explained, when Allison took Lariam for their trip to South America. He described the time it was at its worst: 'I remember it was Potosi because there's a big silver mine there and also we went to another place and watched a soccer match, which was great, and we supported Potosi, and I bought a big flag and waved it around like an idiot as part of the away crowd, and there was a riot afterwards and that sort of thing. But that's another story . . .'

Gerard catalogued the exotic locations they were in when her depression reared its head. She was anxious in a boat in the Galapagos and in the jungles of Venezuela.

After speaking of Allison's feelings of upset after a fatal flood that occurred pretty much on their doorstep during another stint working at Kandersteg, Gerard's mouth was dry from talking and he guzzled water as he moved on to the couple's return to Australia from their extended honeymoon.

'She'd pretty much recovered from most of those episodes, but [was] still a little bit more anxious,' he recalled. 'Before, when we got married, she was just a world-beater, you know? She could do anything. She was just a bit more fragile, I suppose, and she found things with work and everything else a bit stressful. She decided to stop working at the end of June because my job was so good and we could afford to do that.'

But Gerard lost his job. He started working from his garage at home. Their eldest daughter was born in July the following year. Allison's anxiety soared and she would have panic attacks if he left the house. At this point, according to Gerard, he did almost everything bar breastfeeding their baby daughter while Allison lay on the couch. He wired up an intercom between the house and garage so Allison could press the button and he could be in the house in ten seconds flat.

'She certainly would change nappies and that sort of thing. But to be perfectly candid with you, it came to a point where I was doing 80 to 90 to 95 to nearly 100 per cent. Obviously, I couldn't breastfeed, but I was doing everything in the home because Allison was in a depressed state.'

Outsiders would not have noticed Allison's depressed behaviour – she was skilfully hiding it from the world, Gerard said.

'I can tell you 100 per cent why I didn't tell anybody was because I was protecting my beautiful wife. She didn't want to tell anybody because she didn't want to be seen to be incapable.'

His claim to stoic silence was contradicted by statements from colleagues and friends, who said Gerard spoke often of Allison's battle with depression and the extra load it placed on him.

Their second daughter was born in December 2003 and he decided to go into real estate with his parents:

'I went and spoke to all of the agents in the local area and interviewed them to see where I'd like to work.'

The day drew to a close. Gerard's evidence would continue on Monday. It had been an intriguing performance. The biggest sales pitch of his career.

Monday 30 June 2014

Jodie Dann didn't want to get out of bed. Didn't want to face another day of self-serving testimony from Gerard. She rolled over and pulled the covers over her head. It was Monday, and Allison's cousin had spent the weekend dwelling on Gerard's evidence. Was the jury going to buy it? They didn't know Gerard. Perhaps they wouldn't see through him. The prospect of sitting through more of his long-winded stories was making her angry. Maybe she didn't have to go? She thought for a moment before reluctantly getting out of bed and getting dressed.

Phenomenal scenes were occurring at court. Interest in the case had been high in the first three weeks, but Gerard's decision to testify turned the fourth week into a frenzy. Anticipating a rush for seats, *Courier-Mail* morning police reporter Tom Snowdon arrived at court at 5.45 am to reserve a place at the front of the queue. A group of women who had come up from the Gold Coast arrived shortly after him. By the time the building's doors opened at 8.30 am, more than 100 people were waiting. There was still 90 minutes before Gerard's testimony resumed, and people kept flooding in. The record turnout forced a change of plans – the trial would be streamed live on screens in a third courtroom. And it wasn't just any court. The ceremonial Banco court – the biggest in the complex by far, with a capacity to seat more than 200 people – would be utilised. Never before had three courts – plus a media room – been open for evidence in a single court case to accommodate public interest.

Outside Court 11, there was disappointing news for those who had lined up all morning hoping to get into the trial court. A staffer announced the public gallery would be open to family only.

I'd been in court every day with colleague Kate Kyriacou, and Allison's family invited us to stay. Kyriacou had previously covered the Daniel Morcombe trial, using Twitter to report live from the court. She had found it invaluable, and readers wholeheartedly embraced this new era in court reporting. On the Baden-Clay trial, many journalists were using Twitter but no one was as fast or as thorough as Kyriacou. For friends and observers who couldn't be physically present, it offered a simple way to keep up. It was not merely the immediacy this form of social media offered, but its scope for commenting and asking questions made people log on in droves. With no TV cameras allowed in court, one of the most common queries was about Gerard's demeanour: 'What's Gerard doing now?' Our Twitter feeds streamed live on *The Courier-Mail*'s website, with rolling coverage from court reporter Brooke Baskin in the tenth-floor media room.

Gerard's testimony carried on from where he had left off – with a question from Byrne about his success in business. 'We were successful professionally. Personally, it was quite challenging,' Gerard said. His return to work put a strain on Allison. Fortunately, he was able to pick up the slack. The jury learnt it was called 'happy hour' when Gerard came home from work at 5 pm every day. Most of the time he fed and bathed the girls and put them to bed, he said. Allison 'would actually go to bed pretty much as soon as I walked in the door' on many occasions.

Byrne moved Gerard back and forth between his home and work. Gerard revelled in talking shop: 'Very quickly, we did win listings, we got sales, and we became quite successful very quickly,' he said. 'And in fact that very first year, 2005, we won the Quest Business Achiever's Award for the best real estate agency in the western suburbs.'

He was doing all this while looking after his troubled wife. Allison would call him during the day and he'd drop everything and go home. Usually, he did the morning routine with the children as well. Allison put on a façade when she went out, which only drained her further at home – again, an explanation for Allison appearing normal to others.

Meanwhile, her medication was having side effects: 'Allison did certainly suffer a loss of libido. Our sex life basically became non-existent. And she did put on weight.'

He jumped from talking about his sexless marriage to Allison's desperation for a third child – preferably a son: 'She wanted to be able to continue the Baden-Clay name.' Gerard told the court he wasn't keen. The financial pressure of surviving on one income, and Allison's personal difficulties, were already too much.

Byrne asked if he was faithful to Allison at the time, and Gerard began sobbing. He admitted to a month-long affair with former Raine & Horne colleague Michelle Hammond, who until then had not been named.

'I just wanted sex,' Gerard cried, 'and Allison and I hadn't had any sort of physical intimacy for years. It's not an excuse but that's why.'

Gerard quickly regained his composure when discussing his real estate business. He preferred to hire people new to the industry because it 'had a fairly poor reputation for some of its practices', a reputation he considered to be well founded in some instances. He didn't want people who had been 'tainted'.

The couple had their third daughter in September 2006 and Allison was in 'shock' because she had her heart set on a boy, according to Gerard. Again, he couldn't resist damning with faint praise, saying: 'Allison fell in love with her soon, too, which was great.'

Back at work, he was executing his 'big vision' to build an empire across the western suburbs, taking on partners Phill Broom and Jocelyn Frost. Allison wasn't coping, so he was still helping with the morning and evening routines with their daughters. Again, he said, his wife hid her problems in public but would collapse on the couch at home. Allison 'just had no interest in any physical intimacy at all'.

In this environment, he started the affair with Toni McHugh: 'It started one night in the office when we were both working back . . . and then on a couple of occasions we actually met up and had a tryst, I suppose, is the best way to describe it, in my car, which was the Prado, Snowy.'

They'd steeled themselves to sit though all manner of gruesome evidence from scientific experts, but Gerard's testimony proved too much for some members of Allison's family. Geoff Dickie and Allison's uncle Don Moore left the main court and went to sit in the overflow court upstairs. They didn't trust themselves to stay silent.

Gerard told the court he had 'tried to break off with Toni on numerous occasions' but they always ended up back together. Not that he cared for her. Now Gerard belittled his mistress. He was only interested in the sex. Toni left her partner and 'wanted me to divorce Allison'. Gerard's loyalty was to his wife, but it was all very awkward, he said, because McHugh worked for him. He continued to sleep with her because he didn't want to lose a good saleswoman, and because she was volatile and he didn't want her to cause any dramas. He was flattered by the attention, 'but really it was purely for the physical intimacy'. Along the way he had another affair, with Jackie Crane, at a real estate conference in Sydney, but this too was just about sex.

And at work, his business went from strength to strength and award to award, and 'ultimately we were the number 1 office in Queensland'. His business partners were living the high life, buying 'flashy things'. He got caught up in it too, he confessed, buying a new Lexus on a whim in 2009 when Phill Broom bought one. It was the same year Gerard had complained to Allison's psychiatrist that she had wasted money on a treadmill.

Putting the boot into his former partners, he told the court they simply 'stopped selling' before the big move to the new office at Taringa. There was a long, detailed discussion about the business and the Brisbane floods before Gerard came to Allison's discovery of the affair.

His wife reacted with 'just disbelief'. And McHugh 'just couldn't believe it' when he unceremoniously dumped her the same day.

Gerard had duped the two people closest to him – his wife and his mistress. Would the jury accept he wasn't lying now? It was an uphill battle.

Allison imposed a new regime, banning him from working nights. He said she 'needed complete control and access to my phone, so every day whenever I came home I would basically hand my phone to her'. Allison would return the phone in the morning before he went to work.

Gerard tried to spin a positive out of resuming his affair with McHugh. He was worried. He'd 'heard that she was really struggling'.

Trying to downplay his financial struggles, Gerard admitted he cried on the phone to Dr Bruce Flegg's friend Sue Heath when he asked for a loan in March 2012, but they weren't tears of desperation.

'She did ask me, "Are you okay?" and I remember actually breaking into tears at that point, because nobody ever asked me if I was okay,' he volunteered.

Toni McHugh had previously told the court she and Gerard tried to talk every day. Gerard had a different story: 'I was doing my best to distance myself from Toni. So wasn't seeing her at all. Was not calling her. I was responding only to emails that she sent and answering the phone when she called.'

McHugh was 'fixated'. He was trying to get rid of her, to make her 'preferably, go away'.

As to the emails Gerard sent to McHugh telling her he loved her and would leave his wife by 1 July, in the witness box, Gerard insisted that he was merely telling McHugh 'whatever she wanted to hear'.

'I don't honestly know where that came from,' he said. 'I anticipated that that time would come and go and Toni would be frustrated by that. I really wanted for her to be able to make the decision to leave me, if that makes sense.' He lacked courage, he said.

Prompted by Michael Byrne, his defence lawyer, Gerard told the court that two days before Allison disappeared – Wednesday 18 April – he and his wife drove to Mt Coot-tha for the 15-minute session mandated by their counsellor. He said they calmly worked through the questions in Allison's diary. She had asked about Gerard going to the movies with McHugh, and he told her it was only a couple of times. He told her he was 'terrified' of being seen with his mistress, and they 'never showed any physical affection in public'. There were 'a couple of intimate meetings in Snowy' with the seats down, after they had driven to a secluded spot. He drew a map of McHugh's unit in Allison's journal, with it balanced on his knee in the car.

Explaining the toys found in the Holden Captiva, Gerard said the previous week the family had gathered up clothes and toys the girls didn't use any more to give to charity. Allison had loaded them into the Captiva the day before he reported her missing. He had no idea 'whatsoever' how Allison's blood ended up in the car.

The day before Allison vanished was like any other, Gerard said. He'd gone to a chamber of commerce breakfast then to the school cross-country event. He was standing next to the oval when 'all of a sudden something bit me, stung me'. It felt like it went down his shirt too. Previously, Gerard told police a caterpillar had fallen on him. At trial he thought it was a caterpillar but it might have been a spider.

After the cross-country he went to his friend Rob Cheesman's house, which was about to be put on the market. That afternoon he had a parent–teacher interview, which Allison couldn't make because she had work and a hair appointment. That night, he and Allison talked. She was in her pyjamas and they went through some questions from her journal, then discussed more mundane topics.

'I reiterated how I appreciated her strength and forgiveness. It was perfectly normal. Certainly civilised,' said Gerard.

Allison had his phone overnight, as usual, he continued. He didn't put it on the charger at 1.48 am. In the morning Allison was gone.

Next Gerard picked up a highlighter pen for a pivotal piece of evidence. Using it like a razor he attempted to demonstrate how he had cut himself shaving. He talked the jury through it.

'Because it was blunt and I – I was pushing down quite firmly on my skin like that, and I pulled down and then flicked up like that, and that's when I cut myself. I always shave on my right side first, and that's when I cut myself the first time, closer to my mouth. The reason I think that it happened the second time was because I was – and that hurt a lot. When I was coming down again for the second time, I released before the previous cut to be sure that I didn't cut myself there – you know, get involved in that first cut. I then continued to shave and had a bit of an issue shaving around those cuts, obviously, and cut myself again.'

It was a key moment for Gerard. The Crown case turned on the injuries to his face. He needed to convince the jury it was possible they were shaving cuts. Had he done that?

The trial adjourned for the day with Gerard still in the witness box. The next day was Allison's birthday. It was the second anniversary of the date Gerard had chosen as the deadline to leave his wife. It was also the day prosecutor Todd Fuller would get his chance to grill Gerard.

Tuesday 1 July 2014

Before Gerard faced cross-examination, Michael Byrne took Gerard through some final details, trying to tie up some loose ends in his testimony. To begin with, he targeted Gerard's phone calls with McHugh about the conference clash. Gerard had 'no real concern' about the two women in his life meeting at the real estate conference, he said. McHugh had wanted him to tell Allison she would be there, but he never did.

Byrne had Gerard explain why he had called insurers on the day of Allison's autopsy: it was because his father said he was obliged to inform them. On the subject of his finances, he said he had not paid credit card bills between January and May because it wasn't a priority. It was 'not correct' that he was under pressure financially and personally at the time.

Todd Fuller's cross-examination of Gerard began at 11.34 am. In the days leading up to it, there had been much speculation about the approach he would take. Some observers felt the prosecution had been lacking in force and depth in the opening days. Now that Gerard had taken the stand, the gloves would be off. It was Fuller's to win or lose. If surprised by Gerard's decision to testify, he and co-prosecutor Danny Boyle had consequently enjoyed the benefit of a three-day weekend break to prepare, and they obviously hadn't wasted a minute.

Fuller went straight for Gerard's Achilles heel – his credibility. He highlighted his years of deceit. Gerard had lied to his wife, and lied to his mistress. He was a practised liar – the type of person who could lie to police, and lie to a jury, to save himself.

The prosecutor's sarcasm was barely concealed as he noted Gerard resumed having sex with McHugh after she left the business: 'So, you're not having sex with her for the sake of the business, are you?'

Before raking over Gerard's emails to McHugh, Fuller put them on the screens in court. One, sent in the days before Allison's death, had Gerard telling McHugh three times he loved her. The questions were coming thick and fast. And every question was met with a short, sharp response. The tears of previous days had vanished too. Gerard was calm and composed for his interrogation.

'You went on to give her a date when you would be together, the 1st of July; correct?' Fuller asked.

'That is correct,' Gerard replied.

'Which just happened to be your wife's birthday?'

'Which just happens to be today,' Gerard batted back. He added that even McHugh didn't believe he would meet the commitment – she had sat 'in this very chair' and said she didn't believe it. He was ready for a stoush.

Fuller kept returning to Gerard's lies: 'You deceived your family and friends for that four-year period as well, didn't you?'

'Yes, I did.'

The prosecutor went back to Gerard's start in real estate, when he got a job at Raine & Horne then opened up next door: 'So, you took their business and then had an affair with one of their employees [Michelle Hammond]?'

'Correct,' Gerard replied.

Moving quickly along, the prosecutor turned to Gerard's image; he'd barely started his cross-examination and he was getting to the heart of what made Gerard tick. Gerard had carefully built the reputation of a respectable community member over many years. A clash between his lover and his mistress could bring it all undone. That was what set Allison's final night apart from all the others.

The prosecutor highlighted to jurors Gerard's subterfuge: deleting phone calls from McHugh, avoiding text messages and using the secret Bruce Overland email account.

Fuller went back to Gerard's testimony about the early years of marriage – the international travel, the Scouts, his role as acting director while Allison worked in the shops, his well-paying London job while Allison was earning peanuts. It was all about Gerard. He had done little to help his wife at the onset of her depression – he didn't even believe in depression. Before their first daughter was born, Gerard had started working from home because he had been made redundant – it wasn't a sacrifice he made out of concern for Allison, Fuller pointed out.

The prosecutor went through Gerard's financial pressures and his loss of personal freedom after Allison discovered the affair. He had managed to keep his work and home lives separate, until Allison started coming to work to watch over him.

Everyone in the court that day was now watching a verbal sparring match – short, sharp questions met by short, sharp answers. Fuller was jumping backwards and forwards in time, making Gerard work hard to keep the strands of his story from unravelling or snapping off altogether. He brought up his promise to come to McHugh 'unconditionally'.

'It was a bit of a joke,' Gerard explained, 'in relation to a real estate contract being unconditional.'

No one seemed particularly amused.

Fuller asked why Gerard resumed having sex with McHugh after they had broken up in 2011. Gerard had previously said there were only two occasions of intimacy – now he offered that one occasion wasn't strictly sex. Pressed, he appealed to the judge.

'How much sordid detail am I expected to give, your Honour?' Gerard appealed.

'I didn't ask about the sordid detail, Mr Baden-Clay. I asked why you had sex with her,' Fuller said icily.

'Well, it wasn't sex as in intercourse,' Gerard responded. The pair had met at a Coffee Club and then retired to McHugh's car, where an encounter that 'wasn't sex' took place. What exactly the pair got up to in a parked car in the middle of the day was left to the imagination of all in court.

Fuller then turned to a new piece of information. In the previous few days, Allison's friends had retrieved an old post from Gerard's Real Estate Expert blog, written after Allison turned 40. Allison had spent a week away at a health spa. His blog relayed his failed struggle to run the household while she was gone. It starkly contradicted his claims he was the one doing everything at home.

'Mr Mum! The past week I have been trying to do my best impersonation of my dear wife – and struggling,' Gerard wrote. 'Whilst she has been enjoying the rest and quietude, I have been trying to manage the house and transport my three girls to all of their activities – and I am knackered. It's a bit of a cliché that most men have no idea how hard it is to run a household, and I thought that I was pretty in-tune with the day to day routine, but I can honestly say that this week has given me a real insight into the challenges of managing a family . . . I'll certainly be more understanding in the future when I come home from work and find out that dinner isn't on the table with my foot spa pre-warmed.'

But when Fuller tried to introduce the blog, the defence objected and the jury left the room. Behind closed doors, Fuller argued he was entitled to raise it because Gerard had claimed that morning that Allison's depression and episodes on the couch continued until her death. Justice Byrne ruled it should have been presented as part of the Crown case if it was going to be used. The jury would not see it.

With the jury back, Fuller put the blog aside and turned to Allison's journal, asking Gerard to explain her question: 'afterwards, why so mean?'

Gerard said they had resumed a sexual relationship in February 2012, and Allison thought he laughed at her underwear, 'And that's not true.' He didn't tell Allison she smelled, as she had written, it was just that 'neither of us had had a shower' and he'd suggested they should.

Fuller didn't accept Gerard's claim that Allison had asked the crossed-out questions in her diary on the 18th of April. He suggested to Gerard it was the 19th, the night she vanished.

Gerard replied: 'You can suggest it. It's completely untrue.'

Growing in confidence, Gerard started correcting Fuller. In one instance, he told the prosecutor the 'subtle difference that perhaps you're not quite seeing' was that he had borrowed money from longstanding friends, not investors.

'The subtlety hadn't escaped me, Mr Baden-Clay,' Fuller shot back.

Arguing he was not under financial strain, Gerard said he could have wound up his business and emerged 'relatively unscathed'.

Fuller pointed out he was only thinking of himself. Was he not concerned for his three best friends, who would have been left $270,000 out of pocket?

'They are all highly qualified people,' Gerard replied, 'and they went into it with their eyes wide open, with the understanding that there was a risk that they might lose everything.'

The court adjourned. Gerard would have to return for a fourth day, when Fuller would launch a final assault.

Wednesday 2 July 2014

Justice Byrne kept the jury out to deal with an unusual development – the accused had tried to pass him a note. Justice Byrne didn't know what was in the correspondence. Gerard had handed it to a bailiff, but it had been returned unread. Apparently, Gerard had been told he could not communicate with his barrister while under cross-examination so he had tried to pass a message to the judge. Michael Byrne admitted he had no idea what the note contained, and solicitor Peter Shields was given permission to investigate. Shields and Gerard had a brief private chat before Byrne told the court without further explanation that the matter had been resolved.

Gerard looked drained as he started his fourth day on the stand, but his cockiness hadn't abated. When he tried to claim he had answered 'every and any question' police asked, Fuller immediately pulled him up:

'So you answered every question that was asked of you?'

'I did.'

'They asked you to make a formal statement?'

'Yes.'

'You did not?' continued Fuller.

'Oh, I answered them: "No, I will not be making a formal statement." That was my answer.'

The response was a sign Gerard was intent on sparring with Fuller and had forgotten the real battle was to convince a jury he was not the sort of man who could kill his wife, dispose of her body, then lie to friends and family. Gerard was playing into the prosecution's hands by putting his hubris and guile on full display. He was having a battle of wits, but to the jury he may have just looked arrogant.

Fuller homed in on why Gerard used the Holden Captiva to search for Allison on the Friday morning, and not his Toyota Prado, which was parked in a much more accessible spot near the front steps. Gerard said it was because his car had been sideswiped in an accident on the Monday.

'You'd been driving the vehicle Tuesday, Wednesday, Thursday, I assume?' asked Fuller pointedly.

'That's correct.'

'But on this morning you chose to drive the Captiva?'

'Correct,' said Gerard.

Fuller highlighted Gerard's failure to phone Allison's parents and closest friends until late that morning. He dropped in the detail that Gerard had slipped his business card to the GP at Kenmore and raised the fact that Gerard had not told police of the injuries on his torso. He spelt out Gerard's precarious financial position and the difficult consequences should a marital separation have occurred. He suggested Gerard wanted to be with McHugh, who 'offered you things that you didn't get from your wife, the wife that you no longer loved'.

Gerard denied it.

The prosecutor pressed Gerard on the last point, saying McHugh offered Gerard a different life and he resumed the affair because he realised he had made the wrong choice when he stayed with his wife.

Again, Gerard denied it.

Gerard, Fuller persisted, was at risk of a catastrophe if his wife and mistress came together at the conference. His double life would be exposed and 'the façade that was Gerard Baden-Clay would fall'.

The prospect had never entered his mind, said Gerard.

Fuller's voice had been rising. He was working towards a dramatic conclusion, and the court fell silent as he went for the throat in a dramatic exchange.

Fuller: You killed your wife, Mr Baden-Clay?

Gerard: No, I did not.

Fuller: You attacked her and the only way that she could respond was to lash out and claw at your face and leave marks upon it?

Gerard: That is not true.

Fuller: Probably as you smothered her and took her life from her?

Gerard: That is not true.

Fuller: Perhaps she grabbed at your clothing; is that why you had that injury under your right shoulder?

Gerard: No.

Fuller: Why do you have that injury?

Gerard: I don't know.

Fuller: You have no idea?

Gerard: No.

Fuller: You overpowered her pretty quickly, didn't you?

Gerard: I never overpowered her at all.

Fuller: Perhaps her jumper came up as she tried to fight you off, up over her hands and up around her neck, or did that happen later as you moved her body or dumped her in the creek?

Gerard: I never did anything to physically harm my wife in any way, ever, so your supposition to then take it further to suggest that I did other things, as well, is absurd, and I, I object to it. So, I can't answer your question.

Fuller: Her head came into contact with the fallen leaves at the back of your house or at the side of your house, didn't they?

Gerard: I don't know.

Fuller: You put her in the Captiva?

Gerard: I did not.

Fuller: And she sustained perhaps a minor injury to some part of her body that caused her to bleed?

Gerard: I did not have anything to do with anything that you are suggesting.

Fuller: And that's why the blood is on the right hand side over the cowling of the back wheel when the seats are folded down?

Gerard: I had nothing to do with anything that you are asking me.

Fuller: It wasn't enough to be noticed, but it was enough to be found . . . You transported her to Kholo Creek and then dumped her underneath the bridge, unceremoniously?

Gerard: No, I did not.

Fuller: Anxious to get back to your children?

Gerard: The suggestion that I would leave my children for any time in the middle of the night is absurd, let alone do the dastardly things that you're suggesting.

Once again, Gerard's strongest reaction was to the suggestion he would leave his children alone.

The prosecutor continued without pause.

Fuller: That was all done by 1.48 am, perhaps, which is when you put your phone back on its charger?

Gerard: I did not.

Fuller: And you started covering your tracks then, I suggest to you, Mr Baden-Clay: the toys in the back of the car, shaving, cutting yourself just at the bottom edges to help disguise and give some legitimacy to your claim that they were, in fact, shaving cuts?

Gerard: I did not.

Fuller: And then you told everybody they were shaving cuts, anybody who asked. And you were happy for the police to search your house, correct?

Gerard: Yes. I had nothing to hide.

Fuller: Because you knew there was nothing to be found?

Gerard: No, because I knew that I had nothing to hide, and I wanted my wife found, and they suggested that searching the house might in some way be helpful in that – to that end. So, I enabled them to do whatever they wanted to do.

Fuller: And then you kept up the façade of the concerned husband?

Gerard: I was a concerned husband, and I'm a very concerned father. I remain so. It's not a façade.

Fuller: Then you took some legal advice?

Gerard: I did.

Fuller: And you declined to provide a statement to the police?

Gerard: That's correct. I, to be perfectly candid with you, had no idea what a formal statement was and I couldn't see how it was any different to all of the numerous questions I'd answered previously. But my lawyer insisted upon it, and so I followed that advice.

Fuller: And you're certain you never told Allison that she was going to run into Toni McHugh the next day?

Gerard: Absolutely not.

Fuller's interrogation was over. Gerard looked spent.

Defence barrister Michael Byrne had some more questions, and Gerard offered one more piece of unexpected evidence before he left the witness box – intimating he'd had numerous affairs.

'It was purely about the physical aspect of that, that I went to those other women. Some of them over an extended period of time, admittedly. Many of them concurrent.'

It was the last part of the statement that was odd. The jury had only heard of one concurrent affair – when he slept with Jackie Crane and McHugh at the same conference. Gerard was distancing himself from McHugh, but in the process he was raising questions about what else he had been concealing.

At the end of his testimony, the defence called three witnesses. A company called Khemistry had compiled a time-lapse video recording at Kholo Creek spanning ten days, and employee Ashton Ward spoke to the court about how it had been prepared. It showed debris moving up and down the waterway. It was an attempt to suggest the leaves in Allison's hair may have been washed down the creek, and that her body may have floated to where it was found.

The next defence witness, forensic toxicologist Dr Michael Robertson, testified sertraline could bring on serotonin syndrome, which caused profound confusion and other effects. People on antidepressants were also at higher risk of suicide, Robertson said. Under cross-examination he agreed Allison's sertraline levels were not consistent with the majority of sertraline-related deaths.

Finally, psychiatrist Dr Mark Schramm testified people with major depression sometimes took their own lives, did not leave suicide notes, and hid their intentions from medical professionals. Under cross-examination, Schramm readily conceded that Allison's strong maternal attachment went against the idea of her being suicidal. Prosecutor Danny Boyle asked how the risk of suicide was affected by the lack of a triggering event, the existence of short- and long-term plans, willingness to seek assistance, long-term use of antidepressants and absence of prior adverse effects. Schramm had never met Allison. Her psychiatrist, psychologists and counsellors had all testified she was not suicidal.

The defence case ended on a whimper. Had they managed to pull a rabbit out of a hat on Gerard's scratches, it might have been a different story. As it was, they could find no one to testify it *was* likely his wounds were inflicted by a safety razor.

The jury was excused and told to return on Monday for closing arguments. Once they were gone, Justice Byrne had a detailed discussion with the Crown and defence on how he would sum up for the jury the following week. The judge was also considering an interesting direction to the jury – that they should not draw adverse inferences from Gerard's bouts of sobbing in the dock.

'It will have become apparent to the jury,' Justice Byrne said, 'that the sobbing took place in-chief [during defence questioning] and not in cross-examination. It may well be that other observations by jurors of the accused may lead one or more of them to suppose that he was acting.'

Also worrying for Gerard and his team was that Justice Byrne raised concerns about his obligation to spell out to the jury any reasonable scenario consistent with innocence. He was struggling to put one together and wanted the defence to clarify their argument.

'My concern about it, frankly, is this. The evidence doesn't seem to me, at this stage, to identify any possible basis on which she could have died by suicide. She did not drown. She did not overdose. She did not fall from the bridge, because there's no fractures. So what is the suicide hypothesis that's to be put if one is to be put?'

After all the defence efforts to highlight Allison's depression, the suicide theory had no endgame. There seemed to be few positives too from Gerard's time in the witness box. The jury had wanted to see him declare his innocence, but the salesman had failed to close the deal. They wanted to see a broken, remorseful, loving spouse. They saw a confident and boastful man, equally happy to betray either his mistress or his wife as it suited. He was comfortable with deceit and almost seemed to revel in matching wits and splitting hairs with Crown prosecutor Todd Fuller. He had performed like a shonky property spruiker rather than a sincere and likeable widower.

Monday to Wednesday 7–9 July 2014
Gerard's decision to take the stand handed the prosecution a significant tactical advantage. The defence would present their

closing argument first, with the Crown getting the last word before Justice Byrne summed up.

Michael Byrne started with an attack on the media. This was a murder trial 'not a great big media event,' he said. It was a theme Byrne would return to, criticising the 'sensationalist' coverage that appealed to the 'lowest common denominator' and was little more than 'salacious gossip', at times. Jurors may find Gerard's infidelity 'abhorrent' but it didn't make him a murderer, he said. Even Toni McHugh knew Gerard wasn't going to honour his promise to leave his wife by 1 July. Byrne added it was a furphy that Gerard was under financial pressure. Here was a man who had no history of violence. There was no evidence of a struggle at the house. No eyewitnesses. No confession. Byrne said the Crown case simply didn't add up. It seemed fanciful that Gerard had managed to murder his wife without his daughters hearing anything, then left his children home alone while he drove out and dragged his wife's body down to a creek before returning home.

'Do you think such a scenario is even possible?' Byrne asked.

With the presumption of innocence, Gerard's team was not obliged to prove anything. But Byrne suggested one possible scenario for Allison's death. He set it against a backdrop of Allison being deeply upset by the birth of a nephew in Canada, longing for a son of her own.

Is it possible that Allison stayed up watching television . . . thinking about what had gone on between her and Gerard, what had been revealed. She can't sleep. She's up alone. She's supposed to be going to the conference the next day . . . she avoids confrontation. What if she decides to go for a walk at that time to clear her head? What if, because of her depression, she takes her Zoloft tablet around 10 or 11 pm? That would explain, you might think, her changing into the walking clothes which she is found in. She leaves the house, having first placed Gerard's phone, which she had possession of, on the charger at about 1.48 am . . . About 4 am, on the figures Dr Schramm gave you, the drugs would peak in her blood stream, the medication would be absorbed in her system, and was no longer present in her stomach, but we know the levels are in the blood. Maybe with that increase in dosage, we had serotonin syndrome or just the effects of sertraline. Consider that as a scenario. Is it something which is excluded on the evidence? And some time, for some reason, she ends up in the river. The autopsy report can't rule out drowning, it can't rule out a possible fall or jump from the bridge could have rendered her unconscious and that she either drowned or died in the river.

In the courtroom, Allison's aunt Mary Dann just wanted it to be over. She didn't want to listen to the defence 'scenario', so she distracted herself by counting the panels on the court ceiling – there were 65.

Byrne's closing argument finished early on Tuesday 8 July.

Todd Fuller's closing argument also straddled two days, finishing on the Wednesday. Fuller asked the jury to look at the evidence not in discrete pieces, but as a whole, and brought together the threads that when interwoven pointed to Gerard's guilt.

'The scratches on his face show that he was in close contact with his wife, that she was struggling for her life. It was close; it was personal; it was violent,' he said. 'But as I said yesterday, it was effective. What could have been in this man's mind as he carried that out to bring it all to an end? His frustrations from his marriage? The frustrations in his life not going where he thought it would be? The double life, the daily deceptions, the risk to him of it all coming crashing down. You might think that's what was at the forefront of his mind. Like he told Carmel Ritchie, he just wanted to wipe the slate clean.'

Justice Byrne's detailed summing up followed, and continued

into the next day. Fuller and Boyle looked relaxed and confident. But so too did the defence.

Gerard's family had been telling friends everything had gone to plan.

The wait

Thursday 10 July 2014 – wait day 1

Kerry-Anne Walker was in Hong Kong making final arrangements for Flight Centre's Annual Global Gathering, which was to bring together 3500 guests in nearby Macau that weekend. It looked like Allison's best friend was going to miss the verdict, but as the organiser for such a big event, it was unavoidable. Back in Brisbane, her parents Gary and Pam were near the front of the line outside court, as usual. The couple had attended the committal hearing and every day of the trial.

That morning, Pam held up her phone. Kerry-Anne had sent through a photo of a huge arrangement of sunflowers. Staff in her hotel, the Four Seasons, had put the flowers on display overnight. They hoped it was a good omen.

At 11.10 am, after Justice Byrne completed his summing up, the jury retired to consider its verdict. As they filed out of the courtroom, Gerard had his head up and turned in their direction: those 12 good people held his fate in their hands.

The public gallery emptied into the foyer to begin the wait. Verdicts sometimes took hours, sometimes days.

In the jury room, a problem was emerging already. A juror, obviously anxious to do the job right, had downloaded online advice from a US commentator about how to conduct deliberations and had brought along a print-out. Justice Byrne had been told of the breach and, back in court in the jury's absence, he bristled with anger. He had given the jury clear and emphatic instructions twice, plus in writing, not to delve into anything to do with the trial outside of court.

'We will lose this trial if conduct of this nature is repeated,' he stated gravely.

The jury was brought back in and the judge delivered a firm warning: 'We all understand the jurors are often anxious about performing their role; they want to do it well and responsibly,' he said. But 'what was done was wrong', and he repeated his earlier instructions.

After the jury had departed once more, Justice Byrne sighed. 'Let's await the next incident,' he said, standing to leave the court.

The day ended without a verdict. The jury had agreed to continue deliberations on Friday. They were not sequestered during deliberations, and went home, with the judge's stern advice to ignore everything outside court ringing in their ears.

Friday 11 July 2014 – wait day 2

Geoff and Priscilla Dickie were waiting for the verdict at a conference room on the 34th floor of nearby Santos House. Other family members and friends were taking turns to wait outside Court 11 so they wouldn't lose their additional seats should the jury return with a verdict. First thing in the morning, Justice Byrne received a request from the jury to repeat part of his summation. However, when the jury was called back into court at 10.10 am, the foreman didn't know which part needed to be heard again and indicated it was another juror who had asked. At Justice Byrne's request, the other juror told him which section they wanted reread. It related to interpreting lies and deciding between murder and manslaughter.

Justice Byrne repeated his advice from his summing up: if the jury concluded Gerard lied about the scratches on his face because it implicated him in killing his wife, they would still have to carefully consider whether it was murder or manslaughter. Murder required an intention to kill or cause grievous bodily harm. The jury left the court to continue their deliberations.

The prevailing view outside court was that the jury had decided Gerard killed Allison but was unsure whether it was murder or manslaughter. Detectives looked confident, expecting a verdict in their favour before the day was out. The jury was dressed differently, one of the officers noted. 'They're in their drinking clothes. They're ready for a beer after the verdict.'

Confidence was high. But as the hours ticked by and the day dragged on without a verdict, doubts started to creep in. The verdict had to be unanimous. It would only take one dissenter to hang the jury. If that were to occur, there would almost certainly be a retrial and everyone would have to go through it all again.

By 4 pm the jury had not reached a verdict and was sent home for the weekend. They would resume deliberations on Monday, taking the trial into its sixth week.

The meticulous Ewen Taylor sat down at his computer and typed out a group email thanking the team of people who had assisted in gathering forensic evidence in Operation Kilo Intrigue. Taylor wrote that no matter what the verdict, they could all be proud of their work.

Allison's friends and family were dealing with some other difficult news. Kerry-Anne Walker's dad Gary had suffered a stroke. It had affected his vision and he was undergoing a battery of tests in hospital. No one was telling Kerry-Anne because her event was on in Macau the next day and she had to be there. It was to be a long and difficult weekend for Allison's family and friends.

Monday 14 July 2014 – wait day 3

Gerard Baden-Clay arrived at court brimming with confidence. The continuing deliberations had fuelled his hopes of freedom. Television producers were wooing his family, talking extraordinary sums of money for an interview in the event he was acquitted. Industry experts said he could write his own cheque for his story, and by now everyone knew Gerard would want to tell it. His wife's separate $1 million life insurance payout would be his. And his daughters would be back in his care.

'I'm getting out of here today,' he told the guards watching over him.

Gerard had more reason for optimism in the afternoon when he was brought back into court for another redirection. The jury had written a note asking Justice Byrne to repeat his summing up about circumstantial evidence.

Waiting for the jury to arrive, Gerard let his wandering eyes lock onto a television journalist covering his trial. Katrina Blowers, an accomplished newshound and attractive blonde to boot, had to walk past Gerard to reach extra media seats brought into court ahead of the verdict. She felt Gerard's gaze on her but, as she sat down, Blowers tried to keep her eyes on the notepad in her lap. Eventually, she glanced towards the dock and was startled to see Gerard still staring at her. He smiled and raised his eyebrows in greeting – a manoeuvre probably more suited to a bar than a courtroom. Blowers found it extremely uncomfortable. Flustered, she turned bright red and diligently averted her eyes. Like the earlier incident when Gerard had handed his business card to the GP who examined his scratches, it seemed he couldn't help himself.

By the time the jury filed back into court at 3.51 pm for Justice Byrne's clarification, they had been deliberating for 19 hours. And worryingly for Allison's supporters, the latest request seemed a backward step.

'As no one claims to have seen the accused kill his wife, this is a circumstantial case,' Justice Byrne repeated. 'Importantly, to bring in a verdict of guilty based entirely, or substantially, on circumstantial evidence, guilt should not only be a rational inference: it must be the only rational inference that could be drawn from the circumstances. If there is any reasonable possibility consistent with innocence, it is your duty to find the accused not guilty. This follows from the requirement that guilt must be established beyond reasonable doubt.'

The jury member who had asked the previous question was listening intently and reading Justice Byrne's words as they appeared on the screen in front of them. Other jurors had their arms crossed and looked either angry, fed up or bewildered. To those in court, it looked like a jury with at least one person on a separate path.

Outside court, the detectives' calm and confident veneer had vanished. They were worried. This was a much more concerning question. It seemed the jury was still debating guilt or innocence, not murder or manslaughter, as Allison's friends and family had thought jubilantly on Friday. The prospect of a hung jury suddenly loomed large.

The jury deliberated until around 4.30 pm without reaching a verdict, and retired for the night.

Tuesday 15 July 2014 – wait day 4

Allison's extended family arrived at court with heavy hearts. The agony of waiting was taking its toll. The tension was suffocating. No one really knew what to say to each other any more. Small talk was at a minimum as they readied themselves for another day of waiting outside Court 11. The longer the deliberations went on, the more likely it seemed the jury was deadlocked. And in the back of everyone's minds was the additional worry that something could cause a mistrial. Everyone was walking on eggshells.

Outside court that morning, there seemed to be further evidence the jury was split. In the long line to get through security, one juror stood alone while the others milled near the front door. Grabbing the attention of a court official, the solitary juror said it was time for the group to move inside. They had been told but didn't listen, the juror said. A little later, the other jurors moved through together.

Upstairs, I told Jodie Dann about the scene, saying a verdict could be days away. Dann didn't look well. Everyone was exhausted from weeks of relentless stress.

When it seemed the wait would never end, there came stunning news. Word filtered through shortly before 11 am that the jury had reached a verdict.

At first it was only a whisper. Justice Byrne was presiding over another case in a separate court and had abruptly adjourned proceedings. Dann made a phone call and it was confirmed – the jury was due in court in 30 minutes. The wait was over. She burst into tears on the spot. It was the moment everything had been building up to.

Police, family and friends filled the foyer. Kerry-Anne Walker suddenly appeared outside the courtroom and she too burst into tears. She wouldn't miss the verdict after all. Walker had arrived back from Macau only hours earlier. She had been to see her father in hospital then gone to see the Dickies at Santos House when everyone's phones started ringing with news of the verdict. Priscilla and Geoff Dickie and their daughter Vanessa Fowler arrived. Ashley Dickie had been working night shifts and was on the way.

Allison's friends and family could finally dress themselves in yellow. They handed out yellow ribbons, and police put them on too. Mark Ainsworth, public face of the investigation; Brian Wilkins, the former Homicide boss; straight-talking Mal Gundry; arrest team detectives Cameron McLeod and Chris Canniffe; shaven-headed Homicide detectives Peter Roddick and Gavin Pascoe; tireless forensics officer Ewen Taylor; and tower of support Mark Laing – they all made it.

The court doors opened. Family members went in first. Elaine, Nigel, Adam and Olivia took their seats in the front row behind the dock. A dozen extra seats had been brought in for media and they were quickly filled. Michael Byrne and Peter Shields were there. Todd Fuller was in his seat. Danny Boyle made it just in time, looking out of breath from running.

Gerard, in a dark suit, checked shirt and yellow tie, took a deep breath in the dock.

The jury walked in at 11.52 am. Most jurors had their eyes downcast, but a couple looked over to the public gallery. The bailiff announced the jury was all accounted for and the judge's associate asked if they had agreed on a verdict. They had.

'Do you find the accused, Gerard Robert Baden-Clay, guilty or not guilty of murder?' the associate asked.

'Guilty, Your Honour,' the jury's speaker replied.

A cheer erupted in the back of the court. A second's silence was followed by wrenching sobs from Allison's family and friends as it sank in. Gerard looked stunned. His family stared straight ahead, unmoving and silent.

Justice Byrne thanked the jury for their service and discharged them. He invited them to remain in the jury box if they wished, but they all left.

Elaine Baden-Clay stood and walked out too at that point. Those sitting nearby say Elaine was not 'overcome' when she left, but calmly stood, asked Nigel if he wanted to leave with her – he did not – and then headed for the door. She would not listen as Allison's family gave their harrowing victim impact statements. Neither would she hear her son being sentenced.

Outpouring

Nigel, Olivia and Adam stayed in their seats. Gerard was on his feet, rocking back and forth, as Justice Byrne invited Allison's family to come forward one at a time. It was finally their turn to truly speak their minds about Allison's murder.

Allison's mother found the strength to go first and walked forward to the witness box. She stood there in her yellow jacket and ribbon and waited. Gerard was struggling to breathe and a security officer interrupted proceedings, concerned he was about to collapse. Peter Shields checked on him, then Priscilla was cleared to go ahead and address her daughter's killer. Love, pride and sadness for Allison poured out alongside anger at Gerard and a disgust at his base behaviour. She cried as she spoke, but pushed through to the end.

My name is Priscilla Anna Dickie, the grieving mother of the late Allison June Baden-Clay. My daughter was a wonderful mother, a devoted wife, a caring daughter, a loving aunt, sister-in-law and good friend to all who knew her – an incredible achiever.

Because of her life experiences, we had the utmost faith in Allison's ability to handle any situation in her life. This she proved while fighting for her life leaving those telling scratch marks on Gerard's face on that fateful night. God Bless Her.

The impact of seeing those scratch marks on his face the day she was reported missing will remain with me forever. It was obvious to me that one of the last things Allison did was to leave her marks on her husband.

So much has happened since the 20th April 2012, where do I start? The impact of waiting for ten days at the Brookfield Showground, waiting for news, dealing with the realisation that her body had been discovered, organising a funeral, dealing with lawyers, media, counselling sessions, an investigation into Allison's death and ultimately a trial.

Since the 13th June, 2012, we went from being a happily retired couple involved in church and community activities on the Gold Coast to being guardians of three young girls. Every day we willingly deal with school days, special school events and many before and after school activities.

The impact of finding out about the troubled marital relationship over the past few years has been distressing. It has devastated me to know that Allison had been living in a fearful relationship and was trying to handle such a situation alone. His admission of adultery not once but many times during this trial was not easy to digest and goes against everything we believe as Christians. His constant self-interest and continual lying to Allison, his family and friends has disgusted me and my family.

He betrayed her and has made a mockery of their marriage and their life together and we are deeply saddened by this fact. He promised to take care of her and treat her well and again, as is evident, he did the opposite. To kill your wife, take away a mother and to still show no remorse has to us been one of the saddest and most distressing facts from this murder. For the love of her husband and children, Allison stayed and died.

The impact of Allison's murder has had far-reaching effects and the ramifications that have followed have completely and dramatically changed the rest of my life, my husband's, my children and their families.

The sorrow and loss of our precious daughter and the long and stressful journey we have had to take to find her killer has been difficult. Allison did not leave her girls. She has so much to offer them. She just loved them. To be taken from us all so suddenly by such a horrific murder completely devastated me. Not given the opportunity to say goodbye, hug or tell her how much we loved her is shattering and we have all been robbed of Allison's love and guidance. The pain does not go away.

At the command centre set up at the Brookfield Showground, we spent many long days waiting for news. Watching the police, SES and all the volunteers searching and doing all that they could to find her. The support of my family and friends each day gave me the strength to carry on. My hopes were fading, sadness filled my heart with the now likelihood of never seeing her alive again. Then we were told that a body had been found under a bridge. After 10 days of waiting, the anguish, the heart-ache, the discovery of our darling daughter under a bridge was absolutely shattering.

We were shocked that in all that time her husband did not ever come to search or wait at the Command Centre. His complete existence has been for his own self-gratification, which is upsetting for us and for those close to us.

I have been consumed by the enormity of this horrific murder of our darling daughter. No one can take the place of a mother and my heart breaks as I do my very best to fill the gap. I have completely and willingly changed my life as a grandma to adapt to my new situation, which is to now wholeheartedly care for Allison's three daughters.

I have willingly taken on the role of caring for Allison's daughters and I believe that their resilience to this tragedy is a result of her guidance and love. They miss her terribly and cry for her at night. To have Mummy put them to bed one night and then to wake up the next morning and be told that Mummy is missing, what a situation to face. The girls will never see their mother again. Not just now but forever and ever and ever. They have been condemned to a life sentence without the love and companionship only a mother can give.

What can you do or say when dealing with the stress of hugging a little crying girl saying 'I want my mummy!' and answering the question, 'Does mummy love me?' These are heart wrenching moments in my life and theirs which never ever should have happened. Over the coming years, there will be many more times like this to handle. It is heart breaking that these three young girls have been deprived of the love of the most caring and devoted mother The pain of having to bury your child – a mother of three, a daughter, sister, aunt, friend, is just indescribable. The tragedy of it all is that she had so much to offer.

Our lives are so very different. Everything has totally changed. As a grandma, my life now revolves around Allison's daughters and is dedicated to their care. I have no Allison to love, hug, talk to, to take advice from. Throughout this trial I have been deeply hurt by the smear campaign against Allison's name by her husband and those supporting him. My daughter has been robbed of a life. This man murdered one but has in turn destroyed the lives of many others.

You have changed your daughters' destinies and sentenced them to a journey they must take through life without a mother and all I have left are the memories of a wonderful daughter.

Allison's father was next. A man so proud of his daughter, and so lost without her. He bore no blame for her death, but shouldered it anyway.

My Name is Geoffrey James Dickie and I am the father of Allison Baden-Clay, deceased, and the grandfather of her three beautiful daughters, now aged 13, 10 and 7 years.

I have been devastated by the murder of my precious, gifted and talented daughter. Her achievements have been well documented over the past two years since her death. From an early age she studied and strived to achieve perfection in whatever she attempted. Whatever organisation she joined, for example, Flight Centre, she always advanced to become a leader because of her intelligence and friendly personality. Being a Rotary Exchange student, she lived with her host families in Denmark for 12 months and travelled through Europe. This gave her the incentive to travel the world and study various languages.

She was always willing to help others and as such entered the Miss Queensland competition to fundraise for the Cerebral Palsy organisation. She did not have an opportunity to reach her full potential but she changed the lives of many people through her work with Pathways and other organisations.

She gave up her successful career to pursue her dream of having a loving husband and happy and healthy children. She was reduced from a happy, intelligent, capable woman to a woman concerned about saving her marriage and protecting and caring for three daughters.

Allison had always been convinced that she was inadequate and not a good wife and mother. She was constantly trying to improve herself and her appearance to measure up to the expectations of her husband. She tried hard to save her marriage. Finally, in the end, she paid the ultimate price for the marriage and the love of her three daughters.

From the time we received the phone call on the morning of the 20th April, my life has changed. We were living a relaxed lifestyle of retirees and were involved in various charity organisations. As a result of the murder of our daughter, I am living an entirely different lifestyle, mourning the death of our daughter, which leaves an enormous black hole in our lives from which we will never recover.

The memory of Allison and the circumstances surrounding her death are constantly on my mind. I wake up in the middle of the night and find it difficult to go back to sleep because as soon as I wake the thoughts and aspects of the tragedy are always on my mind.

I also constantly try to imagine how she felt at the moment when she was being attacked and realised she was about to lose her life. I know she would have found the strength to fight as hard and long as she could to the end before she was murdered.

During the period of the search, we waited and prayed with family and friends at the Brookfield Showground. We waited day after day, and at the end of each day, when the sun was setting and the light was fading, we left with the thought that we were leaving our daughter alone at night, lying somewhere exposed to the elements.

Our worst fears were realised when her body was discovered. Her death has not only affected our lives, but extends to our immediate family, extended family and friends. No matter what the future holds, our lives will never be the same until the day I die. But I will strive to live life to the maximum due to the fact that I have the immense privilege of caring for Allison's three magnificent daughters who unfortunately do not have the voice to express their feelings about the loss of their mother to the Court. After two years of living and caring for the girls, I would not change my life with them for anything unless I could bring Allison back to care for them herself.

We gain inspiration from three strong, resilient young girls because we want them to live a life like the life that Allison would have wanted for them. On the night of the 19th April, 2012, they said goodnight to their mother and went to bed. They woke up the next morning to find her missing forever. They did not have the chance to say goodbye.

When they are hurt physically or mentally, they cannot call out for mummy, and she will be absent from special occasions, such as weddings, birth of children, Mother's Day, Christmas, birthdays. When other children are talking about their mother, the girls can only absorb the pain and disappointment.

They will grow up into beautiful, intelligent young women who will be strong and contribute to society, because they are a product of their mother's character and love, but they will be without the most important person in their lives, to share triumphs and disappointments.

From time immemorial, it is a known fact that a father's duty is to protect and care for his daughter. Due to the mistreatment and subsequent murder of my beautiful daughter, I have failed in my duty as a father and I will have to live with that for the rest of my life.

He asked me for my daughter's hand in marriage and I gave him my permission, but I didn't give you permission to betray her. We accepted you into our family and you abused our trust with your lies and deceit.

I am devastated, incensed and outraged by the way you have damaged and sullied the memory of my daughter's life by your statements and innuendos when she is not here to defend herself, adding to the pain and suffering of our family.

The girls' father has taken their mother from them forever and I trust that justice will be served for my daughter Allison, and that he gets the sentence that he deserves.

Allison, I love you and miss you and you will be forever in my heart.

At the end he stared directly at the dock, but Gerard's head was down.

Vanessa Fowler had promised Allison at her funeral that the questions around her death would be answered. Now Vanessa could finally bare her fury at the man who had taken her sister's life and denigrated her in death.

My name is Vanessa Anne Fowler and I am the elder sister of the late Allison Baden-Clay. Our Allison left this earth on 19th April, 2012, under horrific circumstances at such a young age. As Allison's sister, I was devastated and deeply affected by her death.

I feel cheated that I never got to say goodbye. I have been robbed of a life together with my sister. We will never get to have that one last cup of coffee together, or exchange parenting advice and share highlights of our children's lives. I miss her, the way she smiled, I look at her photo and wonder what could have been. Her life, her dreams, were cut short and the lives of many changed forever.

Since that day I have changed my life and that of my family dramatically, moving from the Gold Coast to Brisbane in mid

2012. This move was in support of my parents in their care for Allison's three daughters and to accommodate the girls' return to their school, giving them some continuity in their lives.

My role in the family has changed from being the eldest daughter to being a support and carer for my three nieces, with the understanding that in addition to this responsibility, which I have willingly taken on, I have a husband and two children of my own for which to care. My husband changed offices and now drives over an hour to work each way, my children have attended three different schools in the last two years, which has been disruptive to their education and my university studies were interrupted. Due to the events of the 19th April, 2012, my life has been turned upside down and changed forever.

Allison inspired me to be a better person, a better mother. She loved life, loved her daughters, and was loved by all. Allison was extremely capable, hardworking, highly intelligent, strong, resilient, passionate, devoted, confident and generous and had much better dress sense than I, always wearing smart, elegant clothing, in all colours.

With four businesses on the go – real estate, Neways, Pathways and her ballet school – three children to care for, and two mistresses to deal with, all made for one very strong woman. I find it amazing that with everything else she had going on that she still found time to lie on the couch.

Allison never allowed depression to take over her life. She was never so debilitated that she could not function. Like any other mother with three children and a household to run, she was busy, tired and stressed.

I worked with Allison through Pathways. We were a team. We talked about starting a business partnership together, she would work in the Brisbane West area schools and I would do the Gold Coast. She was passionate about building resilience and teaching social and emotional skills to young children and in doing so she changed the lives of so many.

Our lives move forward, we continue with our day to day living, however there is still a hole, a dark void left inside us where Allison touched each of us. We remember her smile, her laughter, her friendship and her love – for this is how she lived her life, always trying to please others and putting others before herself.

My heart breaks for the three precious girls who have been left behind. They look for their mother, cry for their mother, they miss their mother, they loved their mother. To help them deal with the fact that their mother is not coming back, to know that they didn't get to say goodbye, and now to know that their mother has been taken away from them at the hand of their father, is unimaginable.

When I have a little girl snuggle up to me and say 'Aunty Ness, I miss Mummy,' I feel great sadness. My heart sinks and I am even more determined to make their lives happy and full of love, just as Allison would have wanted. Despite the stresses in her life, Allison's care of her children was her utmost priority and she still sang to her beautiful babies as she put them to bed each and every night.

During this trial, there has been an over-emphasis and over-exaggeration on the negative aspects of her life yet we who knew her best know that there are far more positives in her life to focus on. Due to the events which occurred on 19th April, 2012, she is not here to defend herself. She no longer has a voice and in this trial she has been ridiculed, degraded, belittled, demoralised and disrespected. This was inflicted on her by her husband in life and now in death.

Allison was the only bright light in a very dark place that you and those around you created for her. One thing that we have seen from this trial is that Allison was strong and she fought to the death, even when taking the last breath she left her mark to ensure you paid for your evil ways.

It is because of you that I stand here today without a sister. It is because of you that I will never see her delightful smile again. It is because of you that three young girls have no mother. It is because of you that Allison will never get to see her children grow up. It is because of you that numerous lives have been changed forever.

You have shown no remorse for Allison's death. While Allison lay cold, wet and alone out in the elements under a bridge, you enjoyed sleeping in a warm bed, having lavish lunches, dinner dates and in your own words it was 'business as usual', with no regard or concern for your missing wife or the future of three young girls who now face the future without their mother.

But I am not going to allow this statement to be all about you. This is about me and my sister, my sister who today, for the first time since she married you, has come out on top. Today, she is the hero, she is the one who has received justice. The impact that my sister's death has had on my family is indescribable and no one will ever know what we experience every day but we willingly continue forward as we know that everything we do is for Allison's three girls and Allison's legacy.

It has been proven here today that Allison did not take her own life, she did not just 'go for a walk and died'. Allison was a strong, bright and determined woman that just wanted the best for her family. She had an inner strength and endured without complaint more than anyone should ever have had to endure. Some terrible lies have been told about Allison over the past few weeks. A picture painted that could not be further from the truth.

As a result of this trial, some pieces of the puzzle have been matched together and some of the many questions answered, however there is still much more that will remain hidden. Only two people know the answer to those questions – one is dead at the hand of the other.

I hope that justice will be served in more ways than one as my family, including three young girls, are the ones with the life sentence of living without Allison and knowing that her life was cut short because of greed and self-satisfaction.

My life and that of my family will never be the same again and it is my hope that the convicted murderer will be given a lifetime to ponder his actions in taking the life of such a special woman, whose only crime was to love and be loved.

Gerard moved his head violently back and forth as Vanessa spoke. He was shaking and rocking in the dock as if her words were physical blows. And as strongly worded and powerful as Vanessa's statement was, it was actually a second draft, after the prosecution had asked her to tone down her raw, original missive during an earlier review process.

It was Ashley Dickie's turn next. Allison's brother and his wife, Lisa, had rushed to the court but found the doors closed and security blocking their way. He would not be allowed in to face his sister's killer and see him sentenced. Instead, Vanessa read aloud Ashley's victim impact statement to the court. He was a man of few words, but his brief message said it all.

My name is Ashley James Dickie and I am Allison's brother. Allison was a wonderful sister, she was older than me and I loved her gentle heart and her kind nature. We miss her and we think about her every day and how we will never see her again.

Al loved and adored our children, who are now 10 and 7. She will never see their achievements. Their graduations, weddings, everything. She will miss it all.

It is unbearable to think of how she was taken away from my family. Nothing will ever be the same. Our Easters, birthdays, Christmas, will never be the same without her there.

I still find it hard to believe she is gone. My life has been changed forever because of one man's selfish actions. A man who thinks only of himself and whose actions were only to benefit one person himself.

I know you did it and you know you did it. And whatever time you spend in jail will never be enough for taking the life of my beautiful sister Allison.

It wasn't over yet for Gerard. After objectively presiding over all of the evidence, Justice John Byrne condemned Gerard for murdering Allison and everything that followed:

'Gerard Baden-Clay, on the night of 19 April 2012, you murdered your wife, Allison,' Justice Byrne said.

The killing was not premeditated, but it was violent. That night you were under considerable stress. Your financial circumstances were, as you confessed to police, dire. Your domestic circumstances were no better.

You had resumed your affair with Toni McHugh. You kept telling her that you loved her. You led her to understand that you intended to leave Allison and to be with her.

That afternoon you told Ms McHugh that Allison would be at the conference Ms McHugh was to attend in Brisbane the next day. Allison knew nothing about the resumption of the affair. You deceived her into believing it had ended in September 2011. If the two women were to meet the next day, the consequences could have been dramatic, as you realised.

Your unsuspecting wife was doing her best to maintain the marriage. The relationship counsellor had devised a plan. It allowed for Allison to express to you her feelings about the affair in the brief session every second day. You agreed, reluctantly, to that.

The first session happened the night before Allison died. It had turned into an interrogation. Allison remained tormented by the affair. She pressed you for details. On the night she died, Allison again questioned you about the affair.

All the pressures proved too much for you.

The prosecution suggested that you smothered Allison. That looks likely. But whatever the mechanism, your violent attack caused her death. Her fingernails scratched your face, the act of a desperate woman, struggling for life. Those marks are only consistent with your guilt.

Your shameful conduct after murdering Allison bespeaks a profound absence of remorse. You took her body to Kholo Creek. There you disposed of her in an undignified way, dumping her over the ledge to leave her lying in mud, exposed to the elements, insects. Then you put in place, and persisted in, a deception.

You used a razor to cut yourself near where she scratched you, trying to disguise the injury she had inflicted in defending herself. You drove around the streets of Brookfield, pretending to look for her.

You have insinuated her mental illness may have led to drug overdose or suicide. And besmirching Allison's memory in that way is thoroughly reprehensible.

You have no criminal history but you are definitely not of good character. You are given to lies and other deception, so much so that whatever you may say on any application for parole, 15 years or more hence, will need to be assessed with considerable scepticism.

The community, acting through the court, denounces your lethal violence. The impacts on Allison's family have been grave. Their impact statements poignantly express their pain. You took a devoted, loving mother from her three girls, blighting their lives.

The law provides but one penalty for your willful crime. I impose it. You are sentenced to imprisonment for life.

Justice Byrne, like almost everyone else, could not ignore the scratches on Gerard's face. In her final act, Allison had caught her own killer.

After the verdict, Allison's family and friends emerged as one into the sunshine and gathered in the forecourt to release a flotilla of yellow balloons. As the balloons floated off into the sky, one in their number remarked, 'Bye Al'. Walking over to Santos House, they caught the lift to the 34th floor and met in the conference room. Police joined them. Looking out at the spectacular view of the Brisbane River, a flash of yellow caught their eye. One of the balloons had lodged outside the window. After some emotional speeches, Priscilla and Geoff had the difficult task of going home to tell the girls. Others retired to a bar up the road from the courts for a 'debrief'; the venue was appropriately named The Guilty Rogue.

At the end of the night, one of the detectives got home and woke the house singing, 'Gerard fought the law and the law won . . .'

Dear Gerard

Three days after Allison discovered Gerard's affair with Toni McHugh, she started writing a letter. She worked on it for several months, pouring out her feelings. Uncovered by Channel 7's *Sunday Night* program after Gerard was convicted, the letter shows Allison at her most raw. The letter recorded Allison's shock at Gerard's years of deceit. She was bewildered that she could have misjudged him so. Gerard had been a comfortable and skilful liar. The letter also shows Allison was standing up for herself. Although she desperately wanted to save her marriage, Allison was realistic too. Friends are sure she was making back-up plans so that if Gerard followed through on his threats and walked out, she could support the girls on her own. As evidence that Allison was moving towards self-sufficiency, they point to her involvement in the Pathways resilience program, selling Neways products, ballet teaching, investigating business opportunities with Wendy Mollah and going to real estate courses without telling Gerard. Some of her friends believe she may have put a deposit on a property.

> *Dear Gerard,*
>
> *As 2011 comes to a close I wanted to write to you about the year that was and more. This is not meant to be a 'put Gerard down' list neither do I want it to be a 'poor me' letter. My aim is to start the New Year with a fresh start and no longer talk about the affair except in counselling. So I wanted to get as much off my chest as I possibly could. Also I just want to get my thoughts in some sort order for my own sake to clarify what it is that really matters to me.*

I started writing this document on September 17, 2011. Three days after you told me you had an affair. Some things are just snippets of thoughts, some paragraphs etc. You have heard a lot of it before and perhaps answered some of the questions before in the heat of the moment. But I have tried to limit my questions and really would like you try think about them before you answer on paper. I have tried to categorise some things but without much success I'm afraid. It is my hope that you will really read the following pages and where I have asked answer some questions for me (on paper) and with as much thought and clarity as you can. This I believe will truly help me. Well here goes . . .

. . . 3 days ago my husband told me he was having an affair. I get sick just writing the words and am shaking my head as I cannot believe it still. Tonight he has told me it has been going on for more than three years and that he lied to my face that it wasn't happening. I am writing this to try and work it all out in my head. At the moment I am trying to work out what I have done to deserve it – I just don't know. God I just want to be happy – one day I want to just be happy . . .

. . . Well three weeks on and I'm still trying to work out what I have done to deserve it. After all I am just a girl who grew up on the outskirts of Ipswich. The daughter of two very hard-working parents who did everything in order for me to fulfill my potential. I was a gifted dancer and I worked hard to pursue my dancing. In fact I was a good girl that worked hard to please every-one around me. I was smart and found school very easy as I had only limited time to study as I was always studying after school. In year 10 I was still top of my class and mixing it with the best of the students who achieved TE scores of 990 and went onto being doctors. But for me when adolescence hit so did the fat hit my hips and my ballet went out the window in a very slow and painful fashion. In fact I don't know if I am still holding onto that or whether dance is actually my passion that I wish to pursue.

I have blamed my depression and subsequent treatment of Gerard as the catalyst for him going elsewhere but I also wish that when I was sick that he had acted sooner. I often think what if I had cancer, would he have stuck by me or opted for the easy way out? If I had cancer he would have taken me to the right doctors etc. but because he didn't believe that depression was an illness he just ignored it and for too long. I need(ed) him to take me by the hand and get help. I didn't know where I was or what was happening to me and he keeps saying you don't know what it was like watching you and living with you. Well no I didn't and it was his job to help me and get me help!! I was sick!! . . .

. . . I read in a book the other day – as now I am studying coping skills to 'surviving an affair', something I thought I would never have to do. I knew that life wasn't going to be clear sailing but I sure as hell didn't expect this curve ball!! Anyway the book talked about commitment – that without commitment a relationship is doomed. It said that as soon as you are exposed to that choice their commitment to their relationship changes. Gerard was surrounded in his office by people that had chosen the easy way out to not fulfill their commitment so this became an option for G. Of course he also had her in his ear constantly encouraging him to forget his commitment.

. . . Some days I look at him and think what a stupid little naive boy who just wanted to try it with someone else and when the big real world got too hard and he took the easy way out.

And then I think of her . . . the dirty bitch that she is – she knew me and she was sleeping with some-one else's husband even while she was still with her partner – I can't believe they both started f***ing when they were both still in relationships. It just makes me sick the scenes of them crying on each other's shoulder about their f***d up partners and it enrages me that he would talk to her about the intimate details of MY LIFE with some stupid bimbo even before they fucked . . .

Unfairness of it all . . . I get a husband back who is physically and emotionally exhausted, the business is on the brink of bankruptcy and who is left now to support him and save the business – ME – the hopeless pathetic, fat, smelly wife that after 11 years he had enough of . . .

25/11/11 . . . Well I am trying to keep it together on a day to day basis – only to vent and question on a Sunday night. The reason I am doing this is because I don't want to make his life too miserable and risk him looking somewhere else for fun AGAIN. This is the complete unfairness of this whole affair thing – the person who has been cheated on is the one that has to tread carefully in the fear that it will happen again . . .

What hurts most. 1. The length of 3 years and the 100s of choices you made and why you didn't have the courage to end it?? 2. The depth of deceit. This is what I most shake my head about – when you see me having a flash back moment it is nearly almost because I am shaking my head in complete disbelief as to how you could have thought up so many excuses and told so many lied. You could say you are so much cleverer than me I know know??? 3. The complete destruction of trust I thought we had. I believed I could trust you with EVERYTHING and ANYTHING and as I write this the tears start flowing which is an indication to me that this is definitely a key point for me. It really hurts me to think that I looked you straight in the eyes and asked you if you were having an affair and you lied to me! You didn't even blink an eye. 4. You weren't and never will be the man I thought you were when I married you.

Legacy

Jodie Dann froze in her seat. Dann was among around 200 domestic violence workers gathered at Brisbane's four-star Royal on the Park Hotel, overlooking the City Botanic Gardens. US expert Dr David Adams was leading an intensive two-day workshop. It was October 2012 and Adams was discussing the types of men who kill their partners. Adams put perpetrators into five categories, though they often overlapped: jealous; substance abusers; depressed/suicidal; career criminals; and materially motivated. He had a slideshow of high-profile perpetrators as examples. One was particularly close to home.

Up on the big screen flashed a photograph of Gerard Baden-Clay. He had only recently been charged with his wife's murder but was apparently already a poster child for intimate partner homicide. Organisers quickly explained Gerard was yet to stand trial, but the roomful of domestic violence advocates already had him pegged as materially motivated. Perpetrators in that category were obsessed with money and possessions and prone to keeping secrets.

In his research, Adams had worked through the common traits of domestic abusers. Most abusers were never identified because they were different at home and in public. Domestic violence was more about control than anger. Abusive men were skilled at manipulation and image control. Discrediting, blaming and undermining the victim were part of the manipulation. Narcissistic Personality Disorder, Adams says, is a common diagnosis.

Narcissism is a complex disorder. The popular belief is that it is about being in love with yourself, like the young Narcissus after which it is named, who fell in love with his own image.

444

The truth is, it is a more complicated mix of love and loathing. It is characterised by an outrageously overinflated ego but also an extraordinarily fragile one.

Many of the traits seemed to fit Gerard to a T. Narcissists display an unrealistic sense of superiority and importance, a deep need for admiration, a sense of entitlement, a need for control and a lack of empathy. They tended to be snobbish and patronising, made unrealistic demands on partners and children and were given to lies. They have no qualms about taking advantage of others for their own benefit and are drawn to risky behaviour in both business and private. They are prone to extramarital affairs and risky sex. They are often swamped in debt.

In love, narcissists thrive on competition for the affection of potential partners, and lose interest once they have 'won'. In her journal, Allison had written, 'I wish my husband loved me like he did before we were married.' It was unusual. Many women, and men, in unhappy marriages speak of wanting to return to 'when we were first married'. But Allison wanted to rewind further. She knew something had changed the day Gerard put a ring on her finger and she became his.

The narcissist will treat their children as extensions of themselves – to be moulded rather than allowed to develop. They have a habit of knocking others down, to build themselves up. Everything in their life revolves around feeding their egos to maintain their view of themselves as the star performer – the savvy businessman, the attentive husband, the doting father. They cannot bear criticism, real or implied, and can escalate from calm to fury when challenged. A term had even been coined for the explosive reaction triggered when their carefully crafted self-image is challenged: narcissistic rage.

While Gerard and Allison's relationship was certainly emotionally abusive, whether it was physically so is unknown. Allison never wrote in her journal of any physical violence, and didn't raise it in her letter to her husband after discovering his affair, or make any complaints to friends, family or authorities. She was, however, intensely private.

But if nothing else, Allison's murder showed others that emotionally abusive relationships could escalate to fatal violence without warning.

Dann thought if her story could help others recognise danger signs in their relationships, Allison would have left a lasting gift. Dann started writing her own letter, pouring onto the screen the things she would say to Allison in hindsight. The letter formed the basis of a Facebook page, *Dear Allison*, for people dealing with domestic abuse to share stories and seek support.

After the case, the detectives went back to the routine of day-to-day police work. For one of the arresting officers, his next job after Gerard's conviction was charging someone with failing to properly dispose of a needle. Life, and the world, moves on. But this would be the case they would carry with them for life.

Meanwhile, Toni McHugh aired her story on *60 Minutes* and in the *Australian Women's Weekly*, dubbing herself 'Australia's Monica Lewinsky'. Gerard's legal team appealed his conviction within days of the verdict. His family has made no public comment since the verdict was handed down. In private, Olivia Walton is proclaiming her brother's innocence.

Allison's family can never replace what they have lost, but their priority now is raising her three young daughters in a way that would make her proud.

At time of writing, Allison's eldest was excelling at ballet, like her mother. Her middle daughter had a leadership role at school and the youngest was thriving at primary school. Allison lived for her girls and she lives on in them.

PART V – APPEAL

And that's where this book originally finished – but it turned out to be far from the end of the story.

The Murder of Allison Baden-Clay was first published just four and a half months after Gerard was convicted. He had an appeal pending, but few expected it to go anywhere.

We should have known to expect the unexpected where Gerard is concerned, because this most extraordinary of cases had one last, dramatic twist.

The law is an ass

Gerard was never going to accept a guilty verdict. Even so, his appeal was a quick move; his legal team filed just two days after his conviction. The last time Gerard had shown such haste was in claiming Allison's life insurance.

It would be more than a year before the Queensland Court of Appeal got around to a hearing, on 7 August 2015. About 200 people gathered at the Queen Elizabeth II Courts of Law to hear Gerard's team plead their case. Once again, Gerard had an able defence: barristers Michael Copley and Michael Byrne, and solicitor Peter Shields. Although a decision was not expected that day, there was a feeling the long legal process was finally drawing to a close.

Three of Gerard's four grounds for appeal were based on claims Justice Byrne had erred in his summing up to the jury. None of these arguments seemed to find any traction. As Copley spoke, the three appellate judges, Catherine Holmes, Robert Gotterson and Hugh Fraser, showed little interest.

It wasn't going well, but Gerard's legal team had one final argument to make. The aim here was simply to get Gerard's murder conviction reduced to manslaughter, which carries a significantly lighter sentence.

The difference between murder and manslaughter is intent. For a murder conviction to stick, the jury had to be satisfied Gerard intended to kill or cause grievous bodily harm to Allison. So, Copley ran a confounding argument – what if it was all a terrible accident? He outlined a scenario the defence had never raised at trial: What if Allison had lashed out at Gerard, inflicting the telltale scratches, and he unintentionally killed her while trying to fend her off? As for tossing her body under a bridge before rushing home to lie to his daughters, family, friends and police – well, Gerard simply panicked, Copley argued. Of course, Gerard was not actually admitting anything. This was just a hypothetical scenario the jury could not 'reasonably' have ruled out, Copley said.

Except for the fact Gerard himself had ruled this scenario out. He had testified under oath he had no knowledge of how his wife died, unintentional or otherwise. His legal team had told the jury Gerard was either innocent or he had murdered Allison. They were arguing one thing at trial and another on appeal. It would have been laughable, were it not that the three judges were suddenly listening closely. Afterwards, a detective I spoke to had picked up on the body language of the judges too, and was concerned.

But it was just a niggle, and soon forgotten. Senior lawyers told me the appeal had a snowflake's chance in hell. Justice Byrne had made no glaring errors. The jury was apprised of the difference between murder and manslaughter. Crucially, Gerard had spent four days in the witness box and never once opened the door to an unintentional death scenario.

Four months later, on Tuesday 8 December 2015, again about 200 observers gathered for the Court of Appeal's decision. It had been three and a half years since Gerard was arrested, and everyone was looking forward to reaching the end of the legal road. Formal custody of Allison's daughters was in limbo until Gerard's appeal was finalised. Her family was hopeful they could start making plans with some certainty.

For police involved in the case, the daily roster of tragedy rolled on. As people took their seats in court, detectives from Indooroopilly CIB and the Homicide squad were at that moment tied up with a particularly distressing investigation. A woman had brutally murdered her 11-year-old daughter before taking her own life, and an officer who had been meant to pick up Geoff and Priscilla Dickie and take them to court was on the scene. Other arrangements had to be made; none of the other detectives would make it down either. Gerard's parents were also notably absent.

As is the habit of most journalists in the modern age, I'd prepared a brief story in advance, saying the appeal had been dismissed. That way I could just press send when the decision was handed down and the news could be posted online as soon as possible. Usually I would have prepared two alternative versions, but the chances of Gerard's appeal succeeding seemed so remote I hadn't bothered.

Everyone stood briefly as Justice Fraser entered the court-room. Without delay he read the decision: 'The appeal against conviction is allowed. The verdict of guilty of murder is set aside and a verdict of manslaughter is substituted.'

It was as if a thunderbolt had struck the room. There was a confused murmur as people processed the unexpected news. No one seemed to know how to react. Once we had all turned to our neighbours to check we'd heard correctly, there was a rush to a stack of photocopies just outside the door which contained the reasons for the decision.

It had been unanimous. The three Court of Appeal judges had found no fault in the trial judge's handling of the case, but they'd found the jury couldn't be satisfied Gerard intended to kill Allison. There remained 'a reasonable hypothesis consistent with innocence of murder'. Gerard could have inflicted a blow on Allison without meaning to seriously hurt her, leading her to fall and hit her head on a hard surface. The defence and prosecution teams were told to prepare submissions on a new sentence for manslaughter. After everything he'd done, Gerard Baden-Clay was no longer a murderer in the eyes of the law.

Without their usual phalanx of detectives to provide support, Allison's stunned family and friends were ushered into a side room for a debriefing from prosecutors. None of them had prepared for this. While journalists and legal commentators pored over the court's reasoning, Priscilla and Geoff Dickie had more pressing concerns. What on earth were they going to tell the three girls? How could they explain it when they didn't understand it themselves? Everyone in the room wanted to know what the downgraded conviction meant. How long would Gerard spend in jail? Could they appeal the appeal? The prosecution team seemed as blindsided as everyone else and couldn't offer much. An appeal to the High Court was theoretically possible, but they would have to examine the decision. When the Dickies emerged, they had the ashen look of survivors walking from a bomb blast.

The maximum penalty for manslaughter in Queensland is life, but sentences often don't get even close. Within hours, I received a tip-off that Gerard was gearing up to fight for immediate release. There was a chance he would walk out of prison within months, despite his crime and the horrendous ordeal he'd put everyone through.

I conveyed my exasperation in a flurry of tweets over the next couple of hours:

Gerard Baden-Clay spent four days in the witness box denying any involvement in his wife's murder. Court of Appeal overturns jury's verdict.

> *Gerard Baden-Clay has his cake and eats it too. Denied*
> *involvement in wife's death but appeal says it's possible there*
> *was an argument.*
>
> *Phenomenal decision by Catherine Holmes, Hugh Fraser*
> *and Robert Gotterson to overturn jury verdict after 3yrs of*
> *denials by Gerard.*
>
> *No evidence whatsoever before court of unintended death*
> *during entire five week trial.*
>
> (Twitter: @TheMurrayD)

But legal experts were as unanimous as the judges – the decision was sound, even predictable.

Dr Nigel Stobbs, senior law lecturer at the Queensland University of Technology, was asked by media to comment that day. 'It was the outcome I would have expected,' Dr Stobbs said, 'because it seemed a trial in which there wasn't much evidence in relation to intention. If you don't even know the cause of death, it's very difficult to say what was in the mind of the accused. In some sense, it was a predictable outcome.' Barrister Ross Vernon Bowler was also asked to comment on the day and said it would be 'very difficult' for the Crown to get anywhere with an appeal. 'I can't see any obvious points of law,' he said. 'And, goodness me, you're not talking about part-time judges or people with no experience. They are experienced and respected.'

Back in the *Courier-Mail* newsroom, editor Chris Dore was at the crime desk to discuss the decision. I'd covered every day of proceedings with Kate Kyriacou, the paper's chief crime reporter. Logically and legally, it beggared belief. We went through some immediate concerns we had with the judgment.

Gerard had sworn black and blue he knew nothing about Allison's death. Now a scenario he'd ruled out would get him out of jail. The appellate court had also found Gerard had no motive to kill Allison. No motive? Were they being deliberately obtuse? Any detective or criminal lawyer will tell you that when someone murders their spouse there are two motives that crop up time and again: money and sex. Gerard had both motives in spades.

And it seemed the judges had made some alarming assumptions. They stated the jury likely found it easy to conclude there was an 'altercation', probably in the patio area due to the leaves in Allison's hair. (A strange leap. Allison's body could have been lain on or dragged through the patio area after she was smothered elsewhere, perhaps on the couch or in bed, and perhaps without warning.) The judges also decided that 'whatever occurred was quick' because of the lack of noise and injuries. (Again, it seems a dangerous leap to equate quiet with quick. Smothering is quiet, but certainly not quick.) And just where was the evidence to support the court's theory that Allison could have fallen and hit her head? Allison did not have any skull fractures.

There was palpable public anger over the decision. People had engaged with the Baden-Clay case in a way rarely seen in Australian criminal history. Common sense would suggest you shouldn't be able to claim one thing at trial and another on appeal to secure a lesser conviction and sentence.

Dore hadn't missed this sentiment and his mind was ticking over to the next day's coverage. The paper had legal advice that there were few limitations on reporting. A senior staff member reminded Dore the only thing he couldn't do was bring the court into disrepute, as that was an offence in its own right.

'Oh, I'll bring the court into disrepute,' Dore replied to them. It was clearly a joke, but there was no doubt he was going to produce something memorable.

Renowned for his attention-grabbing front pages, Dore produced arguably his best and boldest the next day. The front of the paper was blacked out, with bold white type declaring simply: 'The law is an ass'. It nailed the public mood.

The following day, Dore doubled down with a front-page letter to Gerard. 'You humiliated your wife, the mother of your children, before taking her life. In death, as in life, you continue to dishonour her and disgrace yourself. It's time to stop. Tell the truth,' it read.

Police I spoke to were appalled and genuinely worried by the downgraded conviction. This decision seemed to have dramatically raised the bar for murder.

Meanwhile, public anger was growing rather than fading. In the days that followed, the wave of outrage would turn into a tsunami.

The people v the establishment

Bevan Slattery couldn't believe what he was reading. Slattery's daughter went to the same west Brisbane dance school as Allison's daughters. He'd followed the murder trial and knew how much Allison's family had suffered. The downgrading of Gerard's conviction seriously grated on him. How could a killer claim he had no knowledge of the crime, then argue he might have been the one attacked? What incensed Slattery even more was learning the decision was very unlikely to be challenged. Queensland prosecutors almost never ask the High Court to overrule the Court of Appeal. It had been eight years since the last such challenge.

Slattery typed out a furious post on Facebook. But he wanted to do more, and he had the resources. Slattery happened to be one of the country's most successful tech entrepreneurs and one of Queensland's richest men. (Slattery was on the BRW Young Rich List in 2011 with a net worth of $103 million at the age of 40, and had gone on to bigger things from there.)

A friend put him in touch with Allison's friend Nicole Morrison. Slattery told Morrison he wanted to organise a public rally in Brisbane's CBD to call for an appeal to the High Court. The first thing Morrison did was google 'Bevan Slattery' to check his credentials – she had no idea who he was – then she approached Allison's parents. Morrison told Geoff and Priscilla Dickie it wouldn't go ahead if they didn't want it to. The Dickies gave their blessing.

On the Sunday after the judgment came down, Slattery contacted me through a mutual friend to share the plan. The rally was to go ahead on Friday. A major organised protest against an appellate court's decision was unprecedented. News of the protest hit Monday's front page. In the following days *The Courier-Mail* went out on a limb and backed the rally in a big way, in the face of a barrage of abuse from sections of the legal fraternity.

Legal bodies and some of the nation's most prominent lawyers hadn't taken kindly to the robust questioning of the Baden-Clay decision. They had been lashing the news coverage from the outset. Now, with the prospect of people demonstrating in the streets, the response intensified.

'The reality is that there was no new law in this judgment,' Brisbane lawyer Terry O'Gorman told news.com.au. 'The judgment refers to interstate authority, the judgment is the judgment of the court – it wasn't a split court, the court was unanimous – and, to put it bluntly, the court was comprised of three very experienced appeal judges.' Reaction to the Baden-Clay decision was 'hysteria' fuelled by trial-by-media, O'Gorman said:

> You do not have a murder case or any other case decided by who can yell out the loudest in the media or otherwise about their disagreement with the verdict. The verdict was handed down according to the law of the land and those who don't like it have to cop it because that is the law.

Barrister Greg Barns, a spokesman for the Australian Lawyers Alliance, also thought the Court of Appeal had it right. 'Despite offering and giving briefings to media on Baden-Clay appeal, media still gets it wrong. It's lynch mob stuff by media,' Barns tweeted.

In the eye of the storm was Chief Justice Catherine Holmes. Holmes had only recently been promoted to the position after a period of intense turmoil in the courts. Judges had waged an unseemly internal war in the public arena to oust her predecessor Tim Carmody. Ironically, Holmes had taken the top position with the goal of keeping the courts out of the news. 'My great hope is to make the court itself entirely non-newsworthy, as opposed to the cases which pass through it,' she said at the time of her appointment. So much for that. The Baden-Clay appeal was Holmes's first high-profile case as chief justice and it had thrust the courts in the spotlight like never before.

There was more controversy for Holmes when on the Wednesday, with the rally two days away, the legal profession held its annual Christmas celebrations. Holmes used her speech to thank the Government and Opposition for not letting 'political or populist considerations prevail over the need to respect the court's integrity and independence'. The Christmas shindig became a festival of mutual admiration and media-bashing. Bar Association president Christopher Hughes QC declared the court had faced 'unfair criticism'. Any commentary had to be 'reasoned and reasonable', he said, implying it hadn't been. And Queensland Law Society outgoing president Michael Fitzgerald said the courts had felt the ire of the public on occasion 'due in no small part to a shallow and opportunistic media'.

Rally organisers interpreted all this as an attack on them. A front-page headline in *The Courier-Mail* sought to sum up the overall tone of the comments at the gathering: 'Don't dare judge us'.

The stage had been set for an epic battle. It was The People v The Legal Establishment.

As Friday 18 December dawned, rally organisers were hopeful but a little worried about how many people would turn up in Brisbane's city centre. Allison's case had strong support, but people also had busy lives and Christmas was just a week away. The rally was to go ahead in King George Square, next to City Hall, at 12.15 pm.

Slattery had flown home from Hong Kong earlier in the week to personally oversee preparations. Eight of his full-time staff had been working on it for days. Council and police had been supportive, and Slattery had managed to get approval for the gathering within 24 hours. He'd set up a website and shot a promotional video with Olympic swimmers Libby Trickett and Mitch Larkin.

If the rally failed, it wouldn't be through lack of trying. The organisers wanted an appeal to the High Court but also, if necessary, for laws to be changed so there wouldn't be a repeat of what they saw as a farce. A crowd of a few hundred would avoid embarrassment. If numbers soared to around a thousand, it would send a clear message that the law as it had been applied was unacceptable. The heat would probably keep some people away – it was 28°C but it felt like a thousand degrees in King George Square, a barren concrete wasteland seemingly designed to prevent anyone lingering there.

Nervously, Slattery and fellow organisers watched the crowd build. And build. By the time the rally was due to start, some 4000 people were crowded together under the midday sun. For an event organised in just a few days it was a remarkable turnout. The square was a sea of yellow, the colour that had come to symbolise Allison's fight. Many said they had taken time off work or travelled miles to be there.

Earlier in the year, a young Gold Coast mother, Tara Brown, had been killed after her ex, Lionel Patea, ran her off the road. Patea had beaten Brown's head in with a metal plate as she lay trapped in her upturned car. People were fed up with violent men treating their partners like property and it showed in their placards. One called for 'Justice for women'; another simply said, 'Enough'.

Channel 9 *Today Show* co-host Lisa Wilkinson hastily re-arranged her schedule to fly in from Sydney as MC. Allison's parents, brother, sister and extended family were there. Bruce and Denise Morcombe, whose son Daniel had been murdered 12 years earlier, travelled down from the Sunshine Coast to lend their support.

When it was over, Nicole Morrison was in tears. Criticism from the legal fraternity – who had widely characterised protesters as an 'ill-informed mob' – had hit particularly close to home. Morrison's husband, Simon, was the co-founder and managing director of Shine Lawyers. He was also a past national president of the Australian Lawyers Alliance. He was by her side at the rally.

Meanwhile, Bevan Slattery was hanging back, watching it all unfold. His latest business, Megaport, had listed on the ASX the previous day; its price had immediately jumped 75 per cent. This rally was an achievement on an entirely different level. Slattery's strongest memory from the day would be seeing the Morcombes and Dickies standing side by side in the shadows of the stage. The courage it took these two couples to be there reliving their loss would stay with him forever.

I ran into Slattery and stood with him for a while. He was constantly on his smartphone and I later learnt he'd been messaging the new prime minister, Malcolm Turnbull, whom he had known for 15 years. Slattery had a direct line to the PM and had been filling him in on the rally.

It was kept quiet, but Turnbull and his wife, Lucy, had considered recording a video message about domestic violence for the rally. Slattery called it off two days before, after hearing of the chief justice's comments at the Christmas legal gathering. In an email to the Turnbulls, he'd warned them of bitter recriminations from the legal establishment. 'There is commentary which I find personally disappointing with respect to the rally,' Slattery wrote in the email.

Some commentary from the chief justice today was particularly disappointing in which she appeared to misunderstand how democracy works – and that while the separation of powers is a cornerstone of our democracy, so is the 'will of the people'. Our rights to have peaceful assembly, our rights to freedom of expression, our rights to disagree respectfully with decisions of the court, our rights to seek to change laws. These are as much, if not more so, the foundations of democracy.

Federal Opposition Leader Bill Shorten's wife, Chloe, had her own connection to Allison. The two women were once in a small mothers' group together and had gone on to be mums at the same west Brisbane kindy. Chloe spoke to me soon after the downgrading of Gerard's conviction for a story in News Corp's Sunday papers.

One of Chloe's school friends had been strangled by an ex-lover more than 20 years earlier. The Queensland Court of Appeal had downgraded the murder conviction to manslaughter in that case too. To see the same thing happen with Gerard made her see red. 'It just made me sick and it also outraged and just flabbergasted me that we're still in this kind of space,' she told me.

Populist politics by both sides? Or a genuine will to seize the moment and reduce the unfathomable toll of domestic violence? Whichever way you looked at it, Allison's death had the attention of the most powerful political figures in the nation.

Parallel to the rally, a mum from Crows Nest, near Toowoomba, had launched an online petition calling for a High Court appeal. Nicole Morris (not to be confused with Nicole Morrison) runs the Australian Missing Persons Register, a website that spreads the word when people vanish. Morris, a nursing assistant, set it up after she watched a television documentary and realised there was no national database of the missing. For more than a decade, free of charge and from her own home, she's helped desperate families look for loved ones. When Allison went missing, Morris put out appeals and sent a Facebook message to Gerard's sister Olivia offering assistance. The message went unanswered. She couldn't recall another time where a relative of a missing person failed to respond to an offer of help.

When Gerard's conviction was downgraded, Morris vented online. The readers of her website were all outraged too, so she launched a petition. Less than two weeks later, by the time of the rally, more than 120,000 people had signed it. When Morris printed it to send to state Attorney-General Yvette D'Ath, the petition took up 3200 pages.

Some people took offence to these developments and rushed to defend the courts and criticise the public.

Author John Birmingham used his Fairfax column to attack the 'mob in bright yellow frocks and shirts' at the rally. 'They didn't see themselves as a mob at all. They thought they were decent people coming together to right the wrong . . . But they were still a mob,' he wrote. 'Why bother with courts after all, when a couple of thousand angry punters are on hand with pitchforks and burning branches?' Writing separately on his blog, Birmingham added that *The Courier-Mail* had been 'rubbing itself all over the Baden-Clay murder case'.

Geoffrey Luck's opinion piece for *Quadrant Online* was run under the headline 'Mob rule in Brisbane'. It began, 'A cogently argued decision by Queensland's Court of Appeal that reduced a murder conviction to manslaughter has drawn protests and, to its shame, rabble-rousing front page headlines in Brisbane's local rag.' Not trying to hide his condescension, Luck added that the 'mob' had 'read the headline, but not the judgment'.

As far as I was aware, none of the most strident critics had been to a single day of court proceedings and it showed. They lacked an understanding of the evidence. Falling over themselves to support the establishment allowed them to be intellectually lazy. They seemed to presume the Court of Appeal was correct because it was the Court of Appeal. Enough said. How could the hoi polloi possibly understand anything as complex as the law?

As it would turn out, the mob's understanding of this case would be greater than anyone gave them credit for. The week after the rally, just before Christmas, Director of Public Prosecutions Michael Byrne told the Queensland Government he'd made the call. He *would* take the case to the High Court. The downgrading of Gerard's murder conviction would be one of those exceptionally rare cases challenged by prosecutors in the nation's highest court. After all the bluster of legal experts and commentators, there was a case for appeal after all.

Byrne worked through the Christmas break to ensure the paperwork was lodged on time. On 4 January 2016, he filed documents asking the High Court to set aside the Court of Appeal's ruling.

Not everyone was immediately impressed. *The Australian* newspaper ran a prominent report on 9 January attacking the Crown's appeal. Robert Richter QC, who was described in the report as 'one of Australia's leading and highest paid criminal barristers', had told Melbourne reporter Greg Brown a key argument in the appeal was 'absurd'. The appeal was likely to fail, the headline asserted. Richter's condescension went, well, off the Richter scale:

> As I understand the reasoning makes complete sense legally speaking and the public is really not equipped to make those sort of legal decisions. If you have hysteria in the tabloids it's not based on a proper understanding of the law.

It was a big case, but the cavalry was about to arrive – on a Harley-Davidson. Byrne had asked one of the country's most formidable lawyers to lead the case to restore Gerard's murder conviction.

Vindication

Queensland's leading silk was in his 60s but he hadn't lost his adventurous streak. In his spare time, Walter Sofronoff has been known to cruise around in a Ferrari, roar through the streets on a Harley-Davidson and take to the skies piloting vintage planes. He was perhaps fortunate to survive one such outing, after his 1940s de Havilland Tiger Moth crashed on take-off in 2014. He ploughed through a fence and hit a tree, coming to a halt just metres from a highway. He played it down, saying afterwards he hadn't suffered a scratch and it was no big deal. Sofronoff's father was a Russian Cossack who had fled the communist regime on horseback in the 1930s; his mother had worked in a Brisbane boot factory on what would become the Inns of Court site, where barristers had their chambers. As he rose to the pinnacle of that profession, Sofronoff became universally known as The Cossack, a moniker he uses in his email address.

If anyone was up for a challenge it was Sofronoff. He'd led the Crown's previous appeal to the High Court almost a decade earlier. That case had involved the Queensland Court of Appeal quashing a man's conviction over a drug shooting. Sofronoff won that encounter, with a five-member High Court panel unanimously reinstating the conviction. I discovered another intriguing parallel: Catherine Holmes was one of the Court of Appeal judges in both cases. History was repeating.

It was longstanding convention for the state's solicitor-general to handle High Court appeals. Peter Dunning QC held that position, earning a six-figure retainer to advise the government and act as its chief legal counsel. But Dunning had limited criminal law experience; Sofronoff was Dunning's predecessor and his High Court success could not be ignored. When Sofronoff's role in the Baden-Clay case emerged by word of mouth, lawyers all over town sat up and took notice. 'Walter is possibly our best all-round silk. And he has certainly got the respect of the High Court,' one told me. Another said: 'He's one of the finest appellate advocates we have ever produced. He does everything, but he's exceptional at appeals.' Sofronoff got cracking on the grounds for the High Court appeal with prosecutor Danny Boyle.

I was hearing rumblings of dissent in legal ranks about the Court of Appeal ruling. Some senior figures felt, as the people did, the court had seriously overreached in setting aside the jury's verdict.

A retired judge with more than 50 years' experience in the law analysed the decision in depth. He slammed the appellate court for losing sight of the Crown's case, saying the judges had wrongly jumped to conclusions about the jury's reasoning and that it was 'nonsense' to suggest there was no motive. It was everything that had concerned me all along. He even took aim at the judges for speculating Allison may have died after hitting her head in a fall. 'Death may supervene eventually, or even rapidly, from a severe blow to the head, but it is usually preceded by a period of unconsciousness, brain swelling, subdural haemorrhage and then brain death,' he said. 'One would expect that even an angry or despairing husband who had brought about such a calamity unintentionally would phone for an ambulance or doctor and at least give what aid he could.'

I reported the views of the retired judge on 1 February 2016, but he didn't want to be identified because he didn't want to court controversy. Others said they couldn't speak out because they had to appear before the judges involved. Meanwhile, professional legal bodies were flatly refusing to respond to formal questions. I was starting to view the courts as one giant protection racket.

Later on the same day that the retired judge's comments were published, Sofronoff and Boyle filed their submissions in the High Court.

For High Court appeals to go anywhere, they first have to be granted special leave to appeal. Very few cases clear the first hurdle. Bill Potts, the new Queensland Law Society president, told media the High Court agreed to hear fewer than five per cent of cases brought to them.

The Baden-Clay appeal soared over that hurdle on 12 May 2016, when High Court judges Virginia Bell and Stephen Gageler ruled that it should go to a hearing. A supposedly 'absurd' case had been taken on by the highest court in the land, while the vociferous defenders of the Court of Appeal decision were suddenly awfully quiet.

The hearing went ahead in Brisbane on 26 July 2016. From the moment the Commonwealth Law Courts Building opened, a line formed outside the locked courtroom door. Soon it stretched across almost the entire floor. With half an hour to go before the hearing was to start, more than 100 people were waiting to get in; staff told me they could recall few cases that had attracted such interest. Five judges would hear the case: Robert French, the chief justice; Susan Kiefel; Patrick Keane; Virginia Bell and Michelle Gordon.

Sofronoff walked in confidently in his wig and gown. An aura of fearlessness surrounded him. An amateur theatre fan (he'd earned rave reviews for local productions of *Macbeth*), he was entirely at home in the theatre of the courtroom. On the other side, Gerard's team was unchanged, although Michael Byrne would now do the talking. Proceedings had the formality of a bygone era. The judges entered and sat down in unison, with clerks hovering attentively behind each one to push in their large chairs.

The next two hours were nothing short of remarkable. Sofronoff and Boyle meticulously dismantled the Court of

Appeal's decision, starting with the finding that there was no motive. Sofronoff also pointed out that Gerard ran a 'murder or nothing' defence at the trial. Byrne had told the jury Gerard either murdered Allison or expected her to walk back through the door. Byrne had agreed with the trial judge that, firstly, this was a tactical position, and secondly, that there was 'no suggestion' of a fall because there were no fractures.

But the most memorable moment of the hearing was delivered by Justice Keane, a former Queensland barrister. While Sofronoff spoke, Keane had listened in silence. But after Byrne rose to speak for Gerard, Keane emerged like a crocodile that had been waiting in the shallows for its prey. In a short but devastating burst, Keane unleashed his blunt observations about Gerard's appeal. 'He has had the opportunity to give the evidence; he has given the evidence: it is inconsistent with any notion at all that there was an unintended killing by him,' Keane thundered.

There, in the High Court, Keane had said exactly what the public had been declaring all along. Lawyers and commentators had mocked ordinary people for making the same point. No one mocked Keane.

By the end of the hearing it was clear Sofronoff and the people had come out on top. Still, I'd picked the last appeal wrong. Maybe the judges were just playing devil's advocate.

High Court decisions can take three to six months to hand down, but this one moved quickly. Just over a month later it was announced the High Court was ready to deliver its decision. It was to be delivered in Canberra on 31 August 2016. One way or another the case was finally going to be at an end. There would be no more avenues of appeal.

Geoff and Priscilla Dickie didn't want to spend one more day in court; they decided to stay at home in Ipswich and wait with friends and family for the outcome. Kerry-Anne Walker, Allison's closest friend, flew to Canberra in their place. Nicole and Simon Morrison and Bevan Slattery met her there. The four of them walked into court steeled for anything.

No one apart from Allison's friends noticed at the time, but one other familiar face was there that day. Ian Drayton, Allison's first fiancé, had been at his Canberra home watching the *Today Show* when he saw the High Court decision was to be delivered that morning. More than four years earlier he'd learnt of Allison's death while watching the same show, his cereal bowl slipping from his grasp and smashing at his feet.

Allison had fatefully chosen Gerard over Drayton years earlier, but she had never been far from his thoughts. He got dressed and, on a whim, went straight to court to hear the decision. When Kerry-Anne saw Allison's first love arrive, she was overcome with emotion; they hadn't seen each other for 20 years. She couldn't help but wonder what might have been for Allison.

They all sat together, holding their breath. Nicole Morrison thought one of the High Court judges was looking straight at her and told herself it was a good sign. Kerry-Anne knew the Brisbane hearing had gone well but didn't want to get her hopes up.

Exactly four years, four months and 11 days after Allison was reported missing, the High Court gave its unanimous ruling in *The Queen v Baden-Clay*. The Crown's appeal was allowed. Gerard's murder conviction was restored. This time it was really over.

As soon as they were out of the courtroom, Kerry-Anne and Nicole phoned Geoff and Priscilla and told them what had happened. The mood was ecstatic; after what they'd been through, who could blame them? As far as the Dickies were concerned, an injustice had been set right.

Priscilla knew Kerry-Anne was about to address the media and in the emotion of the moment told her not to hold back on Gerard.

'Stick it to him,' Allison's mum said.

When the call ended, it all started to sink in for Priscilla and Geoff. They needed some time to themselves and left the room to be on their own.

Everyone blamed themselves for Allison's death. Allison's parents thought they hadn't been good enough parents. Her friends thought they hadn't been good enough friends. They all still suffered sleepless nights.

As Kerry-Anne was about to walk outside, two burly, bearded men from the Maritime Union of Australia stopped to check she was ready to face the waiting cameras. The men had just won their case in the High Court too. 'It's a good day for the good guys,' one of them said, smiling.

Kerry-Anne is not the type to crack easily, but those words made tears spring to her eyes. Combined with seeing Ian Drayton and achieving a result almost everyone said was impossible, she only just managed to keep it together as she spoke to the media at the front of the High Court.

'Today's decision in the High Court comes with relief and elation,' Kerry-Anne said in a speech shown live on several networks simultaneously. She continued:

Despite many Queenslanders being labelled as ignorant when they protested the downgrade to manslaughter, the common sense of the original jury has prevailed and justice for Allison has finally been realised.

The ignorance, it seems, lay elsewhere.

The law has acknowledged what we, who were closest to her, knew from that very morning Allison went missing; that is, that she was murdered. Gerard Baden-Clay murdered his amazing wife Allison. The evidence in the original trial displayed his intent as well as his character. Today's decision brings to an end Gerard's attempts to smear Allison's name.

Four and a half years ago, three beautiful girls went to bed with a mother and the next morning they woke without one. He let them and the whole community worry and anguish for days about what had happened. In a fair and open trial a jury found that there was enough evidence to convict Gerard Baden-Clay of murder. They felt there was motive and certainly intent. Thankfully, today Australia's High Court judges agreed with this decision and have reinstated the conviction of murder.

Slattery went straight back to Brisbane. It wasn't until later that night that he read the High Court's decision, and only then did it hit home. His first feeling in court had been relief, but the judgment brought on another. Vindication. If the High Court appeal had failed, he'd planned a lobbying blitz for a change in the law. But no change was necessary – the law just hadn't been correctly applied by the appellate court.

I've heard Gerard was also making plans for what happened if the High Court ruled in his favour. Had the Crown's appeal been rejected, he was going to have his lawyers argue he should be immediately released because he'd been treated so poorly in the media.

The High Court did not pull its punches. Its criticism of the Court of Appeal's decision was comprehensive.

The judges of the Queensland Court of Appeal were found to have delved into 'mere speculation or conjecture'. Their theory that Allison fell and hit her head 'was not based on evidence' and had been expressly ruled out by Gerard and his defence counsel at the trial. On this point alone, the murder conviction would have been restored. But the High Court said it was necessary to go further.

On the claim there was no motive, the High Court said bluntly: 'That was an error.' The Court of Appeal appeared 'not to have considered and weighed all the circumstances established by the evidence at trial'. There was Allison's venting and grilling, the prospect of her discovering the affair was ongoing, Gerard's promises to be free of his wife by 1 July, his inability to afford a divorce and the possible meeting of wife and mistress at the real estate conference the next day. It was also open to the jury to decide whether Gerard's disposal of his wife's body and his lies went 'beyond what was likely as a matter of human experience' to have followed an unintentional killing.

The High Court rapped the appellate court over the knuckles for failing to give due respect to one of the cornerstones of our justice system – the jury system. It warned that the system should never substitute 'trial by appeal court for trial by jury'.

The High Court's remarks were effectively a carbon copy of the submissions of Sofronoff and Boyle. There was plenty more in the judgment, but the High Court's final point was that killing wasn't exactly easy. The 'difficulty involved in killing a human being without the use of a weapon unless the act of killing is driven by a real determination' could also be considered by the jury. 'Upon the whole of the evidence led at trial, it was open to the jury to be satisfied beyond reasonable doubt that the respondent was guilty of murder.'

The people had been right all along.

Someone recently told me the story about what had happened a month prior to this ruling, immediately after the High Court hearing in Brisbane. No one could know for sure how the five judges were going to rule, but Sofronoff had a fair idea. If he'd been supremely confident going into the hearing, he was even more so afterwards. When he walked out of court, he had good news for Allison's family and police.

'I think we got that 5–nil,' he told them. He was dead right.

One of the most remarkable stories to emerge from the High Court appeal was unearthed by *The Guardian*'s investigative reporter Josh Robertson. It concerned the bill for Sofronoff's services. The going rate for a barrister of Sofronoff's standing is up to $17,000 a day. For the entire Baden-Clay appeal to the High Court, he had billed taxpayers just $327. He'd done the appeal as a public service, not for profit. It was possibly the best money ever spent on a lawyer. In an interesting twist, on 31 March 2017 the Queensland government named Sofronoff the new president of the Court of Appeal.

The law

It was an error, plain and simple – actually, a series of them. After the High Court restored Gerard's murder conviction, some people tried to portray the judgment as setting a precedent that rewrote the rulebook. That perception still lingers, but it's actually the opposite. It was the Queensland Court of Appeal that had set a precedent after misconstruing the law. Had their decision been allowed to stand, other courts would have followed suit. The instinct of investigating police was right – the bar for what constitutes motive and intent had been raised, and it would have been harder to get a murder conviction.

The High Court decision refers to prior cases overlooked or ignored by the Queensland Court of Appeal as it went off in its own direction. Their arguments drew on cases cited by Sofronoff during the hearing, among which were two very famous murder cases.

The first was that of Hendrikus Plomp, who drowned his wife Fay in the Southport surf in the 1960s. He'd reported her missing and her body was found on the beach a short time later. Plomp, like Gerard, had been seeing another woman and had promised they'd be together. The High Court found Plomp had 'the strongest reasons to be rid of his wife'. His love affair was a motive for murder.

Plomp is Law 101. Law students learn about it in their earliest university lectures. The Court of Appeal's finding that Gerard did not have a motive to kill Allison – despite his affair and promises to Toni McHugh – was a basic error.

The other significant case Sofronoff applied was that of Johan Weissensteiner, who was convicted of a double murder in the 1990s. Weissensteiner was travelling on a yacht with a couple who disappeared without trace. He chose not to give evidence at his trial. The case went to the High Court, which found Weissensteiner's silence could be used to rule out scenarios consistent with his innocence, as he had been the one person who knew what happened and chose not to offer any explanation.

Gerard went even further – he testified he simply wasn't there when Allison died. The High Court said the prosecution's case against Gerard was stronger than in Weissensteiner because unlike Weissensteiner, Gerard *had* given evidence, but (the jury must have decided) he had lied. This was the same as giving no evidence at all. The result, however, was not only a vacuum in the evidence, like Weissensteiner, but a vacuum that raised a new issue: Why would he lie? Because he was hiding the truth that he *intended* to kill?

Weissensteiner is another landmark case, but no one had previously thought to apply it. The Court of Appeal didn't even mention it.

Some commentators persist with the line that these are issues beyond the public's understanding. Gary Johns, writing in *The Australian*, claimed Gerard's conviction was restored on a 'highly technical point'. Johns wrote, 'The High Court did not reinforce the opinions of the man in the street or of some media. The reasoning in both courts was very fine . . . Reasonable minds may differ on such matters.'

Utter rubbish. The High Court absolutely reaffirmed the views of the man and woman in the street. People protested the Baden-Clay decision because it did not make sense. The people said, 'Why didn't Gerard raise this explanation before?' The High Court agreed.

This was about common sense, not legal technicalities. The best legal minds know the law almost always accords with common sense. When it doesn't, there's been an error and it needs to be corrected.

The High Court's ruling will now stop lower courts from veering dangerously off course in future determinations of manslaughter or murder. Delivering this important clarity is one of Allison's most significant legacies – preventing Gerard and others from getting away with murder.

EPILOGUE

Many true crime authors wait until all appeals are over before publishing, but that process can take years. When we were preparing the first edition of this book we were moving much more quickly. There were some paths that at the time I either couldn't, or didn't want to, go down. With the appeal process over, there's a chance to go into issues that have interested me and, I know, others who have followed this story intently. It's also a chance to address 'Frequently Asked Questions', and to share developments in the lives of some of those named in this book.

Finally, and most importantly, in the few years that have passed since Gerard was convicted, I've come across some startling information that has never been made public. I thought I knew all the major details and then . . . I came across a whole lot more. So, here we go, in no particular order.

Sorry

Gerard Baden-Clay's inexplicable car accident two days after he reported Allison missing has always intrigued people. How could it have happened on that straight road at busy Indooroopilly Shopping Centre in broad daylight? The episode was even more surreal than people realised and possibly the closest Gerard ever came to cracking.

A 17-year-old, who I'll call Mike, was eating McDonald's and waiting for a bus when Gerard's car drove straight into the concrete pylon in front of him. The car had been going about 50 kilometres an hour and didn't brake. Smoke billowed from the vehicle and the airbags had deployed.

Gerard emerged from the wreck, using his arms to drag his body across the ground as if his legs no longer worked. He rolled onto his side. He was moaning as the teenager pulled his own shirt off and put it under his neck for support. Liquid from the car was pooling on the ground. A growing crowd was concerned it might be petrol so they tried to move Gerard to safety.

Mike asked Gerard what his name was, but got an unexpected response: 'I need my lawyer.' At this point Gerard was still pretty much unknown; Allison had been 'missing' for two days. Gerard kept repeating that same strange phrase, 'I need my lawyer', over and over. He was so insistent about it that another bystander retrieved Gerard's phone from the wreckage and found the number for solicitor Darren Mahony.

Someone asked him: 'Why do you need a lawyer so bad?'

Gerard said he was meeting the lawyer at the police station, which wouldn't have made much sense to anyone there.

Mike noticed Gerard's wedding ring and, trying to be helpful, asked if there was a number for his wife. Gerard started crying.

A nurse arrived, then paramedics and firefighters. Gerard's crying intensified. 'Darren,' he moaned.

Paramedics Rindell Manneke-Jones and Louise Winter found Gerard lying facedown, bawling his eyes out. Gerard told them he must have looked down at his phone and hit the pylon. Even for paramedics, who are accustomed to odd conversations, the following exchange must have been bizarre.

Winter:	Do you have any pain anywhere?
Gerard:	All over my body. I need to speak to my lawyer – where's Darren?
Winter:	I need to assess you first.
Gerard:	Tell Darren I'm sorry. Can you ring my lawyer?
Winter:	Do you want me to call your wife or lawyer? What's going on? Is your wife here with you? Your lawyer doesn't need to be involved.

Gerard cried some more. Darren Mahony, the much in-demand lawyer, suddenly appeared out of nowhere. Things got even stranger.

Winter: Can you tell me what's going on? Are you his lawyer?
Mahony: He's been under a lot of stress lately.
Winter: Is there anything I need to know?
Mahony: I'm not allowed to say anything.

But Gerard had something he wanted to say to his lawyer. 'Sorry mate, I'm sorry,' he said.

'I'll talk to your parents and sort it out,' Mahony told him.

It was Manneke-Jones's turn to ask Mahony if there was anything else the paramedics needed to know about their patient.

Mahony wasn't budging. 'I'm not at liberty to discuss anything further without the consent of my client,' he said.

Two police officers, Chris Carey and Glen Hopkins, were on their way to some tasks related to Allison's disappearance when they came across the accident. Gerard was still lying facedown on the ground. They could hardly believe it when they recognised him.

Mahony approached the officers and told them Gerard wouldn't be answering any questions.

Next to show up at this increasingly strange scene was Brendan Flynn, the highest ranked officer at Taringa Fire Station that day. He arrived to find Gerard apologising profusely. Flynn told police Gerard said the same word at least 20 times: 'Sorry.'

When the paramedics said they were going to cut his shirt off, Gerard protested. They ignored him and cut the fabric right down the middle with scissors, exposing Gerard's bare chest and the frenzy of scratch marks inflicted well before the crash. Gerard continued to sob and say he was sorry.

One of the paramedics was holding his head and asked the right question: 'Are you sorry about the accident or something else?'

'There's something else,' Gerard replied.

Gerard was taken away to the ambulance without saying any more.

It was as close as anyone would get to an admission from Gerard, or to an apology for killing his wife.

The hospital

The ambulance left the crash site with Gerard on a stretcher in the back.

'Have they found my wife yet?' he asked as he was taken into the emergency department of the Royal Brisbane and Women's Hospital.

A detective who had arrived answered: No, they had not found Allison.

Gerard was held at the hospital in case he'd tried to take his own life in the crash.

That night, mental health nurse Nat Karmichael paid him a visit for an assessment. Gerard was sharing a large four-bed room with other patients, so Karmichael arranged for him to move to a single room so they could talk privately.

But they were not alone. It was 1.05 am and Olivia was with him. Gerard asked if Olivia could stick by his side, on legal advice. Usually Karmichael assessed people without anyone else present, but said it would be okay.

Asked to rate his mood from one to ten, Gerard said he was a three or four. His wife was missing, he explained. Karmichael asked Gerard how he felt about that. Olivia interrupted, according to Karmichael's account to police. Gerard was 'numb', she volunteered.

Gerard disagreed. He said he was more 'concerned', especially about his children.

Karmichael tried to go into Gerard's relationship with Allison. Again, according to Karmichael's account, Olivia interjected. 'Gerard, do not answer those questions,' she told her brother.

Gerard insisted he was not suicidal; other than that, on legal advice he would not talk about the crash.

Police have often wondered if things would have been different if Gerard didn't have Olivia there that night. Some are convinced he was ready to confess all at the time of the car crash. But Gerard always seemed to have someone present, whether it was his sister, parents, friends or lawyer. Perhaps if he didn't have such rock-steady allies to turn to for support, he would have revealed a lot more about what happened.

There was one final disagreement between the siblings. Gerard said he usually slept for eight hours a night, but had been sleeping poorly since Allison went missing. Olivia disagreed. She'd heard him snoring and thought he'd been sleeping just fine.

*Family – a story**

In late 2008, Gerard sold a home at Kenmore to a couple I'll call Jan and Frank. The home had belonged to Olivia and her husband, Ian. It backed onto the home of Gerard's parents and for a long time everyone got along famously. The only time there was any odd feeling was when Gerard made a rather inappropriate remark after Jan made a joke. 'If we both weren't married I'd put you over my knee and spank your bottom and, let me tell you, you would enjoy it,' he'd said.

Jan got to know Allison through the Brookfield school, where they'd see each other almost every day. It was obvious to Jan that Allison was a devoted mum, never missing a sports day or concert or award ceremony. Gerard had an active role too. Like a lot of people, Jan heard on the school grapevine that Gerard had an affair and she watched Allison soldier on. Jan liked that Elaine Baden-Clay would always speak so highly of Allison, gushing about what a great mother and wonderful person she was.

---

* As told to police by Jan and Frank. Names changed.

Then Allison went missing and Jan mucked in, coordinating a food roster with other parents at school to feed the 11 people now bunking down at Elaine and Nigel's house. Jan would deliver food twice a day, collect groceries and do their laundry.

Two or three times, Frank asked Elaine if Gerard wanted to go with him to the showground to see how the search was going. Elaine would go inside, then come back and say Gerard couldn't go because he was looking after the kids. It seemed pretty strange to Frank, whose own kids were playing with the Baden-Clay children in the yard. He thought Gerard would want to be part of the search effort. The first time Jan saw Gerard after Allison's disappearance, he broke down and sobbed with his head in his hands. There were no tears but Jan left thinking he had nothing to do with it.

Jan and Frank generously lent the Baden-Clays their car and cleared a path through a hedge on their boundary so the kids could come and play at will. Olivia started confiding in them. 'I was lying on the bed with Gerard this morning and I asked him if he'd done it,' she'd said. Olivia hadn't revealed Gerard's response.

That particular comment was made on the morning of 30 April 2012. Hours later, Allison's body was found.

Frank heard the news first. He knew Olivia and Ian had gone for a walk, so he jumped in his car to alert them to the tragic discovery. Ian was disturbed, but not Olivia. Frank remembered Olivia said: 'Good, I'm glad. They would never have been able to clear Gerard's name if they never found a body.' Jan recalled Olivia saying: 'I so hope it's her.'

The next day, Gerard came running up Jan and Frank's driveway, as if someone was chasing him. Frank opened the door and Gerard threw his arms around him in a hug; he was making a crying sound but was strangely dry-eyed.

Sitting at a table inside, Gerard appeared to be sobbing, but then he looked up at the window and his sobs abruptly stopped.

The blind was open about six inches and he asked Frank to close it. When it was down he started sobbing again. To Frank, Gerard's behaviour did not seem genuine – Gerard looked like he was pretending to be upset and playing the part of bereaved husband.

Elaine's comments about Allison changed dramatically after the body was discovered. 'Allison was never a good cook and Gerard was a single parent,' Elaine told Jan about a week later. 'You see, Gerard wasn't only a single parent but he was also a carer.' Jan was shocked and upset. It was ridiculous, not to mention inappropriate, so soon after Allison's death.

Their contact eased after that, but Gerard phoned one day. He wanted Frank to know about a story that was going in the next day's paper. It was going to be about his affair.

A text arrived from Nigel's phone at 8 pm: 'Just wanted to give you a heads-up that there may be an article in tomorrow's *Sunday Mail* about G's affair which ended last year. He told the police about it on day one which was also when WE learned about it. It is also common knowledge in the Brookfield community so be prepared for some salacious commentary – sadly. Love Nigelaine.'

Jan went straight over and found Elaine crying. 'Allison drove him to it. He's my boy, he's my boy,' she said.

'To what?' Jan asked.

'To the affair,' Elaine said.

The dumping ground

Gerard's evidence was he didn't know the creek where Allison's body was found; nor did he know exactly where the nearby Scout camp was, despite his famous ancestry.

They're dubious claims. As a western suburbs real estate agent, it was his job to know the area, and he'd sold and managed properties in the vicinity. His secret trysts in his car with Toni McHugh hadn't been far away either. And family heritage meant everything to the Baden-Clays. It's hard to imagine the town's major Scout camps and their locations hadn't been topics of conversation.

But there's also an amazing untold story about Gerard and Kholo Creek, where Allison's body was discovered.

Sergeant Murray Watson was the second witness called at Gerard's trial. He was the one who described Gerard as 'one of the nicest guys in the world'. Watson gave evidence he had met Gerard several times at a property at Chalcot Road, Anstead, to evict problematic tenants. It was just around the corner from Kholo Creek Bridge, and the fact Gerard had met him there demonstrated Gerard knew the area better than he was admitting.

What Watson wasn't asked about at the trial was his own personal search for Allison. I found out recently that after Allison vanished, Watson had in fact correctly guessed where Gerard would dump her body, or at least very close to it.

This is what happened. Watson was aware Gerard was implicated in Allison's disappearance. He started speculating on where Gerard might have put her body. Watson had been a cop in the Indooroopilly police division for more than 20 years and knew the western suburbs like the back of his hand. He told search coordinators where the local mining shafts were. But because of his dealings with Gerard at the Chalcot Road property, he had a particular feeling that's where Allison's body could be. It was outside the search zone, so Watson took it upon himself to go look around the area.

During one shift four days after Allison went missing, Watson went searching through Anstead bushland. The search took him into Wirrabara Road, the last street before you come to Kholo Creek Bridge when you're driving away from Brisbane. At one point that day, Watson was just 400 metres from where Allison's undiscovered body lay. When Allison's body was eventually found, Watson went straight to the CIB and told detectives he'd been searching there.

Why prosecutors didn't mention any of this at the trial, I have no idea. The jury should have been told. A police officer, who knew Gerard well and regarded him as a mate, had suspected all along that Gerard may have dumped Allison's body in the very area where she was found.

Insurance

Gerard certainly had a financial incentive to kill. Allison's three life insurance policies were worth $1 million, and cash-strapped Gerard was the sole beneficiary in her will.

Evidence gathered by detectives, but never used at the trial, showed Gerard was actively involved in Allison's insurance affairs immediately before her death. On 12 April 2012, just a week before Allison went missing, Gerard was logged as phoning one of her insurers. The insurer's call centre recorded that the operator wouldn't give Gerard any information because he wasn't the policyholder. Prosecutors have never explained why they didn't tell the jury about this. It was significant information that showed Gerard had Allison's life insurance on his mind just days before her death.

Gerard also personally made a number of inquiries about Allison's life insurance after her death that the jury wasn't told about. Chloe Hulbert, a call centre operator with Suncorp in Sydney, remembered taking a call from Gerard on 9 May 2012: just over a week after Allison's body was discovered. Hulbert told police: 'The caller was clearly upset (crying) and indicated that he was worried the policy would lapse.' She apologised to Gerard for the delay and said it was a sensitive case so he'd have to speak to someone more senior.

Gerard also spoke on the phone to a Suncorp executive manager, Mark Bower. Gerard was anxious to find out if he had to keep paying the premium to make sure he got the payout. Bower assured Gerard he no longer had to pay. Gerard, not taking his word for it, asked Bower to put that advice in writing.

From this we can get a picture of Gerard being desperate to secure Allison's juicy life insurance payout. *One million dollars.* It would have solved all his money problems. And with Allison dead there was no costly divorce to deal with. Allison's insurance ultimately included: almost $350,000 from Suncorp's insurance arm Asteron; almost $435,000 from TAL; and $236,000 from IOOF, including a small amount of superannuation.

The Crown decided not to suggest the insurance money was a motivation for Gerard to murder Allison. It seems a strange call. Even if the murder wasn't premeditated, the insurance could have been front and centre on Gerard's mind at the moment he chose to kill.

The insurers did pay up, but the money went into a trust while Gerard's criminal proceedings played out. In February 2017, after an application by Allison's father, the Supreme Court formally declared Gerard had no right to any of her estate. As of March 2017, a court still had to order the insurance be paid into Allison's estate. If that occurs, the insurance will be divided equally between the couple's three daughters. Gerard rightly won't get a cent.

Sources

I'm sure some people would like a line-by-line reference for where the material in this book originated. The nature of this story is that some people would only speak, and provide documents, on the condition of anonymity.

I spoke to literally hundreds of people for this book, and tried to speak to many more without success. One person I particularly wanted to talk to finally and kindly relented, noting he couldn't help but be impressed by my persistence. He even offered me a job in real estate. Imagine.

It's all about Gerard

Probably the number-one question I get asked is: Why the public fascination with Allison's case? It's a fair enough question, except sometimes it carries an overtone that Allison doesn't 'deserve' so much attention. Some almost seem to resent the fuss.

There are many reasons for the interest. A former beauty queen vanishes from a posh suburb and her husband, a descendant of the world-famous Scouts founder, is suspected to be involved. The description sounds like it was lifted from the back of a fictional page-turner.

Then there was Allison herself. A struggling mum of three girls; many could identify and sympathise. But those who run the line that people were only interested in Allison Baden-Clay because she was an attractive, middle-class white woman miss the point.

I've come to believe the real reason this case stirs so much passion is actually the profile of the perpetrator, not the victim. Quite simply, it's all about Gerard. The pillar of the community who wouldn't search for his wife. The holier-than-thou real estate agent who was living a double life. The narcissistic killer who wouldn't admit a thing.

Everyone has known, worked with or dated someone like Gerard Baden-Clay and there was a palpable hunger to see him held to account. It was cathartic to see Gerard brought to justice. When the public thought he was going to wriggle off the hook for murder, they roared their outrage.

Fraud

Not too long ago I was invited to speak about this book at the Queensland University of Technology. Also speaking was Dr Claire Ferguson from QUT's School of Justice. Ferguson had some interesting insights on how killers try to manipulate crime scenes. (Most criminals aren't very bright, like the US man who claimed his wife randomly fell from a height during a walk, but left in his car a map to the exact location where it happened.)

Ferguson also asked an interesting question about Gerard. Many killers have a history of fraud, she explained. Was there any financial dishonesty in Gerard's past?

Sure enough, there are red flags in this area. Kerry-Anne Walker always suspected Gerard had ripped off his workplace, Flight Centre, just before Gerard and Allison left Australia on their extended honeymoon. After Allison went missing, Walker told police Gerard had written cheques from Flight Centre to pay for flowers, vehicles and other expenses for the wedding. Questions had been asked at the time and Gerard left Flight Centre quickly. In any event Gerard wasn't charged and the company later rehired him.

I'd been trying for years to interview Flight Centre founder Graham 'Skroo' Turner. We finally spoke in the lead-up to the rally; Turner described Allison and Gerard in polar opposite terms. 'I remember her quite well. She was highly regarded, successful,' Turner told me. 'Gerard was a bit of a slightly different character but I certainly remember him. He was considered a little bit strange.'

I asked Turner about the persistent rumours the firm investigated Gerard for financial impropriety. 'That was the story,' he said. 'But I think it was one of those things that couldn't be proved. So, he was let go, but not necessarily tried for that.'

Sleaze

This might be hard to believe, but one thing I didn't fully appreciate was just how sleazy Gerard could be. Of course, we all know Gerard was a philanderer who had multiple affairs, 'many of them concurrent', as he had himself testified at trial. But what surprised were his casual sexual remarks and advances towards colleagues and even clients.

Stephanie* first met Gerard when she was househunting and later had dealings with him in the Kenmore and District Chamber of Commerce. She was married with a young son and Gerard knew her husband from the chamber.

At a meeting around August 2006, when Stephanie was chamber secretary and Gerard was vice president, he made his first inappropriate comment. She was lining up for coffee at the time. 'Your clothes are beautiful and I love the way you dress. If I wasn't with Allison, watch out, I'd be with you,' he'd

---

* Name changed

said. Stephanie said something about her husband in reply, and joined the rest of their group.

At the next month's meeting, Gerard spotted her and started stumbling in her direction. When he reached her, he flung his arms around her. 'I was pretending to be drunk to get a hug,' he laughed.

Things escalated at a Century 21 Christmas party, when she told Gerard she wanted to ask a favour. Gerard jumped in first. 'Do you want me to have sex with you?' he said. There were people all around them.

At a family camping trip, Stephanie mentioned she liked condensed milk. Gerard brought out a can to share but only one spoon. 'Don't worry about another spoon, we'll be snogging later tonight,' he said in front of everyone, including Allison. They all groaned awkwardly, and Stephanie's husband wasn't impressed. Their social contact ended soon after.

Some staff thought he crossed the line too. One, Terri Hughes, talked to Gerard about boundaries. She wanted him to stop hugging her and the other women in the office. It was inappropriate.

Mystery text message
Allison's last text message to Kerry-Anne Walker on the night she vanished never rang true. Kerry-Anne had asked Allison to return some borrowed dresses. Allison replied by text at 7.50 pm. Part of the message bugged Kerry-Anne. 'Sorry you had to chase them up,' Allison had texted.

It was a bit formal and Allison would know she never had to apologise to her friend. Kerry-Anne wondered at the time, and still does today, who really sent the text message. Had Allison already lost her life by then? Was it really Gerard who sent the message, giving him a lot more time than anyone has realised to dispose of Allison's body?

Allison's clothes

It has become a common assumption that when Allison's body was found, she was in her walking clothes. But the clothes Allison was wearing – three-quarter pants, a singlet top and a jumper – is exactly the kind of comfortable outfit many women wear to bed.

Tellingly, Allison was not wearing a bra. Her singlet had what is known as an inbuilt 'shelf bra', which is little more than an extra layer of material over the chest area. It seems more likely these were clothes Allison planned to sleep in, rather than walk in.

All Gerard had to do was put her shoes and socks on and tie her laces.

The two cars

A loose end in this book is the sighting of two cars driving towards Kholo Creek Bridge the night Allison went missing. The cars were so close they were almost touching, and the one behind had its headlights off.

Unfortunately, on legal advice, there's not much more I can say about this. Witness Mary Mason has described the drivers to me. She thinks she knows who they are. I'm told police looked into it and the dates didn't match. But Mason is adamant, and has told me she is happy to sign a statutory declaration. I'm not satisfied this has been looked into as thoroughly as it should be.

Prisoner E00477

Gerard's day now starts with a 7.15 am headcount at Wolston Correctional Centre. Dinner's served at 4.10 pm and then the cell doors click shut at 5.30 pm.

It's a regimented existence that resembles his father's boarding school experience. His 50-cell unit in a 'secure' section of the prison provides inmates with a single bed, desk, small shelf, noticeboard, toilet and shower. Like everyone else, on entry into the prison system he was given his own ID: E00477.

When he works in the 'snaps' section, which involves the assembly of metal parts, he earns up to $60 a week. He gets the same rate when he works as a prison trolley pusher, delivering three square meals a day to prisoners from the kitchen.

The biggest surprise has been the bond Gerard has formed with Max Sica, who's serving a minimum of 35 years before he's eligible for parole, the biggest sentence ever set in Queensland, over the slaying of three siblings. One of Sica's victims was a 12-year-old girl. It's odd to think of them together – Sica, a psychopath, and Gerard, the narcissist – but with both claiming they are innocent victims of an injustice, they would have a lot to talk about. According to veteran crime reporter Paula Doneman, Gerard and Sica have regular chats while pushing food trolleys around.

Gerard has been a prolific letter-writer since being jailed. A source sent me one letter he wrote while awaiting trial. In it, Gerard updated his supporters on what he called the 'Four Fs': family, friends, fitness and faith. Gerard signed off with a quote from John Grisham's novel *The Chamber*: 'Weird things happen within our absurd judicial system. Courts rule this way one day and the other way the next.' Given the events that followed in court, it was a prescient line.

Up until his trial, Gerard's daughters regularly visited him in prison. He raved about these visits, telling his parents he didn't know how he could survive without them. These days, Gerard's daughters have nothing to do with him. The moment the jury convicted him of murdering their mother, all contact with the girls was cut off. They have not seen or spoken to him since.

Complete disconnection from his daughters must be the toughest sentence of all for Gerard. After his conviction, he was still wearing his wedding ring and kept a wedding picture on his cell wall.

The High Court's decision was crushing for Gerard. Afterwards, as the reality of his life sentence hit him, he broke down. Sobbing uncontrollably, he had to be helped back to his cell.

He has been seeking to be moved to the prison's residential section, where inmates have more space and freedom.

Will anyone else be charged?
No. To my knowledge, no one else is being investigated over Allison's murder.

The scratches
Gerard's razor story was so blatantly false, from there it was a matter of connecting the dots to why he was lying. But what if he'd said from the outset that Allison scratched him and then stormed off? Would police have shown the same level of interest? I'm told even Gerard's fellow prisoners are obsessed by this point, endlessly discussing what they would have said and done if faced with the same predicament.

That night
So, what happened? Only one person really knows. But we all have theories.

I have no doubt Gerard killed Allison – the evidence was over-whelming. Some people hear 'circumstantial' and think 'weak'. That's not the case; a solid set of facts can reveal everything you need to know. The scratches on Gerard's face spoke of close-quarter combat. The leaves in Allison's hair pointed to death at her house. The blood in the car revealed how Gerard transported her body.

If Allison did fall and hit her head, as Gerard's legal team belatedly suggested was possible on appeal, it's hard to imagine he wouldn't have called an ambulance. Death is rarely instantaneous. To accept that version, we'd also have to accept that, after not meaning to seriously hurt Allison, he would go the next step and dump her body under a bridge. For me it's all a bridge too far.

Some of the most crucial evidence against Gerard came from an unexpected source: his garden. Who would have thought some leaves would play such a big role in a murder trial? But those leaves told a story. Allison, who'd been at the hairdresser's that evening, clearly should not have had half her garden in her hair. Gerard's defence team and supporters certainly realised the power of this evidence during the trial. I'm told one of them, after hearing the expert testimony of Queensland Herbarium director Dr Gordon Guymer, walked out of court and was heard to remark: 'That's a very dangerous man.' Polite, slim Guymer, at five feet seven inches, is possibly the last person in the world you would call dangerous, but the comment showed just how crucial his evidence was seen to be in convicting Gerard.

I haven't previously discussed in this book the *absence* of some plant material from Allison's clothes and body, which didn't come up at the trial. What Guymer didn't find is just as interesting as what he did find. If Allison had been dragged through her overgrown lawn, or if she'd stumbled along road verges or crashed through the tall grass at Kholo Creek, she would have been covered in grass seeds and material from a whole range other plants. There was no sign of that at all; the only plant material that clung to her was from those six species in her garden. Which plays into the following theory: my theory. Others will have different ones, and you probably have your own.

One of the biggest misconceptions is that Allison's death had to follow on from an argument, when in fact it may well have been an attack by stealth. Gerard just may have seen no other way out.

Allison was gaining a little confidence, but she'd never wanted to end the marriage. It's hard to see her threatening to leave and take the children. Much more likely is that Gerard had become sick of being forced to account for his deception. Allison was stripping away his mask, one frustrating question at a time.

Perhaps it was on the couch as she stared blankly at the TV, or in bed as she lay there thinking about her marriage. Smothering is the most likely explanation for the lack of injuries. All she could do was reach out and claw at her assailant. In the process, she marked and caught her own killer, a man who didn't love her and who could only gain from her demise.

Prosecutors didn't say it was premeditated, but perhaps Gerard did plan it. I think the fantasy of being shot of Allison had been bubbling away for years, right back to when he jokingly offered a young real estate worker, Melissa Romano, a job – to 'kill my wife'. Gerard was broke and sick of it. There was a million dollars on the line and he knew it. He had the arrogance to believe he could pull it off.

Allison's body ended up on the overgrown back patio, an area fringed by fishbone ferns and covered in the leaves of crepe myrtle, eucalyptus, lilly pilly and Chinese elm. Some of these fronds and leaves lodged in her hair.

Gerard wrapped her in a sheet or something similar. He no longer had to look at her face. She was just something to dispose of.

He carried Allison down the gentle slope on the side of the house to the carport. A tendril of cat's claw creeper from the beams of the carport caught in her hair as he struggled to manoeuvre her body to the car. He put Allison in the third-row seating area of Sparky, her Holden Captiva, under the cover of darkness. She was bleeding from the head, either from the attack or an injury sustained moving her body. A small amount of blood dripped down the car's side panel.

Quiet Kholo Creek was the perfect dumping ground – lending weight to the possibility that killing Allison was more than a spur of the moment act. Perhaps people would even think she had jumped to her death. Gerard drove her body there, carried her through the tall grass and down the steep slope to a ledge beneath the bridge. She was still in the sheet, which is why she wasn't covered in grass seeds from the bush or garden. With a push, she rolled out of the sheet and down to the muddy bank just below. She lay there through tides and storms, until she was found.

Back at home, Gerard loaded the car boot with old toys. Laying a false trail was a Scouts basic. But he missed the small trail of blood down the side panel.

In front of the mirror, he realised just how bad those scratches were. He tried to disguise them, inflicting more marks on his face with his razor, but only made it look worse. He'd put his phone on charge, having no idea it would log the time it was plugged into the wall. Then he waited for the sun to rise, pressed the panic button early and tried to talk his way out of trouble. He almost got away with it. If it wasn't for those scratches, he'd have been home free.

To donate to The Late Allison Baden-Clay Children's Trust:
BSB: 084-737, ACC: 94-308-4078.

Anyone living with domestic abuse can find support through
the National Sexual Assault, Family & Domestic Violence
Counselling Service on 1800 737 732 (1800RESPECT)

Notes

Scout's honour

1 See www.pinetreeweb.com/bp-listener.htm, citing the pages of the 10th Fife (Cupar) Scout Group in Scotland.

Meet the Clays

1 Ethel Nimmo, Asst Region Commissioner (Qld), *Guiding in Australia*, April 1982, p. 13, cited in www.spanglefish.com/OlaveBadenPowell/index.asp?pageid=531598

2 Ibid. See also Robin Clay, www.guidingworks.com/resources/history/olavememory.html and www.stacycordery.com/juliette-gordon-low/serendipity-the-baden-powells/

3 Robin Clay, www.guidingworks.com/resources/history/olavememory.html

4 http://pinetreeweb.com/bp-family-tree-500-years.htm

5 Phebe Mitchell Kendall, 1896, *Maria Mitchell Life, Letters and Journals*, cited on http://pinetreeweb.com. A digital reproduction is available from the Open Collections Program at Harvard University, Women and work collection.

6 Obituary, Betty Clay, *The Independent,* www.independent.co.uk/news/obituaries/betty-clay-6169960.html

7 Jim Mackie, 'Life with Mum and Dad' (interview with Betty Clay), *The Canadian Leader*, 1975, a facsimile of the article appears at http://s3.spanglefish.com/s/9486/documents/documents/life%20with%20mum%20and%20dad/life%20with%20mum%20and%20dad.pdf. See also www.spanglefish.com/gervasclay/index.asp?pageid=158940 and http://webcache.googleusercontent.com/search?q=cache:aHCZzR37AfUJ:www.achilles.org/ftp/annual/1998.pdf+&cd=4&hl=en&ct=clnk&gl=au&client=safari

Notes

8 Jim Mackie, op cit.
9 Ibid.
10 www.spanglefish.com/gervasclay/index.asp?pageid=158939
11 www.spanglefish.com/gervasclay/index.asp?pageid=158957.
   See also http://en.wikipedia.org/wiki/Betty_Clay and
   www.spanglefish.com/gervasclay/index.asp?pageid=158945
12 Ibid.
13 Nigel Baden-Clay, eulogy for Gervas Clay, May 2009,
   www.spanglefish.com/gervasclay/index.asp?pageid=158939
14 Ibid.
15 Interview with author.
16 Ethel Nimmo, op. cit.
17 Ibid.
18 Ibid.
19 https://groups.yahoo.com/neo/groups/Africa/conversations/
   topics/1571?var=1
20 Ethel Nimmo, op. cit.

Schoolboy
1 *Toowoomba Grammar School Magazine*, 1987.

Boom
Figures in this chapter are from the Johnston Dixon Report
2008/09.

Toni McHugh
1 Allison Baden-Clay cited that date in a counselling session.

Flood
Information in this chapter is from the Queensland Floods
Commission of Inquiry report.

Acknowledgements

During the preparation of this book, an enormous number of people shared their recollections and in various ways gave support. Even though many have asked not to be named, I would like to acknowledge the generosity of those who gave their time, expertise, knowledge and insights. I am extremely grateful to my employers and colleagues at *The Courier-Mail* and *Sunday Mail* for their support and encouragement. A special thanks to those at Random House involved in this book, for their patience, guidance and belief in this story. Most of all, I am grateful beyond words to my partner, Catriona, for being there through many a long day and night.